Roadshow!

Roadshow!

The Fall of Film Musicals in the 1960s

MATTHEW KENNEDY

OXFORD
UNIVERSITY PRESS

OXFORD
UNIVERSITY PRESS

Oxford University Press is a department of the University of Oxford.
It furthers the University's objective of excellence in research,
scholarship, and education by publishing worldwide.

Oxford   New York
Auckland   Cape Town   Dar es Salaam   Hong Kong   Karachi
Kuala Lumpur   Madrid   Melbourne   Mexico City   Nairobi
New Delhi   Shanghai   Taipei   Toronto

With offices in
Argentina   Austria   Brazil   Chile   Czech Republic   France   Greece
Guatemala   Hungary   Italy   Japan   Poland   Portugal   Singapore
South Korea   Switzerland   Thailand   Turkey   Ukraine   Vietnam

Oxford is a registered trademark of Oxford University Press
in the UK and certain other countries.

Published in the United States of America by
Oxford University Press
198 Madison Avenue, New York, NY 10016

Library of Congress Cataloging-in-Publication Data
Kennedy, Matthew, 1957–
Roadshow! : the fall of film musicals in the 1960s / Matthew Kennedy.
    pages   cm
Includes bibliographical references and index.
ISBN 978-0-19-992567-4 (alk. paper)
1. Musical films—United States—History and criticism. I. Title.
PN1995.9.M86K46   2013
791.430973—dc23   2013004811

9 8 7 6 5 4 3 2

Printed in the United States of America
on acid-free paper

In memory of my brother Jim

CONTENTS

ACKNOWLEDGMENTS

I have received enormous support in the research and writing of *Roadshow!*, and it's a pleasure to give thanks here.

I am beholden to Lea Whittington, Barbara Hall, Sandra Archer, and Jenny Romero at the Margaret Herrick Library of the Academy of Motion Picture Arts and Sciences, Jonathon Auxier and Sandra Joy Lee Aguilar of the Warner Bros. Archives at USC, Neil Bethke, Cynthia Becht, and Rebecca Moon at the Charles Von der Ahe Library at Loyola Marymount University, Cynthia Franco at the De-Golyer Library at Southern Methodist University, John C. Johnson at Boston University, Charles Silver at the Museum of Modern Art Film Study Center, Heather Heckman, Emil Hoelter, and Dorina Hartmann of the Wisconsin Center for Film and Theater Research, Ginny Kilander at the American Heritage Center at the University of Wyoming, Albert Palacios and Steve Wilson at the Harry Ransom Center of the University of Texas at Austin, and Lauren Buisson and Julie Graham of the UCLA Performing Arts Special Collections. Special thanks are extended to Karie Bible of Los Angeles and John Fagleson of Austin for excavating at various institutions on my behalf. As for Ned Comstock of the USC Cinema-Television Library, I've exhausted superlatives elsewhere.

Interviews, emails, and correspondence with people who were there enliven the book. My gratitude to Marc Breaux, Leslie Caron, Charles and Peggy Champlin, Carol Channing, Petula Clark, Tony Hatch, Florence Henderson, Arthur Hiller, Norman Jewison, Hayley Mills, David V. Picker, Lee Roy Reams, Dee Dee Wood, and Michael York.

Thanks to friends and fellow UCLA alums Stuart Marland and Tom Schumacher. Jeff Kurtti generously lent his stash of roadshow programs. I extend appreciation to colleagues Stephen Neale, Sheldon Hall, Beverly Gray, and particularly Emily Leider. Thanks also to Jessie Davison, who keeps my website current and visitor friendly, and Michael Fox and Derek McLellan, who both harbor the notion that I can talk about movies. Michael McDonagh, David Ehrenstein, and Will Snyder lent their expertise during research, and Larry Billman of the Academy of Dance on Film and Ron and Howard Mandelbaum of Photofest were extraordinarily helpful in supplying photographs.

My agent, Stuart Bernstein, has guided, advised, edited, pitched, and delivered me from ruination for many years. Oxford University Press editor Norm Hirschy is a gentleman and a scholar; his faith in *Roadshow!* brought it to press. Everyone at the Press, including Richard Kelaher, T. J. Stiles, Geronna Lewis-Lyte, Jonathan Kroberger, and Joellyn M. Ausanka, has been exceptionally friendly and professional. I can never fully thank writer-editor-show business fount Jim Parish for his steadfast mentoring and friendship. Sister Anne Peterson, niece Maggie Kennedy, and friend and movie soulmate Mark Cromwell merit a shout-out for reading the manuscript, applying just the right editorial touches, and offering unwavering love and support. Other patient ones who offered so much as I ruminated and obsessed include Jeff Reid, Edward Hosey, Steven Rowland, Greg and Amy Gnesios, Jim Brown, and everyone at JCC, Ardel Haefele-Thomas, and Dylan Miles. Any errors in this book are mine, not theirs. To all I say thank you, over and over again.

Roadshow!

Overture

There is no feast which does not come to an end.
—Chinese proverb

The lovely art deco ceiling of the Cascade Theatre was obscured by years of dust and cigarette smoke, but in the 1960s there weren't many options in Redding, California, for moviegoing. Two drive-ins, the Starlight and Sky-View, were on the outskirts of town and showed b-rate double bills. Around 1970 came the Showcase, a modern box theater done up in burnt orange inside and out. As the Cascade went neglected, the Showcase marketed itself as the finer house in town, screening exquisite fare such as *The Last Picture Show* and *Sounder*. Management had an annoying habit of splicing their own intermissions into a midway reel change, but that was the price to pay for seeing the day's important films.

It was here at the north end of California's sun-parched Central Valley that I fell in love with movies. My favorites were the musicals, and that love was genetic. My mother loved musicals and had an impressive collection of Broadway original cast recordings. I was a strange kid and took particular delight in those occasions when I had the house to myself and could let those LPs take me where they might. As for film musicals, I remember leafing through the Friday entertainment section of the *San Francisco Chronicle* for the full-page ads for *Camelot*, *Funny Girl*, and *Paint Your Wagon*, each with mail-in coupons for reserve seating. I knew there was something different between the big city moviegoing experience and what we saw in Redding. This thing called "roadshows" didn't come to our town. Our version of *Paint Your Wagon* was not San Francisco's version of *Paint Your Wagon*. There were no program books or LPs for sale in the lobby of the Cascade or Showcase. Musicals or dramas in their roadshow form were abstract wonders, something only great cities could host. My high school had an excellent, hard-driving choir director, Ken Putnam, and the spring productions were a civic highlight. The excitement of performing in *The Music Man*, *How to Succeed in Business without Really Trying* (as J. Pierpont Finch), *You're a Good Man, Charlie Brown* (as Charlie Brown), and *Fiddler on the Roof* (as Motel, hands down my favorite role)

3

was unmatchable. Musicals at UCLA and professional theater and dance were never as thrilling as the hot lights of hometown.

Meanwhile, roadshows died a quiet death in the 1970s as movie tastes and marketing changed. All these years later I want to know why. This book takes its name from the exclusive marketing and booking format begun in the Silent Era to promote Hollywood's most anticipated movies. Sarah Bernhardt's 1912 filmed performance as Queen Elizabeth opened in New York's Lyceum, a legitimate theater in the Broadway district, and ran with three intermissions. A theatrical-style exhibiting of films included an orchestra playing an original score and traveling with the film from city to city, giving the roadshow its most literal meaning.

Some of the most familiar film titles in the world received the roadshow treatment in their first engagements: *The Birth of a Nation, Wings, Show Boat, All Quiet on the Western Front, Grand Hotel, Gone with the Wind, Fantasia,* and *For Whom the Bell Tolls.* Roadshowing allowed studios to maintain a degree of control over film exhibitors, as successful marketing created competition that allow them to set rental prices and terms of distribution. Roadshows reached their peak in the 1950s, when the "big" movie promised grandeur that the newly installed home televisions couldn't. Ancient history was a major inspiration with *The Robe, The Ten Commandments,* and *Ben-Hur,* and into the 1960s with *Spartacus, El Cid,* and *King of Kings.* Musical roadshows came to dominate high-cost moviemaking with *Oklahoma!, Gigi, South Pacific, Porgy and Bess, Can-Can, West Side Story,* and *The Music Man.* By the 1960s, "the roadshow" was a well-known thing, securely attached to high-priced, heavily marketed, eagerly anticipated, reserve seat film aimed for mass audiences. Film historian and roadshow authority Sheldon Hall defined the prestige film as "a product of the mainstream industry at its most earnest, sincere, and respectable (or its most polished in terms of accepted standards of excellence in professional craftsmanship), for which studio executives can congratulate themselves on having fulfilled a cultural rather than (or preferably as well as) a commercial remit."

Roadshow! The Fall of Film Musicals in the 1960s corrects the shorthand that reduces American cinema of the time to *Bonnie and Clyde, The Graduate,* and *Easy Rider.* Equally influential was *The Sound of Music,* which predates them and stayed in theaters for nearly a half decade. Since *Music* was a roadshow and the others weren't, what was that specific experience? Audiences saw the careful marketing of a spectacular new "blockbuster," a movie term coined from a large explosive device of World War II. To generate something akin to the crackling energy of a Broadway opening, roadshow musicals often came with an overture, intermission, entr'acte, and exit music, in addition to a souvenir program and bookings in the most lavish single-screen theaters in large cities. The exhibiting standards were exacting; careful timing of lights, curtains, sound, and projection was critical. Mike Todd, the leading purveyor of roadshows in the 1950s with *Oklahoma!* and *Around the World in 80 Days,* shrewdly took the high and low roads simultaneously. "To show [audiences] got class and appreciate the arts, they'd be insulted if you didn't charge premium prices and make it a little hard to see," he said. "This way they don't have to rub elbows with the gum chewers. Besides, if you get the reviews and have a hot ticket, the gum chewers will figure out how to get in as well. Once you're a hit in New York, you'll have to fight the out-of-town exhibitors off with a stick."

By several measures, including tickets sold and awards won, roadshows dominated the American film industry from the mid-1950s through the mid-1960s. Most of the top money earners were roadshowed in their initial screenings. Of the Best Picture Oscar winners in the same period, eight opened as roadshows, and four were musicals. Some recognized the increased dependency on huge roadshows as a dangerous game. "Without question this new venture finds Hollywood engaged in the greatest gamble of its entire history, the results of which may determine its future forever," noted *Films and Filming* in 1963. "Should these gigantic investments achieve the desired outcome, Hollywood may well have found the definitive and triumphant answer to the threat of television. Should they encounter defeat the whole face of the film industry may be drastically changed. Will the public pay the higher prices made necessary by these colossal expenditures? Is there an audience sufficiently large to permit these pictures to emerge without a loss? How many of these fabulously expensive films can and will filmgoers absorb?"

Good questions. Audiences steadily declined beginning in the late 1940s, while expenses rose. By 1963, the number of American feature films in production fell to a 50 year low. Nothing worked anymore. Derivative plots and aging stars hobbled the Western. Film noir, at least in its classic form, was dead. Poor Twentieth Century-Fox was down to a staff of about 50. If ever Hollywood needed a multi-vitamin containing inspiration, excitement, and creativity, it was in the early 1960s. Musicals were as troubled as anything. "I could feel musicals were dying, because there wasn't a renewal of stories and styles and they kept repeating the same plot," said Leslie Caron, one of the last of the 1950s studio-made musical stars. "Finally the musical died because it was too expensive. Everything was fine when we were under weekly or monthly contracts and salaries were manageable. The set builders were under contract, the costumers, the performers, the dance teachers. It was financially possible. After that, it became too expensive."

Then it happened—the triple whammy of *Mary Poppins*, *My Fair Lady*, and *The Sound of Music* signaling that lavish musicals were the new hope for the industry. In a violent spasm of copycatting, every major studio committed millions to duplicate the success of one or the other, or all three. Roadshowing was essential. In the seven years that followed *The Sound of Music*, it became de rigueur for any film musical to be released in the roadshow format if it wanted to rightfully be labeled "major," "important," or "lavish."

This brings us to *Roadshow!*, a book examining the death of a grand old marketing style alongside the devolution of the film musical. The rickety calculus of cost, marketing, and box office could not last. Big musicals and roadshows essentially destroyed each other, and nearly destroyed Hollywood with them. An astonishing number of variables conspired against them. Public tastes changed so quickly producers couldn't keep up. Since roadshows opened in limited release in large cities, bad word of mouth and howling reviews traveled to the hinterlands, dooming titles to early graves. Beleaguered Hollywood studios seeking tax relief became subsidiaries to large multi-interest corporations, the result being more freelance actors, directors, and producers making movies literally in the streets. Old backlots, the very sites where traditional musicals were shot, were for sale. It was a different game. "The moguls are gone and the movies have entered the era of professional managers, quite as much as Detroit or Akron or the millers of Minneapolis," mourned Charles Champlin of the *Los Angeles Times*.

Musicals dominated roadshow titles of the late 1960s, and when tastes veered toward greater realism, they suffered the reputation of being stodgy and precious, burdened with an irritating artificiality. But the good ones had no such problem. There is more creative pleasure in 1932's 89-minute *Love Me Tonight* than in all the endless hours of late 1960s musicals combined. To watch the classics is to be confronted with the rampant and joyous expression of craft. Establishing shots do not merely set the scene, they luxuriate over the perfectly realized fantasy environments of *The Wizard of Oz*'s Munchkinland or *Meet Me in St. Louis*'s caramelized middle America. The best musicals deter interpretation to become intensely sensual. No one need study the meaning of the *American in Paris* ballet to get drunk on its whirling visuals and music. In the 1940s and '50s, the undisputed prime generator of great classic musicals was Metro-Goldwyn-Mayer, where folk elements were neatly camouflaged in commercial art. When Gene Kelly or Fred Astaire danced with a newspaper, garbage can lid, or hat rack, it had the exhilarating effect of modern art's use of found objects. And every time Judy Garland opened her mouth to sing, we were reminded what a musical star should sound like.

What happened to that once supreme film genre? I have reconciled my childhood memories of the late 1960s musicals with the adult realization that most of them aren't very good. The misjudgments piled up like a freeway collision disaster. Broadway adaptations were often literal and stage bound, as though anything too cinematic would destroy rather than enhance artistic integrity. People who had no business starring in musicals were hired simply because they were movie stars. And genuine talent in front of and behind the camera was not well used, much less nurtured as in the Studio Era.

As the last roadshows are too static to be embraced as camp, most are neglected today, odd castoffs of a bygone era. Plenty of non-musical roadshows flopped, too, but musicals offer the most graphic and consistent examples of films hopelessly out of step. *Camelot, Star!*, and *Hello, Dolly!* offered little more than a celebration of excess and the exploitation of nothing. What *are* all these singing and dancing people getting so excited about? And why do they have to be so excited for three hours, when two are more than enough? The 1960s musicals succumbed to the allure of self-importance, replacing the virtue of craft with the burden of size.

Hollywood has always looked to technological breakthroughs or gimmicks (sound, color, 3-D, widescreen, Dolby Sound, feature animation, 70 millimeter, IMAX, 3-D again) to arouse a fragmented, bored audience. But by 1967, piles of money went to an art form tied to the old while moviegoers hungered for the new. Musicals came to represent the disconnection between what Hollywood was producing and what the public wanted, while audiences themselves became ever less cohesive. Parents were hanging onto their Frank Sinatra and Rosemary Clooney LPs while the kids were devouring *It's Alright Ma (I'm Only Bleeding)* and catching *Wild in the Streets* at the nearest drive-in. When *Sgt. Pepper's Lonely Hearts Club Band* appeared, Warner Bros. was throwing its prime resources at *Camelot*, while Fox was doing likewise with *Doctor Dolittle*. Hollywood did not outright ignore youth music, but musicals with big money behind them adamantly resisted new sounds.

Quick changes in music and film were symptomatic of something bigger. What do people routinely confronted by death want to see and hear? "It is fashionable to see the boomers' '60s obsession as a reflection of their own narcissism, their inability to get over themselves," noted a 2007 *Newsweek* cover story on the reverberations of 1968. "But this does not do justice to a truly traumatic decade. In the midst of adolescence, an entire generation was presented with repeated reminders of its own mortality: the Cuban missile crisis; the assassinations of the Kennedys and Martin Luther King Jr.; the violence in the cities; the 58,193 Vietnam War dead. So much death and killing, too much to simply put aside." While some eras of woe inspire divine escapism, the 1960s did not. The antiwar movement, emerging drug culture, sexual revolution, and civil rights movements for African Americans, women, and homosexuals point to a society grasping at self-reflection and reinvention.

After the cruelties of war, assassinations, moral compromise, and political fraud, the cultural shift was complete. Business as usual was rejected at the movie marketplace in favor of the masculine arts of war, crime, and meditations on violence that rose to prominence in the early '70s. The industry shift was complete. New Hollywood had triumphed, signaled by a rising dark tone that mirrored public disillusionment. Only one musical caught that wave. *Cabaret* could not have been released in 1965 any more than *The Sound of Music* could not have been released in 1972. And by then nothing could save the roadshow.

Roadshow! had a long development as I struggled to give it form. Why hadn't these films been the primary subjects of a book? Did other writers on film know something I didn't know? Do we shrink too readily from an extended look at failure? Other more practical questions persisted. Where's the story's through-line? Where does it end? The roadshow format stayed in the back of my mind until I realized that every big musical of the era was released as such. It then became the symbol and theme of the entire phenomenon of too much money and not enough contemplation of time, place, talent, and a fast-changing American society. The roadshow hook also excited me because it was such a major part of film distribution and exhibition in the 1960s, yet is all but forgotten today. I very much enjoy shining a flashlight into the dank attic of neglected film history.

Researching and writing *Roadshow!* became an exercise in blind faith. I grew overwhelmed at the volume of reporting in *Variety* and other primary written sources. So many factors threatened to pull the project in a dozen directions. There was the selling of the studios to conglomerates, boardroom deals, aging executives, box office figures, distribution plans, studio and location shooting, renegade directors, and unstable, egomaniacal actors. "Tell the story of how the films got made" was my eventual mantra. While writing a biography of actress Joan Blondell, I researched at the University of Southern California (USC) Warner Bros. Archives, a fantastic repository for the studio's production files. Each of Blondell's 1930s films typically yielded files less than one-inch thick. *Camelot*'s was closer to ten feet, organized in carefully numbered boxes. Upon inspection, I didn't know whether to laugh, cry, hire a small army of readers, or run to the nearest exit. Firming my resolve and rolling up my sleeves, I was alternatively numbed and amused by the nonsensical minutiae of production planning. The files in other archives for other roadshows, including *Hello, Dolly!, Star!, Goodbye, Mr. Chips*, and *Doctor Dolittle*, were equally swollen. The "Bigger Is Better" roadshow philosophy extended to the quantities of paper generated, internal studio warfare, and collisions of artistic temperament. In the hush of one or another archive, I occasionally emitted an involuntary "*aahh!*" upon discovering a precious tidbit that would add zest to the manuscript.

I was as hungry as a cub reporter and eager to secure interviews with eyewitnesses. Alas, many have passed, but several honored me with their recollections. How sweet it was to hear the unmistakable tones of Leslie Caron, Petula Clark, and Michael York coming through the phone. Borrowing a line from Caron's *Gigi*, I tried not to "gush and jabber" as a longtime fan, but to converse with each as actors holding precious memories. Director Norman Jewison (*Fiddler on the Roof*) is an interviewer's dream, rattling off stories and insights with dizzying speed. Michael York faxed relevant pages of his autobiography as my homework. No one pulled rank or displayed unbecoming levels of ego. Talking with each was a pleasure, and sometimes a joy.

Since there are so many films, each with its own story, how was I going to organize this thing? I thought about concentrating on three important careers (actress Julie Andrews, producer Arthur Jacobs, and director Joshua Logan), but that seemed too narrow. How about a film per chapter? That seemed too segmented, and falsely suggests these films neither overlapped in time nor influenced one another. I finally settled on the structure that awaits the dedicated reader, with several of the major films (*Camelot, Doctor Dolittle, Finian's Rainbow, Funny Girl,*

Star!, Paint Your Wagon, Hello, Dolly!, Goodbye, Mr. Chips) braided through the book by planning, production, and release dates. This offers a rough chronology of roadshows in the making and/or in the market. The effort may fairly be called Altmanesque, honoring a director whose career ascendancy owes something to the death of the roadshow. As such, *Roadshow!* taxis all over Hollywood between 1965 and 1972. It visits executive meetings, rehearsal halls, and sound stages, with each studio laboring in vain to make "the next *Sound of Music.*"

Roadshow! is an elegy—for the lost "event" of cinema going, the classic musical, the grand old theaters, and most important, the place of moviegoing in American life. It's quite different now. *Big* theaters and *big* screens have been somewhat lost to new audiences who may love their computer-generated spectaculars but are amenable to watching them on smart phones and laptops. The grand showmen of the past, the Cecil B. DeMilles, Mike Todds, and Darryl F. Zanucks, must be spinning in their graves.

And *still* the musical lingers as an instantly recognizable and peculiarly lovable American thing. Now's the time to tip our hat to the exuberant world of Henry Higgins, King Arthur, Dolly Levi, and Charity, and to assess the damage that was done by their misappropriations.

CHAPTER 1

The Musical That Ate Hollywood

When Richard Zanuck went searching for a movie to produce, he found the Broadway musical *The Sound of Music* in the Twentieth Century-Fox script library. "It was a studio head's dream, especially a studio that had been pronounced dead," said the production chief son of studio kingpin Darryl Zanuck. When agent Irving "Swifty" Lazar accompanied a Fox executive to a performance of *Music* in New York, the reaction was dramatic. "He was crying like a baby," said Lazar. "I knew I had a customer." Others were also impressed. Over clam chowder at a Howard Johnson's during intermission, screenwriter Ernest Lehman told his wife, "I don't care what anyone says about this show; someday it's going to make a very successful movie."

In 1964, *The Sound of Music* was just another hopeful in a list of green-lit features at Fox that included the Sistine Chapel drama *The Agony and the Ecstasy* and Steve McQueen as a gunboat engineer on the Yangtze in *The Sand Pebbles*. Fox had already profited from producing four Rodgers and Hammerstein adaptations, so the studio was predisposed to embrace *The Sound of Music*, a property they had paid $1.25 million to adapt. Lehman's optimism at its potential won him the screenwriting assignment, which was news in itself. The fact that the screenwriter of *West Side Story* was on board proved that Fox, bled nearly to death by the obscene costs of 1963's *Cleopatra*, was still in business. When Lehman asked where his office would be, Zanuck surveyed the devastated studio and asked, "Where would you like it to be?" Lehman compared it to "calling a theater and asking, 'What time does the movie go on?' and they say, 'What time would you like it to go on?'"

In an early meeting between Lehman and Zanuck, William Wyler was suggested as director, though the great veteran of *The Best Years of Our Lives* and *Ben-Hur* had never directed a musical and was hard of hearing. He was reluctant to accept, but Lehman thought he would be won over by the stage show. When the final curtain fell, Wyler turned to Lehman and announced he hated it. This story of a 1930s postulate nun turned nanny who fills her seven charges with the joy of singing was just too sugary to bear, particularly since she marries her widower boss before the family escapes Nazi-infested Austria. "I remember *The Sound of Music* had a certain—well, stink is not quite the right word—about it," he said. Maybe stink *was* the right word. When he told Burt Lancaster he might direct, Lancaster shook his head and said "Jesus, you must need the money." When Lehman sent Wyler a first draft screenplay, and it was returned without notes, he knew the courtship had failed. "He's never going to do the picture," Lehman sighed.

West Side Story's director Robert Wise likewise found the plot too schmaltzy. Billy Wilder then passed. So did Stanley Donen, director of the previous decade's buoyant *Singin' in the Rain* and *Funny Face*. Gene Kelly dismissed Zanuck and Lehman by telling them "to go find somebody else to direct this shit." Then Wise read Lehman's treatment and reconsidered. Perhaps not coincidentally, he had not seen the stage version. Playwright Robert Anderson had, and gave Wise a suggestion: "Can't you run those kids through a whorehouse, or something?"

Together with Lehman, Wise showed immediate good judgment in handling tricky material. They were most sensitive to the sentimentality and *gemütlichkeit* that worked on stage but would be smothering on the big screen. Both men envisioned opening up the movie to take advantage of its setting in the Austrian Alps. There was also the matter of casting leading character Maria von Trapp. Fiftyish Mary Martin had originated Maria on Broadway, but was never seriously considered; she would not pass as a dewy postulate in close-up. Wise jotted a few names on a yellow pad to see how they looked—Anne Bancroft, Shirley Jones, Angie Dickinson, Leslie Caron. Doris Day was a foregone conclusion to Richard Rodgers, but Zanuck was keen on the very British Julie Andrews, Broadway star of *My Fair Lady* and *Camelot* with the heaven-sent four-octave voice. Her present notoriety, however, came with the job she did *not* get. When Warner Bros. bought *Lady*, Andrews had yet to make a movie, and Jack Warner wanted the insurance of a star as Cockney flower seller Eliza Doolittle. Audrey Hepburn was a safer bet, though her singing abilities were limited, and she was eventually dubbed. The job was given to soprano Marni Nixon, whose vocals for Deborah Kerr in *The King and I* and Natalie Wood in *West Side Story* already made her familiar to the ears of musical fans.

There were other forces justifying Warner's elitism. Andrews was never costar Rex Harrison's first choice on stage or screen. He found her wooden, and director Moss Hart shouted insults at her to that effect in rehearsals. "I never got that part under control," admitted Andrews later. But Walt Disney was not so ready to forsake her film career before it began. He saw her in a matinee of *Camelot*, and was certain she would be ideal for *Mary Poppins*, a rare original musical his studio was readying. However, that did not begin any "get me Julie Andrews" virus among producers. When her London manager suggested her for Maria, Richard Rodgers scoffed. "I suspect that, for picture purposes, she may not have a big enough name and I don't even know how she photographs," he wrote to Lehman. A change of heart came when Disney sent rough footage of *Poppins* over to Fox, and Wise and Zanuck promptly cast her as Maria. She signed a two-picture contract at Fox for a fee of $225,000 each, with no share of the profits for either.

In casting other key roles, Wise and Zanuck practiced a reversal of what old Jack Warner knew to be true. Male lead Captain von Trapp was assigned to Christopher Plummer, a relatively unknown non-singing stage and television actor from Toronto. Key supporting roles went to Richard Haydn and Peggy Wood, neither widely known. Several of the children had never appeared in a movie, including Charmian Carr, who had the featured role of eldest daughter Liesl. The only real movie name in the cast was Eleanor Parker as the Baroness, Maria's competitor for von Trapp's affections. She was a three time Oscar nominee in the 1950s, but was not at the top ranks of stardom by the mid-1960s. So do stars make movies, or do movies make stars? Wise and Zanuck were going to find out. Here was an $8 million extravaganza with nary a big name in sight.

With *Mary Poppins* in the can, rehearsals for *Music* began on Fox's Stage 15 in Los Angeles on February 10, 1964, and lasted six weeks. On March 26, the first musical number, "My Favorite Things," was shot, and all was well. "Robert Wise was a dream," recalled Dee Dee Wood, who choreographed with her husband Marc Breaux. "He was fascinating to watch. He was so calm and knew exactly what he wanted. He had a stopwatch and kept on schedule, never yelled, ran things beautifully, which is difficult with so many children on the set." As planned, the company took advantage of gorgeous Salzburg and environs during location shooting. The baroque Mirabell Gardens became a backdrop for the "Do-Re-Mi" montage, and the Benedictine Nonberg Abbey was used for exteriors. In late June, all the actors except Andrews returned to Los Angeles, while she and a skeleton crew filmed the opening number in Bavaria atop what came to be called Maria's Mountain. Though it was summer, the temperature was freezing and the rain was unrelenting, causing expensive delays. The crew would pass the time under makeshift tarp tents, singing or playing cards, and hoping the clouds would separate long enough to get a shot or two. When the sun came out, a helicopter was dispatched to capture Andrews cresting the hill. Over the noise, Breaux yelled, "TURN!" to synchronize her spin with the passing overhead camera, but she was swept off her feet by the downdraft. Her playback was on precise cue, so that she could faultlessly mouth her own voice from a recording she made back in Los Angeles several weeks earlier. It was a hellish few days, and the inherent stop and start nature of filmmaking made for an unsatisfying experience. They were filming the title song, but who knew if it would work on film?

The company had just one weekend to rest after returning to Los Angeles, recover from jet lag, and report to the Fox studio for additional shooting. Everyone was fatigued from a shoot that was now 22 days behind schedule and $740,000 over budget. In fact, the movie was nicknamed "S & M" by weary participants, but everyone was carrying on gamely, except perhaps Christopher Plummer. He began calling it *The Sound of Mucus* and kept the children at a distance. When he learned his songs would be dubbed, he threw a tantrum and threatened to quit. His actor's insecurities manifested in the heavy imbibing of schnapps, which brought weight gain, necessitating a refitting of costumes and extra makeup. Wise remained patient and Andrews held Plummer's hand to calm his nerves, and he eventually reformed. He and Andrews shot their last scene, the romantic "Something Good," in Fox's manufactured gazebo. By then, there was intense press interest in the movie, with reporters on the set every day. That stink William Wyler once smelled was replaced with something more fragrant. Plummer recalled "a distinct scent of success in the air." Andrews sensed it, too. She took him aside and whispered, "Do you get the feeling we might be famous one day?"

Andrews received her answer two weeks later. In the midst of postproduction dubbing and looping, she was chauffeured to Grauman's Chinese Theater on Hollywood Boulevard to attend the world premiere of *Mary Poppins*. On that night, August 27, she became a movie star. The public love affair was ferocious and immediate, and the film was greeted as enthusiastically as its star. Sam Goldwyn wrote Disney after the premiere, "You have made a great many pictures, Walt, that have touched the hearts of the world, but you have never made one so wonderful, so magical, so joyous, so completely the fulfillment of everything a great motion picture should be as *Mary Poppins*." The fantasy of a nanny who descends from the clouds by her open umbrella was essentially a 140-minute stroll through the park, but no one seemed to care that the story was perilously thin, or that costar Dick Van Dyke's London dialect was patently ridiculous. With influences from English music hall, Gilbert and Sullivan, and folk songs, the score contained two instant classics, "Spoonful of Sugar" and the joyfully overextended neologism "Supercalifragilisticexpialidocious." And, most important, it was a movie that delighted children and left their parents, if not enraptured, at least entertained by so much exuberance and creativity on the screen. It was an eye-popper, made with uncommonly high production values, and ace special effects combining live action and animation.

The Andrews voice was celebrated as liquid sunshine, with a direct style honoring lyrics and emotions above her ego. Often vexed and always hyper-efficient, she embodied Mary's starchy self-assessment as "practically perfect in every way." Her screen charm was overpowering, so much so that the *My Fair Lady* casting question was reborn. Why was this family-friendly enchantress denied the opportunity to reprise her Eliza Doolittle on screen? *This* is the girl Jack Warner rejected for a $1 million dubbed Audrey Hepburn? Hepburn was a huge star, but was he *crazy*? *Mary Poppins* cost a relatively low $5.2 million to make, and it returned that amount at the box office quickly. And though it did not run as a hard ticket (industry slang for roadshow) feature in the United States, it did in London to great success.

Mary Poppins could not have arrived at a better time in *The Sound of Music*'s gestation. Andrews's sudden vault into movie stardom made her Fox's most prized commodity. There were other good omens for *Music*, as it appeared the public had a strong appetite for musicals. *The Unsinkable Molly Brown*, MGM's raucous adaptation of a middling Broadway show, did exceptional business. The Beatles rushed onto the screen in *A Hard Day's Night*, and if that was not a conventional genre entry, it at least demonstrated that audiences could relish extended music in their movies. It cost a mere $500,000 to make and grossed $10 million even before United Artists sent 1,000 prints into general release. Elvis Presley appeared in three features that year, singing in each one. The swooning *Umbrellas of Cherbourg* was an art house hit, and its every word was sung in French.

The sure test of musical endurance was the upcoming *My Fair Lady*, Warner's $17 million colossus bowing at the picture palace Art Moderne Criterion Theatre at Times Square. On Broadway, *Lady* had been a bigger hit than *The Sound of Music*, and its George Bernard Shaw–based story and music were of far greater wit and sophistication. *My Fair Lady* was considered such a near perfect piece of musical theater that neither Warner nor director George Cukor dared tamper with the source material. Its virtues as cinema are accordingly limited to ravishing costumes and sets, and the presence of a bona fide movie star in Audrey Hepburn. To Warner's consternation, she became the primary sore point. Though she worked hard, the inescapably regal Hepburn never fulfilled the description of her as "so deliciously low, so horribly dirty." Unconvincing as a guttersnipe in her early scenes, and obviously dubbed throughout, the new conclusion held that Andrews should have played Eliza. Pretty much everything else looks and sounds like a deluxe hologram of the stage version. There are all the illustrious Lerner and Loewe songs, Broadway holdovers Rex Harrison and Stanley Holloway, and every last lyric preserved on film for eternity. That suited most everyone. *My Fair Lady* was a critical and popular triumph, raking in millions through roadshow engagements worldwide.

Julie Andrews was on her own upward spiral when *My Fair Lady* opened without her. Though *Mary Poppins* was not a roadshow in the United States, it was doing equivalent business. Then came *The Americanization of Emily*, an antiwar drama that Andrews had wedged into her schedule. It tested her as an actress, not just a singer who acts, and she proved credible in a grown-up role. By New Year's 1965, Andrews was on fire. When she picked up a Golden Globe for *Mary Poppins*, she tartly thanked "the man who made all this possible, Jack Warner" and drew a roar of laughter. Then the Oscar nominations were announced. She was on the Best Actress list for *Mary Poppins*, while *My Fair Lady* was nominated for everything *but* Best Actress.

With fine attention given to audience experience of Todd-AO, widescreen, and multi-track stereo, *The Sound of Music* sneak previewed in January of 1965 in Minneapolis. "The weather was miserable, and we thought nobody would show up," said Richard Zanuck. "But the theater was full, and at intermission the whole audience stood up and applauded for five minutes. They did it again at the end. . . . Bobby Wise and I looked at each other, shell-shocked." That freezing winter night in Minneapolis was the first time Zanuck imagined that he was sitting on a major hit. "We came back to the hotel and waited in my suite, Bobby Wise and some of the executives and distribution guys, everyone from the picture," he said. "We got drunk and we waited for the comment cards to arrive.... By the time we got them, we were all pretty smashed. We divided them up and everybody started reading them off: 'Excellent! Excellent! Excellent! Excellent! Excellent!' In my pile was one 'Very Good.' I was so tanked up that I got enraged—I wanted to call [exhibitor] Ted Mann and find out if there was any way of tracing who could have possibly written the card." Zanuck cabled his father that the preview was "nothing short of sensational. . . . there is no question in my mind but that we have great commercial hit of the smash category." After a like reaction in Tulsa, publicist Mike Kaplan told Wise, "You could get rid of me tomorrow and you'd still have a smash. Just open the doors and get out of the way."

Kaplan decided on the tag line "The Happiest Sound in All the World" for print ads, and they began to appear in February. Dominating them was Julie Andrews, swinging her guitar case in one hand and her overnight bag in another, running up a grassy hill with her exuberant charges behind. All are smiling broadly, while off to the side is an improbable, glowering Christopher Plummer with arms akimbo. When early *Music* ads ran in the *New York Times*, they shared a page with *My Fair Lady*, heralding its twelve Oscar nominations. When *Lady* earned Best Picture by the New York Film Critics, the Criterion announced it was taking reserve seat mail orders through 1965. Now expectations were rising for *Music*. *Film Bulletin* announced that it "*has the makings of a first-rate roadshow attraction*, possibly a staunch competitor for the phenomenally successful *My Fair Lady*. . . . It is *a potential blockbuster* for every market, except where action is a prerequisite."

The Sound of Music, scheduled for its world premiere in New York on March 2, played by the rules expected of roadshows. The opening night gala champagne supper dance benefited a worthy cause, the March of Dimes. For the klieg-lit opening, attendees were an Old School hodgepodge of show business and politics. The souvenir program included two-page color spreads accompanied by lyrics, neatly mimicking the widescreen sweep of the movie. Most noteworthy was *Music*'s venue, the Rivoli on Broadway in the theater district. Designed by master architect Thomas White Lamb and erected in 1917, the Rivoli had a Greek revival exterior with eight fluted white Doric columns and a monumental isosceles pediment. The tympanum housed over two dozen statues from Greek myth, all in service to the glory of motion pictures. Two box offices of marble, glass, and stainless steel were fitted to accommodate all weather conditions. Inside, Miro and Picasso knockoffs adorned the foyer walls. Heavy glass doors opened onto the sidewalk, but solid doors into the auditorium prevented unwanted sunlight. Nineteen speakers delivered the finest in audio fidelity and the 1,600 mohair seats were more than comfortable. The sweeping widescreen was gently curved on both sides to offer a seductive and grandiose effect.

As Twentieth Century-Fox publicist Mike Kaplan would learn, his *Sound of Music* tag line "The Happiest Sound in All the World" was hardly an exaggeration. From the collection of Photofest.

Ever since *Oklahoma!* premiered there in 1955, the Rivoli was *the* place for roadshow musicals. *South Pacific, Can-Can,* and *West Side Story* had played extended runs. On *Music's* opening night, the audience filed in to find the house lights up and screen curtain closed, its fabric gently undulating across a broad expanse. A roadshow screen could *never* be bare. The crowd was seated, and a faint noise of wheels on tracks was heard while the curtain opened and the house lights dimmed. The garish blue-and-orange Twentieth Century-Fox spotlight logo lit the screen. But—the first sound was not music but a high wind blowing through dense white clouds. No overture? Isn't this a Rodgers and Hammerstein musical? Savvy filmgoers knew that *The Sound of Music* and *West Side Story* were both directed by the same man, and he appeared to be aping himself. Like *West Side Story, The Sound of Music* begins airborne. But all similarities end there. Instead of vertiginous shots high above the gridded canyons of Manhattan, the clouds thin to reveal a flight over serrated, snowy alpine peaks. We're above the tree line, but as wind gives way to chirping birds, we're zooming over a high forest ridge, then a reflecting river valley, lush pastures, and storybook castles. A barge glides on a shimmering blue lake. A piccolo mimics the birds, then the horns play a 12-note phrase. The earth is getting closer and the screen is dominated by forests and grass. Soon a lone figure tops a hill in the distance. The camera approaches from above, and we see she is wearing a dirndl and striding purposefully onto an open field. Nearer to her we fly as her arms outstretch and she spins in exaltation, the strings and brass swelling. Cut to a medium shot to confirm that she is the star, pretty young Julie Andrews. Her extended arms span the length of the screen, and they seem to enfold not just the beauteous scenery, but everyone gathered at the Rivoli as well. She is ready to burst with gladness:

The hills are a-liiiiiive, with the sound of muuuu sic . . .

Over the next minutes came the pristine rendition of the title song, then the gold-tinted opening credits ("A Robert Wise Production") set against the glorious backdrop of Salzburg, harmonizing nuns, precious love-starved children, the Captain, the Baroness, curtains to play clothes, accidental romance, and the intermission at one hour, 42 minutes. Following the entr'acte came reconciliation, marriage, growing Nazi threat, a tense concert, return of the nuns, and finally the "Climb Ev'ry Mountain" escape along a high ridge as the curtains of the Rivoli rolled shut and the last images flickered to dark. Exit music from the score accompanied the moviegoers as they rose to crowd the aisles.

During the premiere screening, Wise excused himself to get an early edition of the *New York Times*. He sat alone on one of the upholstered seats in the lobby and read Bosley Crowther's tepid-to-cold review: "[Andrews] provides the most apparent and fetching innovation in the film . . . [she] brings a nice sort of Mary Poppins logic and authority to this role, which is always in peril of collapsing under its weight of romantic nonsense and sentiment. . . . [She] seems to realize that the whole thing is being staged by Mr. Wise in a cozy-cum-corny fashion that even theater people know is old hat. . . . The septet of blond and beaming youngsters who have to act like so many Shirley Temples and Freddie Bartholomews when they were young do as well as could be expected with their assortedly artificial roles, but the adults are fairly horrendous, especially Christopher Plummer . . . looking as handsome and phony as a store window Alpine guide . . . a couple of new songs (both forgettable). . . . Its sentiments are abundant. Businesswise, Mr. Wise is no fool."

Crowther, whose stodgy tastes were out of step with many critics, might have been a champion. Instead, he continued to find fault, solidifying his opinion in a later article. "Where *My Fair Lady* and *Mary Poppins* have more or less held the ground achieved by *West Side Story* (at least, they have shown such style and grace that they cannot be charged with retrogressing) . . . *The Sound of Music* [has] set the musical film back 20 years." A similar tenor was heard from others. "Calorie-counters, diabetics and grown-ups from eight to 80 had best beware," warned Judith Crist in the *New York Herald Tribune*. "All that was a sugar-lump on stage has, courtesy of the super-spectacular screen, become an Alp. . . . The movie is for the five to seven set and their mommies who think their kids aren't up to the stinging sophistication and biting wit of *Mary Poppins*." Fox executive Seymour Poe became thin skinned whenever his cash cow was insulted. He was "sizzling" over the "unwarranted and vitriolic attack by Crist on a picture as superlative as *Sound of Music*," and "Insofar as Bosley Crowther is concerned, I think he has reached a point in his life when he is living in the 'never-never' land of 'precious' little movies—the kind with a $100,000 negative cost which probably play 300 bookings in the United States in cute little bandbox theaters." Darryl Zanuck stressed forbearance, believing "the public itself will take care of Miss Crist. After the film has been running one year at the Rivoli, then it might even be worthwhile reprinting her review as an advertisement." Dividing lines were drawn. The East Coast journalists were brutal, while the West Coast–based dailies and trade papers were enthusiastic.

The naysayers were louder, more plentiful, and ultimately more interesting, as they reveal the beginnings of a culture war that would grow more heated in the coming years. *The New Yorker*'s Brendan Gill positively foamed at the mouth: "A huge, tasteless blowup," he wrote. "When one adds the falseness of the plot to the falseness of the dialogue and then observes that the standard of acting maintained by Julie Andrews, Christopher Plummer, Richard Haydn, and Eleanor Parker is well under ordinary high-school level, it becomes obvious that an equal degree of verisimilitude could have been attained by shooting the picture at the nearest Walgreen's." He saw something vaguely sinister in this chipper family songfest, excoriating Ernest Lehman for penning the words "Salzburg, Austria, in the last Golden Days of the Thirties" that appear immediately after the opening credits.

Gill reminded his readers the late '30s were decidedly *not* golden, least of all in Austria, where resident Nazis were readying the death of 200,000 Viennese Jews. He and others were not begrudging people their entertainment, they just did not want it to dishonor the past. "*South Pacific, The King and I, West Side Story*: They have all been a little embarrassing, but perhaps *The Sound of Music* is more embarrassing than most, if only because of its suggestion that history need not happen to people like Julie Andrews and Christopher Plummer," noted *Vogue*. "Just whistle a happy tune, and leave the *Anschluss* behind." Apart from its avoidance of history, it was still too glycemic for critics and other onlookers. Actor Doug McClure put it succinctly: "Watching *The Sound of Music* is like being beaten to death by a Hallmark card."

The cacophony of outrage over *Music*'s gooey sentiment is a curious thing. The film is no sweeter than Disney's 1960s offerings with Hayley Mills or the beach romps of Frankie Avalon and Annette Funicello. But something about *this* musical appearing at *this* time caused blood-freezing yowls. Did they sense the coming end of the old style musical? And were critics unhorsed by a creeping awareness that their words had no apparent effect on box office queues? Critics then and now often dwell on its cloying sweetness while sidestepping its many assets. Underneath the syrup glaze is a shrewdly conceived cinematic reworking of operetta bathos. Unlike the claustrophobic and set bound *My Fair Lady*, this musical takes in great gulps of clean, fresh air. Moments that were merely pleasing on stage became rapturous, as Wise took maximum advantage of what the screen has to offer. When Mary Martin sang "the hills are alive" at the Lunt-Fontanne Theatre, she did so perched on a papier-mâché tree in front of a painted backdrop of snowy mountain tops. Andrews, caught in that inspired opening, benefited from the full glory of location. The ascending major scale of "Do-Re-Mi" is hardly more exciting than "Chopsticks," but its deficits are erased on screen by jump cut editing and a thoughtful selection of Salzburg's loveliest sights. On Broadway, "My Favorite Things" was sung by Maria to the Mother Abbess. In the movie she teaches it to the kids, growing closer while distracting them from a withholding father and fearsome thunderstorm. Turning "The Lonely Goatherd" into a marionette show advances the children's adoration of Maria while enlivening the lyrics and framing the song neatly on a proscenium stage within a widescreen ratio.

Wise and Zanuck's casting gambles did and did not pay off. Both Christopher Plummer and Eleanor Parker managed somehow to be stiff and oily simultaneously, but most everyone loved Julie. She attacked her lines with a brisk efficiency that echoed Mary Poppins, yet there is a greater joviality to her Maria. Her bobbed hair lengthens her face and narrows her chin unflatteringly in profile, but her "radiance floods the screens, warms the heart, and brings back the golden age of the Hollywood musical," noted *Life* in a cover story about the new star. To James Powers at the *Hollywood Reporter*, she is "a whole whirling dazzling constellation. She is not just an ordinary movie personality, she is a phenomenon. Once there was Mary Pickford, then there was Garbo, now there is Julie. She is very likely going to be the object of one of the most intense and sustained love affairs between moviegoers and a star in the history of motion pictures." As the coming years would confirm, Powers was only half right about the whirling dazzling constellation. Intense, yes. Sustained, no.

The Sound of Music was rolled out quickly. From its early March openings in New York and Los Angeles, it arrived at more than two dozen premiere theaters in cities larger than 200,000 across North America by the end of the month. All were equipped for 70-millimeter widescreen projection and six-track stereophonic sound. The experience at Rivoli was replicated at the Italian Renaissance Michael Todd Theatre in Chicago, the art deco wonderland Fox Wilshire in Los Angeles, and the Mann in Minneapolis, Fox's good luck charm since *Music* previewed there. Then on perfect cue, Julie Andrews won the Best Actress Academy Award for *Mary Poppins*, and her certain arrival as a major new star was complete.

With so much wind in his sails, Zanuck exercised perfect instincts in distributing Fox's singing money machine. By the end of the month, *Music* was doing sellout business on 33 screens, twice a day in the biggest cities at high tickets prices of $2 to $3. Zanuck then delayed a standard release and spread *Music's* reserve seat engagements over a two-year period, extending its life in the urban centers while compelling theater owners in America's small and mid-sized cities to exhibit their first movie in the hard ticket format. *Music* expanded to another 98 screens, bringing the roadshow experience to such uninitiated townships as Harrisburg, Billings, Waco, and Sioux Falls. Records were broken everywhere.

The foreign business was no less impressive. *Music* began its international distribution at London's Dominion Theatre, and its non-English debut as *La Novicia Rebelde* (*The Rebellious Novice*) at the Ambassador Theater in Buenos Aires. When it moved to a global market, it trickled into 261 theaters over two years, dubbed for dialogue and songs in French, Italian, Spanish, and German. It benefited inestimably from repeat customers. Fox devised a "Certificate of Merit" to theaters where tickets sold exceeded the local population. Twenty-five certificates were issued to cities as large as Syracuse, Orlando, and Atlanta, and in the United Kingdom in Birmingham, Cardiff, and Newcastle-upon-Tyne. Before the end of its first run, *The Sound of Music's* 106 million domestic tickets sold would numerically equal 55 percent of the American population. Then came the backlash, albeit toothless. Germany, reportedly outraged by the cardboard Nazi villains, rejected it, and became the only market on the planet where *The Sound of Music* flopped. *Mad Magazine* titled its satire *The Sound of Money* and sent up its profitable sweetness, while college students in the one-screen town of Moorhead, Minnesota, picketed for relief. Protesters circled under *Music's* unchanging marquee with signs reading, "49 Weeks of Schmaltz is Enough" and "Don't Get Caught in the von Trapp."

By the end of 1965, *Music* was playing on 131 screens in America and had been number one at the box office for 30 consecutive weeks. It had amassed $65 million in worldwide receipts by week 35, and was inching its way up the list of all-time moneymakers presently occupied by top-ranked *Gone with the Wind* and the opulent 1950s roadshows *Ben-Hur*, *The Ten Commandments*, and *Around the World in 80 Days*. As the number of screens grew exponentially in 1966, data gathering and reporting became ever more inexact, with money figures a jumble of gross receipts, distributors share, and film rentals. But however they were derived, the numbers were huge. So huge, in fact, that *Variety* estimates had *The Sound of Music* eventually becoming the all-time top moneymaker.

The 1965 film awards were a standoff between populism and elitism, the masses and the critics, and old guard versus new, with the Academy caught in the middle. The critics ignored *The Sound of Music* in their awards, but it collected the Comedy or Musical Golden Globes for Best Picture and Best Actress. When Oscar nominations were announced, *Music* was up for ten. So was *Doctor Zhivago*, MGM's roadshow epic of the Russian Revolution and formidable box office competitor.

Screenwriter Ernest Lehman was not nominated, but there were fault lines deeper than his snub. Best Picture nominees *Darling*, a stylish defamation of London's *la dolce vita*, and *A Thousand Clowns*, a low-budget American anti-Establishment comedy, sat in startling opposition to the lift up your hearts and sing optimism of *The Sound of Music*. In the end, *Music* and *Zhivago* each picked up five awards at the Santa Monica Civic Auditorium at the first Oscar telecast in color. Best Actress went not to Julie Andrews, but to *Darling*'s mod, incandescent Julie Christie. Andrews had the affection of the world, but she could not erase the déjà vu of another singing nanny. Prizes for Picture and Director, however, went to *Music* and Robert Wise. The Best Picture victory was ultimate acknowledgment that *The Sound of Music* was critic-proof, that their venom was not fatal, and that the Academy was as enamored of old-fashioned false nostalgia as any audience in Middle America. As it had most everywhere else in the world, *The Sound of Music* made a great number of people in Hollywood very, very happy.

In August of 1966, *The Sound of Music* surpassed *Gone with the Wind* as the number one box office movie of all time. It took 26 years of releases and rereleases for *Gone with the Wind* to amass its income. It took *The Sound of Music* 18 months. And some associates became very rich. Lehman's estimate was $1,000 a day for two years. Wise and his Argyle Enterprises, and associate producer Saul ("Solly") Chaplin, received 10 percent of the profits, meaning Wise deposited at least $8 million. Richard Rodgers and the estate of Oscar Hammerstein received 10 percent of the gross after exhibitors took their share. And by the end of 1966, nearly two years after its premiere, it was still playing with reserve-seat high priced tickets. As of November 1966, *Music* had played only 275 screens in the United States, and only 3,164 out of a potential 35,000 worldwide. Still ahead were neighborhood theaters, drive-ins, and rereleases at lower prices.

Lehman recalled that he and Dick Zanuck were walking back from the Fox commissary one day when Zanuck smiled and said, "It's a great picture, isn't it?'"

"I just don't make a habit of getting too enthusiastic," said Lehman.

"I want to hear you say it," said a goading Zanuck. "Say 'it's a great picture.'"

"Yes, Dick. It's a great picture."

It seems inevitable in retrospect, but Dick Zanuck had his doubts. "It was a gamble for us," he said, "because $8.2 million, which is what it cost to make, is a lot of money; it was not the most distinguished show Rodgers and Hammerstein had ever done, and our cast was relatively unknown." William Wyler did not see it coming. "The very things we were on guard against are the things that appeal to so many people," he said. "In a world which has changed enormously in the last few years, the movie is a kind of fantasy about a world which no longer exists, where everything comes out right, the Nazis aren't really Nazis, and it's happy-ending time. Our astronauts have succeeded in getting out of this world, but those who haven't go to see *The Sound of Music* one more time." *My Fair Lady* director George Cukor had to admit that his movie's success looked wan in comparison. "In spite of [*Music's*] naiveté, you find yourself caught up," he said. "There's a tug at the heart. My principal emotion is jealousy."

In accessing the film's popularity, Andrews said, "It's refreshing and not too complicated. A love story, with children and music. That word 'joyous' has an awful lot to do with it." To Zanuck, "It deals with good, wholesome subject matter—kids, nuns—and it entertains in a charming, romantic way." To Lehman, "We had no formula. When you think of a picture's success, you have to think of the world market, and there's no formula for that. I was surprised it was so successful in Tokyo, but what do I know of the Japanese, huh? Maybe they want to escape, too; maybe they're tired of making transistor radios." Wise aimed for more lofty words, saying the success "reminds us that film is truly a medium more powerful than we are capable of understanding." Their summations aren't revelatory, so does *anyone* know what ingredients stirred in what proportions resulted in the addictive cocktail known as *The Sound of Music*? Wise all but threw up his hands in stupefaction. "I wasn't trying to say a damn thing," he admitted. "No message. That's as good a face as I can put on it."

It has since been made clear that *The Sound of Music* was the pinnacle of the American screen musical's viability, winning Oscars and dumping mountains of cash on Twentieth Century-Fox even as it was spit roasted by the critics. What most of them missed was its monumental confidence in the power of song to move us beyond a drab existence. *London Times* pointedly asked, "How far, perhaps, is the awful eagerness to see this pleasant film a sign that simple and basic things are lacking in many people's lives?" While *Music* was becoming the most popular movie in the world, Malcolm X was assassinated, the United States increased its military presence in Southeast Asia, the worst race riots in the nation's history took place, Vietnam protesters surrounded the White House, and the United States dropped its first bombs on Hanoi. *The Sound of Music*, it seems, gave shape to sweet dreams in an era of nightmares.

When *Music* left the Rivoli in December of 1966, it had played there for 94 weeks. It could have kept going, but Fox was itching to showcase its newest Robert Wise roadshow *The Sand Pebbles*. *Music* was only the second-longest running film in Rivoli history; *Around the World in 80 Days* ran 103 weeks, but *Music* was the highest grossing. Only after it closed at the Rivoli did it play at nine theaters in greater New York City at regular prices. It was not until mid-June 1967 that it expanded to a mere six theaters in greater Los Angeles. More than two years after the premiere, *Variety* was still reporting *Music* among the top grossing movies in circulation. By final count, it booked more than 600 roadshow engagements and ran four and a half years in its original release, finally closing in December of 1969.

The Sound of Music legitimized the hit-driven blockbuster mentality that had come to rule Hollywood since Mike Todd and *Oklahoma!* "The beauty of the big picture nowadays is, of course, that there seems to be no limit to what the box office return may be," noted *Fortune* magazine in 1955. The words were even truer 10 years later. Rather than rely on a steady output of mid-budget modestly profitable movies, one studio could feed off the meaty carcass of a super-hit for years. And with the diversification of American entertainment, the potential for secondary markets was enormous. Besides profitable afterlives on television, successful roadshows could spawn reissued novels, comic books, clothing, and toys. The soundtrack sales alone were breathtaking. *Poppins*, *Lady*, and *Music* all sat comfortably on *Billboard*'s annual top 10 best-selling albums list, *Music* remaining there for three years.

These three arrived with a sudden gale force, their premieres telescoped into a period barely more than six months. They were nominated for a combined 35 Academy Awards, and won 18. As one filmmaker put it, they are "going to give virtue a good name in Hollywood." Richard Zanuck could hardly believe his luck. "To come back like this [after *Cleopatra*]," he said, shaking his head in amazement. "It unquestionably marked the dramatic turnaround of Twentieth Century-Fox. Everything about this picture has a happy ending."

Or does it? The influential critic Pauline Kael was getting the heebie-jeebies, and she was not one to be silenced by so much box office and so many Oscars. "The more money these 'wholesome' movies make, the less wholesome will the state of American movies be," she wrote. "'The opium of the audience,' Luis Buñuel, the Spanish director, once said, 'is conformity.' And nothing is more degrading and ultimately destructive to artists than supplying the narcotic." Kael upbraided Wise for inciting Pavlovian responses in his audience. While we may produce moisture about the eyes during a well-placed emotional climax, some of us nonetheless "loathe being manipulated in this way and are aware of how self-indulgent and cheap and ready-made are the responses we are made to feel." She was a self-appointed Cassandra to Hollywood's Troy, and, true to script, her words were ignored. "'The Sound of Money' . . . was probably going to be the single most repressive influence on artistic freedom in movies for the next few years," she prophesied.

Dick Zanuck did a reversal and essentially agreed with her, but only after the fact. "*The Sound of Music* did more damage to the industry than any other picture," he said years later. "Everyone tried to copy it. We were the biggest offenders."

The Singing Nun starring Debbie Reynolds arrived from MGM in 1966 as the first *Music* knockoff. It tells the true story of Belgian sister and one-hit wonder Jeanine Deckers, who stole hearts when she sang "Dominique" on *The Ed Sullivan Show*. It was not a musical strictly speaking, but it was unintentionally funny, polluted with lines like "the guitar is the only family she's ever known." There were the nun comedies *The Trouble with Angels* and its sequel *Where Angels Go . . . Trouble Follows*, the atrocious Elvis Presley vehicle *Change of Habit*, and the TV series *The Flying Nun*.

Variety wondered if the wimple craze wasn't "a form of audience rebellion against too many sexy-spy, ultra-adult efforts on the market," but the nun business was a minor affair compared to *Music*'s impact on musical roadshows. The ensuing gold rush nearly equaled the madness over sound following *The Jazz Singer*. The world craved musicals, or so it seemed, and Hollywood was going to deliver. There would be original musicals, Broadway adaptations, musical biopics, English imports, and revivals. There would be musicals for grown-ups and musicals for kids, live action and animation. Jack Warner went forward with his film version of *Camelot*, confident it would be a worthy follow-up to *My Fair Lady*. For the youth market, he also planned a singing version of *Rebel Without a Cause*, with suggested casting of Bob Dylan or Troy Donahue. Paramount soon announced four upcoming eclectic, expensive musicals, three of them from stage originals: *Half a Sixpence, Paint Your Wagon, Darling Lili*, and *On a Clear Day You Can See Forever*. Disney, intensely pleased with the over-achieving *Mary Poppins*, announced its next musical would be the original all-star *Happiest Millionaire*. MGM raided its own vaults for inspiration. Musical versions of *Goodbye, Mr. Chips, The Great Waltz*, and *Random Harvest* were announced. Universal went forward with the original *Thoroughly Modern Millie* and the Broadway transfer *Sweet Charity*.

Most committed of all was a smug Fox, which now referred to *The Sound of Music* as "The Mint." Dick Zanuck announced that its musical offerings over the next few years were to include *Doctor Dolittle*, based on the children's stories; *Bloomer Girl* and *Hello, Dolly!*, based on Broadway originals; and a biopic of English stage star Gertrude Lawrence for Julie Andrews. Each of these were to be lavished with all the money, capital resources, and talent available to its producing company. And each was designed to be a reserve seat, hard ticket extravaganza. Few among the executive wise men paid attention to the rise in cheap "teen pics," the increased visibility of underground films, or the new hunger for European titles on university campuses and in small neighborhood cinemas. What did any of that matter? A blazing new era of screen musical entertainment had begun.

CHAPTER 2

"I, Too, Can Sing"

Camelot arrived on Broadway in 1960 on a golden chariot. Its creators were no less than Alan Jay Lerner and Frederick Loewe, lyricist and composer of the skyrocketing hit *My Fair Lady*. Its director was Moss Hart, whose genius segued from librettist to playwright, and producer, as well as director. Its stars were the charismatic Welshman Richard Burton, Julie Andrews, and Robert Goulet as good King Arthur, his faithless Queen Guenevere, and the man who came between them—the brave, dashing, but vain Sir Lancelot du Lac. As if *Camelot* needed additional marketing petrol, President Kennedy, a Harvard classmate of Lerner's, was moved by its utopian vision set to music. According to Jackie Kennedy, he was spellbound by the Knights of the Round Table as a boy and played the Broadway cast album in the White House. When she spoke to *Life* magazine just one week after Dallas, she implored the world to embrace the title song "Camelot" as the symbol of her slain husband's administration. "He loved 'Camelot,'" she said. "It was the song he loved most at the end." The last line of the final reprise haunted them both:

> *Don't let it be forgot*
> *That once there was a spot*
> *For one brief shining moment*
> *That was known as Camelot.*

The reality of *Camelot* the musical, its making and unmaking as Broadway show and movie, lives much closer to the ground. In the months leading up to its pre-Broadway opening in Toronto, Moss Hart was hospitalized with a heart attack, Lerner suffered a bleeding ulcer and the breakup of his second marriage, and costume designer Adrian died. When it ran over four hours, Noël Coward proclaimed it "longer than *Parsifal* but not as funny." When it was scheduled next in Boston, Lerner quipped, "It would have been easier to move Toronto to Boston than *Camelot* to Boston."

Despite the less than enthusiastic early notices, *Camelot* sold over $2 million in advance ticket sales. When it opened one week late in December of 1960 at the

Majestic Theatre in New York, it still faced major rewrites in adapting T. H. White's gigantic Arthurian tetralogy *The Once and Future King*. "It was really half baked on stage," said Joshua Logan, the eventual director of the film. During its torturous two-year run on Broadway, Lerner said it was "plagued with enough misfortune to send everyone connected with it into the desert for 40 years." Kennedy's tastes notwithstanding, there were dull battle scenes, anachronistic humor, romantic clichés, and a distractingly bombastic chorus. In attempting to preserve both the farce and tragedy of White's book, Lerner and Loewe fell short of their flawless musical interpolation of Shaw with *My Fair Lady*. Logan, an avuncular man with silver hair and a paunch, found something of integrity there. "Lerner describes it as a story of a woman in which human passions destroy human dreams. That's the tragedy of *Camelot*. But Arthur learns his dream will live, even after the Round Table is destroyed, and that is its triumph."

Camelot's most powerful champion was in the White House, but its next most powerful was at Columbia Broadcasting System. Ed Sullivan presented the *Camelot* stars on his Sunday night TV variety show, and the result was an instant spike in ticket sales. *Camelot* eventually became a hit, running on Broadway for 873 performances, and touring extensively. Its original cast album sold well, and the songs "Camelot" and "If Ever I Would Love You" became standards. Rumblings of a film transfer began. The ultimate classic movie musical producer, MGM's Arthur Freed, urged studio president Joseph Vogel to buy the rights to both *Camelot* and *Paint Your Wagon*, a 10-year-old Lerner and Loewe musical. For *Camelot*, Freed envisioned the original cast with Vincente Minnelli (*Meet Me in St. Louis*, *Gigi*) directing. But Vogel was not enamored of either property, and said no to Freed's requests.

Jack Warner was hungrier for *Camelot* than Arthur Freed or anyone at MGM, and in February of 1961, Warner Bros. bought it for a hefty $2 million, with the agreement that the movie would not be released before April of 1964. That gave Warner some free time, so he went after *My Fair Lady*, which was still on Broadway and was a hit of greater magnitude. *Lady* was in fact the longest running production in Broadway history at the time Warner Bros. forged a movie deal. CBS, the stage production's underwriter, was open to offers, and MGM put in a bid for $4.5 million. But wily Jack Warner made a backroom deal with CBS guaranteeing $1 million over any competing offer. *My Fair Lady* was sold to Warner Bros. for $5.5 million in 1961, making it the highest cash payment ever made for source material for adapting to the screen.

In his voracious acquisition of two big musicals, Warner was absolutely certain of public demand. He made his tastes more than clear at the kickoff dinner party for the making of *Lady*. This son of a Jewish immigrant cobbler saw an opportunity to purvey decency again. Facing a roomful of industry professionals, he said "I think the American producers have learned a helleva lesson to stop aping the Italian, the French, and the Spanish and other undesirable films that have caused all this censorship and legions and seals and no seals and art and all that hokey-pokey." *Camelot* eventually found its angle of repose as a stage production, with its message of peace and reconciliation welcome during the Cold War. It thrived on tour, buoyed by lilting songs that received much airtime. Movement toward making the film version didn't resume until late in 1965, a full year after *My Fair Lady* was confirmed as a blockbuster. Suddenly the film version of *Camelot* took on the weight of higher expectations, as the recombining of Warner Bros. and Lerner and Loewe was anticipated to produce something just as grand. But, as Warner reluctantly came to accept, *Camelot* never approached the caliber of *My Fair Lady*, and no amount of money, talent, and time could wish it into greatness.

Lerner began punching out a screenplay without Loewe, who was happily retired and had not "the slightest intention to write another note." Robert Wise was offered the opportunity to direct, but in reporting to Warner, production chief Walter MacEwen noted, "He does not want to type himself as a director of musical subjects—and he still has *The Gertrude Lawrence Story*, which falls in that category, on his slate for next year." Then came the Texas born, Princeton educated Joshua Logan, who had impeccable credits as stage librettist, producer, and director of *South Pacific* and director of *Annie Get Your Gun*. His screen credits (*Mr. Roberts, Picnic, Bus Stop, Sayonara, Fanny*) were respectable, and he handled actors well, having guided three to Oscars and three more to nominations. His previous venture into film musicals was 1958's *South Pacific*, an artistically misbegotten effort that nonetheless brought huge revenues to Twentieth Century-Fox. Logan was suitably keen to the challenge of directing, and he signed for $250,000.

Logan was known to be efficient, a coveted trait considering that *Camelot* was already booked for an October 1967 roadshow premiere in New York. He was enthusiastic about Lerner's first-draft script. "The magic was eliminated," he said without a trace of irony. "What tore the musical apart was that you were dealing with real people having real problems, and suddenly Arthur was put under a spell. I liked the new approach without magic." He believed *Camelot* could make a great movie. Lerner was confident that Logan could deliver that great movie, too, as they both actually *liked* his handling of *South Pacific* on film. "[Lerner] had chosen me for *Camelot* with no demands as to how he wanted it done—simply gave me carte blanche," said Logan. "His job of writing had been completed before my work began. He had improved the stage play, I felt sure."

Warner and Lerner approached Richard Burton to reprise his stage role as Arthur, but when he demanded a salary twice that of what the studio was prepared to pay, talk of casting him ceased. Other big names were tossed around, including non-singers Peter O'Toole, Gregory Peck, and Marlon Brando, but they were rejected, not interested, or not available. Richard Harris learned of the screen transfer of *Camelot* while shooting the screen adaptation of James Michener's long best-selling novel *Hawaii* with Julie Andrews. "It took me about 15 seconds to say, 'I want that,'" he said. Unlike Eliza Doolittle, Guenevere on screen was a role Andrews viewed with antipathy. And the timing was wrong. After *Mary Poppins* and *The Sound of Music*, Andrews felt the need to develop as a dramatic actress, not a singing one. And she was in such demand that who could say when she'd be free to make *Camelot* anyway? "Guenevere I did hear about," she said. "Having not done *My Fair Lady*, it would be perhaps compared in some way. . . . For some reason, I said I'd rather not do it." Warner mulled over casting her, but doing so came with the tacit admission that he was wrong about Audrey Hepburn for *My Fair Lady*. Was Jack Warner wrong? Hadn't Andrews benefited amply from that "injustice"? *Lady* was undercut by an ossified treatment of the stage original more than by Hepburn's performance. As noted by musical historian John Springer, it was done "in high style, with all of its great stage moments lovingly preserved, and a big, big box office success to boot, what more could one have asked? We don't know, but we think there is something. Like excitement, perhaps."

When Andrews played Guenevere on stage, there was no sexless film image to overcome. Now she was the whole world's singing nanny, and hormonal Queen Guenevere is supposed to incite men to war. Logan told Warner he wanted "a ravishing bitch" in the role, and felt Andrews did not suffice. "She was never a dangerous Guenevere," Logan said of her stage performance. "She was cozy and little girlish and adorable. When I heard her sing 'Lusty Month of May'—the word 'lusty' had nothing to do with the ingénue way she sang or with the cute way her courtiers danced. Somehow, it all looked like the yearly maypole dance at Mansfield Female College back in Louisiana."

The casting of Guenevere is an example of the sudden temperature change that occurs when publicity turns an unknown into a star. A Warner Bros. memo listed a dozen not too famous young British actresses for the role, including Vanessa Redgrave, all below the "obvious names" of Julie Andrews, Audrey Hepburn, and Julie Christie. On yet another list Warner contemplated Polly Bergen, Ann-Margret, and *South Pacific*'s Mitzi Gaynor. Then Redgrave became the latest mod British bird to enchant America with the release of the quirky low-budget comedy-drama *Morgan: A Suitable Case for Treatment*. Suddenly the *New York Times* swooned over "tall and majestic" Vanessa, who came with extraordinary credentials. Her mother was actress Lady Rachel Kempson, and her father was Sir Michael Redgrave, both the sorts of British actors who invite the word "distinguished" in front of their names. Press attention grew with the simultaneous ascension of younger sister Lynn, making her own mark in *Georgy Girl*, yet another appealingly oddball British entry. Logan's son saw *Morgan* and told his father to have a look. Redgrave *is* Guenevere, he believed. She was not known for her singing, but Logan was impressed enough by a recording of folk songs she had sung. And she certainly could act; Logan saw in her a feral sex appeal he believed would serve the project well. The frenzy was on. "Every producer in the world seems to be after her," noted a studio memo from production head Walter MacEwen. "She's the answer to our industry," gushed Logan.

Warner was unconvinced, and none too pleased with her outspoken politics. "I voted Labor but feel pretty low about it," she told a reporter. "It's so shortsighted of them to back America in Vietnam. I feel the American government is making a terrible mistake." He was further concerned about her commitment to *The Prime of Miss Jean Brodie* on the London stage for the next several months. "Do we really have to wait for that tall Communist dame until November?" he asked Logan. Then he saw *Morgan* and became yet another one of her champions. Logan negotiated shrewdly, noting that the company could shoot Lancelot's quest on medieval locations in Spain while Redgrave fulfilled her obligations in London. Warner agreed.

Andrews and everyone else faded in the sudden blinding light of Vanessa Redgrave. But she was reticent about *Camelot* not so much because of her vocals but because of the artificiality of its old-fashioned ways. "I've never even worked in a *studio* before—it's all been on location," she said. She bounced all over London in *Morgan*, accompanied by British New Wave's loose structure and camera trickery. She was free, improvisational, outdoors, and very sexy. With *Camelot*, she would be weighed down by cumbersome queenly finery on a cavernous sound stage, and she feared such domestication would "rule out accidents and they're often the most fertile moments of all." She eventually overcame her own reservations. "It seemed exciting to find if I could beat the problems of not being in a natural state." She signed for $200,000 and two demands: that she get two weeks rest following *Jean Brodie*, and that she do her own singing.

Richard Harris waged a vigorous four-month sales pitch on Lerner, Warner, and Logan. In his quest for Arthur, he besieged them with cables, letters, offers for screen tests, and "I love you" cards. "You have to hand it to him, he left no stone unturned," said Franco Nero, the chiseled, wavy haired, blue-eyed Italian who was cast as Lancelot. Given Warner's past struggles with free-living actors like Errol Flynn, his acceptance of Harris took some convincing. Of the dozen movies Harris had done, only one, the uncompromising rugby drama *This Sporting Life*, had made a strong impression in the States. Warner reasoned that what he needed was a lucky break, since even by the emotive standards of classic British acting, he was uniquely commanding. The six-foot tall, 200-pound Limerick Irishman came with a booming voice, penetrating blue eyes, and a fallen mop of red hair. "A critic once described my face as five miles of bad Irish country road," he said. "Every wrinkle tells a tale. I wouldn't eliminate a single wrinkle for $1,000." Casting a potentially brilliant Harris came with huge risks. "I swim in a pool of my own neuroses," he said. "I carry love, grief, and wrath deeply like an Irishman." An unrepentant drunk, he had broken his nose multiple times while brawling, and was well acquainted with various members of English law enforcement, once knocking over a double-decker bus with a small Ford. His bad boy offscreen high jinks had benefited his career so far, in that they were an extension of the rough types he'd played effectively on film. But that convenient association, that melding of the private man and public actor, wouldn't do for King Arthur. Warner knew how to deal with insubordinate actors, but he did not enjoy it. For a salary of $300,000, he expected model conduct from Harris.

For traitorous Mordred, Arthur's bastard son, Logan cast 25-year-old David Hemmings, a doleful-eyed actor with credits already stretching back more than a decade. Roddy McDowall, the stage Mordred, was too old at 37; his "father" Richard Harris was two years younger. Robert Goulet, the stage Lancelot, was unsuitable for different reasons. Though he had a mellifluous baritone that caused romantics to hyperventilate, Logan felt he was not "ascetic enough to suggest the holy or spiritual, and his lustiness was that of a red-blooded American boy. Only his name suggested the French background Alan Lerner demanded." Franco Nero claimed that both he and Harris were hired on the recommendation of John Huston, who was directing Harris as Cain and Nero as Abel in *The Bible: In the Beginning.* . . . If he was not French, Nero at least exuded a continental air, and his good looks would compensate for inauthenticity. Warner abandoned his desire for a top French actor and agreed to Nero. Logan was concerned that Nero's English was insufficient, but his prejudice was destroyed when Nero delivered a speech from *Romeo and Juliet* that he learned phonetically. When asked if he could sing, Nero responded, "Everyone sings in Parma! I, too, can sing; as a boy I worked many times in opera choruses." As if it was his decision, he announced that *Camelot* is to "definitely" feature his voice. "I'm an actor—but if somebody asks can I sing, I can sing!" It seemed Warner had lost his instinct for casting, and perhaps even his taste for confrontation. Ever since Marni Nixon had done ghost vocals for Audrey Hepburn, dubbing had been a dirty word. But rather than hire stars with musical credentials, Warner simply let his stars take on the score themselves, imperfect pitch and all.

Camelot preparation required extensive research, with a log kept of queries from Logan, production designer John Truscott, or any one else in charge of one of the film's creative departments. Truscott, a distractible and wildly inventive 29-year-old Australian, had never made a film, but his designs for the London production of *Camelot* so captivated Warner that he insisted Truscott get the job. Truscott was excited by the opportunity, perhaps too excited. *Camelot* the film was a complete visual reinvention, and no detail was too minute. The research log book contained inquiry records of, among many other topics, the spelling of "guenevere," cosmetics in the time of King Arthur, archaeology and Camelot, books on tapestries, necklaces, heraldry, Punch and Judy, castles in Scotland, drawbridges, clocks, lights, horns, gargoyles, falconry, when were celestial globes first made?, does the Queen sit on the right or the left of the King?, handbags and pouches, the archbishop's ring, door hinges, Norwegian houses, Breugel pictures, soap, towels, brushes for Arthur's bath, and fruit in England circa 1200.

Warner told MacEwen he wanted sets, costumes, and props under way before he left to oversee production in Spain. "This is a very serious project," he wrote in his authoritative "Papa Jack" style. "We must get the finished script, the breakdown of the scenes, the budget, the shooting schedule, etc. You know exactly what

I mean and all concerned know what I mean so let's get moving." Warner's marching orders incited Logan and Truscott to think on the grandest scale, and the sets came to represent an entire self-sustained kingdom. There was tremendous range in the legerdemain for the interiors. Warner and Logan envisioned something that combined the factual and historic with the imaginary and fantastic, while Truscott borrowed visual elements from Saxon, Viking, and Gothic interiors. As Logan put it, "Since it is patently impossible to recreate with any accuracy the period from Arthur's legendary past, the whole picture will have the aspect of a period no one has ever known, but which may be identified in the onlooker's eyes and mind as something surely out of a colorful past."

Truscott, who lacked all instincts to economize, began constructing an array of non-working gadgets and set pieces, such as a sundial, astrolabe nautical navigation aid, and a fanciful stargazer. Within the castle courtyard were a tinsmith, blacksmith, silversmith, carpenter, tailor, and sculptor, each with his own shop. Outside were butchers, greengrocers, bakers, weavers, ceramists, cobblers, undertakers, candlestick makers, apothecaries, and assorted livestock. As script drafts appeared, the Production Code voiced its concern for animal safety in the jousting scenes and suggested that the production consult the American Humane Society. In matters of sex and nudity, its directive sounds alarmingly retro: "In the love scenes, among the 'Visions of Their Past,' on page 89, scenes 158 through 165, we could not, of course, have our lovers in the nude. They should be properly and decently clothed."

Logan was obsessed with avoiding clichés—no illuminated manuscript head-dresses, gold banners, or embroidered lion silhouettes. "The fact that Alan Lerner uses modern nicknames for his characters, much wit and rather informal speech at times plus the fact that it is 'musical' rather than 'straight legitimate drama' and that it is based on T. H. White's fanciful book, gives us much license to experiment," he wrote to Warner. "I feel we should make use of all of the modern techniques of photography, cutting, sound recording, set decoration, and laboratory work that some Italian, English, and French directors have made enormous strides in recently. This picture should help show the world that Hollywood is still capable of being the style setter of the motion picture industry." To that end, Logan's wish list included "vast forests," "wild animals," "elaborate materials for decor," "sophisticated costumes," "young peasants working in plowed field," "wrestlers, acrobats," "stained glass windows," "pointed Gothic arches," "frescos," "tapestries," "fleur-de-lis-esque elegance," and in "The Lusty Month of May" sequence, emphasis should be placed on "lusty," not "May."

Warner's faith in the project, and in Logan's stewardship, was so high that he said yes to almost everything. Soon the backlot was teeming with building in preparation for the late November start date of 17 weeks of studio production. Fifteen of Warner's 23 stages were consumed with *Camelot*. There were 20 white oaks, sycamores, cottonwood, and elm newly planted, as well as seedlings and shrubbery. Models and work drawings were under way, and portions of the set were already in the mill. Costumes would be constructed through purchases Truscott made in Spain and California, with the rest to be rented from Western Costume. "Things seem to be coming along very nicely," reported associate producer Joel Freeman from the studio in Burbank to Warner at his villa in Cap d'Antibes in the South of France. "C'est Moi" and "Camelot" were prerecorded and as Truscott prepared to leave for Spain, "he will leave plenty of work to keep his crew busy while he is gone."

Production documents for *Camelot* read like planning notes for an East Hampton lawn party. Here is a movie hell-bent on making clutter. Notes on the design of "The Lusty Month of May" include "jonquils, daffodils, lily of the valley, forget-me-nots, violets, bluebells, briar roses, wild clematis, mock orange, hawthorn, buttercups," but "it is also suggested that we don't go too wild with the quantity of flowers on the set itself, save for a mass of *real* daffodils, for fear of becoming too pretty pretty, too precious, too picture postcard. Although it seems impossible at the moment, somehow we *must* have a field of bracken fern." (The official count of daffodil bulbs was 2,400.) Picnics should include tablecloths, hampers, peasant pies, dried (not fresh) fruit, a side of beef, spit-roasted pork, truffles, breads, jams and jellies, and, of course, a potpourri of spring flowers (see earlier) so profuse that all that food can hardly be seen. Arthur's bath would contain a carved, ornamental copper tub with embroidered washcloths. His study was to be filled with an abundance of stuffed mammals and fish, rock quartz, collections of butterflies, eggs, hourglasses, maps, star charts, and rocks, a hawk on a stand, caged English thrushes, tapestries, scrolls, manuscripts, a dragon skeleton, "books and more books," fur rugs, fossils, seashells, paperweights, and candles and holders "smothered with molten candle wax to the point of overdoing it."

While nails were pounding into sets in Burbank, and Redgrave was earning raves onstage as Miss Jean Brodie, production began in Spain on a 30-day shooting schedule. Beginning in "Madrid's lung," the verdant Casa del Campo, the crew visited eight locations in total, with an emphasis on various magnificent Spanish castles. With Warner's full commitment, the money flew out of California and into Iberia. The Castle of Coca was the inspiration for *Camelot*, now being duplicated in Burbank. But when set designer Edward Carrere deviated from the original, about 1,500 pounds of cobblestones were shipped to the Castle of Coca to match those already in place at Warner's. If that seemed like taking coal to Newcastle, Logan explained "It was absolutely necessary since we expect to do everything right in this picture—even to matching Spanish and Hollywood cobblestones." The finished castle was the largest set ever built on the Warner backlot, measuring 400 by 300 feet, and nearly 100 feet tall with a reported cost of more than half a million dollars.

The cast and crew on location numbered more than 100, with nearly as many horses, and a full complement of costumes and accessories. A production budget

Camelot production designer John Truscott reviews the wall of fabric swatches he collected for the film's costumes. From the collection of Photofest.

was generated during the weeks in Spain. Sets were currently estimated at $1,482,549, with "miscellaneous" at $1,640,606. *Camelot* would now cost $11,093,750, based on holding firm to the 30-day shoot in Spain, with a seven-week hiatus, and 82 additional days in the studio. Warner was uncharacteristically quiet during the rebudgeting, but he did issue an edict stating that all travel to and from Spain must be via the Polar Route, with no stopovers in New York or anywhere else.

Production in Spain began at a leisurely pace and was only mildly disrupted by the weather. When it was not raining, temperatures rose past 100 degrees and strained the mobile kitchen's water supply, but no dehydration of cast or crew was reported. The early action focused on Lancelot as he recruits the best of knights to the cause of Arthur and the Round Table. The first scene to be filmed included his song "C'est Moi," which he lip-synched atop a horse to a playback recording done by a professional. His boyhood experiences in Parma notwithstanding, Nero's singing voice was judged to be inadequate for Lancelot's soaring ballads and Logan decided he would be dubbed by tenor Gene Merlino. Nero's speaking voice brought a related challenge. He was no more proficient speaking English than singing it, and was tutored daily by exported UCLA professor Daniel Vandraegen, credited as "speech consultant."

Truscott was overseeing costume and set construction in Burbank when he saw the first raw footage from overseas. In a memo of barely contained panic to MacEwen, he was "horrified" by what came back. "I feel most sincerely that I should return to Spain instantly to try and get into this picture the distinction and quality that we all so earnestly hope for," he said. "The past few rushes that I have seen have been amateurish, dated, and straight out bad.... I consider [returning to Spain] a *must*." Truscott arrived in Madrid the following day.

In direct contradiction to Truscott, Logan wrote to Freeman expressing his pleasure at the performances being turned in by both Harris and Nero. "If [Nero] seems a bit too much at times, I have always shot or will shoot protecting close ups where his diction and true dedication will cut through." He did admit to some problems with art direction, but Truscott's return improved things "when the Spanish art director had botched it." Logan was thrilled with the beautiful shots capturing the hot blue skies and burnished countryside, and dismissed a few days delay from rain as a minor setback.

With barely a week left of shooting in Spain, Harris boarded a plane in Madrid and flew home to London. He told Freeman to expect his return in three days, with the sudden departure "caused by some legal caper in connection with his divorce." Harris was distraught at the possibility of losing his three young sons. This disregard for an expensive production brought Freeman to a boil with "The Mad Irishman." He had already relinquished his location apartment to Harris's astrologer, and had to contend with an irate restaurateur who barred Harris and threatened to call the police because of his behavior. Redgrave, meanwhile, was caving under stress in London. She reportedly suffered a mental breakdown during a performance of *Jean Brodie* and could not remember her lines. The vacation written into her contract was no indulgence of a pampered star. It now seemed a necessary restorative against future attacks.

The great hopes of Spain disappeared rather quickly. Harris returned to finish the shoot as promised, but Logan was despairing toward the end. To lower Freeman's expectations, he wrote, "I wish we could have given you only great film in Spain but with this setup and this weather it's absolutely the best we could do." Increasing rain delayed what could be filmed, and Spain finished 12 days behind schedule. Logan came home with just 30 minutes of printed footage, a tiny amount to show for more than a month on location.

Warner hosted a press luncheon for 400 to rouse excitement for *Camelot*. Smitten with his leading lady, Logan said to the assemblage, "Ladies and gentlemen, I give you Vanessa Redgrave, the most beautiful girl in the world." With that, she entered, her jewels, gown, and hair consistent with a young actress grabbing at Hollywood stardom. Her claim to Logan's superlative was boosted by the premiere that very evening of Michelangelo Antonioni's *Blow-Up*, an opaque murder mystery she made with *Camelot*'s David Hemmings. Both found themselves at the height of vogue when *Blow-Up* became a much discussed art house hit. Avant-garde cineastes revered its chic avoidance of conventional meaning while traditionalists scratched their heads. Jack Warner was baffled with Antonioni's success, though whether he believed Hemmings and Redgrave going topless would help *Camelot* revenue is anyone's guess. No longer could Logan put on a happy face, and still ahead was a great portion of the film's shooting. "The enormous production went on its huge, lumbering way, like a mammoth juggernaut about to crush us all," he wrote.

With nothing left to do but build sets and wait for Redgrave to finish *Jean Brodie*, the production went on hiatus. Warner might have hoped for a smooth studio finish to his musical opus, with no more Harris nonsense or Redgrave breakdowns, but he was preoccupied. A bombshell rattled Warner Bros. and immediately explained his curious detachment from *Camelot*. Seventy-four-year-old Jack Warner had agreed "in principle" to sell his 1.6 million shares in Warner Bros. Pictures, Inc. to the Toronto-based film and television distribution company Seven Arts. Details were yet to be announced, but Warner was expected to receive $32 million from the sale. "Not bad for a butcher boy from Youngstown, Ohio," he said with his familiar toothy smile.

Jack Warner did not step down as president hurriedly. He would oversee the completion of *Camelot*, but the buyout was shocking news. He had been there at the studio's founding in 1923 with his three brothers, but Jack became the dominant face of Warner Bros. There was ample speculating about why he voluntarily stepped down. For him, television was the adversary ever since the Federal Communications Commission prevented his studio from getting an early hold on production for the small screen. With court decisions disfavoring monopolistic studios, and unions exercising greater control, hierarchy and power were redefined. "It isn't fun anymore," he told his son-in-law. "Casting a picture is a pain in the ass nowadays; I've got to deal with all those fucking agents." Nudging from his wife to relax and get his estate in order was further incentive. And behind his decision was the reluctant admission that he was not only aging but growing irrelevant as well. Between the new corporate men roaming the studios and the independent producers working with small budgets and low overhead, the mighty overseers of classic backlot production studios were nearly extinct. The Burbank studio did not buzz with busy sets the way it used to. Perhaps Warner's distribution chief Ben Kalmenson played on Warner's disillusion by making it worse. "Ben kept feeding him stories of how bad the picture business was going to be," said studio publicist Max Bercutt. "If Warner had held out for a couple of years, he could have sold his shares for 70 million dollars instead of 20. I asked him if he regretted that. He said, 'What's a few million, more or less?' But I really think selling broke his heart." His heart would endure another ordeal when *Camelot* went into release.

CHAPTER 3

The Animal Kingdom

While Jack Warner was free-spending on *Camelot*, Twentieth Century-Fox led the roadshow charge. Studio head Darryl Zanuck was its most vocal advocate. With *The Sound of Music* newly installed as the world's top money earner, he possessed evangelistic zeal:

> Roadshows have put motion back in motion pictures. For too many people, the definition of this maneuverable word, Roadshow, stops with "reserved seats at fancy prices." But to me, Roadshow means moving the motion picture industry back into high gear, leading the entertainment field once more by making films which could never have been born without this new production concept. It changes budgeting, financing, and in turn new availability of talent, ideas, technical and engineering feats—a whole new horizon of production possibilities. . . . We all know too well how past abrupt changes in the country's entertainment habits—spelled *television*—broke up a lot of "easy" industry patterns. Suddenly the public could see in their own parlors the reality of space shots, race riots, political conventions, even heaven forgive us—assassinations. The world of illusion as created in the Hollywood studios and photo labs, or the excitement of a thousand screaming extras, no longer matched the day-to-day drama piped into homes throughout the world.

Zanuck was convinced that revenues would support their size and lead to technical and aesthetic innovations that only big money could buy. "We are deeply committed to this fundamental concept of making and presenting films. It is fully reflected in our '67–'68 production program of roadshows. We expect *Doctor Dolittle* to have a great chance of repeating *The Sound of Music* appeal for total family business." Based on the children's stories written by Englishman Hugh Lofting in the first half of the twentieth century, the *Doctor Dolittle* books told of a pudgy, lovable country veterinarian who spoke 498 animal languages, but was finding Goldfish a challenge. "That's the trouble with fish languages," the good doctor said. "They only work under water."

Fox bought the *Dolittle* rights in 1963 through Arthur P. Jacobs, a former press agent now fledgling independent producer. Jacobs was a colorful figure even by Hollywood standards, known for his highly developed organizational skills, a cigarillo in one hand and a Fresca in the other, and an enviable track record of shaping the public images of many top stars and directors. With a new production company named APJAC for its founder, Jacobs was given an initial $6 million budget. *Dolittle* would reunite the *My Fair Lady* duo of star Rex Harrison and screenwriter-lyricist Alan Jay Lerner, with *Lady* music supervisor André Previn writing the score. Harrison's interest derived primarily from the involvement of Lerner, who soon suffered something like writer's block exacerbated by an ugly divorce from his fourth wife. "He worked on the picture 15 months on and off, mostly off," said Jacobs. "We painted an office for him, painted his name on a parking space, and then we waited. And waited some more. I get him on the phone, he tells me he knows what he wants; it's all in his head. More phone calls. He tells me he wants to see me here, I go see him, he tells me he's leaving for New York, I go to New York; they tell me he's in Rome. That's it. So I signed Leslie Bricusse to write the script and do the score."

Bricusse was an affable composer suddenly in demand with the onset of musical fever. A Cambridge man considerably younger than Lerner, he was a true wunderkind, getting heard on the West End by age 19. His friendship with entertainer Anthony Newley resulted in the stage production *Stop the World—I Want to Get Off* that multiplied its return and begat the standard "What Kind of Fool Am I?" Bricusse, then in his early 30s and hungry to crack the movie business, was thrilled at Jacobs's offer to write the *Dolittle* songs. After the two met and conceptualized, the feelings were mutual. "He had more specific ideas than the other gent has had in 14 months," huffed Jacobs. Bricusse and his wife moved to Coldwater Canyon and in no time he hammered out "Talk to the Animals," a simple tune in keeping with Harrison's singing inabilities. Fox recorded early demo tapes of his tunes with a 75-piece orchestra, then sent the results to Harrison in Portofino on the Italian Riviera, where he kept a villa.

Doctor Dolittle was positioned as the biggest movie of a two-year horizon. Fox printed a countdown calendar for exhibitors as well as monthly mailers of *Dolittle* news, stills, talent search, fun facts and figures, and behind-the-scenes machinations. The animals provided a panoply of marketing hooks. Whatever parrot was to play Polynesia should be trained to give interviews, take screen tests, and behave appropriately for all attending press. Through Licensing Corporation of America, Fox orchestrated the biggest merchandising tie-in campaign in film history. New York–based Patricia Newcomb, the top woman in the business, was hired as Director of Publicity for a two-year stint, with a full staff under her. Jacobs's background as a press agent gave him confidence in big ideas. He wrote to

Pablo Picasso's representative asking the master to do a watercolor interpretation of Dolittle's world that would be auctioned off at a UNICEF benefit, and subsequently mass produced as a 1967 Christmas card, to be timed with the opening of the movie. But the ultimate conversation starter, and potential merchandising star, was *Dolittle*'s fantastic Pushmi-Pullyu, a llama-like creature with two opposite-facing heads and no ass.

Bricusse visited Harrison in Portofino. Christopher Plummer accompanied him, and recalls Bricusse serenading Harrison with *Dolittle* songs, while "Rex was glowing, his excitement rising by the second—you could almost see the money clicking away in his head as he added several grand more for each new song he would be obliged to sing." For directing, Richard Zanuck considered William Wyler, the man who avoided *The Sound of Music*, and John Huston, who was being driven to the brink by Fox's other unmanageably huge roadshow of the moment, *The Bible: In the Beginning*. . . . In reviewing the script, he cautioned his son against *Dolittle*'s heavy reliance on fauna, since *The Bible*'s Noah's ark sequence alone, with its 35 animal trainers on payroll for 18 months, was costing the studio $3 million. "I know of no motion picture that needs more careful and expert preparation than this one," he wrote to Richard. "When you deal with a number of almost uncontrollable items, it goes without saying that you have to *know* exactly what you can and what you can't do from a practical standpoint, otherwise it can be an economic disaster."

Neither Wyler nor Huston, nor third candidate George Roy Hill, had musical credits. Vastly more qualified was early suggestion Vicente Minnelli, who showed up on the short lists of directors for nearly every big musical of the late '60s. Zanuck wanted Richard Fleischer, a soft-spoken, unassuming Brooklynite and director of *Compulsion*, a homicide drama Zanuck had produced. Jacobs had the pleasure of offering the job to Fleischer, who was overwhelmed by the energy of the fast-talking neophyte producer. "His appearance always gave me the impression of a stick of dynamite enclosed in a thin turtle neck sweater covered by a handsome sports jacket," wrote Fleischer of Jacobs. Fleischer fancied himself a risk taker and was confident that today's kids will "dig" *Dolittle*. "I'm sick and tired of films which tell me how black and sad life is," he said.

Fleischer and Bricusse flew to Portofino and waited to rendezvous with Harrison in the elegant Hotel Splendido. The meeting was critical, since Harrison was given director approval and had never met Fleischer. Tensions were increased since a cagey and paranoid Harrison was at the height of his popularity, yet smarting from *My Fair Lady*'s humiliating salary inequities favoring Audrey Hepburn. He swept into the Splendido 90 minutes late. Awkward silences followed, as everyone could feel him lording his contractual rights over Fleischer and the entire production. Fleischer at last jumped off a cliff, announcing, "Rex, I hate to say it, but I've got something to tell you." More silence. "I'm sorry, but I don't think you're right for the part." It was Bricusse who broke the thick air with an explosive laugh, giving everyone permission to acknowledge Fleischer's nervy role reversal. Abundant wine and lasagna followed, and Harrison approved Fleischer. With that blessing finalized, a gargantuan *Dolittle* was populated by a cadre of middle-aged tyros. It was Jacobs's second movie, Bricusse's second as composer, Fleischer's first story musical, and Harrison's second.

Conflict surfaced when Harrison did not approve the casting of Sammy Davis Jr. in a supporting role. Davis had already agreed to the part, but Harrison was insistent. "I don't want to work with an entertainer. I want an actor. A real actor, not a song-and-dance man," said Harrison. He suggested Sidney Poitier, and he liked his idea so much that he threatened to quit if Poitier did not sign. Having been "Rexed," Fleischer and Jacobs went to New York to break the news to Davis while hoping that an actor of Poitier's stature would even *read* a part named Bumpo Kahbooboo, crown prince of Jolliginki. Poitier arrived at Fleischer's room at the Sherry-Netherland, and Jacobs proceeded to do the best sales job of his life. After the pitch, Poitier said, "I like it. I like it very much. Yes, I'll do it." That night, Fleischer and Jacobs had house seats to Davis's Broadway musical *Golden Boy*. It was hell, as Davis was playing directly to his two guests in an effort to ingratiate. Backstage was worse, as Poitier was there to congratulate his friend Davis on a fine performance. Jacobs finally told Davis the whole sad story over a late dinner. Davis was irate and threatened to talk to the press, sue Harrison, and complain to the National Association for the Advancement of Colored People (NAACP). The next morning, with everyone fully informed, Poitier phoned Jacobs and refused the part out of loyalty to Davis. But Poitier met with Bricusse, and, by some miracle, was talked back in. Jacobs wrote Poitier a note "to tell you how thrilled all of us are that you have agreed to be Bumpo."

Poitier was to be paid $250,000, a heavy sum for a role that was to appear only in the last third of the movie. Fleischer was to be paid $300,000 plus 5 percent of net profits. Harrison was to be paid $650,000 for 24 weeks, plus $25,000 per week overtime, $50,000 in expenses, 7.5 percent of the gross over $12 million, and 10 percent of the gross over $17 million. "The budget was beginning to look like a bloated stomach ad for Alka-Seltzer, but we hardly noticed it," wrote Fleischer. As Jacobs recalled, "So now Rex had a contract, he was getting more money than God, we were in business. Then Rex says, 'Good-bye, sue me, I'm not going to do it.' We had a picture called *Doctor Dolittle*, $12 million going in, and no one to play Doctor Dolittle." The mercurial Harrison told Jacobs the script was "bloody marvelous," then two days later rejected Bricusse's lyrics and the script, announcing he does not do pratfalls, will not be sung to, and wanted out. "Why don't you get Cary Grant to do it?" he asked. After much back and forth between agents and lawyers, Fleischer suggested approaching Harrison directly. "NO!" shouted Dick Zanuck. "I don't want anyone talking to that son-of-a-bitch. He forced us to get rid of Sammy Davis, who would have been terrific in the part, or he'd walk off the picture. So we hire Poitier, because *he* insisted on him, and he walks off anyhow."

We've been jerked around enough. Fuck him! I don't want him in the picture. We'll find somebody else." Zanuck was resolutely against reengaging Harrison, "as he will drive us all to an asylum."

The final alternates for Dolittle were Peter Ustinov, Alec Guinness, Peter O'Toole, and Christopher Plummer, an actor with fewer musical gifts than Harrison, but who was hot by association with *The Sound of Music*. Based on Zanuck's enthusiasm, Plummer was selected, and hired for a fee more humble than Harrison's. Harrison was wired with the message that he has been relieved as requested. Then in a moment of abject if dreaded honesty, Zanuck and the others admitted that Plummer was not right, and this time they weren't joking. In a long distance phone call, Fleischer negotiated Harrison's return. He "could be mean-spirited and very excitable, and he'd have a few drinks and fly off the handle," said Zanuck. "And on top of it all, he was an egomaniac at the height of his clout. But when he heard about Christopher Plummer, he temporarily turned into a human being again and begged his way back. And from that point on, I had him." Plummer, who was paid off for a princely $300,000, sniffed on his way out "no one enjoyed playing hard to get more than [Harrison]."

Harrison was soon the fully committed star, offering script revisions to Fleischer and the Zanucks. He now felt Dolittle should be someone like his Henry Higgins of *My Fair Lady*, that is, a man of "amusing irritability." Then he turned sour again, his primary complaint this time being Bricusse's "banal" music and lyrics. He wanted Bricusse replaced by the "Have Some Madeira, M'Dear" songwriting team of Michael Flanders and Donald Swann. Given the high stakes, Jacobs had few options but to coddle him. Bricusse was out; Flanders and Swann were in. When their test songs were recorded and shared with Fleischer and Harrison, both found them lightweight and precious. So they were fired, and Bricusse was rehired. Bricusse knew that Harrison was behind his on again off again employment, which brought great working anxiety. "The next nine months were absolute misery," he said. "The problem wasn't so much writing it but in dealing with Rex Harrison. Our relationship at first was extremely difficult—like a headmaster (Rex) and pupil (me). I would tell him what I had done and he would say in effect, 'Could do better.'" Harrison promptly rejected three songs put before him. "Rex is a bully, a snob, a perfectionist, and a magnificent professional," said Bricusse diplomatically. "He won't let one syllable go into the picture that he doesn't feel is right, even if it means fiddling for hours over a tune or discarding it completely."

Fox held a press conference announcing the *Dolittle* principles: Rex Harrison, Sidney Poitier, and Anthony Newley, who had such a fine relationship with Bricusse that they called each other "Newburg" and "Brickman" to honor their shared admiration for each other and director Ingmar Bergman. Also cast was child star Hayley Mills, poised at 19 for young adult roles. Sensational new entertainer Barbra Streisand was considered, but when Fox called her people, they shot

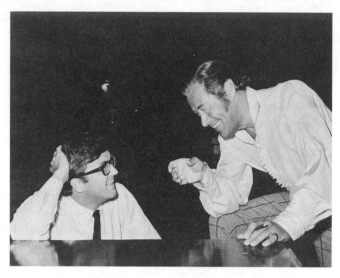

Composer Leslie Bricusse and star Rex Harrison share a rare moment of synchronized smiles during the troubled making of *Doctor Dolittle*. From the collection of Photofest.

back with a price of $500,000. Even though *Dolittle* had the largest starting budget in Fox's history, an internal memo to Zanuck called the price "ridiculous," and Streisand was nixed. Expense was not spared elsewhere. *Dolittle* was to have the biggest advertising and publicity campaign in the history of Fox. Seven months of animal training was soon to begin at California's Jungleland. "I think Rex Harrison and Dick Fleischer interviewing 20 pigs for the role of Gub-Gub is something that must be covered," wrote Jacobs to Fox's director of advertising.

Darryl F. Zanuck's faith in roadshows, or at least *this* roadshow, began to waver. As he advised his son, he likened *Dolittle* to *The Sound of Music* even while admitting the comparisons "are not really justifiable." He noted that, unlike *Music*, *Dolittle* lacks suspense, danger, and conflict. Its only hope was comedy and music. Furthermore, "I am deeply concerned about the overall cost. This is a big physical picture with enormous mechanical problems. . . . I believe you are taking a hell of a gamble." Others at Fox began to express doubt as well. Associate producer Mort Abrahams voiced his misgivings at *Dolittle*'s size, as did production executive David Brown, who reminded Zanuck that American musicals typically perform badly overseas. But the voices of pater Zanuck and others grew dim once production began and the budget seemed to grow to a million dollars per pig.

Rehearsals began in mid-April 1966, the same week champagne corks popped at Fox for *The Sound of Music*'s Oscar victory. The primary *Dolittle* creators met once a week, with the pale and stocky Jacobs forever arranging his color-coded 3x5 organizational index cards. "Only APJAC himself fully understood how his card system worked, and he was constantly reshuffling his deck like a demented Las Vegas dealer," wrote Bricusse. In a letter to the uncast Barbra Streisand,

Newley wrote, "We started rehearsing the dances for *Doctor Dolittle*, or as it's known amongst the Hebrew elements, 'Dr. Tagoornicht'!! (a rough Yiddish translation of do little). I shall have the pleasure of working with that well-known anti-Semite, Rex 'George Rockwell' Harrison." (Rockwell was the leader of the American Nazi Party.) Soon Harrison's anti-Semitism flared in Newley's presence, with "Jewish comic" and "Cockney Jew" spit within earshot. Lines were drawn. Newley grew close to Samantha Eggar, the lovely English actress replacing Hayley Mills. Harrison considered both of them "twits" for joking on the set and disturbing his concentration. Harrison and Fleischer managed a decent working relationship, despite Harrison's ongoing threats to quit. "He was like a Humpty-Dumpty who kept falling off the wall," said Fleischer. "Each time all the king's horses and all the king's men would put him back together again."

According to Eggar, Fleischer did not know what he wanted from his actors, or how to foster camaraderie on the set. "It was always them and us and that is how we went through the film," she said. "Like schoolchildren. We were the young ones and they were the prefects, and we didn't like them, and they didn't like us." Harrison explained himself through his signature role. "I find it less difficult than some actors to be irascible without being unpleasant. And Higgins triumphed, perhaps, not only because *My Fair Lady* was such a hit, but because he treated most everyone around him with rudeness. He was an undiscriminating prig."

Dolittle took its toll in short order. Jacobs, who had a habit of signing his letter with "love and kisses," was hospitalized with a sinus infection. And in just three months, budget estimates grew by more than $1.5 million, while the original $6 million figure became downright quaint. A demo record with a 45-piece orchestra cost $100,000. The 2,500 costumes came in at an estimated $500,000. The scope of the project required that each costume be numbered, indexed, and cross-referenced in a guide to the collection, lest anything be lost or forgotten. The largest line item of the budget, the animals, was now at $2 million. And as if by unholy curse, a giraffe died the day before insurance coverage began. "The strain of *Dolittle* is beginning to show," Bricusse wrote to Newley. "I do so desperately want it to be good. This is our first cinematic outing in Hollywood, Newberg, so how can I expect you to be as good as I want you to be unless I give you something to be good with? Deep down beneath several crusts of misery that have been heaped on to me during the past few months is the same happy, laughing idiot we all used to know and love."

Some of the anxiety was relieved when Fleischer and Zanuck decided to fire Poitier before he completed a day of shooting. Bumpo had been expanded to fit Poitier's stardom and salary, but thousands could be saved by cutting the role altogether. The only hurdle would be Harrison, a.k.a. "Tyrannosaurus Rex," who had insisted on Poitier originally. Just as Jacobs and Fleischer considered their approach, a cable arrived from Poitier's agent outlining "22 points still open" in the contract that must be resolved in 24 hours or it is "null and void." And on hearing that Poitier was out, Harrison actually reacted with reason. In *Dolittle's* entire sorry production history, Poitier's retreat was the only break it ever had. Jacobs side-smiled as he wrote to Poitier: "I'm terribly unhappy and distressed that the *Dolittle* situation ended as it did." Jacobs and Richard Zanuck then publicly announced "with deep and genuine regret" that Poitier would not be appearing in *Dolittle*. "We simply had a script which ran well over four hours," said Jacobs. "In pruning, it was essential to find ways to cut without making the story unworkable. . . . We will miss Mr. Poitier's great talent and drawing power, and it is my heartfelt hope that we shall be associated with him in some important future venture."

No one fully anticipated the unique challenges of mounting a film with more than 1,200 costars who would rather bite, dart, scratch, defecate, urinate, lunge, or kick than act. "We have many, many outstanding problems in regard to animals," wrote Jacobs, noting the script called for a goat to climb the neck of a giraffe and two lions to play patty-cake. Featured *Dolittle* players Chee-Chee the chimp, Jip the dog, Polynesia the parrot, Sheila the fox, Toggles the bespectacled horse, and Sophie the lovesick seal would all need understudies. Gub-Gub needed frequent replacing as piglets outgrow their cute stage quickly. Some of the stars were uncooperative. A group of cats would not follow Newley down the street, even when lured by a rolling barrel of fish. A goat ate Fleischer's script and kicked props all over the set. Mary the rhino suffered a viral attack requiring a penicillin injection by elephant gun and would have to be replaced. "Do you know how much it costs to fly a rhino from Mombasa to Hollywood?" asked Jacobs. The report of giraffe whiplash has the ring of urban myth to it, as does a parrot who learned to squawk "Cut!" But Jacobs rightfully asked, "How do you tell an elephant what to do, even if he's the best trained in the world?" Harrison recalled a horrific scene involving a huge flock of sheep. "First, they had to spray me down for flies," he recalled. "Then the sheep were constantly peeing all over me. The ground was so wet. Oh—agony!!"

In August 1966, Harrison, Newley, and Eggar flew by private jet to Castle Combe, the idyllic village in Wiltshire in the West Country that was to double as Lofting's make believe Puddleby-on-the-Marsh. Animal problems dominated as they had at Fox. Fleischer remembered one shoot calling for ducks on a pond. "What could be easier?" he asked. "As soon as they turned the birds loose on the water the pathetic creatures apparently had forgotten how to swim. There they were, sinking like rocks. It was terrible. Everybody jumped in to save them—it seems it was the molting season and they'd lost their water-repellent feathers." Additionally, Harrison received bites from four species. After his year on *Dolittle*, he announced, "My love for animals came to a remarkably low ebb."

All signs of modernity, including cars, antennas, Coca-Cola signs, and stoplights, had to be removed or hidden in Castle Combe, and various barriers, including shrubbery and a sandbag dam, had to be installed. This caused consternation among the locals. "Half the villagers were in a state of righteous indignation and wanted us hanged, drawn, and quartered," said Harrison. "The other half were making a fortune out of us." Among them was Sir Ranulph Twistleton-Wykeham-Fiennes, Third Baronet, who produced a homemade bomb intended to destroy one of the film's sandbags and flood the set with river water. He spoke of the spoiling of Castle Combe by mass entertainment before being arrested. War metaphors crept into the cast and crew's ever darkening humor. "We are deep in the heart of British Occupied Wiltshire making a grand Todd-AO Classic," wrote Newley to a friend. "You will probably be seeing it in 1984!"

Just as the baronet incident was resolved, it began to rain. And rain. And rain. August is the wet season in the West Country, a fact known to all Englishmen, but known to no employee of Twentieth Century-Fox. "Castle Combe is a gorgeous place, but everywhere you walked there was either cow shit or mud," said costume designer Ray Aghayan. "It rained every day except the one day we needed it to rain—we had to shoot that day with phony rain." After five days of sunshine amid 53 days of downpours, Fleischer saw little choice but to pack and move to a studio-constructed Puddleby on Fox's ranch in California. Castle Combe was abandoned with the production 15 days behind schedule. "It is the weather, not the bombs, which has made life intolerable," said Fleischer. A sodden crew lashed their tonnage and motored away. A team of tradesmen stayed behind to restore the village to its pre-*Dolittle* charm, but the ill feelings lingered. "I doubt if it will ever be the same again," said one townsman as the *Dolittle* gang drove toward the airport.

As both Zanucks grumbled about runaway costs, Jacobs was hospitalized. "Arthur would always insist he had indigestion," said a friend. "But we knew it was heart trouble. He was not a well man." Conditions were hardly more agreeable at the controlled environment of Fox. Exhausted choreographer Herbert Ross was shuttling between New York, where he was staging dances for *The Apple Tree*, and Los Angeles for *Dolittle*. When he returned to rehearsals in New York early, he explained why. "We postponed for three days," he said. "The giraffe stepped on his cock." It was all too much for Jacobs, who was in London when he finally suffered a heart attack. Many were seized with the reminder of mortality. "Take this warning seriously," wrote Bricusse. "You have so much to look forward to in your life and career." Jacobs was smoking again before leaving the hospital, and his wife was given nitroglycerin tablets and "something like Demerol" to inject in him should he need it during the flight to California. He obeyed doctor's orders to keep away from the studio, if not the cigarettes, while he convalesced at home.

A visit to Fox might have caused another heart attack. Harrison complicated the shoot by repeating his *My Fair Lady* demand to sing live as scenes are shot, rather than lip-synch to a prerecording with a full orchestra. He argued that a playback recording would inhibit his performance. So he sang his songs live, accompanied by one piano on the set, with the orchestral arrangements to be mixed later. It was tedious and expensive. "He's the star, so what are you going to do?" asked arranger Lionel Newman. The arrival of Harrison's wife, thorny actress Rachel Roberts, made things worse. She had won acclaim for her powerful turns in British kitchen sink dramas, but she was a troubled woman prone to suicidal depression, dipsomania, and destructive or odd public behavior, such as howling like a basset hound in fine restaurants. *Dolittle* and *Camelot* were shooting in Los Angeles at the same time, inspiring Richard Harris to host a party for the Harrisons. Roberts thanked Harris by opening the cage of his expensive Chinese mockingbird and setting the creature free. "I doubt whether Rex could talk to the animals," Anthony Newley said, "but I'm certain he was married to one."

Inching his way back on the job, Jacobs did not show great concern that *Dolittle*'s budget was now nearly double the original estimates. "Everyone wants to be identified with this picture. *Everyone*," he said. "All the big companies, they want to do some kind of tie-in promotion. You won't be able to go into a store without seeing *Doctor Dolittle* advertising something. You got to figure that's going to bring people into the theater. I mean, these are big companies. They don't do this just for *any* picture." The merchandising interests were indeed colossal, with 50 licensees ready to spend $12 million on advertising. Ten thousand retail stores would carry *Dolittle* wares, while two food companies were ready to display 35,000 large standup images of Harrison. Approximately 300 items with an estimated retail value of $200 million would be part of the *Dolittle* campaign.

Some found the production reports more than a bit gauche. In an early bit of negative publicity, essayist William K. Zinsser wrote a piece in the *New York Times* suggesting that the marketing of *Dolittle* was misguided. "It is still 13 months until the release of *Doctor Dolittle* as a movie musical, but already the amiable doctor is beginning to slip away from us, his round and foolish face merging into the urbane features of Rex Harrison. . . . It was hard to miss Harrison, for instance, on the cover of *Life* not long ago, riding a giraffe, just as it becomes harder every day to miss the publicity campaign proclaiming the $15 million film as one of the most expensive in history and heralding the *Doctor Dolittle* clothes, toys, books, and other merchandise that will inundate our children in 1967. Obviously Twentieth Century-Fox does not share John Dolittle's cardinal belief that 'money is a nuisance.'" Dolittle was a modest man who lived simply, while Harrison was quite the opposite. He was not right physically or temperamentally, being too worldly and unctuous. Similarly, the books were unpretentious and therefore at odds with the elephantine production. In short, Zinsser suspected that Fox was making a botch of it. "Harrison was absolutely livid about [the article]," said publicist Patricia Newcomb. She and Harrison believed that a portion of the marketing budget should go to distancing the lavish movie from the humble books.

After the misadventures on the Fox lot and at Castle Combe, the company moved to its next location of Marigot Bay at Santa Lucia in the Caribbean, doubling for the tale's Sea Star Island. There, after dumping 250 loads of sand and planting 210 palm trees, the production was revisited by rain. Santa Lucia's weather was every bit as volatile as Castle Combe's, but the warnings were ignored. If there wasn't a tropic deluge, complete with thunder and lightning, there was bright sunlight accompanied by a plethora of biting airborne insects. Newley missed his children terribly but was implored not to send for them, as the flying pests brought sores and infections, and the area was a hot spot for amoebic dysentery. A production assistant bought all available cans of Off! in Barbados, but a thorough shellacking of the insecticide failed to relieve cast and crew. Typical production notes for a single day are pathetic. On November 21, 1966, it rained, and Eggar was good for one shot while Newley was bedridden with the flu. Eight crew members were stricken with vomiting, diarrhea, and fever that lasted for two days. No one was electrocuted, though the danger with so much water and so many currents was ever present. "On good days, there were only eight or nine showers," said Fleischer, who was on the verge of nervous collapse. "This is really a runaway production. We've run away from every location we've been on."

Fox bought an island schooner to transport cargo from Trinidad to Santa Lucia. Then it was virtually rebuilt, 10 feet longer, and the deckhouse was made to resemble an English country cottage surrounded by flowers. "The work with animals, the squabbling and backbiting behind scenes, and my own private troubles had among them already nearly finished me," Harrison wrote. "My own private troubles" was code for "my wife." While at Santa Lucia, she had learned how to swim. Mastering the breaststroke, she reached the point where *Dolittle*'s trained seals were kept. In a move reminiscent of the mockingbird incident, she loosened the netting in an effort to let them escape. An outraged Jacobs said to Rex, 'We should have taken out an insurance policy against your wife setting all our animals free!'" She was also rude to Geoffrey Holder, the commanding Jamaican-born actor who was the approximate replacement for Sidney Poitier. "I don't have to talk to you, do I?" she asked when they were introduced. Harrison responded to a nightmare shoot and unstable spouse by becoming further isolated and adversarial, sabotaging scenes, and treating Newley with renewed contempt. "As with all insecure bullies, they lash out," said Samantha Eggar. "It's only once you stand up to them that they back down. And nobody stood up to him."

Jacobs was not well enough to travel to the Caribbean, and his reaction to the location footage was appropriate horror. A late highlight of the movie is the arrival of the rare, wondrous Great Pink Sea Snail, yet the contraption looked more like fiberglass and plywood than anything invertebrate. "How is it possible to go so far wrong from what we saw in the prop shop?" he wrote to associate producer Mort Abrahams. "Even in black and white long shots it does not look right, so certainly in 70-[millimeter] it will look worse."

Leslie Bricusse was nearing the breaking point as well. Holed up alone at Thanksgiving in the Dorado Beach Hotel in Puerto Rico, he wrote to Jacobs: "Eighteen months ago today I was a fresh-faced youth, arriving in California to begin work on my first and perhaps only Hollywood film. Today, 18 years later, my gnarled and arthritic old fingers stammered out the final screenplay changes, and the script, music, and lyrics for *Doctor Dolittle* are complete. Typing out these final changes, I felt as Jennifer Jones and Gregory Peck must have felt as they dragged themselves through the dust for the final death agonies of *Duel in the Sun*. There is blood everywhere, but I can't stop shooting. As I gaze proudly at the 247,659 pages of screenplay and the four thousand songs that I have written, I realize that I shall never write anything ever again except blue pages for *Doctor Dolittle*. The film will come and go, succeed or fail, but old Brickman, as they will lovingly remember him, will still be burning the midnight oil in his Motion Picture Relief Fund Cottage, muttering to himself about Giant Yellow Grasshoppers and two-headed actors. . . . Love, Brickman"

Then, to pass the time away, he wrote his final lyrics for *Doctor Dolittle*, sung to the tune of "Sixteen Going on Seventeen":

> *The budget's 16*
> *going on 17*
> *APJAC, it's time to think.*
> *Better beware,*
> *be canny and careful.*
> *APJAC, we're on the brink.*
> *When it was 13*
> *going on 14*
> *everyone wore a smile.*
> *Let's stop pretending—*
> *you started spending—*
> *like it was out of style.*
> *Totally unprepared were you*
> *for rain in Castle Combe.*
> *Timid and shy and scared are you*
> *when entering Zanuck's room*
> *to tell him*
> *Now it's 19 going to 20*
> *Please will you sign these checks?*
> *Though the film is costing us plenty*
> *Most of it goes to Rex!*

Dolittle finished production in early 1967, and by then its costs were reportedly $13 million. Harrison decided he should rerecord every one of his seven songs. "The head of the music department exploded with fury at the very idea," said Harrison, "and said that because I had insisted on recording my songs live, and not, as everyone else always did, and should, to playback, it would be impossible to rerecord." Harrison got his way, and both Fleischer and Jacobs admitted that the results were superior. By now Richard Zanuck could do little but half-heartedly banish all comparisons to Fox's money pit *Cleopatra*. Against all evidence, he claimed that the studio had "much better control" over expenses this time.

Jacobs, meanwhile, was nothing if not aggressive. He ordered the soundtrack album distributed to every major newspaper in every large city across America with an accompanying cocktail party for leading disk jockeys. The original pressing was the largest in history at 500,000. "Bigger than *Sound of Music*," he told Abrahams. "Bigger than *My Fair Lady*, bigger than anything."

"I like it," said Abrahams.

"You better like it," said Jacobs.

So had millions of others, if Fox had any hope of recouping.

In contrast to Fox, Universal Studios took a middle of the road approach, rarely investing in huge budgets. Though *Spartacus* was a hard ticket hit in 1960, the studio didn't bank on another roadshow for a half-decade. The enormous Musical Corporation of America (MCA) completed its takeover of Universal in 1962, with the conglomerate headed by Lew Wasserman. The studio was smart to diversify its slate of movies and commit to television.

One of Universal's more visible men was Ross Hunter, a showy producer who made the kinds of movies financiers backed without losing sleep. At their best, they were exquisite high-gloss melodramas (*Imitation of Life*) and comedies (*Pillow Talk*) reflected through a perfectly manicured and increasingly uncommon romanticism. "A producer has to have a handshake with the public to find out what will tear them away from their homes," he said. "I went out there saying, 'you're going to see a picture with real stars looking glamorous in beautiful gowns on beautiful sets. No kitchen sinks. No violence. No pores. No messages.' And it *worked*." It worked so well that his cultural identity as the son of Austrian-Jewish immigrants and his sexual identity as a happily coupled gay man became irrelevant. What mattered was that the "RH Factor" spelled big revenues. His success can be measured in a massive $75 million seven-year contract at Universal signed in 1964 when the industry was dominated by independent producers and single picture deals.

The idea for *Thoroughly Modern Millie* came to Hunter during a 1954 Broadway performance of *The Boy Friend*, an affectionate musical spoof of the 1920s starring just-getting-started Julie Andrews as a naïve heiress and perfect young lady. Since Hunter was in the habit of making Universal a great deal of money, his wishes were readily fulfilled, and production on *Millie* began in May of 1966. He bagged Andrews for the title role, which was an achievement given her impossibly crowded schedule. Screenwriter Richard Morris threw everything into his script to see what stuck. There was mistaken identity, white slavery, drag, aerial stunts, poison darts, firecrackers, and an homage to Harold Lloyd, among so much more, all to be shot on the Universal backlot. An industry observer said the finished script "sounds as if it might have been inspired by producer Hunter or writer Morris saying 'wouldn't it be fun if . . . and then . . . a bit of this . . . and don't forget . . . ' and so forth."

Universal turned to George Roy Hill to direct. One of his producers described him as a "tall, mean-faced goy" with "a habit of banging down the phone at the end of a conversation, even if the call is relatively innocuous. He doesn't see himself as an auteur, but an administrator." He had a temper and wasn't above walking off a set, or telling producers to "perform an anatomically impossible act upon themselves." The man briefly considered for *Doctor Dolittle* had a varied background, flying transport planes in the South Pacific during the war, and studying music at Trinity College in Ireland before flying for the Marines in Korea. When he sat down at the piano, he played nothing but Bach, and when he picked up a book, he read nothing but history. If he was going to break into musicals, *Millie* was a better fit than *Dolittle*, as it combined his three passions of movies, flying, and music. He showed immediate confidence on the set, thoughtfully choosing standards from the era to set the mood. Elmer Bernstein, who composed original music for *Millie*, said Hill was "the most knowledgeable director in the business in the use of movie music." Hill made no denial.

Hunter and Hill plowed through stacks of old yellowed magazines, brittle newspapers, sepia photographs, cartoons, films, and pen-and-ink art work of James Montgomery Flagg. Hunter read every issue of *Vogue* and *Harper's Bazaar* from 1920 to '25, but neither took themselves too seriously. "This is no 'message' film," wrote Hunter. "We aren't searching for the great sociological truths of the 1920s." Primary concern was the "chest question"—flat or full? Flappers were expected to wear beads, and they must hang straight. Corsets did the trick, while nervous bra manufacturers countered with ads glorying in female curvatures. Such controversies were hardly academic as *Millie*'s Jean Louis, the Parisian costume designer who virtually defined Hollywood glamour in the 1950s, began drawing sketches of an era still within memory.

Millie was not conceived as Andrews's movie alone. Puppyish James Fox and statuesque John Gavin were cast as leading men. The real support came with three women who had triumphed in one medium or another, but whose film credentials were close to nil. Mary Tyler Moore, playing the delicate flower Miss Dorothy Brown, had been a fixture on American television and was just finishing a five-year run as Laura Petrie on *The Dick Van Dyke Show*. Carol Channing, housed in Chicago with her super smash *Hello, Dolly!*, was cast as Muzzie Van Hossmere, a Gatsbyesque multimillionaire and champagne-swilling jazz baby. *Millie* was only her second film, her first being the exceedingly painful *First Traveling Saleslady* 10 years prior, in which she was romantically paired with male ingénue Clint Eastwood. "We called it *Death of a Saleslady*," said Channing. Rounding out the principals was Beatrice Lillie, the peerless British stage star who was coaxed into a rare screen appearance. "I run a hotel for single young ladies," she said in explaining her role as the comically wicked Mrs. Meers. "I'm [also] a purveyor of merchandise for an Oriental white-slave ring—and I'm a bungler." Lillie at 72 was suffering from early Alzheimer's disease, resulting in disorientation and endless retakes. She had "enormous problems retaining the lines," said Morris. "George Roy Hill was infinitely kind, and Julie Andrews was awfully good to her."

Millie had a generous budget of $5.3 million, and Hunter and Hill saw that the production ran just three days over schedule. The polite working relationship ended during editing. Active hostility broke out when, according to Hill, Hunter "wanted to put back 20 minutes of meaningless cream puff I had cut out of the picture." Hunter saw *Millie* as a roadshow with all the trimmings, but Hill was striving for something else. Musically, Hill wanted an old-time radio sound, tinny but evocative of the 1920s. Hunter disapproved, and "rescored it with André Previn and a thousand strings!" said Hill. He was further dispirited by Hunter's insistence on an intermission. "It was like taking a soufflé out of the oven half way through and asking 'how's it doing?'" As a grab bag of self-conscious clichés, *Millie* needed to be light, funny, and small. "I knew it had to float on its own mindless nonsense," said Hill. It's "more of a cartoon than a real movie." Hunter didn't fully disagree, but he wanted *Millie* to be light, funny, and *big*. *The New Yorker*'s Brendan Gill believed that for Hunter, "twice as large is twice as good, twice as loud is twice as convincing, twice as long is twice as funny."

With his outstanding record at Universal, and his friends in executive positions, Hunter was free to sack Hill. In defining who's boss, Hunter maintained that Hill was, "very difficult" and "very demanding, and very . . . by difficult, I mean he wanted what he wanted. . . . I think all directors need producers, like all producers need directors. And I think sometimes a lot of directors want to do it on their own, and they really can't. They do need that wall to throw that ball against." After hearing the news of his discharge, Hill climbed into his 1930 open cockpit biplane and took to the sky. Upon reaching full altitude, he looked down and saw that he was high over Universal Studios. "I must have been seized by a demon at that point," he said. He put his plane into a steep dive and whipped it around the corporate office where the men who had fired him were conferencing. Terror briefly shook the building. "That'll show those sons of bitches," he said in a glorious adrenaline rush.

Millie was now out of Hill's control, and Hunter supervised its finish without interference. Previn continued his job of giving *Millie* a big musical sound. Hunter kept much of what Hill wanted excised, including a pointless wedding scene. Also included was an overture, intermission, and two plus hours' running time. It was delivered as such for its benefit premiere at the Criterion in New York, while *The Sound of Music* was still playing in first-run theaters. The cast was in attendance, as were such Old School stars as Myrna Loy and Ethel Merman. Bea Lillie, at risk of running away with the movie, was beaming when her hapless Mrs. Meers left the audience in a fit of laughter. Though Hill had no say in the final product, his trickery is found throughout the film, revisiting the 1920s through technology of the 1960s. Brimming with a shiny professionalism typical of the "RH Factor," *Millie* abounds with fast motion, silly title cards ("I wish my bust wasn't so full" is the first one, with Millie fluttering her eyelids and staring into the camera), iris-in, iris-out, and changes in color saturation to suggest Millie's modernization.

With Andrews in her low-waist dresses and cloche hats, and Moore giving a studied imitation of Lillian Gish, *Millie* would more favorably impress if it did not scream "aren't I just the cutest movie?" every three minutes. Some blame goes to Hill, who directed Andrews and Moore to a stalemated preciousness. *Millie* draws attention to 1960s youth culture by being a syncopated lampoon of the silly child-like exuberance of another era, but Andrews and Moore are the wrong embodiments of such an effort. Their attempts at 1920s virginal innocence are more than a bit strained. Both Andrews and Moore were thirtyish, and *The Boy Friend* happened more than 10 years earlier. When 1920s "It" Girl Clara Bow was their age, she was retired. Universal did Fox a favor in using Channing, offering them a de facto audition for their upcoming film version of *Hello, Dolly!* However entertaining she was in a small role, the thought of spending more than two hours with this wide grinning, shock-wigged creature in giant screen format left more than a few people a mite queasy. Bea Lillie, however, endeared herself. Done up in Grand Guignol arched eyebrows, lacquered scalp with tight bun, and blood-red lips, she's a fantastic amalgamation of Amerasian blue-eyed dragon lady lunatic villainy. Whether trundling her squeaky laundry hamper through the narrow halls of the Priscilla Hotel for Single Young Ladies, dispensing toxic powder through her oversized ring, or preparing mayhem by dart gun hairpin chopsticks, hers is one of the funniest deadpan performance since Buster Keaton. Unfortunately, her inept yet unscrupulous Chinese henchmen now look more offensive than their antecedents from the 1920s and offer a reminder of entrenched racial stereotypes. Equivalent treatment of African Americans in 1967, the year of the Sidney Poitier triumvirate *Guess Who's Coming to Dinner*, *To Sir, With Love*, and *In the Heat of the Night*, is fairly unimaginable.

Positive reviews for *Millie* were rare. Most interpreted it as the harmless piffle it intended to be. "The film will not help in the slightest degree in alleviating poverty or ending the war in Vietnam, but audiences are going to know what they paid for and get value in return," noted the *Saturday Review*. "Ross Hunter's *Thoroughly Modern Millie* probably comes under the heading of what is now called Camp," noted *The Hollywood Reporter*. No one expected *The Village Voice* to love it, but its review was outright hostile. *Millie* was "simple-minded," and cursed with a "tasteless, uninspired" script. Hill's direction was "slipshod," while Moore, Channing, and Gavin were a trio of "no talent types." Its one saving grace was the one participant who actually experienced the '20s. "Too bad it wasn't called *Thoroughly Modern Lillie*." In expressing the odd movie juncture of 1967, when old and new sensibilities clashed with unusual force, supercilious Bosley Crowther found himself loving *Millie* as much as he detested *Bonnie and Clyde*, decried as "a cheap piece of bald-faced slapstick comedy that treats the hideous degradation of that sleazy, moronic pair as though they were as full of fun and frolic as the jazz-age cut-ups of *Thoroughly Modern Millie*." His attacks on forward-looking films (*Doctor Strangelove*, *Goldfinger*) hastened his retirement. "I am very fond of Bosley Crowther," said editor Arthur Gelb, "but it had to be done. We had to have someone who could look at movies from a fresh perspective." Crowther had loved *My Fair Lady*, tolerated *The Sound of Music*, and wrote glowing press for *Camelot* while most others plugged their noses. With Crowther gone, big musicals lost their last friend at the *Times*. His replacement was young *New Yorker* transplant Renata Adler, who had next to no experience as a film critic. With Crowther's departure, the critical environment for roadshow musicals became more unwelcoming. Certainly no one at the *New York Times* was going to be so misguided as to defend a limping art form. There were no more major champions for the musical's decorative, apolitical wonderfulness.

With various old tunes, composing and scoring contributions of five men, and a jaunty original title song that owes something to Cole Porter's "Anything Goes," *Millie* does not hold together as a unified creation in the Rodgers and Hammerstein tradition, but it was not so designed. The dancing is only adequate, and clearly not the strength of any of the principles. Perhaps Hill was right and *Millie* needed a lighter touch. At 138 minutes, it is too long and a strange choice for Universal's first roadshow seven years after *Spartacus*. It does exactly what Hill feared. At some invisible moment, it moves from cute to cutesy, the good cheer curdling into labored gaiety. The heroine's chipper exclamations of "terrif!" and "delish!" could send moviegoers screaming up the aisles, hands clamped over ears.

Millie was much more than tolerated. It did sell-out business on its premiere run in New York, and was similarly received during its national roll out, leaving critics as bemused as they were at *The Sound of Music*. Jane Wilson of the *Los Angeles Times* sat in a Hollywood theater and found the scene enlightening. The draw was Julie. "I have never seen so many middle-aged housewives in hats gathered together in one place as I saw at a packed afternoon showing of *Thoroughly Modern Millie*," she wrote. "'Oh, isn't she cute! Isn't she just darling!' they whispered to one another throughout the film." Like it or not, Andrews led the counterrevolution for moviegoers wary of the profanity-strewn *Who's Afraid of Virginia Woolf?* or the bullet-riddled *Bonnie and Clyde*. Andrews "may drive her station wagon 'round Beverly Hills with a "Mary Poppins Is a Junkie" bumper sticker on the back (and she did) but she lacks the necessary decadence of the day," wrote Wilson. That lack, apparently, is precisely what filled theaters. "Critics tend to be mystified by her success, and to attribute it either to foolishness of the general public or to the size and spectacle of her vehicles," noted *Sight & Sound*. "[But] what critic ever really loved Jeanette MacDonald as she deserved? Or Deanna Durbin?"

Between the making and release of *Millie* came Universal's *Torn Curtain*, Andrews's only film for Alfred Hitchcock. Though one of his lesser efforts, it was a startling box office hit, playing on Cold War anxieties and perfectly timed to the apex of Andrews's and costar Paul Newman's popularity. *Millie* brought in even more cash, and it, too, made no claim to greatness. It was billed as Universal's highest grosser ever and did not leave roadshow release for a year. *Variety* reported a more humble success as the fifth top rental of 1967. But in either case, it was an effective moneymaker. The RH Factor had struck again. Ross Hunter was certain it would be successful "not because of the quality of the movie, but because we needed so badly again, to laugh and enjoy ourselves and not worry about what we were seeing on the screen."

The Andrews film resumé now consisted of *Mary Poppins*, *The Americanization of Emily*, *The Sound of Music*, *Torn Curtain*, *Hawaii*, in which she played the sympathetic wife of a rock-ribbed missionary, and *Thoroughly Modern Millie*. All were hits, some huge, and adoration for her seemed boundless. In a cover story on Andrews, *Time* sounded more like a love-struck schoolgirl rewriting "My Favorite Things" than a reputable news magazine. "She is everybody's tomboy tennis partner and their daughter, their sister, their mum. To grown men, she is a lady; to housewives, the gal next door; to little children, the most huggable aunt of all. She is Christmas carols in the snow, a companion by the fire, a laughing clown at charades, a girl to read poetry to on a cold winter's night." She was also declared the number one box office star by the *Motion Picture Herald* poll of exhibitors. "Andrews-musical-roadshow" remained the three safest words in Hollywood.

As for *Millie*, it became one of the first movies to mine the nostalgia boom of the '20s and '30s that would intensify through the early '70s. Hill found the end product, cut to Ross Hunter's liking, rather embarrassing. "I think *Thoroughly Modern Millie* would have been one of the best things I've ever done in terms of technique if they had just left it alone," he said. His residual bitterness was not widely heard. The maxim that a good movie is one that makes money, and a bad movie is one that does not, went into effect. *Millie*'s success confirmed the roadshow format as supreme. Ross Hunter won this round, crowing that Universal's decision to roadshow *Millie* was "like cream in the coffee." The message was clear. No musical, even one as slight as *Thoroughly Modern Millie*, could be too expensive or too long.

CHAPTER 4

Movie Stars

When Julie Andrews signed for *The Sound of Music*, she agreed to two movies at Fox. "When we heard that, we said, 'Oh boy,'" said Robert Wise. "We rang the front office and said, 'We want to put dibs on Julie. [But] we had to come up with a story.'" With the voluminous input of story editor Max Lamb, Wise concocted a biopic of the late British stage star Gertrude Lawrence. Lamb and Andrews went to lunch, he made the pitch, and she said yes before coffee. Wise and producer Saul Chaplin then bought every song Lawrence ever sang in public.

Wise and Chaplin noted facile similarities between Lawrence and Andrews. Both had come from deprived childhoods with broken homes, and both had long stage careers beginning when they were very young. Both were world famous, and both had played Eliza Doolittle, Lawrence's 1945 production of *Pygmalion* scoring nearly as strongly as Andrews's *My Fair Lady* in 1956. But they were worlds apart as performers. Lawrence triumphed on the magnitude of her personality, not the excellence of her singing. She was irresponsible, promiscuous, stylish, and acerbic, hardly adjectives that spring to mind for Andrews. Alan Jay Lerner observed "the indefinable substance that is the difference between talent and star. The substance is not always the same. Gertrude Lawrence was electric. Julie was all that is endearing." But Wise was unperturbed by the contrasts. "The aim was to celebrate Julie, with whatever feeling of Gertrude she could get into it," he said, sounding dangerously like someone who believes his leading lady is impervious to miscasting.

Wise approached the screenplay as a Julie Andrews showcase, not as an authentic recreation of Lawrence's glittering career amid Beatrice Lillie, Noël Coward, and Cole Porter. "The great drive was not to do the Gertrude Lawrence story, and we were interested in it only as a starring vehicle for Julie," said Wise. He bought the rights to Lawrence's autobiography, *A Star Danced*, and the book her husband Robert Aldrich wrote, *Gertrude Lawrence as Mrs. A*. English playwright and Coward friend William Fairchild would co-author the screenplay with younger writer David Stone. After both of them met with Coward in Jamaica, they drafted separate screenplays, much to the pleasure of Robert Wise: "It was certainly encouraging to learn that you had such a rewarding session, and it's really marvelous that our approach seems to agree so completely with Noël's version. I'm so glad that he feels Julie Andrews is the best person to play the title role. Good show chaps!" That was the last kind word anyone at Fox said about Stone, who kept dithering with the screenplay, extending deadlines, and finding excuses to be non-productive. It got so bad that Chaplin reported to Wise that Fairchild is "very upset at the prospect of being in the same city with David Stone." Using language that evokes organized crime, Chaplin instructed a staff person at Fox "to pay him off and get him out of the way." Three months later, David Stone had exploratory surgery for a stomach ailment, and died under anesthetic. He received no posthumous writing credit for *Star!*

When Chaplin, Wise, and Fairchild met again with Coward, this time at the Savoy Hotel in London, the delicate matter of casting a Noël Coward was raised. Among those considered, Daniel Massey had pedigree on his side. His father Raymond had starred with Lawrence in *Pygmalion* on Broadway, and Daniel was Coward's godson. The casting of a Beatrice Lillie was significantly more troublesome. Much to the shock of everyone at Fox, Lillie wanted to play her much younger self. When it was politely suggested that she was too old, her manager pooh-poohed such concern with, "Oh, but you Hollywood people can work wonders with your lenses and filters." He also sent eight pages of criticisms of Fairchild's early screenplay draft. By his rewrites, "We would've had to make it *The Gertie and Bea Story*," said Chaplin. That was the breaking point. "After a single meeting with Beatrice Lillie and her personal manager, John Philip, and endless, most unpleasant correspondence with Mr. Philip, we have reluctantly decided to write Bea Lillie out of the script," reported Wise.

Coward was a vivid memoirist, and when asked to describe Lawrence, he said, "She could wear rags and look ravishingly beautiful. She was irresponsible. Magical but quite mad. Exaggerated her humble beginnings. Lonely offstage. As a performer, she needed great control. Wonderful sense of humor. She had many affairs—with just about everybody. Treated her beaux abominably. Made everything around her seem platinum-plated." Alone with his thoughts, Coward accessed his feelings for the proposed film. It was "a project of which I heartily disapprove," he wrote in his diary. "[Wise, Fairchild, and Chaplin] stayed for ever. We argued back and forth." He also identified the problem that should have been glaring to anyone ready to pledge multiple millions of dollars. "*Why* they are doing the film I shall never know," he wrote. "There isn't any real story behind the fact that she started young in the theatre, became an understudy, then a star, lived with Philip Astley, Bert Taylor, etc., married Richard Aldrich, and died. I really do think that the Hollywood film mentality is worse than ever." As for Andrews, she "is about as much like Gertie as I am Edna Ferber's twin, but what can one do? I like her athletic, careening, wholesome nun in *The Sound of Music*. She is a bright, talented actress and quite attractive since she dealt with her monstrous English over-bite. It will be interesting—more interesting, I hope, than dear Gertie's actual life."

At $625,000, Andrews was contracted below her highest asking price (she was paid a cool million for *Thoroughly Modern Millie*), but she was compensated with first-class air travel and $1,000 per week for living expenses. And there was the understanding that she would look more ravishing than ever before, thanks to Lawrence's well-established reputation as a fashion trendsetter. Securing a worthy costume designer was nearly as important as guaranteeing Andrews and Wise. Owen McLean, primarily a casting director, steamrolled the hiring of Donald Brooks and instructed an underling to "prepare the necessary papers" for his employment. The terms were exceptionally generous: $1,500 per week with a 20-week guarantee, as well as $500 per week in living expenses and screen credit at 50 percent size of the title.

McLean's end run would be unheard of in the studio era when talent worked under long-term contracts with controlled pay scales, and it sent production department head Stan Hough into a tirade. He found the compensation "outrageous" as he "had never heard of Brooks in Hollywood and was certain we were paying a great deal more than was necessary." Hough was outraged his office "had been bypassed unnecessarily" in the selection of Brooks. He reminded Richard Zanuck that costumers spend huge amounts of money on wardrobe-heavy movies such as this one, and for that reason the production office should be closely involved in hiring. Costumers "must feel a responsibility to this office and, frankly, they must understand if they fail to design wardrobe within budgetary limits there may not be another time or another job.... It is important for them to know that this office is responsible for their employment." Indeed, Brooks had a short list of credentials, his immediate prior assignment having been a small Warner Bros. film for which he was paid a flat $750. But Wise initially found the Brooks deal fair, as he was reputed to be one of the up-and-comers among Hollywood costumers. He had been Oscar-nominated for *The Cardinal*, and was Jacqueline Kennedy's designer for the historic 1962 *Tour of the White House*. Wise was satisfied, and Brooks was hired.

Top-rank talent climbed aboard, including choreographer Michael Kidd, cinematographer Ernest Laszlo, and production designer Boris Leven. And just as they were being signed, Andrews and her costume designer husband Tony Walton announced their divorce. They had had precious little time together as their careers took them everywhere but to each other. Since *Music*, Andrews's schedule had been torturously full, with barely a weekend between productions. Few marriages could have survived such stress, and when *The Gertrude Lawrence Story* began production just as *Thoroughly Modern Millie* went into release, Andrews had solidified her position as the world's biggest movie star. Despite the collapse of her marriage, she began enthusiastically: "When I got into the role and read the script, I couldn't wait to get my hands on all the things she had done. She was an incredibly multitalented lady. What we'd come up with was a rattling good story, credible rather than realistic."

First up for shooting on the Fox lot was "Piccadilly," Lawrence's 1915 Brixton music hall debut song. Delays began immediately. Wise reported to Zanuck, "Although we are starting off at a slower than scheduled pace, this opening sequence is in most ways the most difficult one, physically, in the picture with the number of extras, the need for a smoke-filled atmosphere, and the complexity and movement of the number itself." A 150-day shooting schedule was drawn, with 23 days at Fox before the company moved to locations in New York, Cape Cod, the French Riviera, and London. A staggering 24 musical numbers were planned, and all but three of them featured Andrews. Brooks was told to design 114 costumes for her alone, and Leven was to design 105 sets, not including any temporary structures built on location. But this movie was all about clothes as worn by a fashion sophisticate. As such, *The Gertrude Lawrence Story* sounded dowdy and meaningless to those who didn't know of her. To most Americans, Gertrude Lawrence might have been the inventor of oven mitts. To capture the glamour and excitement of her life and milieu, and comment on the Andrews phenomenon, publicist Mike Kaplan put forth *Star!* as a catchy title. It stuck.

There was still the problem of selling Lawrence when, as *Los Angeles Times*'s Charles Champlin diplomatically noted, she "was not a major American enthusiasm." Those who had no memory of Lawrence, and they were legion by the

Producer Saul Chaplin, star Julie Andrews, director Robert Wise, and choreographer Michael Kidd pose early in the making of *Star!* Andrews is costumed for the production number "Piccadilly." From the collection of Photofest.

mid-1960s, had to take on faith her particular magnetic charm. While filming in New York, the marketing department ran a two-page ad in the *New York Times* announcing that "although the opening night of *Star!* is more than 17 months away, we are taking this unusual advertisement because there is already such an overwhelming interest in this attraction." The ad featured a line drawing of the Rivoli Theater façade and marquee done up for *Star!* with throngs of moviegoers outside. The ad included hoary copy ("that shimmering era of Broadway") and a priority mailing list form. A one-page ad appeared in *Variety* three days later. In it Fox crowed that "seventeen months in advance of its New York Premiere Twenti-eth Century-Fox launches its roadshow attraction for 1968 with this double truck ad in the Sunday *New York Times*." Included was a reproduction of said ad, with a "FLASH!" announcement that over 2,000 priority mailing list forms had been received in the two days since the *New York Times* ad ran. Eventually, 15,000 pri-ority forms came in. *Star!* was so hyped, even the hype had hype.

In a parallel world at Columbia, another musical biopic was gestating. Its origin can be traced to the moment Ziegfeld Follies comedienne Fanny Brice approved Norman Katkov as her biographer. After Brice's death in 1951, Katkov found the "endless process of excision and revision that was in turn exasperating, stultify-ing, and (I think the professional writer will agree) crippling." When the book neared publication, Brice's son-in-law, former Forest Lawn floral wreath arranger Ray Stark, bought the manuscript for $50,000, and it was never published. Stark also swore Brice's surviving husband, raffish gambler Julius W. "Nicky" Arnstein, to silence. Stark, who was married to Brice's only daughter, planned to turn his mother-in-law's life story into a film, not a book. He oversaw a screenplay by MGM writer Isobel Lennart, and attempted to sell *The Fanny Brice Story* for Judy Holliday, with Dirk Bogarde as Arnstein. The script also passed by Judy Garland, who was not interested. When no one bought, and with the suggestion of several readers, Stark asked Lennart to retool the script as a Broadway musical. Only then did *Funny Girl* gather momentum. Stage producer David Merrick came on as Stark's business partner, and Jule Styne, who had secured his place among Broad-way giants with *Bells Are Ringing* and *Gypsy*, agreed to write songs. Jerome Rob-bins and Stephen Sondheim came on as director-choreographer and lyricist, respectively.

The casting of Brice was perilous and required an actress-singer of tremendous range. The show would succeed or fail on the magnetism of its star, whether or not she had any resemblance to Fanny Brice. She would have to amuse as Brice did on stage, but also pull off the drama of her stormy marriages and private life. Anne Bancroft was a strong contender. When Mary Martin's name was raised, Sond-heim voiced his disapproval to Styne: "You've got to have a Jewish girl, and if she's not Jewish she at least has to have a nose." David Merrick first suggested uncon-ventional songstress Barbra Streisand, whom he worked with in her Broadway debut in *I Can Get It for You Wholesale*. When Styne caught her act at Bon Soir, a

Greenwich Village cabaret, he was entranced. "I went down [to the Bon Soir] every night for a month, and said to myself, 'this has to be Fanny Brice.'" Stark was still pushing for Bancroft. To settle matters, Styne wrote several songs, then presented them to her. She backed out, believing they weren't right for her.

Styne took Robbins to the Bon Soir, where he was impressed with Streisand. After she auditioned, she was cast, and Robbins was set to direct. Then he backed out, and Garson Kanin (*Born Yesterday*) came on board. After New York rehearsals, *Funny Girl* went on an out-of-town tour, with extensive tinkering on the road. Robbins rejoined the production, much to Kanin's consternation. Songs came and went with disturbing speed, and the show nearly died during its tryout in Boston. "It was never really bad," said Stark, "but it lacked something." The "lack" was discharged with Streisand's growing command of her character. "Somehow the two personalities have come together," said Stark. "I don't know what is Barbra and what is Fanny. Barbra plays Fanny as an extension of herself—which is something that Fanny could never have done. Fanny wasn't an actress, but a satirist." After five postponements for still more revisions to songs and book, *Funny Girl* opened at Broadway's Winter Garden Theatre on March 26, 1964. The tortured gestation was nowhere in evidence on opening night. *Funny Girl* was an immediate hit, and Streisand was an immediate star.

Brice was not well known by anyone but elders when *Funny Girl* premiered. That worked in Streisand's favor. Far from being a musty tribute to a half-remembered star, *Funny Girl* used its lead character to display the blazing talents of someone new. The story was not very exciting and followed both the standard rags-to-riches and laugh-clown-laugh formulas. Humble, homely Brooklyn girl Fanny becomes an unlikely Ziegfeld Follies star, and finds adoration on stage while enduring private heartache in her marriage to the morally dubious Arnstein. Backed by an orchestra heavy on strings and brass, Streisand made every song a tour de force, sometimes overwhelming the melody with bravura technique when a simpler interpretation might have better served the lyrics. She is not made to be beautiful, but is rather transformed into beauty by the magnitude of her talent—and ambition. "I remember a long time ago when I was a kid," she said, "I had to be somebody. And, I decided I didn't want to be just the best of one thing. I would be the best singer, best actress, best recording star, best Broadway star, and best movie star. That was my challenge." Streisand's voice dominates the *Funny Girl* original cast album, which stayed on the *Billboard* charts for nearly a year, at one point reaching the number two spot.

Before Streisand ended her Broadway run, Columbia Pictures head of production Mike Frankovich announced that the studio had purchased the rights to *Funny Girl*. Frankovich, a former child actor reputed to be a decent man in an indecent business, believed *Funny Girl* fit right into Columbia's varying inventory. "We've got away from arty-smarty pictures, to films that are artful but have a strong accent on entertainment," he said. Stark was adamant that Streisand would star as her film debut, thereby offering her the challenge she set for her self to be the "best" in multiple wings of show business. He shrewdly hitched his wagon to her quickly rising stardom. His deal with Columbia had him receiving 10 percent of the gross plus 50 percent of the net profits, inciting the *New York Times* to comment, "It's quite apparent that before he became a producer he was an agent."

Streisand closed *Funny Girl* on Broadway on December 26, 1965, then took it to London in early 1966. "It just seemed I was in prison," she said of her engagement abroad. "I disliked it intensely." She was happier on the move, and after London, she signed to a 20-stop American singing tour backed by a 30-piece orchestra for a minimum payload of $1 million. One million was also the magic number for her guarantee on *Funny Girl*, a record for a film debut. Before the movie rolled, she would knock off four million-seller records, be seen by 70 million on her TV specials, and sing before a crowd of 130,000 in Central Park.

Columbia went in search of a major director to wrangle Streisand. She was more confident and experienced at singing than acting, so the choice had to be someone who worked with actors supremely well. There was one man who epitomized the actor's director above all others—William Wyler, the very same who let *The Sound of Music* slip away. Before Columbia signed him, Streisand needed educating on who he was. It was not difficult to sell him, the triple-Oscar winner who had guided 13 actors to Oscars of their own. Actresses were his specialty; how could novice Streisand *not* be flattered by the director of *Jezebel*, *Mrs. Miniver*, and *Roman Holiday*? But he had no musical experience and, at 65, was hard of hearing and did not have the energy often called upon to direct a film of large magnitude. But Streisand need dramatic, not musical, guidance, and he was a fan even before production started. He had seen *Funny Girl* in London, and remarked, "I wouldn't have made the picture without her." He came to the movie with the perfect attitude under the circumstances. "What interested me," he said, "was this girl, this fascinating creature, and how to present her on the screen. My principal job was to present her in the most advantageous manner possible. Not to draw attention to myself, but to draw it to her." Vincente Minnelli thought Wyler was an inspired choice for Streisand's film debut, despite his lack of musical experience. "William Wyler is one director you don't fool around with," wrote Minnelli, who would direct Streisand in *On a Clear Day You Can See Forever* two years later. "[He] doesn't like to be told what to do. . . . [I] talked to Wyler once in Europe—I said about a certain person, 'I got along with him very well.' He answered, 'the important thing is when they get along with me. I'm the boss.'"

Wyler and Streisand did not start congenially. When he arrived late to a meeting with her and Stark, she was displeased. Stark was moved to write a curt inter-office memo, reminding Wyler of her "fetish about punctuality." Streisand's ego was ever present. "At the beginning, I guess, before we started the picture, we had the usual differences most people have," she said in speaking of Wyler. "At that point, I think I knew more about *Funny Girl* than Mr. Wyler. I had played it a thousand times and had read all the revisions of all the scripts—for the movie and the play. But once we started . . . well, it couldn't have been a more creative relationship."

Streisand arrived in Hollywood on May 2 and began rehearsals on *Funny Girl* two days later. As of May 10, her Nicky Arnstein had not yet been cast. Sydney Chaplin, Charlie's son, was Streisand's costar on Broadway, but he would most certainly not appear in the film. He sparred with Streisand and did not have the movie credentials Columbia wanted. Many were suggested, from George Segal, Cliff Robertson, Dirk Bogarde, Rock Hudson, and Peter Lawford, to Omar Sharif, Paul Newman, and Warren Beatty. Stark offered the role to Newman, who found a self-deprecating way of saying "hell no!" in his rejection: "I am grateful for the offer and the interest, and I hope it doesn't seem like an act of arrogance to turn all that affection down, but the truth of the matter is that I can't sing a note, and as for that monster, the dance, suffice it to say that I have no flexibility below the ass at all—I even have difficulty proving the paternity of my six children. Would you also please convey these sentiments to Barbra, with whom I would one day like to do *Macbeth*, which is to say, I have the feeling we play a different game. . . . Most Sincerely, Paul Newman." Sharif, the man who sent romantic hearts fluttering as Doctor Zhivago, was cast as Arnstein. Anne Francis was cast as chorus girl friend to Brice, with Walter Pidgeon as Flo Ziegfeld, lending the film a degree of nostalgic dignity by his presence. Wyler considered stunt casting the role of Fanny's mother, floating names like Rosalind Russell, Lucille Ball, and Bette Davis, before returning to the stage originator Kay Medford.

The score received an overhaul, with the end goal of more singing time for Streisand. Tunes were cut, but the instant classic "People" remained. Additions included "My Man," a French torch song Brice had made her own. Cast was set, as was director and musical numbers. Rehearsals began at Columbia's Burbank studio spread over 105 acres in the San Fernando Valley north of Hollywood. *Funny Girl* arrived at a time that the studio was feeling anxious. Even though Columbia was relatively healthy financially, buyout fears were epidemic. Aggressive investments by Banque de Paris from Switzerland had the look of a takeover. A sale was averted, but restructuring throughout Hollywood gave everyone the jitters. "It is," as one Columbia employee put it, "nervous time around here."

When *Funny Girl* opened on Broadway in March of 1964, *Hello, Dolly!* had opened barely six weeks earlier to stellar business. Playwright Thornton Wilder used an old Austrian comedy as inspiration for *The Merchant of Yonkers*, a 1938 play about a lovable but conniving middle-aged woman who "arranges things," specifically romances. It was rewritten and presented more successfully as *The Matchmaker* in 1954, which then became a modest 1958 film with Shirley Booth.

When producer David Merrick, director Gower Champion, and composer-lyricist Jerry Herman endeavored to musicalize *The Matchmaker* as *Dolly, a Damned Exasperating Woman*, they encountered more than their share of creative differences, backstage dramas, and polite if unenthusiastic out-of-town audiences. Merrick tormented the less-experienced Herman, who had his confidence shaken to the ground when Merrick enlisted four more seasoned songwriters to clean up his music and lyrics. "It was like being tossed into a pool of show-business sharks," said Herman. Egos be damned—*Dolly!* was cut here, expanded there, sliced, recast, and retitled *Hello, Dolly!* When Louis Armstrong recorded the title song before the Broadway premiere, it took its composer by surprise. "I thought I'd written a pleasant score, and a song that fitted a spot in act two rather well," he said. "It was warm and nostalgic, with a simple lyric and melody, but I had not the slightest idea that anybody—let alone Louis Armstrong—would ever record the tune."

Dolly!'s plot concerns the professional matchmaking services of meddlesome Yonkers widow Dolly Gallagher. She sets up the wealthy Horace Vandergelder with the milliner Irene Molloy, but Irene and a friend meet two of Horace's shop hands and fall in love during one romantic night in New York. All convene at the opulent Harmonia Gardens restaurant, with Dolly snagging Horace for herself. That's about all there is to it, but the easy score, able cast, Champion's energetic staging, the infectious title tune, and its old-fashioned charm fueled *Dolly!* to delirious success all out of proportion to its merit as theater. It won a record 10 Tony Awards, including Best Actress for irrepressible raspy-voiced Carol Channing, whose idiosyncratic good humor and warmth turned Dolly into a musical comedy immortal. Her Tony competitors included *Thoroughly Modern Millie* costar Beatrice Lillie in *High Spirits*, and Barbra Streisand in *Funny Girl*, who would never again lose *anything* to Carol Channing.

Dolly! was bound to get Hollywood's attention. Paramount, as producer of *The Matchmaker*, had controlling rights, and passed. As testimony to Richard Zanuck's exceptional faith in musicals, and *Dolly!*'s unparalleled achievement, a mammoth deal between Fox and Merrick was struck. *Variety* reported that Fox bought *Dolly!* for at least $2 million plus a percentage of the gross. As front-end deals go, it was reportedly the second largest in history after the $5.5 million Warner Bros. paid for *My Fair Lady*. The terms were harsh: The film version could not be released within five years of signing the contract, or longer if the Broadway production is still running at that time. The film rights sales alone represented a 170 percent profit on the show's investment.

Producer-screenwriter Ernest Lehman took a six-week Palm Springs sojourn to conceptualize *Dolly!* on film. He then flew to Chicago to watch Channing on stage in four performances. He then returned to his newly furnished suite of offices at Fox to pound out a film outline on his typewriter. Next he went to New York to see Ginger Rogers essay the role. Only then did he begin to write a draft screenplay, which received lavish praise from executives. "It is absolutely a brilliant job in my opinion and has every ingredient necessary to reach the kind of goal and figures set by *Sound of Music*," wrote Richard Zanuck.

There was still no cast, and Zanuck was getting barraged with suggestions at every appearance he made in Hollywood that spring. "Everyone over the age of six, it seems, wants to play Dolly Levi," he said. Casting took place during the production of *Thoroughly Modern Millie*, and Ross Hunter sent rushes of Channing to Fox via helicopter to convince them to sign her. Lehman had initially favored her, but Hunter's lobbying backfired. When Lehman saw the rushes, he grew certain Channing would *not* work on film. Rather than consider other actresses of her generation, Lehman and Zanuck began to toy with a radical makeover, with Dolly considerably younger as an excuse to cast meteoric Barbra Streisand. But she did not care for the stage version, or at least did not appreciate it trouncing *Funny Girl* at the Tonys. "It actually annoyed me," she said. "It was like fluffy musical theater, you know, typically American, it had no real life or guts or emotional contribution." She liked the score, however, except the title tune. When she was approached to play the part, she told Lehman and Zanuck they couldn't be serious. "I was just as flabbergasted as everyone else by their choice," she said. She suggested (in jest?) 35-year-old Elizabeth Taylor as an alternative "older woman" whose "time is running out." But when disapproving rumors of her taking the role circulated, their negative tone firmed her resolve to accept. "When everybody was against me as Dolly I took up the challenge," she said. "Once I resigned myself to the fact that I was going to do it, then it was a lot of fun."

On May 9, the *New York Times* reported that 25-year-old Streisand would play Dolly in the screen version. As no director was yet announced, Lehman spoke to the *Times*, eschewing details of her terms, but remarking that her contract represented "the largest single film deal in film history with a performer who has never before appeared in a motion picture." He was careful not to defame Carol Channing. "I am not implying criticism of anyone who has done the role previously," he said, "but I chose Miss Streisand because I'm convinced she's one of the most exciting talents to come along in the recent past and I know she'll be perfect for the role."

Channing had scant film experience, but she was more vetted than Streisand. Who could say in 1967 that Streisand would read better on film than Channing? In photographic terms, both of them were as odd as they were theatrically gifted. "We wanted Carol Channing," said Lehman in masked insincerity. "But the trouble was Carol didn't photograph too well; it had nothing to do with the fact that she wasn't as big a marquee name as Streisand. . . . After seeing *Thoroughly Modern Millie*, I honestly felt that I couldn't take a whole movie in which Carol was in practically every scene. Her personality is just too much for the cameras to contain." Channing learned of Streisand while in Montreal doing *Dolly!* at Expo 67. The news brought thoughts of death and dying. "No one even called me and told me," she said. "I read about the casting in the newspaper. Well, of course I felt suicidal; I felt like jumping out of a window."

Streisand's casting in *Dolly!* became the second great musical film controversy of the decade after Julie Andrews, Audrey Hepburn, and *My Fair Lady*. "Would you believe Barbra Streisand for the screen's *Hello, Dolly!?!*," shouted the *Washington Post*. "Well, that's the knuckleheaded fact. . . . With all due respect to young Miss Streisand, the mournful Nefertiti is clearly not the outgoing, zestful Irishwoman whose vitality brightens Wilder's mature, life-loving Dolly Gallagher-Levi. The perversity of not choosing to get Carol Channing's musical comedy classic on film is hard to fathom." To further Channing's sorrow, *Hello, Dolly!* ended its 29-city tour in Houston. Hers was the longest stay of any musical star in history, and *Dolly!* in New York and on the road had made over $17 million. Though she had logged 1,272 performances, she was in no mood to leave, especially with no movie to anticipate. Weeping in front of the audience after a final Sunday night curtain call, she said, "don't ever say 'Goodbye, Dolly.' Maybe David Merrick will have a grand *Hello, Dolly!* revival in the year 2000, and we'll all come back. It'll always be *Hello, Dolly!*"

Channing was awash in humiliation. Streisand was guaranteed $1 million of *Dolly!*'s $10 million starting budget. Tiring of her role as thief, she publicly trivialized Channing's position by saying, "Carol can do any movie she wants to that year and get an Oscar for it." Julie Andrews sent a telegram that read "Don't worry, Carol. You'll get your *Mary Poppins*." *Thoroughly Modern Millie* had been released only a few weeks when the *Dolly!* casting shocker broke. Streisand was a recording artist and Broadway actress who had yet to sell one movie ticket. It made no sense—if you are going to bypass Channing, as least do what Warner Bros. did with *My Fair Lady* and cast a movie star. Of course that is exactly what Ray Stark at Columbia and Richard Zanuck at Fox proposed. The investments to make Streisand a movie star were nothing if not extravagant. She had arrived in Hollywood to film her debut, and a week later she is cast in her second feature for $1 million.

On May 14, Stark hosted a backyard party in his Holmby Hills mansion to welcome Streisand to Hollywood. She could not decide what to wear and had guests waiting for two hours. She then kept to herself, requiring aging film royalty such as Cary Grant and Jimmy Stewart to approach her. The journalists present were not kind in their reporting, and so continued the love-hate, mostly hate, relationship she had with the press. Comments she made did not distinguish shyness and anxiety from arrogance and narcissism. "People are so self-centered [in Hollywood]," she said to a reporter. "Such utter self-concentration. It's very boring. Here performers are images and commodities. . . . [Hollywood] is like a small town. It has its own set of values, narrow and small. . . . I wouldn't want to raise my son here, in a town where people are judged by the size of their swimming pools." She refused to treat Channing delicately and came just shy of calling her a phony. "When I got the role of Dolly, they announced that I got yellow roses from Carol. I was very touched. I called my husband up and said, 'you know, I got yellow roses from Carol Channing?' And he said to me, 'I know, I read about it this morning in the paper.' So it was just publicity. This whole thing about her campaign after I got Dolly, a terribly destructive journalistic campaign, which I think is in terrible taste and bad faith and so forth." Asked if she believed Channing had something to do with it, Streisand shot back, "I *know* she had something to do with it."

Amid all the press attention was the need to film *Funny Girl* on a four-month schedule. Omar Sharif proved to be a problem when the Six-Day War between Israel and Egypt broke out on June 5, just as principal photography was beginning. The Arab-Egyptian Sharif was a pariah in a pro-Israel environment, and there were demands he be fired against threats of picket lines at the *Funny Girl* box office. One letter to Wyler stated, "As a Jew I can assure you that if Omar Sharif plays the part of Nicky Arnstein, although a gangster is unquestionably more suited to an Arab, you will be offering a greater insult to the Jews than even the appeasers in our State Department, and I shall ask every Jewish organization to ask its membership to boycott your picture. We may be the smallest minority in the world, but a very devoted one." Wyler was not cowed. "People lost their heads," he said. "There was a story in one column that said, 'Omar Kisses Barbra—Egypt Angry,' to which Barbra said, 'Egypt angry! You should hear what my Aunt Sarah said!' Because he was an Egyptian, what were we supposed to do—fire him, or hang him?"

In July, the *Funny Girl* cast and crew left Los Angeles and flew to New York and New Jersey for location shooting. Streisand complained about the arduousness of filmmaking. "They gave me a chair with my name on it," she said. "So when do I get to use it?" Particularly stressful was the elaborate "Don't Rain on My Parade" sequences done over 10 days at an East River pier below the Manhattan Bridge. It's 1915, and Brice, dressed in an ankle-length coat dress and high heels, is running to catch a tugboat while carrying one suitcase, a makeup case, and a fistful of yellow roses. Musical numbers director Herbert Ross said, "She's not the athletic type," before insisting on a retake. "Boy, am I gonna sue you," she said. "My back hurts. My feet hurt." Touching her dress, she said, "this is wool—W-O-O-L. You know, from a lamb." Aboard the tug, and with a successful take finally in the can, Streisand shouted "wheeee" and, complaining of thorns in her fingers, threw the roses into the East River. Columbia began to grind out the publicity. Unlike *Star!* at Fox, *Funny Girl* began immediately selling reserved seats rather than soliciting interest order forms. With a premiere slated for September 1968 at the Criterion, 44 performances promptly sold out. The *Funny Girl* company meanwhile returned to Los Angeles from the East to continue principal photography at Columbia's studio on Gower Street. By now Streisand's attitude was grating on nerves. She was self-taught in movie technology, and used her newfound knowledge in confrontation with more seasoned colleagues. "The only thing she hasn't learned is tact," said Stark. Screenwriter Isobel Lennart found work on *Funny Girl* "a deflating, ego-crushing experience." Some were outright appalled at Streisand's hubris, defying a director of Wyler's experience and stature. "Wyler was fallible and aging, but he'd been making movies for over 40 years, and she was telling him what to do."

There were fractures elsewhere. Wyler was admiring Herbert Ross's work with the songs and sought to have him credited as "Director of Musical Numbers" rather than the more standard "Staged By." Columnist Joyce Haber reported that Ross directed half the movie and should be given co-director credit as was done for choreographer Jerome Robbins with Robert Wise on *West Side Story*. Haber's piece was discomforting for both Wyler and Ross, who exchanged notes of apology with "no hard feelings." But anger flared when Ray Stark used his friendship with Haber to intimidate Wyler. In an outbreak of pettiness, Stark rode Wyler, overseeing details and inundating him with less-than-friendly production notes. Wyler jotted a response that he never sent: "Dear Ray: .... You can write me all the memos you want—for the record, for your file, and for your publicity, but any future memos from you will go unread straight into the trash basket, where most them belong. . . . Don't try to be a David O. Selznick—it's hopeless. And don't let thinking go to your head—there isn't room. William Wyler." Then the "no hard feelings" between Ross and Wyler hardened. Most of the musical numbers, and the script, were set before Wyler came on. As a result, Ross and

Director William Wyler and star Barbra Streisand confer during the filming of "Don't Rain on My Parade" in *Funny Girl*. Body language suggests the two have switched jobs. Streisand is sitting in producer Ray Stark's chair. From the collection of Photofest.

Wyler each had their own cutters. Ross conceived, choreographed, and directed the songs, but Wyler had authority over him as director. "Wyler just didn't like musical numbers," said Ross. "He doesn't understand that you can progress a story through indirection, through atmosphere. I had somewhat the same problem with Dick Fleischer on *Doctor Dolittle*. But Fleischer was always there, on the floor. He either took my ideas, or he didn't. It was his responsibility. Willie wasn't on the floor for *Funny Girl*. He wasn't present at recording sessions, either."

Funny Girl finished production in late November. When asked how she did, Streisand perpetuated a perfectionist reputation by saying, "I'm not pleased." Asked to elaborate, she said, "The first few weeks were tense, but nothing terrific. They're not used to an actress speaking up. But I *feel* things like lights. I *know* a light should be two inches to the left, and so on. And that goes into other areas, like dialogue. I remember every line of every script on *Funny Girl*. I played 42 different last scenes. The one I did opening night on Broadway was a new scene that day." As for clashes with Wyler, Streisand said "Sometimes he'd agree, and sometimes not. Sometimes we'd try a thing my way and his way, and see which worked better. He's marvelous. He learned to trust my first instincts. My first take is always my best." As for rushes, the movie neophyte said, "One time I can only see the color of my lipstick. Another time I worry about my hair. I know all the pieces, but I don't know. It's like anything. I'm sure but I'm in doubt, you know? I'm sure what I think but I'm not sure that I'm right. I mean, there's no absolute truth; it's all variable." When she saw Wyler's edited version of the "Swan Lake" travesty, she was unhappy, and fought (and won) to use Ross's version. She was vindicated when preview audiences loved it, and it stayed in the final film.

Streisand had about a month to relax after *Funny Girl*, enjoying the holidays with actor husband Elliot Gould and their infant son. Production on *Hello, Dolly!* was due to commence in January on location in New York's Hudson Valley. Its director was to be Gene Kelly, who would appear to be an inspired choice. As actor-dancer-choreographer-director, he was arguably the greatest multi-talented American musical entertainer of them all. And he was eager for the job—curious about Streisand, as was everyone, and delighted at Fox's grandiose commitment. He had turned down *The Sound of Music*, and he was not about to say no to another potential smash. "Gene had exactly the qualities we needed on the picture," said producer Ernest Lehman. "Tremendous energy and vitality, and a maddening cheerfulness. Whether he *felt* all that cheerful as the production got under way and encountered certain difficulties, is another matter." Behind his supreme musical credentials were some troubling realities. Kelly had not had a success in musical films since *Singin' in the Rain* 15 years earlier, having followed that hit with the disappointing *It's Always Fair Weather* and the utterly rejected *Invitation to the Dance*. When the MGM musical died, he found supporting actor roles on film and television, but there was no escaping a trace of obsolescence in his name.

Original plans called for the gigantic New York 1890s sets to be build at Fox's Malibu ranch, but that was abandoned under consideration of high transportation and hauling costs, and when the Santa Monica Mountains got in the way of every camera angle. Somewhere in Europe was suggested then quickly rejected. "Jesus, you can get away with shooting *Cleopatra* in Rome," Lehman said. "But *Hello, Dolly!* is a piece of hardcore Americana. You shoot that in Rome and the unions back here will raise such a stink you'll have a hard time getting over it." Lehman thought the charred railroad station from *Gone with the Wind* that still stood on the Desilu lot had possibilities, but Zanuck bristled at the idea of building an expensive set as a gift to another studio. *Dolly!* would need eight sound stages in addition to many locations in California and New York. For the rousing Act I finale, "Before the Parade Passes By," Zanuck envisioned a literal reading of the title with a huge procession marching down the front of the Fox Administration Building off Pico Boulevard. Immediately there were concerns about construction and safety, given that the set was designed to be the biggest in Fox history. Rehearsals began as the logistics of gargantuan sets continued. Then Carol Channing resurfaced. "On the day they started rehearsals, I called Gene Kelly and said '*please* let me do *Hello, Dolly!*'" she recalled. "He said he had nothing to do with it. I had dinner with him that night—he felt sorry for me." She remained conflicted about Streisand for decades. "A barrel of laughs she ain't," wrote Channing. "My opinion of Streisand is completely warped. What opinion would have you if someone . . . kidnapped your baby? My baby was *Hello, Dolly!*" But, she added, "I can't stop admiring her."

The problems born of miscasting soon appeared. The title song concerns the return of cherished Dolly Levi to the Harmonia Gardens restaurant.

I said hello, Dolly, well, hello, Dolly
It's so nice to have you back where you belong

In doing the math, Streisand's Dolly would have last dined at the Harmonia Gardens when she was 12. Streisand was just eight years older than a typical star of a high school production of *Dolly!* More troubling was the lack of promise in the raw material. "*Hello, Dolly!* is a pretty infantile story, and very early in adapting it to the screen, I realized my biggest problem would be how to make it less silly," said Lehman. "On the stage it was absolutely asinine." From the beginning, *Dolly!* had its producing and distributing studio willing to spend its way to success. Great movies may be made from offbeat casting, creative conflict, production adversity, and an open wallet. But they are not guarantees.

CHAPTER 5

Smoke and Gold

The Walt Disney Studios kept its fiscal health in the early 1960s. It had already diversified into multiple areas of show business and opened its unique fantasy theme park Disneyland in Anaheim, California, in 1955. From its well-manicured country club style studio compound in Burbank, it was also cranking out family products such as *101 Dalmatians*, *The Swiss Family Robinson*, and *Pollyanna*. The financial success of *Mary Poppins*, Disney's super-smash of 1964, was a particularly happy surprise. "Walt Disney Studios continue to reflect, entirely, the multifaceted and evidently unflagging genius of Walt Disney himself," wrote Charles Champlin in the *Los Angeles Times*. "He continues to have the industry's surest instinct for the taste of the particular audience at which he aims."

Poppins convinced Disney that he should enter the roadshow musical business. Like Ross Hunter with *Thoroughly Modern Millie*, he believed that a lengthy musical with intermission could also be light and airy, with good clean fun shining from every corner of the screen. It was in that spirit that he bought *My Philadelphia Father*, a 1955 book by Cordelia Biddle and Kyle Crichton about the real life exploits of Cordelia's father, the late Colonel Anthony J. Drexel Biddle. *My Philadelphia Father* had also been a short-lived play on Broadway, and neither version contained the faintest shadow of family disharmony or psychological complexity. The real Biddle was supposed by *Esquire* to be "one of those truly monstrous eccentrics, a man of brutal insensitivity and slyness, who was able to indulge his whims until they were swollen like goiters." When he wasn't palling around with Teddy Roosevelt, Kaiser Wilhelm, and various Dukes and Vanderbilts, he was befriending punch-drunk prizefighters, ex-cons, and alligators, which were kept in the family conservatory. He fancied himself a novelist, explorer, publisher, jujitsu master, and arts patron. He even tried singing, but his *Pagliacci* was judged the worst ever heard in the Western hemisphere. A devout amateur boxer, he founded a movement called Athletic Christianity while advising the United States Marine Corps on myriad forms of death and mayhem.

"Uncle Walt" asked writer A J Carothers (he preferred no periods) and producer Bill Anderson, a 25-year company man at Disney, to musicalize Biddle's story. Their unassailable response was to assign Richard M. and Robert B. Sherman, the brother composing team behind *Mary Poppins*, to begin writing. Burt Lancaster, Brian Keith, and Rex Harrison were mentioned as Biddle, but studio favorite Fred MacMurray won the part. This was his sixth outing for Disney, and the star of *The Absent-Minded Professor* and *Son of Flubber* actually had musical credentials. In addition to singing and playing the saxophone, he had done a Bavarian slap dance at RKO back in the 1930s. Director Norman Tokar, who had worked at Disney with MacMurray, was signed.

Disney had the esteemed Greer Garson, Geraldine Page, and Gladys Cooper fill the elder women's roles. Juvenile leads went to Paul Peterson, an alumnus of TV's *The Donna Reed Show*, and singer John Davidson. Davidson's dimpled, well-scrubbed boyishness, coupled with a pleasing baritone, made him an ideal live action Disney prince. Tall, freckled Lesley Ann Warren, star of a beloved TV production of *Cinderella*, was making her film debut as Cordelia. In his first American film was pop singer turned musical comedy star Tommy Steele. With a varied background as merchant marine, guitarist, TV star, and Shakespearean actor, he made his biggest splash on the West End in the 1963 musical *Half a Sixpence*. Disney saw Steele in *Sixpence* on Broadway, and, much as Julie Andrews was courted during *Camelot*, he made an offer to Steele for *The Happiest Millionaire*. He would play John Lawless, the Biddle's fun-loving singing and dancing butler, who would also function as the movie's narrator.

As rehearsals were under way, Disney's 28,340-square-foot Stage Two was converted into the Biddle's 1916 Philadelphia mansion with a budget of $450,000 for crystal chandeliers, walnut paneling, and antique furniture. "Fabrics photograph in exact relation to what they cost, so we can't skimp on materials," said *Millionaire*'s Oscar-winning costumer Bill Thomas. He designed 250 costumes for the featured stars, plus nearly 3,000 additional for the extras.

With more than 80 minutes of song and dance, co-choreographer Marc Breaux's first memory of *Millionaire* was that it was too long. Working with George, an eight-foot, 200-pound resident of the California Alligator Farm in Buena Park, presented its own problems. "We had to choreograph a number for Tommy Steele and an alligator. Oh, my goodness! It was very weird," recalled co-choreographer and Breaux's wife, Dee Dee Wood. "To dance with an alligator, you've got to be one of two things—out of work or out of your mind," said Steele. "One never worries whether the alligator will walk away with the scene. It's whether he'll walk away with you."

Walt was not present on the set every day as he had been with *Poppins*, but he remained congenial with cast and crew, making an effort to learn everyone's name. With the production going smoothly, he had little reason to worry. "He usually held court in the hallway afterward for the people involved with [*The Happiest Millionaire*]," said Robert Sherman. "And he started talking to them, telling them what he liked and what they should change, and then, when they were through, he turned to us and with a big smile, he said, 'Keep up the good work, boys.' And he walked to his office. It was the last we ever saw of him." It was not well known that Disney's absence from the studio was due to late-stage lung cancer. Employees and even family were not informed of his illness. Disney himself kept an optimistic outlook despite weight loss, zero energy, and great pain. Very near the end he watched a rough cut of *The Happiest Millionaire*, and conferred with staff on how to edit it to something below three hours.

Disney died before *The Happiest Millionaire* was finished. Remarkably, the studio continued without serious disruption. Roy Disney, Walt's brother and business partner, issued a statement, "We will continue to operate Walt Disney's company in the way that he has established and guided it." He added that his brother knew how to hire people "who understood his way of communicating with the public through entertainment." With that directive, *The Happiest Millionaire* went on its merry if overpriced way, with Tokar guiding it as he had *Leave It to Beaver* on TV and a number of Disney films earlier in the 1960s.

Millionaire tried to capitalize on a wistful longing for more genteel times as expressed by Geraldine Page, who played John Davidson's imperious mother. "The period of this picture is one of elegance," she said. "World wars had not upset standards, people were polite, women were feminine, they moved with grace and

Fred MacMurray, Greer Garson, Walt Disney, and Tommy Steele pose rather stiffly on *The Happiest Millionaire* set very soon before Disney's death. From the collection of Photofest.

talked softly. We have to re-examine elegance today." Disney Studios quite agreed, announcing its intentions to roadshow *Millionaire* and give it a marketing campaign and premiere bigger than anything in its history. At the preview, *Millionaire* clocked in at just under three hours, including overture, intermission, and exit music. It was long to be sure, but the studio was increasingly confident of another *Mary Poppins*-sized hit. Original costumes, props, and a stand-in for George the alligator were displayed at Bullocks Department Stores in Torrance and downtown Los Angeles in advance of the premiere at the Pantages Theater. Even in a town built on hyperbole, Disney marketers went overboard, proclaiming the premiere as quite simply "the most exciting event in the history of Hollywood!" There was such belief in certain success and unprecedented demand that the Pantages was booked as the only screen honored with exhibition rights. Even New York would have to wait several months to see *The Happiest Millionaire*.

On a clear and warm early summer night, spectators in bleachers on Hollywood Boulevard enjoyed a parade of Disney characters while guests and stars arrived in antique cars. Upon entering the Pantages, women were given gold alligator pins, and men gold alligator tie tacs. Following the premiere screening, guests ambled two and a half blocks to the Hollywood Palladium on the longest canopied red carpet promenade in Hollywood history. The Palladium was done up for a 1,500 guest benefit for the California Institute of Arts, with a replica of the Biddle mansion on prominent display. In addition to more vintage cars and the 36-piece Disneyland Marching Band, George welcomed guests in an alligatorium near the front doors. Cordelia Biddle Robertson, Biddle's surviving daughter, was overcome and could only say, "It's chic, divine. It's all a dream. It makes me want to cry." Tommy Steele had nerve enough to acknowledge so much flaunting of wealth. When he was asked to lead the crowd in a chorus of the film's tune "Fortuosity," he borrowed a line from John Lennon: "Everybody who wants to sing, sing, and those who don't want to just rattle your jewelry."

The party was a hit, but *Millionaire* wasn't. The problem was the character of Biddle, who directed comic setups rather than occupying the heart of the movie. "*Mary Poppins* was *Mary Poppins* and also Julie Andrews and everything that happened related directly to her fantastic talents (fictional and personal). There is no such unity of interest and identification in *The Happiest Millionaire*," noted Charles Champlin. MacMurray does not summon enough humorous goodwill, and when he sings he makes a doleful noise. The ingratiating character actors and ingénues are in service to themselves and their subplots, but not to any story of consequence. Miscast in a dull mother role, orange-haired Garson wanders through the movie offering little more than an erect posture and round vowels. In startling contrast, Steele delivers a performance at perfect intensity for a live performance in a huge concert hall, with an overworked smile that blazes like a fluorescent lamp. "[He] has just about the widest, toothiest smile I've ever seen," reviewed a young Roger Ebert for the *Chicago Sun-Times*. "It is too much of a smile even for a Walt Disney movie. Along toward the third hour of *The Happiest Millionaire*, you begin to suspect it's a fully automated smile that pops open and snaps shut in response to a transistor concealed somewhere in Greer Garson's hair."

Variety expressed hesitancy over its earning potential, specifically as a roadshow: "Hardtix pix mean advance planning by patrons, yet a typical Disney audience unit—a carload of juves with parents—might be more properly considered an impulse-type of attendance . . . [but *The Sound of Music*] struck gold in the family market on roadshow." There was little chance any of the immediately forgettable Sherman tunes would become hits, save perhaps "Fortuosity" and "There Are Those," a duet-spat for Page and Cooper. But when the two formidable actresses suggest a worthwhile exploration of class antagonisms, the movie jerks back to humor derived largely from pugilism in the parlor. Lost in the mix are a few awkward points of ideology incongruent with the 21st century. While Biddle is contentedly odd and void of aspirations of power, he does join the Marines as part of the film's happy ending. Aunt Mary (Cooper) drives an electric car, but she is mocked for being old-fashioned. As a forward-looking young man, Angie Duke (Davidson) wants to go to Detroit, "the land where golden chariots are molded out of dreams." The high-spirited exit music heard over a hideous matte painting of Detroit's belching smokestacks leaves no doubt that *Millionaire* was a protracted love letter to the auto industry. Carothers thought this would sell big, metaphorically suggesting that trends in entertainment were more toxic than petroleum-based effluvia. "Great numbers of people all over the world will enjoy [*The Happiest Millionaire*] and appreciate a breath of clear air in a heavily polluted atmosphere," he said in apparent seriousness.

As *Millionaire* chugged through its run at the Pantages, aided by senior citizens bused in on group sales, Disney Studios opened its animated musical feature *The Jungle Book* as a standard release. It became one of the top 10 box office hits of the year, and played on everything Disney does best, bringing vivid characters to life by exquisite animation, strong voices, and a catchy score, then wrapping it up with a supremely friendly cross-generational appeal. *Millionaire* looked particularly deficient next to the charms of *The Jungle Book*. "My present advice is to let the little ones see *Jungle Book* twice, find a rerun of *Mary Poppins*, and leave the millionaire with his process-shot alligators," wrote *Life*.

The great hopes for *Millionaire* were ludicrous when put alongside *Mary Poppins* and now *The Jungle Book*. Those two were delivered fully and lovingly formed. Not so *Millionaire*, which submitted to endless scissoring and splicing. Its overture, entr'acte, and songs came and went, while its exhibited length was variously reported as 181, 172, 170, 164, 159, 155, 144, 141, or 114 minutes. As befitting a roadshow, it played just twice a day at the Pantages through 1967, leaving in January to begin its citywide release. It did not open in New York until November as the holiday feature of Radio City Music Hall. The 141-minute version was screened, but a loss of up to 40 minutes did not endear the movie to critics or audiences. The growing up lessons so effectively coursing through *Old Yeller,* *Pollyanna,* and *Mary Poppins* are absent here. Take them away, at least in a Disney film, and all that is left is dross. "Anyone exposed long enough to [Disney's] serene myths would have some trouble with reality," warned *Esquire.* "The Disney formula is perhaps more glaringly apparent in this film than in any of the others," noted the *Christian Science Monitor.* "Impossibly beautiful girls and boys with impossibly 'cute' younger siblings and impossibly quaint parents are placed in impossible situations that solve themselves with impossible ease." Business tapered off dramatically after Christmas, and soon very few were interested in *Millionaire.* "How regrettable and downright depressing it is to see the Music Hall brought to the point of being compelled—or even seeking—to show a cheap, gimcrack film such as this at this time of year when it is pulling its most hopeful and trustful audience," wrote a churlish New York reviewer. Originally slated for 12 roadshow engagements, *Millionaire* left Radio City in mid-January and went "on grind" (industry jargon for a roadshow's wide release) in February. To appease wary exhibitors wanting more than two showings daily, the 114-minute version was provided.

The Happiest Millionaire became another swept-under-the-rug megamusical late in the career of a movie giant. As clean as a Sunday school sing-along, it makes sense only as a cynical product of avarice in the wake of *Mary Poppins.* In that respect, it laid a big egg. After all roadshow and standard priced bookings were tallied, the approximate domestic rentals for *Millionaire* came to $5 million, barely 15 percent that of *Mary Poppins.*

The Happiest Millionaire had a story that was too thin, but *Finian's Rainbow* had a story that was too thick. Lyricist E. Y. Harburg explained how the 1947 Broadway musical *Finian's Rainbow* came to be. He was working on two non-musicals, one about a wish-granting, pot-o'-gold seeking leprechaun, the other about a white Southern bigot who magically turns black. Harburg was floundering with both until he asked himself, "Why not combine the two stories by having one of the leprechaun's wishes used to turn some senator black? Then I knew I had something." Deep in the green of Ireland, Finian McLonergan steals a crock of gold from leprechaun Og and sets sail with daughter Sharon for the Appalachian hamlet of Rainbow Valley, Missitucky. Since Americans can get rich by burying gold at Fort Knox, so can Finian, or so he reasons. Og follows them and falls in love with Sharon, but she is more interested in Woody, a sharecropper and union organizer. Only Finian and Woody's sister Susan know where the gold is hidden, but she is not talking—literally. She's mute, and communicates only through dance. Enter the racist Senator Billboard Rawkins, who plans to buy up Rainbow Valley and thwart Woody's dreams of decent wages and brotherly love. Then Sharon turns the senator black when she makes a wish over the buried pot of gold. From there, the plot begins to get strange.

Finian's Rainbow is a farrago pulled in the opposing directions of social criticism and fairy dust illusion. As Nina Hibbin stated in the *Morning Star,* "How on earth, I kept wondering, could this Irish-American hoe-down, set in a homespun village community in the Deep South, and topped up with a phoney black-and-white togetherness theme, be projected as entertainment for anyone over the age of five and a half?" The question was answered when it opened at the 46th Street Theatre with Broadway's first racially integrated chorus and ran for a respectable 725 performances. If its book was frankly ridiculous, its saving grace was and is Burton Lane's music and Harburg's lyrics. "How Are Things in Glocca Morra?," "Look to the Rainbow," "If This Isn't Love," and "Old Devil Moon" are still lovely, with inventive and playful lyrics and corkscrewing rhythms:

> My heart's in a pickle,
> it's constantly fickle,
> and not too partickle, I fear.

Some buoyant phrases approach the élan of Cole Porter:

> When I'm not facing the face that I fancy, I fancy the face I'm near.

Discussions with MGM for a screen version with Mickey Rooney as Og go back to 1948, but racial politics and McCarthy era fears kept it from getting a film deal before the 1960s. An unrealized cartoon version would have combined the superordinate vocal talents of Frank Sinatra, Ella Fitzgerald, Judy Garland, and Louis Armstrong. Warner Bros. saw its own pot of gold, given that *Finian* came in for a fraction of *Camelot*'s costs. Even during the musical buying craze, a 20-year-old qualified success on Broadway did not demand top dollar to purchase. Warner Bros. jumped at the low price of $200,000, and immediately analyzed its potential for a new generation. *Finian*'s concern for racial justice, redistribution of wealth, and organized labor would seem to translate well from Broadway to the screen.

On June 2, 1966, production chief Walter MacEwen wrote to Jack Warner about casting. Dick Van Dyke would cost $300,000 and Julie Andrews twice that much. Sixty-seven-year-old Fred Astaire was less expensive, as was British pop tune hit maker Petula Clark. Astaire, whose last musical was *Silk Stockings* nine years earlier, signed for $150,000 and 5 percent of the profits. Clark, the sterling voice behind the smash "Downtown," had acting experience going back to British films as a child. And while *Camelot* was very much Jack Warner's baby, *Finian's Rainbow* was not. Though he continued as studio overlord, he left decisions to the younger men in charge. One thing was certain. *Finian* would have no *Camelot*-style location boondoggles. It would be shot on the Warner sound stages and backlot, and receive a general release pattern.

Producer Joseph Landon, a handsome and graying former World War II Air Force navigator, sought to make *Finian's Rainbow* "in bold and unsafe fashion." He believed a young director would be eager and cooperative, sensitive to new audiences, and filled with fresh ideas, but Warner favored a veteran like *My Fair Lady*'s

George Cukor. Now that Warner was semi-retired, the new Warner Bros.-Seven Arts chief executive Eliot Hyman flexed his muscles and okayed Landon's pursuit of an up-and-comer. Hyman was looking to save money, and a hungry young director would be cheap and defer to producers. The new vice-president in charge of world-wide production was Kenneth Hyman, a 38-year-old film producer and son of Eliot. In his ascension, Eliot said he had every intention of continuing with "big, important roadshow type of films, as well as the odd and off beat films" known to come from Seven Arts. As for accusations of nepotism, "I learned a long time ago that I don't have to explain myself to my friends. The others are out to kill you anyway."

The name Francis Ford Coppola materialized. The unkempt, creative young Italian-American already had a resumé peppered with interesting material. A graduate of the UCLA Film School, he was an assistant to *Little Shop of Horrors* director Roger Corman and had written screen adaptations of Tennessee Williams's *This Property Is Condemned* and the best seller *Is Paris Burning?* He began directing with *You're a Big Boy Now*, a well-received low-budget comedy of counterculture appeal. Seven Arts gave him a three-film contract, with the hope that he could direct the first splashy musical of the era that looked and sounded big, but was actually made under controlled spending.

Coppola was guaranteed 30 weeks of work at $97,300, while the film was given a $3.5 million budget. As the first university film school graduate to break into mainstream filmmaking, he brought youthful passion to the set. "From as far back as I can remember, my whole purpose has been to make movies," he said. By accepting middlebrow entertainment, Coppola demonstrated that he would and could work within the Hollywood machinery, positioning himself as a young filmmaker with commercial aspirations. Let his idealistic classmates rebel themselves into unemployment. Coppola did not hesitate to announce his love of musicals, Fred Astaire, and Petula Clark. He was familiar with the *Finian* score and was compelled to direct "by the goddamn thought of doing all those wonderful musical numbers." So what if this assignment was far removed from Roger Corman and *You're a Big Boy Now*? "I'm the original sell-out," he told a reporter. He reflected years later, "At 29 I was making an older man's picture."

When *Finian's Rainbow* received a New York revival in the spring of 1967, it was panned as a moldy relic. This alerted Warner, who told MacEwen to update it. Coppola quite agreed it needed something. "When I read the book, I was amazed," he said. "I thought it was sort of ridiculous, a cockamamie story." Still, he believed the movie should stay true to the original. "It can only be treated successfully now as a sort of period piece," he said. "In its period it has its own coherence, and its comment on color, for instance, was perfectly acceptable, but now it would be completely inadequate. So I decided that it had to be handled as what it is, a fantasy without time or place."

Coppola may have resisted change, but the story would not function without rewrites. In the wake of the civil rights movement, Watts riots, and assassination of Malcolm X, its attack on racism was patronizing and naïve. A reworked script that added a San Francisco hippie folksinger met with his disapproval. The compromise subplot was bizarre enough to render the stage plot coherent in comparison. In the screenplay, a black botanist creates a mentholated cigarette from a tobacco and mint blend, which offers a contemporary illusion to marijuana. But it had a tacked-on quality, with no relationship to the songs or the story. With his task looking evermore futile, Coppola's initial excitement waned. "The only reason I got the job was because I was young," he said. "Warner's had this creaky old property lying around, and they wanted a young director to modernize it." There was no escaping the book's infeasibility. "A lot of liberal people were going to feel it was old pap," said Coppola, while "the conservatives were going to say it was a lot of liberal nonsense. I knew I was going to get it from both ends." Coppola also had to cope with a studio in no mood to spend money. Scrimping is a grand tradition at Warner Bros. reaching back to the Depression. With *Camelot* sucking up thousands of dollars every day, *Finian* had to be done cheaply. Coppola's budget was barely enough to pay for Julie Andrews's *Star!* wigs over at Fox.

The cast had three weeks of rehearsals in a small practice studio before shooting began on Stage Six using the leftover forest set built for *Camelot*. On June 21, 1967, production began with a picnic lunch at "Rainbow Valley" on the Warner backlot. Behind a shaded rostrum, Jack Warner welcomed one and all, and assured them he was not walking quietly into the sunset with his sale of controlling interest in Warner Bros. When someone shouted that he looked to be a healthy 55, he shot back "I feel 14." At the same gathering, Warner announced that *Finian* would be roadshowed at a cost of $6 million. The decision was also made, less publicly, to shoot the film in 35-millimeter to save money.

Coppola's inexperience added to Astaire's mounting discontent with the production. "I had a good time with Francis and enjoyed him as a director, because I knew he was a talented guy," said Astaire. "I don't believe he was quite 'up' at that point to what musicals needed. Technically he was always trying to change the way the sound was being picked up and had to redo a lot of it. . . . We weren't allowed to shoot in Ireland—'we can't afford to spend the money.' I thought, 'Jesus, Warner Bros. can't afford to spend the money?' I don't think Warner Bros. ever wanted to do the damn picture. . . . At one point they didn't want Finian to dance, because he hadn't danced in the stage version. That's the kind of thinking that was going on. I said, 'Wait a minute, for God's sake. If I don't do a dance, the people will throw rocks at this thing. They'll say, 'What's the matter with him—is he sick or what?'" Sanity prevailed, and Astaire danced, guided by Hermes Pan, the very choreographer who defined early film musical dance with Fred and Ginger in *Top Hat* and *Swing Time*.

Coppola was among the youngest on the set, an unenviable situation for a director attempting to build authority and trust. "I was like a fish out of water among all these old studio guys," he said. The performances were not coming in as he hoped either. Don Francks, Clark's love interest, and Tommy Steele as the leprechaun, were bothersome, while Astaire and Clark had a mutual unease born from respect. She was nervous at having to dance with him, and he was nervous at having to sing with her. Tensions eased after a recording session when he jumped up and shouted, "I sang with her! I sang with her!" Clark remembered, "Francis was the new kid on the block, and Fred was used to the old grammar of Hollywood, every chair being in place, that sort of thing. Francis wasn't so interested in that. He was looking for some kind of reality with shooting outdoors under semi-controlled conditions. He wanted Fred to dance through a real field, and Fred told him, 'I don't dance through a real field. You build a field in the studio.' But that clash didn't last long. They adored each other. And I think we all knew early on that Francis was someone special. *Finian's Rainbow* was a peculiar story, with its leprechauns and race relations, but it was the most wonderful experience to make."

The biggest production crisis came with the dancing. Pan felt the *Camelot* forest set was unsafe for strenuous dance numbers requiring sprung floors and level surfaces. Warner Bros. refused to budge, as did Pan, leaving Coppola in the middle. Pan found Coppola to be "a real pain. . . . He knew very little about dancing and musicals. He would interfere with my work and even with Fred's. . . . These schoolboys who studied at UCLA think they're geniuses, but there is a lot they don't understand." Coppola decided to fire Pan and go it alone. After Pan, "there

The *Finian's Rainbow* gang: director Francis Ford Coppola, stars Petula Clark, Don Francks, and Fred Astaire, producer Joseph Landon and star Tommy Steele. From the collection of Photofest.

was no planning, no set choreography," he said. "It was a matter of doing what seemed right at the time." Coppola made anti-choreography, resorting to high crane, helicopter, and tracking shots from cars and horses in an effort to distract the viewer from the chaos on the ground. "Move to the music," he told the crowd. Coppola took a crash course not only in choreography, but in Hollywood obsequiousness as well. Just when he needed some honest appraisal, he found none. He later noted that he was working "in a methodology I didn't understand very well and over which I had no control. I'd express some doubt about the way things were going, and the people around me would say, 'It's going great.' We had no sour notes on *Finian's Rainbow*; everyone kept saying how terrific everything was all the time." The dance improvisations made it difficult to match shots in editing. The problems of continuity were enlarged by Coppola's success at taking the production on location for just eight days of pickup shots around central California. The results open up the film, but matching real exteriors with the forest set was beyond any editor's capabilities. "Look what we're competing with," said a defensive Coppola. "*The Sound of Music*, where they go and sit on the Alps for a month."

Finian was the only feature shooting at the studio, as production had nearly ceased while Seven Arts was assuming control. George Lucas, a 22-year-old USC film student interning at Warner Bros. that summer, wandered the empty sound stages once teeming with the cowboys, Indians, gangsters, molls, and g-men emblematic of the studio. When Lucas was on the *Finian* set, he struck up a casual dialogue with a crewmember. "You know what today is?" he asked Lucas. "It's Jack Warner's last day as boss of the studio. Think of that!" Lucas was not overjoyed, as his esteem for the new type of movie executive would lessen just as his own career took off. "They're people who have never made a movie in their lives, agents and lawyers with no idea of dramatic flow," he said several years later. "But they can come in, see a movie twice, and in those few hours they can tell you to take this out or shorten that." In a direct reference to Darryl F. Zanuck and Jack Warner, he added, "The movie industry was built by independent entrepreneurs, dictators who had a very strong feeling about movies. They knew what they wanted and they made it happen."

When *Finian* ended principal photography in late September, Coppola was sick to death of leprechauns, sharecropping, pots o' gold, Fort Knox, race swapping, and mint-flavored tobacco. He was only too happy to leave postproduction to the studio while he went on to make *The Rain People*, a low-budget Warners film he packaged with *Finian*. He could take pride in his business negotiations as well as his efficiency. *Finian's Rainbow*, unlike many of its contemporaries, never suffered from elephantiasis. It ran two weeks over production schedule, but costs were not astronomical. In fact, Kenneth Hymen was so pleased he offered Coppola half a million dollars to direct a screen version of Broadway's *Mame*. Coppola said no, as his attention was on the small world of a discontented housewife in *The Rain People*. "*Finian* made *The Rain People* possible," said Coppola. "The fact that *Finian* was made and everyone at the studio liked it meant that I could then go and do *The Rain People*." With an odd duck original drama as his next project of choice, Coppola did not look like anyone's idea of a sellout.

While the new corporate men heading Warner Bros. expressed satisfaction with *Finian*, it was not predominant in their thoughts. The terrifyingly expensive *Camelot* was looming. In *Finian*, Astaire said, "Things are indeed hopeless—hopeless—but not serious." It became a favorite line for Coppola, but its mood is closer to *Camelot*. Executive satisfaction at *Finian* could have been the result of Coppola bringing it in for $4 million, rather than any quality coming off the screen.

For now, faith in the roadshow was widespread. "Filmgoers these days scanning their local pix pages in search of an evening's celluloid diversion had better be prepared (1) to book a seat in advance and wait a week, perhaps a month, or more; (2) check their bank balance for at least $8.50—the current roadshow tariff for two evening ducats," reported *Variety*. "With roadshow marketing examples infecting even the indies, the urban filmgoer will find, under the picture listings, no less than 10 films on hard ticket policy in most key city locales. . . . The industry's current infatuation with the ploy . . . has never been topped." Reasonable questions were asked. Can such a glut sour the public on roadshows? Are all 10 features really that special? Are they worth the high ticket prices? Will they doom general releases to second-class standing? One industry executive told a *Variety* reporter that the current inflation of roadshows accompanies a deflation in quality. "It's impossible to produce more than 10 really good roadshows every two years," he said. But Hollywood also took audience loyalty for granted, even amid declining numbers. "The public's memory is short. One winner and everything in the past is forgotten," reported *Variety* in its roadshow analysis.

Is that really so? In early 1967, a survey in *McCall's* asked, "What Do You Think of Today's Movies?" One thousand random surveys were analyzed from 12,000 received, with most of them completed by 18- to 34-year-old women. The results did not conform to historic stereotypes, but did reveal ever-widening diversification of movie tastes. More than two thirds said they were "almost always" or "sometimes" offended by "sex scenes or overly frank dialogue." Many also "largely showed a negative reaction to today's 'liberated' screen, feeling that it is out of step with their personal and parental attitudes." The popularity of such TV fare as *The Beverly Hillbillies, Bonanza*, and *The Lucy Show* would suggest that Richard Nixon's soon to be defined "Silent Majority" wanted its nightly entertainment safe and bland. Makers of the upcoming *Camelot, Doctor Dolittle, Star!, Funny Girl*, and *Finian's Rainbow* could be encouraged by such observations, as well as reports that the best-liked features, at least among *McCall's* survey participants, were roadshow musicals. But the study was skewed. Its least-liked features were *Darling, What's New Pussycat?*, and *Who's Afraid of Virginia Woolf?*, three box office winners. So—did Hollywood even know who was buying movie tickets anymore?

CHAPTER 6

Over-Egg the Pudding

For all of the location shooting in Spain, precious little of *Camelot* was in the can. Some now sensed an urgency and excitement at the labors ahead, and well understood the magnitude of risk and reward. "I feel that we are off to a healthy start on this enormous undertaking, which is actually a much bigger and more expensive picture than *Fair Lady* if you take out the difference in story cost plus overhead," wrote production chief Walter MacEwen to Warner. "Moreover, this one is 'all ours' until we reach a gross where we are far ahead of the game. It could be our *Sound of Music*, and then some."

He could wish for his own *Sound of Music*, as "enormous" was the fitting word. Whatever *Camelot* used, it used excessively. Every department was bursting. The hair stylist had 25 assistants. Terrestrial animals were represented with 73 dogs, 12 rabbits, three cows, two foxes, a deer, and a monkey. But those numbers are modest compared to the avian presence: 200 pheasants, 24 ducks, 12 geese, two ravens, an owl (an essential accoutrement for Merlin), hawk, and assorted parrots, magpies, thrushes, and finches. Master carpenters chiseled a 150-seat Round Table 38 feet in diameter, 119 feet in circumference, and weighing nearly a ton and a half. The Great Hall, where Arthur knights Lancelot, was built on Stage Seven, the very spot where Eliza Doolittle sold violets at Covent Garden. It was now the biggest set ever built at Warner Bros. With a kit of 400 pigeons flying overhead, the Great Hall had a ceiling of rough-hewn beams, rare for a studio set. When Warner calculated that the whole thing cost $500,000, he approached a cameraman, pointed skyward and said "you better get the ceiling on film" in a faintly threatening tone. Accountants took a hard look at the bills from Spain and presented a revised total estimate of $12,182,500, more than a million dollars larger than the budget calculated barely two months prior. Sets were now $1,688,874, and "miscellaneous" grew to $1,705,069.

Vanessa Redgrave arrived on the set as scheduled, energized from her rest following *Jean Brodie*. "She has always been beautiful," director Joshua Logan said, "but suddenly she became five times more beautiful on camera." For one key romantic scene, he had her appear at Lancelot's bed chamber backlit to silhouette her body under a sheer white nightgown. He wanted "The Lusty Month of May" to be sung slowly and with insinuations. "That's a good idea," said Frederick Loewe. "You want a 'Dirty Month of May'—and Vanessa Redgrave will be very good at it." Though Logan professed adoration of Redgrave's looks, their working relationship grew strained as she posed a number of odd suggestions. She wanted to wear one costume for the entire film, believing it would be "terribly chic and original." Logan firmly vetoed that idea. Then she wanted to sing "Take Me to the Fair" in French as a way of mocking Lancelot and his native language. She believed that audiences would get the joke. Logan did not. "They won't know, Vanessa," he said. "They never know anything that isn't spelled out."

While shooting *Camelot*, Richard Harris took full advantage of Los Angeles at night, squiring one or another date to various celebrity haunts such as the popular Daisy Club discotheque in Beverly Hills. "I was indifferent to The Beatles, I hated The Beach Boys, they're so *American*," he said. "The vibe around Sunset Boulevard and LA at that time was exceptionally vibrant. It was cool to be 'Brit,' even if I was Irish-Brit. And the scene was full of David Crosby and Neil Young and Paul Simon and Brian Wilson. . . . All you were ever hearing was about this-and-this act being at the Fillmore or the Hollywood Bowl, and bringing the house down. I was hanging round with hippies who thought the scene was *just* about music. It got to feel like music, and only music, would change the world. Movies were old hat."

Despite the disregard his cohorts had for the movies, Harris was committed to playing Arthur, at times outfoxing Warner to get what he wanted. Like Rex Harrison on *Doctor Dolittle*, Harris was adamant on singing his songs live, rather than lip-synching to a prerecording. So he called Warner and said, "I don't care what they say about you. From now on I will defend you. You are a great man. Thank you for letting me do the songs live!" He was meticulous with looping and audio fine-tuning, spending one hour dubbing three syllables ("*Cam-e-lot*") for one scene, not satisfied until he had done 72 takes. But he was also an alcoholic, with Logan observing he would need "a bit of grog in the afternoon to keep up his high spirits." Then there were the pranks, including a display of his erect penis in preparation for a bathing scene. "I wanted to have something handmade for my queen," he announced to thunderous laughter from the crew.

Production designer John Truscott may have been pleased that *Camelot*'s botched Spanish footage occupied a diminishing place in the film, but he was still gravely dissatisfied with the visual results of his art direction. He complained that associate producer Joel Freeman was the heavy who made impossible demands in an effort to stay on schedule while he begged MacEwen for extensions, rescheduling, and added personnel. For costumes, he collected materials from around the world, reworking the fabrics with multiple dyes to achieve a unique hand-loomed appearance. Redgrave and Harris each had 40 costume changes, and Franco Nero's body armor studded with sterling silver took an hour to assemble every day. Redgrave's $12,000 wedding dress was its own epic production, with a dozen women crocheting the overdress and 11-foot train for two months, then decorating it with thousands of dried pumpkin seeds and tiny pearl shells. Her Great Hall robe was something out of a sadomasochistic gift catalogue, weighing 64 pounds and made of 682 diamond-shaped golden plaques, backed with copper and fastened with metal rings. Merlyn's hirsute cloak was dotted with snail shells, leaf skeletons, and spider webs. Warner's tin shop struck 7,942 pieces of armor for 361 suits. And with Truscott's liberal use of goatskin, monkey fur, deer hide, and yards and yards of leather, no animal was safe on the *Camelot* sets.

It was all too much, as Truscott eventually cracked under the strain of overseeing 3,500 costumes valued at $2,250,000 and 45 sets now spread over every sound stage on the lot. The one-minute wedding scene alone, illuminated by more than 1,000 candles requiring 10 men 45 minutes to light, was enough to make anyone buckle. Truscott finally sent a letter of resignation to Warner. "The reasons are large and numerous," he wrote. "Unfortunately, your beautiful movie can only suffer a fate of ugliness under these present conditions." MacEwen assured Warner that he and Freeman would do everything possible to "pacify our young genius." Their methods worked; Truscott stayed on. Logan was noticeably relieved, as he had come to value Truscott immensely. "His dedication and priest-like passion contributed more to the final film of *Camelot* than anything else," he said as a compliment. Back on the job, more raw nerves were exposed. At the end of a day's shoot, most of the armored suits were strewn across the dressing tents, resulting in delays and added expense for repairs. But not all news from the production front was bad. While those playing Knights of the Round Table behaved like perfect slobs, it was reported that the peasant extras hung their blouses, pantaloons, and all other apparel items properly and with respect.

On a Sunday afternoon, Richard Harris fell down in the shower of his Malibu rental, hit his head, and blacked out. Varying reports had him discovered by a staff person or his brother-in-law, unconscious and bleeding copiously over his right eyebrow from a gash the size of a poker chip. A doctor was summoned, Harris was medicated, and the wound was closed with 12 stitches. Against orders, the sybaritic Harris went out that night to party. By Monday morning, however, his stitches had partially reopened, making him unfit to work for several days.

Without contacting the doctor for confirmation, Warner called Harris and unburdened himself. "You're a lying, drunken crook!" he yelled into the mouthpiece. "Get back to work or I'm going to sue you for everything you've got." A cooler MacEwen took a tough stance with Harris's agent Dick Shepherd. McEwen concluded drunkenness caused the accident. He noted that Harris drinks on the job, with empty bottles cleared daily from his dressing room. MacEwen also complained that Harris has not made himself as available as he should for a production of this complexity and expense. Shepherd asked for a tally of hours Harris was to be available for early mornings, through lunch, and past quitting time. There was an impasse of sorts, while dizzy spells and headaches confirmed that he

Composer Frederick Loewe and lyricist Alan Jay Lerner, the creators of *Brigadoon*, *Paint Your Wagon*, *My Fair Lady*, *Gigi*, and *Camelot*. From the collection of Photofest.

suffered a mild concussion. Freeman wondered if the wound could be sealed temporarily and covered with makeup. He was told that would bring infection. A plastic surgeon labored to graft skin from Harris's scalp onto his forehead to give the impression of a natural wrinkle rather than a fresh scar. Meanwhile, *Camelot* waited and the clock ran. Surgery delayed production another three or four days.

While recovering, Harris picked up the phone and called Jack Warner. In a calm tone, he demanded that Warner come to his home to apologize for his fictitious accusations. As Warner saw his $13 million swan song idling, he knew what he had to do. Gritting his teeth, he made the trip to Malibu to endure what was possibly the most humiliating moment of his career. Following his apology, Warner wrote to Harris that he "was deeply in sympathy with you not only as a producer but as a human being. If there is anything we can do to get you back on the high road we will do it." He even joined the chorus of flatterers in saying that "all of the film I have seen assembled to date is magnificent and will do everyone much good in their future careers." That was more than enough to satisfy Harris. When he returned to the set, he performed his obligations ably over the final weeks of production. But he never explained how he came to fall, nor did he gloat about the full nelson he performed on Warner. He merely offered a cryptic, "You've got to run the length of your wildness, that's what I always say."

After dining on crow, Warner was in no mood to further humor Logan, Harris, or anyone connected with *Camelot*. He applied heavy pressure on Logan to finish, but there was much left to shoot. Then Warner pulled the plug, and informed Logan he had to finish within one week. Logan pleaded for two, but Warner refused. Logan and company shot with frenetic speed, working until dawn on the last night of production. Finally Logan said "we're done," and could only hope that any loose ends could be picked up in editing or stock footage. He and Alan Jay Lerner had a warm friendship and shared a dislike for Warner. When filming ended, Lerner sent a bedraggled Logan a photo of Warner with the words "Fuck Him" engraved in its gold frame.

With irretrievable lost time in Spain and at home, suddenly the production had gone into overdrive. "It was amazing," recalled Nero. "In our first two months in Spain, we shot wonderful stuff, none of which ever reached the screen. In our last one week in Warner's Burbank studios we shot almost one hour of used screen time." Expenses rose as quickly as the raw footage. "I've spent $2,599,023.14," remarked stupefied set designer Edward Carrere when his job was through. When the marathon-sprint of principal photography was completed, Harris gave every cast and crew member a pricey silver piece from Tiffany's as a parting gift. He then pilfered two items among the many thousands constructed for the film. He took King Arthur's crown and the squeaky bike he used to get around the lot, complete with its "King Arthur" placard written in olde English lettering.

The final cost estimate, including marketing, came to $15 million, the second most expensive production in Warner Bros. history after *My Fair Lady*. Under the weight of such high stakes, flattery and pep talks ran thick. "When you see *Camelot* as a finished picture, I am confident you will judge it to be a great motion picture, with a marvelous cast of principals," said MacEwen to *Doctor Dolittle*'s Arthur Jacobs. "[Our] two pictures will no doubt be fighting it out for all the honors and all the money in 1968." Warner Bros. President Wolfe Cohen wrote MacEwen that he predicts "the best motion picture in our history. . . . I anticipate that *Camelot* will be a top grosser throughout the world."

Warner made a major push toward marketing cooperation with the sleepwear industry. Representatives from 30 companies were flown from New York, put up in the Beverly Hills Hotel, and fed a nonstop banquet of *Camelot* propaganda. Other merchandise included lipstick, ship models, birdcages, vases, wooden soldiers, chess sets, eggs in claws, and hourglasses. There was interest by Ford motors in buying out early performances for their own promotions and to feature their new line of cars photographed against *Camelot* sets. Warner liked the idea, charging Ford more than $26,000 per screening. For the home decorating market, there was the *Camelot* burlap and cork Sinclair wall coverings that came in "nine dashing designs" and added "a spark of elegance to the decor with an almost magical versatility."

On July 14, Bastille Day during the Summer of Love, Warner Bros. was bought for $178,122,000 and formally dissolved as a corporation. In its place was Warner Bros.-Seven Arts Ltd., to be ruled by the parent company in Toronto. Brothers Harry and Albert Warner had retired and sold their interests in the 1950s, but Jack held on as a king without a realm. Now, during the critical months of production and marketing for *Camelot*, he was an independent producer. "I intend to go on doing just what I am doing," he announced, though his function in the new company remained undefined. "If I quit here, where would I go? What would I do? I'm not going to retire until I drop on the job." His last memo on *Camelot* was sent to Walter MacEwen, and it concerned his quest to relive past glory. "We must have a minute or more of the overture and the proper music before the intermission and the coming out of the theater music," he wrote. "The whole ball of wax should be similar to what we did with *My Fair Lady*."

There were signs that *Camelot* would not enjoy even a third of *My Fair Lady*'s success. None of the lyrics had been translated for dubbing in foreign languages, while the original Broadway cast album had little sales and exposure outside English-speaking markets. When at last the lyrics were translated into major European languages, it was too late to saturate those markets in advance of the premiere. More ominous was the distribution plan that played out as if *Camelot* had the muscle of *My Fair Lady* or *The Sound of Music*. Warners identified 10 principal cities for premiere engagements to start between October 25 and December 22, with another 150 and 200 theaters booked as roadshows, but only after the premiere engagement in a particular major market was finished. For example, Oakland's reserved seat engagement would not play until San Francisco's had closed. This plan of exclusivity supposed that *Camelot* would keep large theaters packed for months on end.

Logan believed *Camelot*'s price was a bargain. "We spent it for beauty, texture, and originality, not just for epic size," he said. "I know there are those who scoff at musicals. It's an attitude that prevailed throughout Europe until *West Side Story* broke down the barriers against American musicals." As the first gigantic musical to appear since *The Sound of Music*, anticipation was exceptionally high. The Bill Gold poster design was a bright full-color collage drawing of scenes from the film, fairly drunk on its own sumptuousness. The souvenir program ran 52 pages, the thickest ever for a roadshow musical. Original LA reserve seat tickets sold from $2 to a record-setting $6. The *Camelot* trailer dripped in pageantry, with a rolling royal yellow pronouncement over a medieval castle. Stylistically it looked 10 years older than it was: "We take great pleasure in extending an Invitation to enter a whole New World of Magnificent Musical Entertainment." Logan never betrayed himself to the press, but he had serious doubts. He did not see the completed film until it was screened for the New York critics, and he knew they were displeased. He offered to recut it, and eliminate 20 minutes, but Warner said no. Without alternatives, he pasted on a smile and told one reporter that his only argument with the finished product was the fire engine red opening titles.

Daily Variety columnist Army Archerd hosted the premiere outside the geodesic Cinerama Dome Theater on Sunset Boulevard. While he congenially talked to arriving stars on live TV, the scheduled start time came and went. *Camelot* began nearly an hour late, which may dissuade an audience from liking a movie even before it starts. Sure enough, most of the reviews veered from bad to awful, which did not appreciably hurt *The Sound of Music*, but neither did it help *Camelot*. While the critics of *Music* concentrated on its sweetness, attacks on *Camelot* covered a wider range of sins. Most everyone carped about length, a defect harder to tolerate than too much treacle. The *New York Times* found Merlin's forest, the very same used in the upcoming *Finian's Rainbow*, to be so much "grossly whimsey-whamsey Disneyland." The *Los Angeles Times* posited that the souvenir program was "a far more successful work of art than the movie itself." *Time* found it "carious" and *Films in Review* called it "a gaudy, mawkish, pretentious, disorganized bore. Logan's direction, if it can be called that, reveals little appreciation of how to use the screen for a musical." *Monthly Film Bulletin* groaned that "a dull play has become an even duller film. . . . one wonders if the fashion for musicals in which only the chorus can actually sing may be reaching its final stages." Even Jack Warner joined in the hooting. "The schmuck," he mumbled at Harris in the *folie de grandeur* unwinding upon the screen. "Some king. All he does is scream lines. I shoulda stuck with Burton—and Andrews. Yeah, why did I let Josh Logan con me into casting this English asshole, Harris, as Arthur? And Redgrave . . . scrawny broad . . . Franco Nero as Lancelot? He's an Italian, for chrissakes! *Hell, none of them could even sing!*" Logan began to distance himself from *Camelot* soon after it opened as he took sideswipes at Jack Warner. "On these reserved seat affairs, the director does not have the right of final cut as he does on conventional films," he explained. "The producers apparently feel that the investment comes first. Money is the main consideration. The producer is anxious to get back the millions he has put into the production. . . . The production was sold in advance to theaters and opening dates were specified. We had to meet that deadline, ready or not."

Camelot had its admirers who saw a finely rendered world that might have been. The most flattering minority opinion came from *Variety*, which declared it "one of Hollywood's all time great screen musicals" with sets and costumes that bear "the creative use of research that is constantly visible." *Commonweal's* reviewer was dazzled by John Truscott's "magnificent" sets and costumes, and the scenes of "extraordinary beauty," but took a defensive posture on its old-fashioned virtues rapidly losing favor in popular entertainment. "Perhaps a little sentiment and idealism is what we need in these trying times," he wrote by way of confessing that he rather liked *Camelot*. It does have its share of mellifluous songs, with veteran music supervisor-conductor Alfred Newman leading a full orchestra of as many as 67 instruments in the making of lovely listening.

Underlying the cacophonous reception was a battle for the heart and soul of American movies. The traditionalists who found something to admire were met by a larger mob of critics and audiences hungry for innovation. *The Sound of Music* was already looking anomalous, as *Help!*, *Who's Afraid of Virginia Woolf?*, *Bonnie and Clyde*, and the James Bond empire had all since arrived. It was easy to embrace cinema's new cynical realism and hip escapism when the alternative musical fantasy world was so bloated and dull. Logan never met a five-minute scene that he could not stretch into 10. Worse is the depressing litany of all that is *not* seen but merely discussed: a full assembly of the Knights of the Round Table, the withdrawal of Excalibur from the stone, and the metamorphosis of Arthur into a fish and a hawk, that is, the very magic that Logan consciously suppressed. Those moments that involve actually *seeing* something happen, such as a jousting match and the rescue of Guenevere from the burning stake, are brief and uninvolving. *Camelot* did musical entertainment no favors, and whatever attempts it made at contemporary political, sexual, or aesthetic relevance were laughable.

The stars were very much "In" at the moment, putting them somewhat at odds with the family audience sought by Jack Warner. Redgrave never looked so radiant and she is touching in her romantic scenes with Nero, but that did not make her an effective Guenevere. Logan's ravishing bitch appears more as earth-mother-in-training, and rather too placid to disrupt a grand social experiment. Redgrave's singing voice is not actively bad, but it is bland and lacks Julie Andrews's bell clarity. She slides uneasily into high notes, arriving at the right pitch by approximation. Harris, too, distracts in the early scenes with a vague effeminacy highlighted by purple eyeliner and a blow-dried Caesar hairdo. He alternates between a play-to-the-last row bravado and a Brandoesque lisping drawl, both undone by Logan's nostril-flaring close-ups. Dental work, enlarged pores, and Ben Nye pancake fill the screen, while the devil is in the details. During one of Logan's camera rapes, a drop of mucus glistens on Redgrave's right nostril.

Overhanging the movie is a feeling of abject waste. It gets better as it goes, or is that surrendering to the torpor of "magnificent entertainment" stretched over three hours? Fifteen million dollars just sits there on the screen, proud, gauzy, and inert. It has no spark of life, just tremendous visual busyness. *Camelot* works against itself in part because no one put the brakes on John Truscott. Its olio of visual and dramatic moods, the dark, dank forest, medieval realism, musical fantasy, costumes as fashion parade, and flavorful crowds entertain as if Arthur's court was the Renaissance Pleasure Fair. It is buried in its own bric-a-brac, a victim of Truscott's fiendishly crowded designs and Logan's cack-handed direction.

Camelot rolled out over several months as planned, opening nationally and internationally to bad reviews and insufficient box office. When its first run ended, Warner Bros. reported rental income of less than $7 million, meaning that *Camelot* would have to more than double that sum in reissues and TV showings to break even. It was trimmed down to 150 minutes for general release, a whittling unthinkable to the sacred frames of *My Fair Lady* and *The Sound of Music*. Even so, optimism in roadshows was still high. "There seems little doubt that the really big film—the two-a-day, reserved-seat, roadshow picture with the intermission to restore circulation in the lower back and to relieve the tedium at the candy counter—is here to stay," wrote Charles Champlin in the *Los Angeles Times* soon after *Camelot* opened. That was not cause for rejoicing, as Champlin became one of *Camelot*'s detractors. "[Roadshows] are thought to restore some dignity to movie going, in that you are assured a seat and don't have to trip over empty pop-corn cartons to get to it. They command premium prices and the exclusive first-runs presumably whet appetites for the subsequent runs at regular prices. And they justify financially the greater length, high costs, starrier casts, and whatever else is big about bigness. The roadshow contagion is now so epidemic that almost any picture deal which comes along is very carefully mined for its intermission potential." Therein lies a major problem with *Camelot*. Its bigness made it small. The littering of the sets with so many inessentials resulted in a "claustrophobic closet drama" in which the dancing between Harris and Redgrave becomes "a bit like Astaire and Rogers doing a production number in the dinette of a tract house."

Given the contemporary horrors in America, much of *Camelot* was out of step. The maintenance and glorification of monarchy, no matter its ideology of peace, did not sell in 1967. *Camelot* did not just contradict an era; it contradicted itself. Lerner infuses "The Simple Joys of Maidenhood" and "You May Take Me to the Fair" with sexism and lighthearted allusions to violence. Lyric use of words like "thrash," "smash," "whack," and "crack" approach bad taste and contradict Trus-cott's flower child hippie costumes of "The Lusty Month of May." Its sexual mo-rality was outmoded, not for its polite treatment of infidelity as much as its maintenance of traditional gender roles. Much of *Camelot* was both old-fashioned and counterreactionary. If you want to make a movie of forbidden love in 1967 with a femme fatale that will resonate with audiences, make *The Graduate*.

Something else maligned *Camelot*. It was sodden with reverence for the state in all its pageantry, now under siege. "For any generation born before World War II, rituals, ceremonies, and social institutions have an inherent validity that makes them intimidating—a validity that has priority over human feelings," noted Philip Elliot Slater in his landmark study of American dysfunction *The Pursuit of Loneliness*. "Many young people no longer share this alliance.... This change was responsible both for the character of radical protest in the 1960s and for the angry responses of older people to it. Sitting-in at a segregated restaurant, occupying a campus building, lying down in front of vehicles, pouring blood in office files—all depended heavily on a willingness to make a scene and not be intimidated by a social milieu." *Film Quarterly*'s William Johnson asked if select recitations of Arthur were relevant to Vietnam. Indeed, there are soliloquies that have the potential to soar, if only they were embedded in a movie of greater moral consis-tency and artistic integrity. When contemplating the betrayal of his Queen and Knight, Arthur summons a noble forgiveness. "Could it possibly be civilized to destroy what I love? Could it possibly be civilized to love myself above all? We reach for the stars! Violence is not strength and compassion is not weakness. We *are* civilized!"

The dreamy political idealism of *Camelot* found too few admirers, and came with a "who are they kidding?" cynicism. Memories of John F. Kennedy and his affection for the Broadway recording were still raw. There are moments when Harris's kingly voice and bearing nearly elevate *Camelot* into the zone of moving drama and do justice to the powerful associations for a recently slain and newly mythologized president. But then Truscott's obnoxious designs, or Logan's direction, or Redgrave's not quite good enough singing voice intrude. The moment of aesthetic virtue is gone, much like the faded glories of "one brief shining moment that was known as Camelot."

Roadshow musicals were made by best estimates to what would be popular two or three years hence. In the last half of the 1960s, that was too long a turnaround to play what was a safer game in less volatile times. Imitating past hits with high investment had worked before, most recently with historic epics and musicals, but extreme money coupled with fast and unknowable changes doomed this one. The question of the moment: Was the low return on *Camelot* an anomaly or an early sign of a shift in American moviemaking?

In the years since *The Sound of Music*, the first baby boomers turned 21, and they were ready to be heard. "The young have already staked out their own minisociety, a congruent culture that has both alarmed their elders and, stylistically at least, left an irresistible impression on them," wrote *Time* in a cover story on the generation of Americans 25 and younger, now comprising nearly half the population. "No Western metropolis today lacks a discotheque or espresso joint, a Mod boutique or a Carnaby shop. No transistor is immune from rock 'n' roll, no highway spared the stutter of Hondas." Though political activists form a small minority on college campuses, "For the first time, commitment seemed to pay off, and a New Left was born: a grass-roots populist mélange of organizations and splinter groups that struck in all directions—antipoverty, anticensorship, antiwar, antiestablishment." The young, decrying Vietnam and distrustful of President Johnson's Great Society, are freely experimenting with drugs and sex, and doing so with music that "reflects a uniquely lyrical view of the world." It ranges from "the controlled venom" of the Beatles to "the Eliotesque elegance" of Simon & Garfunkel, and "goes far beyond the moon-June lyrics of the past in pop." Like it or not, "the world today is committed to accelerating change: radical, wrenching, erosive of both traditions and old values. Its inheritors have grown up with rapid change, are better prepared to accommodate it than any in history, indeed embrace change as a virtue in itself."

It was industry belief that the majority of filmgoers were in the "young adult" category of 16 to 24, but could anyone who needs two years to ready a product see this much change coming? And where else to place *Camelot*, and most other roadshow musicals, but at the losing end of a newly defined cultural and generational divide? As the ancien régime, Jack Warner and Darryl F. Zanuck unapologetically aimed their roadshows at middle-aged adults, or parents who see such films as a treat for the children. That huge 16- to 24-year-old crowd might choose *Camelot*, but a safer guess has them lining up for *You Only Live Twice*; *To Sir, With Love*; *Cool Hand Luke*; or the brilliant new revisionist crime drama *Bonnie and Clyde*.

Jack Warner could not help but feel out of date. On November 26, when *Camelot* was still in early release, 83-year-old Albert Warner died at his mansion in Miami Beach. The retired studio treasurer was happy to live and work outside the spotlight that kid brother Jack so coveted. With Albert's death, only Jack remained of the four, and he was an ever-diminishing presence on the lot. The fate of *Camelot* embarrassed him, but it was only the first jumbo musical to go down. Very soon others throughout the film industry would feel something of Warner's chagrin and regret.

CHAPTER 7

Do Little

Darryl Zanuck was rarely in California, instead spending his days overseeing Twentieth Century-Fox Studios from his Paris apartment. He was the last standing old studio titan, with *Newsweek* describing him as "something of an anachronism—his chauffeured Jaguar and dark glasses and glossy aura are the trappings of a cultural dinosaur dragging his legend like some long, spiky tail." Fox was doing very well in 1967, with net profits of over $150 million. More than two dozen productions were in the pipeline, and the television wing had nine hours of prime time per week. Though father Darryl and son Richard had a complicated relationship, they forged an agreeable division of labor, with Richard head of production with David Brown. If nepotism was present, so be it. Richard's management of *The Sound of Music* spoke for itself.

Both Zanucks were present at the annual stockholders meeting at the Starlight Roof of the Waldorf Astoria Hotel in New York. The mood was festive, the future bright. David Brown expressed a bit of caution, gently reminding everyone that *The Sound of Music* was no guarantee of like returns for Fox's next three big musicals: *Doctor Dolittle*, *Star!*, or *Hello, Dolly!* "You've got to be careful about musicals," he said. "They're very soft in the foreign market. In the old days, you didn't have to consider that much. But you do now. We get over 50 percent of our rentals abroad. You take a massive hit like *Sound of Music*. Even there two-thirds to three-quarters of the rentals have come from the English-speaking world." Richard was not blind to the risks. "There's really no playing it safe," he said to a reporter. "You're putting yourself on the line, taking the chance and hoping for the big reward. If a big picture doesn't work, you're in real trouble."

Dolittle was in the throes of postproduction. The nightmares of Castle Combe and St. Lucia were playing out in the assembling of many miles of raw footage. When editor Marjorie Fowler announced that a hard deadline on cutting *Dolittle* "quite possibly carries the same validity as a tea-leaf reading," she was fired. Her successor's job was made no easier when Rex Harrison insisted on reshooting scenes to better highlight himself, and Dick Zanuck asked Leslie Bricusse to pen two more songs.

With editing almost complete, Fox marketing went into high gear. While *Dolittle* was still in rough cut, Richard Zanuck wrote of his admiration to producer Arthur Jacobs: "It has been three days now since I've seen *Doctor Dolittle* and I cannot get it out of my mind. It is simply magnificent in every respect." Zanuck mapped a plan of release. *Dolittle* would open at New York's Loews State Theatre on December 21, with tickets for the first 19 weeks available by reserve seat orders. The final edits were complete by early September in advance of the sneak preview in Minneapolis, Fox's "lucky city" ever since *The Sound of Music* first screened there. Director Richard Fleischer and Jacobs met at the Los Angeles airport in advance of their flight. Just before boarding, Jacobs said to Fleischer, "I just don't want to go to Minneapolis. Let's go to Vegas instead."

"It would be less of a gamble," Flesicher said.

Later, Fleischer turned to Jacobs and said, "What I like about you, Arthur, is your calm."

"Why should I be nervous? It's only 18 million dollars."

Publicist Perry Lieber, wearing a tie clip shaped like a musical staff with sharps and flats spelling out "The Sound of Music," booked the Fox crowd at the Radisson. Fox had bought out the Mann Theater, where Universal's *Thoroughly Modern Millie* was playing to robust business. When Jacobs entered the lobby, he was aghast to see a large display for *Camelot*, the competition from Warner Bros. Since this was a sneak preview, audiences did not know what they were to see that night. "Oh my God," he said. "Oh, my God, *Camelot*. That's what they'll think they're going to see. Oh, my God."

As the patrons settled in, and came to learn that they were watching *Doctor Dolittle*, not *Camelot*, they were largely unresponsive. As *Dolittle* played, they sat mute, while the only applause came from the Fox staffers planted in the theater. The intermission was similarly sedate, with mumbling conversations void of enthusiasm. "This is a real dead-ass audience," said Richard. Summoning all his optimism, he added, "[But] this isn't *Sound of Music* or *My Fair Lady*. The audience hasn't been conditioned to the songs for five years like they are with a hit musical."

The second half saw no improvement in response. Audience members, who had shelled out a costly $2.60 per ticket, dutifully filled out their preview cards. Rex Harrison's agent came up to Jacobs and said ambiguously, "Arthur, you've got yourself a picture here." Theater owner Ted Mann was more upbeat, predicting a year run minimum. At the post-party in Zanuck's Radisson suite, Fox personnel tallied the preview cards. One hundred and forty-eight called *Dolittle* "Excellent," 76 "Good," and 45 "Fair." Associate producer Mort Abrahams comforted the group by deciding that "The 'Fairs' were all over 45." Some decided that the audience was low energy because it lacked children. But others could not gild the tepid response. Richard thought it was a bad idea to hold a sneak preview at all, since they often do poorly in the Midwest. In comforting him, Fleischer said, "I'd be mystified if I came into the theater and didn't know what the picture was and the first scene was a guy riding a giraffe." While many believed salvation would come with a younger crowd, one Fox vice-president was not convinced. "We mustn't forget the older people," he said. "They're the repeaters. The children won't get there unless their grandparents take them. The grandparents, they're the repeaters. Look at *The Sound of Music*." Despair gave way to action, with meetings and plans hatched for edits before the Fox people left the Radisson. Darryl meanwhile assessed the situation from afar:

> Of course, I was disappointed after Minneapolis. It was a bad preview. . . . Dick sent me a wire, "I haven't lost confidence," he said. We know what was the matter with the picture now, and it taught Dick one thing. Never take distribution people or sales people to a preview. I've been telling him that for years. They don't know a goddamn thing except selling pictures and they're not going to do you any good going around with long faces in Minneapolis or any other goddamn place. We've got $50 million tied up in these three musicals, *Dolittle*, *Star!*, and *Hello, Dolly!*, and quite frankly, if we hadn't made such an enormous success with *The Sound of Music*, I'd be petrified. You're never sure of a hit in that category. You're never sure of a hit any goddamn time, but when you're talking $20 million, it's a bigger gamble.

After Minneapolis, Fleischer wrote Harrison, "We all feel that we have a huge success on our hands and one of the all-time money makers." Then he proceeded diplomatically over the matter of "our lovely prologue." It landed with a thud on preview audiences, but to cut it meant removing the only time Harrison rode a giraffe, which became the major visual element in marketing. The favored solution was to cut the prologue, insert the giraffe ride in a later transition shot, and hope that audiences did not notice a mismatch of costumes.

With the prologue gone and other cuts made, a revised *Dolittle* screened in San Jose and San Francisco. Unlike Minneapolis, these previews were not sneaks, with gushing ad copy in the *San Francisco Chronicle* heralding *Dolittle* as "something very special" at the cavernous Orpheum Theater. Private jets flew the Fox entourage, with Jacobs removing himself from *Goodbye, Mr. Chips* planning in Europe to attend.

The audience was younger and livelier in San Francisco than Minneapolis, which Zanuck and Brown took as a good omen. Back at Zanuck's suite at the Fairmont, the 800 comment cards were read with a little hope and a lot of Scotch. Jacobs picked up the first one and read it aloud. "'Impossibly bad,'" he said. When calculating the overall percentages, Abrahams discovered that 57 percent of the San Francisco audience rated it "excellent," a mere one point higher than Minneapolis. The "Good" ratings often came with complaints that the movie was too long. In between San Francisco and San Jose, the Anthony Newley song "Where

Are the Words?" was axed, and "Beautiful Things" shortened. The San Jose screening was in a smaller theater, and the cards were the most favorable yet. Zanuck decided the San Jose version of the film was the one to unleash on the public, but he knew what was coming. "When a picture previews badly, there's very little you can do," he said. "You can make it a better picture by putting some things in or taking some things out, but you can't save it. The hand has been dealt and there's no way of putting the cards back in the deck."

Arthur Jacobs hid his panic well. He seemed reborn after his heart attack, having lost 30 pounds on a diet of cigarettes and vodka. He boasted of the $12 million in licensing agreements collected for *Dolittle* merchandise so far, and his plan to saturate radio airwaves with the score. The great idea man even conceived of a screening at the Vatican, a Peruvian national honor for Harrison at the Lima premiere, and a *Doctor Dolittle* school holiday. The Hollywood tradition of raving about a movie in the presence of its producer extended to father and son. In a cable Darryl sent to Richard, he reported "Screened final version *Doctor Dolittle* last night and it was an absolutely thrilling experience. . . . It is my prediction that, even though at the beginning adult audiences may not break down the doors to get in, it will eventually end up having every child in America insist that their parents take them at least three times." Fox's Vice-President of Advertising Jonas Rosenfeld told Richard it was "an enchanting masterpiece," while the edits since Minneapolis are "nothing short of miraculous and have lifted a very good film into a truly great one." Another Fox man believed "This picture has [the] potential of *Sound of Music* and will be enjoyed by audiences of all ages everywhere."

The Los Angeles premiere took place at the Paramount Theater on Hollywood Boulevard as a benefit for the Motion Picture Relief Fund. Tickets were $125 each, with the screening followed by a black-tie reception in a tent erected in the Paramount parking lot. As a unique touch, Fox decided to dress up some of the *Dolittle* animal stars in evening wear, and shuttle them and their trainers to the premiere in limousines. "It's really cute as hell," said Perry Lieber. "The animals are the stars of the picture and they'll be the hit of the evening. Sophie the Seal will arrive in a limo, and she'll be wearing a rhinestone harness and walk right into the Paramount just like she was a star. And Chee-Chee the Chimp, we'll have him dressed up in white-tie and tails and special patent-leather pumps." Later he added, "Oh, yeah. All the animals will be wearing pants. They better be, or you'll have some messed-up limos."

Jacobs was hoping for live national television coverage of the Los Angeles opening with Rat Packer Joey Bishop as emcee, but Richard nixed the idea due to recent lessons learned. When Army Archerd hosted the live premiere for *Camelot*, the audience was left waiting for nearly an hour after its scheduled start time. Zanuck was not going to let that negative publicity attend the unveiling of *Dolittle*. "If we blow Joey Bishop, we blow Joey Bishop," said Jacobs. "It's disaster to make an audience wait 55 minutes. We got to get him to tape it." Jacobs micro-managed

Rex Harrison and director Richard Fleischer pose a mite uneasily with an unbilled cast member of *Doctor Dolittle*. From the collection of Photofest.

the LA opening, ordering free soundtrack albums for every attendee. No speeches, he said. "And the goddamn food at the *Camelot* party was inedible. We've got Chasen's, so that's no problem. But we need two orchestras. The *Camelot* party fell apart because they only had one orchestra." Fourteen hundred guests attended against a convoy of limousines and barricades controlling hundreds of fans. Governor and Nancy Reagan were there, as were *Dolittle*'s human and animal stars. Joey Bishop hosted for a taped replay on his late-night talk show.

Reviews were mixed at the Royal World Premiere on December 12, attended by Queen Elizabeth and held at the Odeon Theatre at Marble Arch. *Los Angeles Times*'s Joyce Haber flamed rumors that *Dolittle* is a disaster. Expenses were known in advance of the opening, with published estimates of $27 million in ticket sales necessary to break even. Advance sales at Loew's State Theater were a heady $400,000, but *Variety*'s review was a study in ambivalence. "Is it a 'good motion' picture?" it asked. "The answer varies according to what the individual expects for his money. Action fans won't 'dig' it."

Fox marketing made a full-throttled attempt to bluff its way into a hit. The original soundtrack album had the biggest first pressing in history, with half a million records installed in stores four months before the movie's premiere. Versions in a multitude of languages were released. "Talk to the Animals" was recorded by Sammy Davis, Jr., Andy Williams, Dizzy Gillespie, Jack Jones, Tony Bennett, and André Kostelanetz. Even thunderous Kate Smith was interested in doing a cover. "Don't knock it, Arthur," music promoter Happy Goday told Jacobs. "She's very big with the 'God Bless America' crowd."

The final product is loaded with *potential* charm, but, like *Camelot*, *Dolittle* refuses to take flight. Its delight in all creatures great and small is overwhelmed by a lumbering production. It does have assets, none of which elevate *Dolittle* to genuine entertainment. Castle Combe as Puddleby is not without visual enchantment. Top-ranking cinematographer Robert Surtees avoided the antique shop look of *Camelot* by employing crisp 70-millimeter camerawork. The movie is packed with fauna, but real animals standing about are dull to the eye, rather like watching a movie shot at the zoo. The fake ones created a greater problem. Sheila the Fox moves like a creaky figure in a museum diorama. When Harrison communes with an octopus, its creators do not even attempt verisimilitude. The giant lunar moth resembles an overdressed kite, but hardly a living thing. When a whale head butts a floating island, we see plastic trees, enamel, wood, and stucco lurching in a studio water tank. But the biggest technical fiasco of *Dolittle* is the fabled Pink Sea Snail. The 40-foot contraption is so unenchanting that when Samantha Eggar squeals, "I've never seen anything like it!" she might as well be exalting a Greyhound bus.

The players lack the spirit of fun that *Dolittle* so achingly needs. Harrison's 1,000 performances as Henry Higgins had entered his bloodstream, and there was no escaping the air of shtick in his Dolittle *sprechstimme*. While Newley's Matthew Mugg is uncomfortably affected and too often dim-witted, his rough-hewn Irishman was relegated to supporting player by edict from Harrison. Young William Dix, playing little Tommy Stubbins, is so underutilized he belongs in the props department, not the cast. Richard Attenborough as a jovial carny is not half bad singing "I've Never Seen Anything Like It," but Eggar remains irritable and conflicted. Does her aristocratic Emma Fairfax desire Mugg or Dolittle? Her opening number, all about the crossroads in her life, is blunted by the fact that we do not know who this stranger is, or care two cents for the juncture she approaches.

Dolittle, perhaps more than any musical of the era, carries itself like Frankenstein. Everywhere you look there are parts borrowed and stolen, with a script that cannot decide where to go. Harrison's "Why Do We Treat Animals Like Animals?" sounds like the impoverished twin of "Why Can't a Woman Be More Like a Man?" from *My Fair Lady*. The Oceania of *Dolittle*'s second half is pure *South Pacific*, while the sedated island children look like a pandering to white audiences wanting *King and I*–type human faux exotica. Geoffrey Holder, as a clichéd movie island chief, is either a hero or a villain. One minute he is sympathetic to the cast-aways, the next he has them prepped to be dinner. The best of many subplots has Dolittle reuniting Sophie, a depressed circus seal, with her husband. As Harrison prepares to cast her into the sea, he sings, with admirable restraint, a plaintive song to her called "When I Look Into Your Eyes." The highlight of *Dolittle* is a love song to a *seal*. The love song between two *humans*, "After Today," is alternatively dowdy in sound, staging, and execution. As a celebration of sudden love, it attempts to function as another "The Trolley Song," "Singin' in the Rain," or "Gigi," but in it you can hear the traditional musical go on life support.

In merchandising *Dolittle*, Arthur Jacobs sought nothing less than the whole-sale takeover of America's popular commercial outlets. With inexplicable pride, he said "You won't be able to go into a store without seeing *Doctor Dolittle* advertising something." With 300 items worth $200 million retail, he was hardly exaggerating. There were clocks, watches, sweatshirts, card games, luggage, pencil sets, hats, balloons, combs, brushes, sunglasses, place mats, toy medicine kits, musical instruments, scrapbooks, lunch boxes, ceramics, notebooks, tumblers, play money and billfolds, change purses, color slides with viewers, night lights, animal print bikinis, greeting cards, coloring books, yo-yos, animal crackers, costumes, robes, cereal, furniture, jigsaw puzzles, charm bracelets, animal cuff links and tie clasps, pet food, and a collector's set of nine free *Doctor Dolittle* statuettes inside specially marked boxes of Royal Shake-A-Pudd'n. There was also Mattel's talking Rex Harrison doll that said "*how-do-you-do-I'm-Doctor-Dolittle*" with the pull of a string. Other promotional campaign suggestions included a tie-in between the song "Fabulous Places" and airlines and travel agencies, the playing of the soundtrack at airports and in flight, and a movie brochure in every seat pocket. Most all of the products sprang from Jacobs's exuberant mind, but little of it was sold. "That fucking *Doctor Dolittle* killed off merchandising tie-ins for the next decade," said a Fox promotions staffer years later. "I'll bet there are still Mattel warehouses in California bursting at the seams with that crap."

Given the realities of *Dolittle*'s potential market, this time Fox was too selective in the premiere engagements. In December, it opened in North America in just four theaters in as many cities. It would add nine in January, 15 in February, eight in March, and 14 in June. Among other English-speaking countries, it opened initially in 26 first-run houses. It opened on a mere 35 screens throughout the whole of Europe west of the Iron Curtain. It was even more rare in the Middle East, showing twice daily on one screen in Iran and Israel. The Far East premiere engagements totaled two in Hong Kong and Malaysia, three in the Philippines, and five in Japan. South America's only first-run engagements were on three screens in as many countries. No initial bookings were made for huge multi-national regions of the Middle East, South and Southeast Asia, or all of Africa. Final theatrical gross was in the neighborhood of $9 million, with $6.2 million returned to Fox in rental fees. That put it below *The Happiest Millionaire* in domestic rentals.

As if *Dolittle* did not have big enough public relations problems, it also came under allegations of racism. A New York high school librarian wrote an excoriating piece in the *Interracial Books for Children* quarterly that received wide exposure. She stated that *Dolittle* comes off as "the personification of the great white father nobly bearing the white man's burden" and that *Dolittle* creator Hugh Lofting was "a white racist guilty of almost every prejudice known to modern white Western man." The African characters "emerge as quaint, comic, childlike figures with simple minds and ridiculous customs and funny-sounding names." Even the animals are shown to feel superior to the Africans. Efforts to censor the reissued books and take the movie off the market went nowhere, but the complaints did little to stimulate ticket sales.

"You look back now and ask, how could you have been so stupid?" said Richard Zanuck years later. "*Doctor Dolittle* was conceived in a period of euphoria. We were all riding a musical wave that we didn't realize was going to come crashing down on the beach all at once. Sure, there were probably signs and warnings out there, but you're already so committed financially and emotionally that it's very hard to pull the plug on these big undertakings."

Fox's second of the three giant post–*Sound of Music* musicals was no less elaborate than *Dolittle*. Preproduction for *Star!* was already falling behind schedule due to Robert Wise's responsibilities on *The Sand Pebbles*, a complicated drama that required his full attention. *Star!* producer Saul Chaplin made several flights to *Pebbles* location in Taiwan to confer with Wise, and their meetings inevitably focused on the sheer girth of the film. Preliminary sketches included 20 wigs and 36 separate makeup designs for Julie Andrews, just as she did fittings for some of the 94 costumes designed for her by Donald Brooks. It was during these preproduction months that *Star!* grew from huge to colossal. One wig to be worn in one production number alone came to $650, and the budget now loomed at $13,604,700.

An exhausted Wise reported to Fox, where *Star!* was commencing production on a revised schedule. Andrews came to the set accompanied by a small entourage of hair stylist, makeup man, and dresser. Everyone doted on her. Set too hot? Two large electric fans appear within seconds. Shoes ugly? A new pair will be supplied by morning, with a bright plastic flower in each. When Dick Zanuck implored Wise to cut costs, Wise essentially said no. "I wish I had some brilliant idea of a way to get several million out of the budget, which is what I'm sure we would all like very much. However, we have this script and this story and we have to do it mainly here rather than in England; so I'm afraid any giant elimination is out of the question." He and Chaplin did find a way to cut five and a half days of shooting and save expenses on over 600 extras, but in a film of *Star!*'s magnitude, that reduction was hardly felt.

Actor Robert Reed joined the cast 10 days before everyone checked into the St. Moritz and Regency in New York to begin location filming. Fourteen sites in

Manhattan and on Long Island were used over 18 days in May without significant hardship or delays. But nothing was cheap—one week at the Lyceum Theater on West 45th Street cost $34,400 in rental alone. While filming went smoothly, and Andrews, Wise, and Chaplin formed a congenial trio, costs were added to an additional shooting day in New York, and more extras, staff, operations, makeup, and transportation. Location personnel receiving per diem grew from 6 to 40, and hotel rooms, including office space, grew from 8 to 50.

From New York, *Star!* moved to the Cape Cod Playhouse, still owned by Richard Aldrich, Gertrude Lawrence's widower played by Richard Crenna. From there, trouble could be anticipated. London was less than accommodating for location filming. Regent's Park was only available in the mornings, Westminster School (St. James) on Saturdays only, the Railway Station, Carney St. Courts, and Strand on Sundays only, while permission was flat-out refused for St. James's Palace and at Speaker's Court, where filming would snarl traffic and create an attractive nuisance near Marble Arch.

Before negotiating London, the crew moved from Cape Cod to the South of France for eight days of filming in and around the Villa Serena at Cap Ferrat. In London, *Star!* did manage early morning shoots at Marylebone Train Station and Regent's Park. Noël Coward was present, quietly editing the screenplay without credit. According to screenwriter William Fairchild, when Coward reviewed Daniel Massey's dialogue, "He changed three words, cut out a few 'dear boys,' and poured me a whopping drink."

By early July, everyone returned to the Fox Studio for interior dramatic scenes and production numbers. Wise and Andrews were very nearly at the end of their endurance. On a particularly vexing day of shooting, when the blue screen lights kept burning out, costumes were mismatched, and delays were causing everyone to be irritable, Wise confessed a fatigue at being Fox's roadshow director of choice. "Three years," he said wearily. "I didn't really want to do another big picture. Period pictures take so damn much time. For *The Sand Pebbles*, we had to build our own junks and our own rickshaws. . . . I want to do something where I don't have to take down television antennas in order to shoot." As for Andrews, she sang sixteen songs in *Star!*, in contrast to a mere seven in *The Sound of Music*. "This is the most difficult film I've ever made," she said. "It's like going into training. I must take care of myself or I'd be *dead*. I get up at 5:45 A.M. every day, and sometimes I don't get home till eight at night."

Budgets and schedules were forever being revised, always with more outlay of time and money. By late July, two production numbers, "The Physician" and "Parisian Pierrot," added 11 unscheduled days for rehearsal and shooting. This was, if one believed Fox's marketing, an Andrews vehicle bigger than any vehicle ever concocted for any star. Wise maintained the lavishness was justified. Lawrence was a fashion giantess and a client of the world's leading designers. In keeping with Lawrence's penchant for luxury, Andrews wore $3 million worth of perpetually guarded Cartier jewelry air-shipped to locations in California and Europe. Additionally, predictions were made that the effects of *Star!* would be gargantuan, with Donald Brooks's costumes shaking the fashion world. Couture was already favoring the plucked eyebrows, green eye shadow, and red lipstick of the era between the wars, according to *Look*. "For women who do not want to follow the hippie road or slick moon-blast trail to fashion, here is salvation." As for Andrews, this will vanquish the sexless nanny image once and for all. Surely her millions of fans want to see her expand her repertoire into Lawrence's chic and stylish world.

The demands of being the biggest movie star took a price on Andrews. When engaged in a discussion of urban riots in America with choreographer Michael Kidd, she said "Why don't the people just work hard and get out of the slums? They're not very intelligent, are they?" She softened that remark by confessing an ignorance and regret that her formal education ended at 15. "I feel that someone in my position really ought to know more." Her inclinations toward caution extended to interviews, where she began delivering canned answers, verbatim from one journalist to another. "You would be *amazed* at some of the things they invent about me!" she said. "If I did all the fan magazines say, I would be the most promiscuous lady in town!" She was nothing if not stressed, and quietly began seeing a psychiatrist. And there *was* something for the gossip sheets. Andrews met *Pink Panther* director Blake Edwards, and soon after he pitched *Darling Lili* to her, all about an English rose who spies for the Germans during World War I. "Professionally and romantically, things kind of started from there," she said. But she asserted that her private life was none too spicy. "I would think that most people would suppose that it might be a little difficult to make it with Mary Poppins!"

Though he had high respect for Andrews, Wise feared that her innate reticence was getting in the way of her performance. "If Julie has anything it is a quality of honesty and truthfulness, and it is this that has made her doubtful, given her difficulty with some of the 'theatricality' of Gertie Lawrence's behavior," he said. "If she has had to work hard on anything it has been on the volatile and 'hammy' aspects of Gertie." Challenging, too, was a script requiring her to pass out drunk, which Wise chose to indicate off camera. "I'm too cautious, too careful a person," Andrews said of acting so inebriated. "I'd be terrified of what I'd reveal if I ever really let go."

After all non-musical scenes were completed, Andrews was alone with bit players to complete the production numbers "Jenny," "Limehouse Blues," "Someone to Watch over Me," and "Parisian Pierrot" over the final eight weeks. Most elaborate was "Jenny," the gaudy display of a loose woman pulled from Lawrence's *Lady in the Dark*. Dressed in a decidedly un-*Mary Poppins* black sequined body stocking, Andrews had to hang from an overhead cable and slide down a rope suspended above the stage, then burst through a flaming hoop to balance on the feet of circus jugglers, all without benefit of a body double. "Jenny" took two weeks to rehearse and film, and brought Andrews to the limits of her underdeveloped dancing abilities. "Limehouse Blues" was the last number of *Star!* to be shot, and was followed by a wrap party on the set. A Dixieland band of middle-aged musicians played "Hello, Dolly!" as Wise was being interviewed. When asked how he felt about *Star!*, he responded "marvelous and nervous."

Darryl Zanuck wrote to Wise suggesting cuts. He felt that after the "sensational" first half, when Lawrence was working her way out of the slums, she grew to be "an unpleasant bitch and a repulsive alcoholic." He added, "This girl, this talented idol, had become a social 'tramp.' I knew Gertrude Lawrence personally and I didn't like her either." Wise responded by reminding Zanuck that he made suggestions for cutting *The Sound of Music*, too, which were not followed. Zanuck backed off, a move he would come to regret. Darryl's choice not to be more insistent with changes in *Star!* came largely from the enthusiasm of son Richard and fellow producer David Brown. "Sometimes where I'm nervous on a project and I know they're high on it I have the authority to say, 'No,' but it's difficult for men so valuable to the company," said Darryl. He added that perhaps they were right, or that they were blind to reason. "We were all punch drunk with the overwhelming success of *The Sound of Music*."

When the hard numbers were tallied, they read like a military campaign. *Star!* completed principal photography 1,197 days after Andrews said yes to playing Lawrence. There were 1,400 camera setups, and Andrews appeared in 1,372 of them. Shooting took 149 days, 10 over schedule, with Andrews on camera for 132 of them. This broke down into 143 first-unit shooting days, six second-unit, five travel days, three lineup days, three holidays, four inactive days, and 28 rehearsal days, not including rehearsals in advance of production. Twenty additional first-unit crew members were added in New York, London, and France. One hundred and eighty five sets were built over 20 locations. And despite the film's worship of Julie Andrews, there were 44 speaking roles, 345 bit parts, and 10,000 extras. "'Star!' nears finish line," shouted the headline of *Spotlight*, a studio newsletter devoted exclusively to marketing the film. The communiqué was partly for the instructional benefit of the press. "'Star!' is entertainment with a bang," wrote a Fox staffer. "But in the pressure of deadlines, some of our friends forget this—and refer to us only as 'Star.' Please don't take the bang out of our title. It's 'Star!'; Bang!" The directive was only fitting for a production "designed as the biggest musical of all time."

Throughout the making of *Star!*, Wise faithfully responded to the mountains of fan letters he received for *The Sound of Music*. "People who don't like it must be hard-faced, with wrinkled foreheads and foreboding frowns," wrote a housewife from Malawi. "I saw it four times. I was ecstasied," wrote a schoolboy from Malaysia. "I'm worried—it's cheaper than therapy," wrote a psychiatrist from California. Wise's standard replies of "thank you" and "we're thrilled at its success" eventually came with a new sign-off: "I hope you will enjoy *Star!*"

Arthur Freed, the great emeritus musical producer at MGM, hoped to work with Andrews. He sought her through the invention of a biopic of Irving Berlin and his women. Berlin's lawyer told Freed that a deal could be struck for $1 million, which came with six new songs and availability to Berlin's entire catalogue. Screenwriter Arthur Laurents (*West Side Story, Gypsy*) was reportedly employed to write an original story, and Vincente Minnelli would direct. Laurents had concocted a screenplay called *Say It with Music*, about a man who romances four different women.

Plans unraveled as Laurents backed out, and Leonard Gersche (*Funny Face*) tried but failed to fashion a workable screenplay. Then Betty Comden and Adolph Green gave it a shot over two years. They overhauled the screenplay with a twentieth-century panorama, with cross-cutting used to tell three stories from various eras. "*Say It with Music* will be the greatest physical musical ever made," said Freed to *The Hollywood Reporter*. "It will cover all of Irving Berlin's career with his songs to be used in medley, ballet by Jerome Robbins and Bob Fosse, vocal and imaginative forms."

With a $10 million budget, Julie Andrews, Sophia Loren, Ann-Margret, and Robert Goulet were originally announced as the stars. Then it was Andrews alone, with boyfriend Blake Edwards as director at MGM in 70-millimeter, Super Panavision, and reserve seats. Andrews signed for $1,000,000 against 10 percent of the gross plus 35 cents from each cast album sold. The script, such as it was, remained problematic. Most recently doctored by director-screenwriter George Axelrod, it now concerned a vain and needy woman who becomes suicidal with the death of her Svengali-like husband. Encumbered with a screenplay that would not gel, MGM finally abandoned *Say It with Music*, but not Julie Andrews. In March 1968, the studio announced her as the star of *She Loves Me*, an adaptation of the 1963 Broadway musical. Edwards would write, direct, and produce. *Darling Lili*, another Edwards brainchild for Andrews, was meanwhile being shopped at Paramount. Andrews had already fattened the coffers of Disney, Fox, Universal, and United Artists. Naturally, MGM and Paramount wanted in on the action.

CHAPTER 8

Casting About

The musical remake of *Goodbye, Mr. Chips* burned in Development Hell with particular ferocity. Its turnstile of personnel was constant, and disadvantageously coincided with Metro-Goldwyn-Mayer's advanced corporate meltdown. Composers and lyricists were hired and fired, 51 songs were written and rejected, and for a time it seemed that everyone in Hollywood with or without musical credentials was announced to direct or star. *Chips* suffered enormously—from timing, shell games at MGM, a producer of intense caprice, and profound shifts in public taste.

Goodbye, Mr. Chips began as a short 1934 novel by James Hilton and was adapted for the English stage in 1938. Louis B. Mayer produced the first film version at the newly opened MGM Elstree Studios outside London. The elegant results were greeted with high praise. As Arthur Chipping, the dry teacher of fictitious Brookfield public boarding school, Robert Donat gave his signature performance, and won an Oscar for it over Clark Gable's Rhett Butler. It also made a star out of Greer Garson, appearing in her film debut as the woman who awakens Chips to the joys of romantic love. It was delectable filmmaking. *Chips* is one of those stately, well-crafted, warmly felt dramas that gave the studio system a good name.

A draft of *Chips* the musical was on file in the MGM script department since 1951, but it wasn't until 1964 that the idea took off. Former studio messenger boy Arthur P. Jacobs, the high-strung producer behind *Doctor Dolittle*, was offering MGM a marketing and distribution package of three big movies to be made through his APJAC productions. None of them were made, but *Chips* materialized instead. Jacobs approached director Vincente Minnelli and dramatist-screenwriter Terence Rattigan, himself public-school educated, for their early appraisals. In his "Memorandum on *Mr. Chips*," Rattigan wrote to Minnelli and Jacobs that he believed "the original version is far too *obviously* sentimental for today" and that an updated treatment must be more "astringent." This, he believed, would come through casting and a reconsideration of period. The book covers Chips's fictional lifetime from 1848 to 1934. Rattigan advocated moving forward, running through the 1930s and ending soon after the Blitz. The main action is to take place when Chips is 45 in 1923, a time Jacobs defined as "long cigarette-holders, Oxford bags, Tallulah Bankhead in London, and *No, No Nanette*."

Rattigan saw the emotional heart of the story in Chips overcoming his fear of being in love and coming to realize that wisdom is not derived exclusively from books. Comparisons to Henry Higgins must be assiduously avoided, he cautioned. He felt the love interest Katherine was underwritten in the first movie, and she must be better defined. How that was to happen, he wrote, remained "hazy." Though he admired the 1939 film, Rattigan believed it avoided the novel's "gentle irony," which should probably be reintroduced.

In between *My Fair Lady* and *Doctor Dolittle*, Rattigan initially championed Rex Harrison as Chips, and Jacobs was agreeable. The husband and wife composing team of André and Dory Previn meanwhile began negotiating terms with Jacobs and MGM to write the music. Then Jacobs met Rattigan, Minnelli, and Harrison in Paris to conceptualize. Jacobs assured Minnelli that Rattigan's participation as screenwriter "is set and I think that Rex is 99 percent set. I also think we can convince him Julie Andrews is not too young to play Katherine." But then Rattigan had second thoughts, that Harrison should *not* play Chips, suggesting alternatives Laurence Olivier, Richard Burton, and the younger actors Peter O'Toole and Albert Finney. Harrison had a nasty reputation, and Jacobs wanted to stay open to other actors as well. As he wryly noted, "Just supposing disaster strikes and Rex is actually taken off to that asylum for megalomaniac actors that has been awaiting him . . . and just supposing Julie Andrews goes to that other asylum reserved for actresses who refuse to play opposite Rex Harrison—then we would at least have at hand a musical version of *Goodbye, Mr. Chips* which should commend itself not only to other actors and actresses of status and distinction but also—which is far more important—to audiences all over the world."

Pairing Harrison and Andrews was marketing gold after their denied partnership in *My Fair Lady*. Still, Rattigan wondered why Katherine had to be English. She could be American (Shirley MacLaine, Lee Remick, Jean Seberg) or Continental (Romy Schneider, Leslie Caron). With Rattigan's suggestion that Katherine be more three dimensional, and the group firmly picturing Andrews, it was decided to turn her from a governess to a fun-loving music hall entertainer. Here, now, is a love story of opposites, an Apollonian-Dionysian contrast set to music. She's sensual; he's cerebral. She's streetwise; he's bookish. She's impetuous; he's deliberate. The poignancy of the tale will be derived from their reconciliation of temperamental differences and mutual redemption. He will emerge from his cocoon, and she will learn of contentment not as a soubrette, but as the loving wife of an honorable man. With a general concept materializing, a budget was made. Expenses were high, but not alarming. *Chips* was to cost barely less than $4 million, not including the two star salaries. It would have a 90-day shooting schedule that would take cast and crew to England, MGM facilities at Culver City, and Greece.

While Rattigan labored over a first draft screenplay, casting the two leads became a dizzying game. Andrews cooled on the idea and was consumed by *Star!* Burton supplanted Harrison, with both of them aiming for $1 million dollars plus percentage deals. With Andrews out, producer Carlo Ponti lobbied for his wife Sophia Loren, with Jacobs responding with a polite but noncommittal reply. Then Burton was out, but no alternative was named. Audrey Hepburn was in. Then she was out.

The Previns got to work on the songs. Dory's first set of lyrics sent to Minnelli and Jacobs were all in lower case, and reflect some kind of an attempt to draw out the personality contrasts between Chips and Katherine:

Sung by Katherine:

he's a master, met a phoricly, [sic]
rhetoricaly [sic], historicly [sic],
he knows his ABC's and H20's!
but, don't add him up corporeally
or question him sartorially,
he doesn't know his knickers
from his nose!

That was good enough for MGM and Arthur Jacobs, and a contract was drawn for the Previns. The young maestro John Williams was employed as assistant for a flat sum of $15,000. Despite his low earnings, he had great responsibility, overseeing arrangements and conducting.

Minnelli then excused himself from the project, which brought Gower Champion to the director's seat. In development meetings, associate producer Mort Abrahams reported to Jacobs that Rattigan and Champion were collaborating well, but he found Dory "very difficult in terms of changing lyrics." He felt that Dory was so problematic that unless she agreed to different working methods, "we will have to take steps to replace her. . . . It has been very tricky here, what with Terry [Rattigan] walking in one door and the Previns in another, and it's really been pretty funny trying to keep them apart."

For Katherine, Jacobs was considering Samantha Eggar, who had less name recognition than Loren but was more congruent with the stereotype of an English public schoolmaster's wife. She signed to star opposite the on-again Richard Burton. She would take second position to him and be paid $300,000 for 24 weeks. Burton approved Eggar and pushed for filming in Ireland and Greece, with vocal prerecording in England or Rome. Or, he said, the entire film could be shot in the United States if there was a favorable tax ruling. The Previns and Champion were pacified for the present, while the company began the logistics of corralling hundreds of English schoolboys as extras. Jacobs now focused on the terms of his remuneration, and was granted a $300 per week assistant and office space in London.

Burton would not sign a contract until he heard an expensive demonstration recording of Previn's score made at RCA Hollywood Studio. The question of where *Chips* would be filmed was also unresolved. Ireland, the United States, Spain, France, and England were all being juggled as principal locations, with a vacation sequence to be shot among the ruins of Greece. Audrey Hepburn's name surfaced once again, though she would be more expensive than Eggar. And since Eggar had signed a contract, she would have to be paid off. Burton's participation in *Chips* ran up against production delays and scheduling conflicts. He was currently distracted by the long-run intersecting drama of his life and work. While Jacobs dithered, Burton kept busy as one half of the most famous couple in the world, dodging paparazzi while making five movies in prompt succession with Elizabeth Taylor. Not surprising, Burton finally withdrew from *Chips* due to "contract disputes," while production was delayed until sometime in 1968. He never heard the demo recording.

With the role of Chips up for grabs again, Jacobs went back to thinking like a producer. He put forward various names to studio president Robert O'Brien: Peter O'Toole, Albert Finney, Peter Sellars, Richard Harris ("Should be very hot after *Camelot*"), and Paul Scofield ("Should be very important after *Man for All Seasons*"). The inevitable comparison to that *other* musical came when Jacobs told O'Brien, "It is the subject matter in music which hopefully will give us another *Sound of Music*." Jacobs even suggested Christopher Plummer as Chips based on the dubious "fact" that he "has been seen by more people than any actor in history."

MGM was in a delicate place while *Chips* was so fitfully pulled together. Saddled with a $57 million debt, company stock prices were falsely inflated due to the competitive bidding of a supermarket tycoon and smelting company president. With a proxy war in progress, it was nail-biting time. Several overseas projects, including *The Dirty Dozen* and the tightly guarded *2001: A Space Odyssey*, were running over budget. O'Brien sought to pacify shareholders and the public, reminding them of strong revenues for the gooey *Singing Nun*, the pulse-pounding hard ticketed *Grand Prix*, and the seductively cryptic *Blow-Up*. He projected further confidence in the upcoming roadshow *Far from the Madding Crowd* and the summer reissue of *Gone with the Wind*, but could not rule out a Warner Bros.-Seven Arts–type merger. If it happened, he said a company in the communications field would be preferred.

Given the ping-pong of *Chips* casting, and the present condition of the studio, executives grew cautious. When development money and final approval of the *Chips* score were withheld, Jacobs sent a scathing telegram to O'Brien. "If MGM is unwilling to make necessary commitments to move project forward at this point then strongly urge APJAC be permitted to purchase property and make picture elsewhere," he cabled in typically stilted Western Union style. "We are aware of your company and stockholder problems and in light of the widespread publicity already given this picture and its casting, we do not believe that these problems are in any way helped by your *Chips* decision considering that MGM and APJAC's substantial investment may be totally lost in contrast to the excellent opportunity to make this picture in January 1968 with top stars who are prepared to commit now."

Jacobs spoke out of turn to O'Brien, since top stars and a start date of January 1968 were but pipe dreams. He warmed to the idea of Peter O'Toole, but he was no more ready to commit than anyone else. The *Chips* casting game was now the subject of much industry gossip, and Samantha Eggar had reason to wonder if her contract was worth anything. O'Toole voiced concerns about her experience, while Champion objected to O'Toole based on his lack of musical training. At this juncture, Jacobs reconceived much of *Chips*. Gower Champion and the Previns were still aboard, while two non-singers, O'Toole and Hepburn, would star.

The coordinating of schedules and salaries was made more challenging by Jacob's flip-flopping. As soon as he settled on Hepburn, he rethought Sophia Loren. "The idea of a non-English lady being thrown into a typical English public school certainly makes for a more interesting situation," he wrote to Ponti. Jacobs was even prepared to fly to Rome with Rattigan and Champion to discuss the "new approach" with Loren and Ponti. Though Jacobs had secured neither Hepburn nor Loren, he was certain that Eggar was now out. Two days after releasing her, MGM and Jacobs fashioned a deal for Hepburn, which included 30 weeks of employment at a guarantee of $750,000 plus 10 percent of the gross film rentals over $20 million.

The original *Chips* start date came and went, and Jacobs remained the very epitome of indecision. Ignoring Rattigan's protestations, he returned to Rex Harrison. Perusing the songs Previn had written, Harrison was not favorably impressed. "My Boys" went "nowhere" and "I Like the Little Fellows," he felt, "should be called 'I *Hate* the Little Fellows.'" He did like one number called "With Her," but on the whole, he was in a temper. It seemed that Jacobs never stopped wanting Harrison and he moved forward with a deal while trying to sell the difficult star to O'Brien and the MGM brass. "I should like to go on record on behalf of myself, Gower Champion, Terence Rattigan, and the Previns that we are absolutely convinced that Rex Harrison is the perfect Mr. Chips," he wrote to O'Brien. For *Chips*, Harrison would accept nothing less than $750,000 against 10 percent of the gross from the first dollar earned. In addition, he would have an expense account of $2,000 a week, and would receive 5 percent of all royalties on the soundtrack album. Most important, he had final approval of costar, composer, and lyricist. If Harrison did not like the Previns, now deeply invested, he could insist they go, thereby forcing the production to start over. As if by royal edict, Harrison announced he is "committed now with the protection of Rattigan's involvement." With Harrison ready to sign for a start date, it was time for MGM to increase its participation. But weeks, then months, had gone by, and APJAC attorneys were impatient. Attempting to place blame on MGM and not on his own work methods, Jacobs claimed the studio has "stalled, delayed, and extended this project at their own whim, to the detriment of APJAC. The picture has been put together with different combinations and fallen apart, primarily due to their own internal problems and not because APJAC in any way failed to deliver."

MGM granted Jacobs a $125,000 salary, lease on a London office and flat, consultants' fees, and various secretarial, overtime, and incidental expenses. As with *Doctor Dolittle*, he would receive the credit line "An Arthur P. Jacobs Production" above the title and at 60 percent of its size. An additional "Produced by Arthur P. Jacobs" in the standard position would be 75 percent of the title's size, and "An APJAC Film" would follow the MGM logo. With Harrison in mind, Jacobs returned to the ever-nagging question of Katherine. He prepared an entirely new list of names, but where once Jacobs bemoaned MGM's lack of involvement, he now regretted it. Apparently Robert O'Brien went around APJAC and cast American actress Lee Remick. "Despite the fact that Shirley [MacLaine] is a bigger name, Gower and I feel Remick is better for the part," wrote O'Brien to Jacobs.

Harrison enjoyed the sport of changing his mind and focused renewed attention on *Chips* after wrapping *Dolittle*. Exercising his right at costar selection and believing an American would be wrong for Mrs. Chips, he lobbied for Maggie Smith. Then he changed his mind. Smith had turned down a play with Laurence Olivier and a film role because of a supposed firm offer to star in *Chips*. There were threats of suing MGM and APJAC, especially when Jacobs went public with intentions to cast Remick. Indeed, how many times can a producer go back on his word and still hope to make movies? Smith backed off her threat, while Harrison went to work at sabotaging Remick's chances. When compromising photos of her appeared in Italy, Harrison loudly expressed his disapproval. They were never published in the United States, and though Jacobs did not find them shocking, he told Harrison "I don't think any future pictures like this would be helpful to her image as Mrs. Chips, and she assured us that no such pictures will be done in the future."

The next wave of Previn music and lyrics arrived, and they were unfit for a greeting card. The quest for simplicity and introspection resulted in verb conjugations that would bore Chips's remedial grammar students:

> *He smiled . . . I smiled . . . we smiled . . .*
> *And the sky smiled, too*
> *We walked . . . he talked . . . I talked . . .*
> *And the sky was blue.*

A new production schedule estimate was pushed forward to the spring and summer of 1968, while location scouting was under way, and Remick was sent drafts of her songs. Then Harrison began to make trouble again. After meeting with him, a defensive André Previn wrote Jacobs that "none of us expected him to like every new song and every new change in the script. However, none of us ever dreamed that he would simply turn down every word either. . . . I just cannot believe that after all the discussions and rewrites we all did before Rex ever was presented with all the stuff were for nothing; after all, Gower is not exactly ignorant about musicals, and if he liked everything he read and heard, what could be so completely wrong about all that work?. . . . This was, to me, willful and spoiled, and more than slightly demented and egomaniacal. . . . I think we should, if at all possible, dump Rex once and for all, and try desperately for O'Toole or someone else, before Rex drives us all into a premature grave."

Jacobs was desperate to anchor *someone* to this production, and that someone was Harrison. He reasoned that if Harrison was rejecting Previn as composer and Remick as costar, then it's the Previns and Remick who must go, not Harrison. He talked to O'Brien about keeping Harrison, firing the Previns and Remick, rewriting the score with *Dolittle*'s Leslie Bricusse, and starting yet another search for Mrs. Chips. O'Brien issued an emphatic no, and Jacobs had few options but to release Harrison. "I am sure, however, sad as this is, it will not effect [*sic*] our friendship," wrote Jacobs. Then as a sedative, he added that *Doctor Dolittle* was marketed to the sky at Fox's recent world film convention. "The mini film received a standing ovation," he reported, "and if anything exceeded the reaction which we received earlier this year when the domestic distributors were here. Everything is coming along marvelously on the campaign, and the advances are staggering."

As recalled in John Gregory Dunne's *The Studio*, Harrison's departure from *Goodbye, Mr. Chips* was his doing. Confident he could succeed where Previn had failed, Jacobs met with Harrison in early September to finalize everything and get a contract signed. "It was all set," Jacobs reportedly told Dunne. "Gower and I even went to Paris to see Rex. We drive out to his house in the country and he meets us at the door. 'Marvelous day,' he says. You know the way he talks. 'Bloody Mary, anyone, Bloody Mary.' He gets us the Bloody Marys and then he says, 'Now let me tell you why I'm not going to do *Mr. Chips*.' That's the first we heard about it. It was all set. Well, Gower looks at me, picks up his attaché case and says, 'Sorry, I'm going to the airport, I'm going home.' It was all set. *All set*."

While the Previns remained (for now), Remick did not. She was fired when Champion saw rough footage of former child star and current pop song sensation Petula Clark in *Finian's Rainbow*. Clark was English, and she could dance, act, and sing with a sweet but not cloying purity. Perfection! O'Brien and Jacobs were similarly enthusiastic, and APJAC worked quickly to get her. As for the pinwheeling negotiations that preceded her, Clark had heard the rumors that others vied for Mrs. Chips, but no one shared details. It didn't much matter, as she was quite moved by what she read. "The original script was extraordinary," she said. "Terence Rattigan had written something beautiful."

Jacobs now went after Peter O'Toole with equal determination. O'Toole was initially appalled at the very idea of a musical of *Goodbye, Mr. Chips*, but like Clark, came to respect it through Rattigan. "I saw the original film with Robert Donat when I was about eight and loved every second of it," he said. "But at first the thought of its being done again as a musical filled me with horror. The only thing that caused me to read it was the fact that the script was by Terry Rattigan. Now Terry isn't an oil painter so much as a line drawer and he's written a beautiful script for the film, elegant down to the last detail." As for the musical demands, O'Toole announced that he did not dance, but he would like to try his own singing for the first time on camera. Jacobs was certain at last that he found the winning star combination. He and Mort Abrahams met O'Toole in London, concluding that his acting would compensate for any inadequacies in his singing. Meanwhile, production supervisor David Orton and designer Ken Adam worked out a shooting schedule. They then toured England in search of the ideal gray stone school as primary location.

There was still the matter of the Previn's score. Harrison had a point—the music was problematic. Abrahams wrote to Champion outlining which songs should go and which should stay. He also supported the plan to hire Bricusse to write backup material. "While all of this may seem a bit cloak-and-dagger, it has to be carefully designed to give the Previns the maximum opportunity to complete the scores by themselves," Abrahams wrote to Champion. "And while the involvement of Leslie must be kept completely confidential, his consultation at this stage of the game is designed for the same purpose. Nothing could make us (and that includes you and Leslie) happier than if the Previns came in with smashing new material, and we could thank Leslie and buy him a new color television set." All in all, he remained in the Previns' camp. "Let's face it," he wrote, "the Previns and their music are the reason [sic] I agreed to do this picture."

Past indiscretions began haunting the production. Apparently the last one informed of Petula Clark's engagement was Lee Remick, whose agent asked if she was dependent on Harrison or not. "My main concern now must be whether MGM acknowledges or denies its commitment to Lee Remick to play the female lead in Goodbye, Mr. Chips," wrote her agent, with the whisper of a threat. She filed a breach of contract suit against MGM and APJAC, while MGM and Jacobs asked the New York Supreme Court to bar Remick from their books and records, claiming they are irrelevant to the suit. Jacobs was relieved when supporting roles were cast without incident. Reliable British players Michael Bryant, George Baker, and Alison Leggatt were brought on. Sir Michael Redgrave, father of Vanessa and Lynn, was cast as the headmaster, and O'Toole's wife, Siân Phillips, had a small role as an eccentric actress.

The problem of music reached a crisis in November. The Previns learned of Bricusse's stealth composing and went on strike, refusing to put pencil to paper until they met with Champion to discuss the replacement songs and the use of their own music. They also insisted on hearing a demo tape of O'Toole's singing. Abrahams felt the demands were unreasonable, noting that Broadway musicals are often written before a star is cast and the music has already been largely approved. In addition, the Previns were distracted in Houston as their show *Happy Time* prepared for its pre-Broadway premiere, and with the holidays approaching, a meeting before January was unlikely. Why, Abrahams wondered, couldn't the Previns make progress on their re-revised material? "Arthur and I were doing everything conceivable to give the Previns the opportunity to do the score by themselves, but their position was making this very difficult to accomplish," he said.

The Previns held the music hostage, unwilling to complete the score if Bricusse was simultaneously at work. That did it—Jacobs fired them, and Champion walked out two weeks later. "We will make every effort to find a piece of material that you will like," Jacobs wrote perfunctorily in accepting Champion's resignation. For Jacobs, finding a director was now even more urgent than addressing the Previn-Bricusse imbroglio. His newly released *Doctor Dolittle* was not performing well, and packaging *Chips* was agony. He admired the work of American choreographer Herbert Ross on *Dolittle* and was hearing praise about his handling of the dance sequences in *Funny Girl*. Jacobs picked up the phone and made a few calls. Ross, who had never directed a movie, found himself the emergency hire of a woebegone project led by a producer who could not make up his mind. Just five days before Christmas, and as if it was the easiest negotiation in the world, MGM announced its big budget musical remake of *Goodbye, Mr. Chips* would be directed by first-timer Herbert Ross, and star Peter O'Toole and Petula Clark.

CHAPTER 9

Buying and Selling

During the Studio Era, executives like Paramount's Adolph Zukor "could afford to be high handed," according to a piece in the *Wall Street Journal* about the decline of Hollywood in the late 1960s. "Actors and directors, locked into long-term contracts with the majors, functioned as hired hands and were often treated as such." Not surprising, many of the old lions were nostalgic for their early days. "The whole industry misses the phenomenon of the big studio," asserted James Stewart. "When you were part of a studio, you were part of a family. Now you don't even know who you're working for." Moreover, the reduced studios were skittish. "[They] have a tremendous fear of offending the people who can make them millions," said one publicist. Freelancing talent are now "walking, talking corporations orbited by agents and business managers." Filmmakers spend most of their time packaging actors, directors, and crew into something that won't bankrupt financiers but still please high-priced independent stars, directors, and producers.

By the early 1960s, Paramount was suffering. There was a tax assessment pending from the U.S. Treasury Department, a disastrous Jean Harlow biopic, an over-budgeted *Hurry Sundown*, and infighting among board members. Its headmen were aging; president Barney Balaban was well into his 70s, and chairman emeritus and studio founder Zukor still had a hand in at 90. About the only thing Paramount had to be proud of was 1964's *The Carpetbaggers*, a high-earning piece of designer trash. Sixty-three-year-old George Weltner took over as president that year and firmly believed that to court new audiences, Paramount must cast off old ways, and old board members, and be unafraid of films that are "vital up-to-date and daring." He sought to capitalize on the youth market, articulating his beliefs in a letter to the board. "These young people are independent and sophisticated," he wrote. "They shape their own world and they also tend to shape the rest of the world. They are not like any previous group of teenagers. These people dash off to Canada to ski or to Fort Lauderdale at Easter for other purposes. . . . Let us not sit back in criticism of our young people, misjudging their energy and ebullience and let us not try to feed them *Alice in Wonderland*, *Little Red Riding Hood*, pablum, pap, and balderdash. If we want to stay in business, we must move with the times, with the arts and with the . . . raising of the intelligence levels of our audience."

Awareness of the all-important youth market accompanied the corporate take-over of Hollywood. "After World War II, American business underwent a period of consolidation as large numbers of firms merged and as corporate control and decision making became centralized among a relatively few companies," wrote film historian Tino Balio. "Mergers had been common to business before this time, but growth had proceeded along rational lines. A book publisher, for example, might have merged with another publisher, or a steel company might have acquired an appliance manufacturer. After World War II, however, a new type of corporate entity came into being—the conglomerate, which can be defined as a diversified company with major interests in several unrelated fields." Seven Arts was already in the movie business when it bought Warner Bros., but not so Gulf + Western when it bought Paramount for $165 million. Gulf + Western began as a car bumper manufacturer in Grand Rapids and grew to an auto parts manufacturing and distribution company with an aim toward diversification. In buying Paramount, it made films part of a widening portfolio.

"People said we're going Hollywood," wrote Gulf + Western chief Charles Bluhdorn. "But we saw in Paramount the opportunity to take a great name, an institution, to put some zip and energy and drive into it and to restore it to its old pride and glory." Paramount fit into Gulf + Western's newly defined "Leisure Time Group" that included features and TV movies, music recording, publishing, and travel. Bluhdorn was also ready to lead the film industry into a new era of austerity. "We fought the system, this thinking that we're living in a river of money," he said. "Hollywood is not Fort Knox." Bluhdorn rolled up his sleeves, ousted old studio executives, and appointed himself chairman, president, and CEO. He kept the New York office on Broadway and devoted approximately a quarter of his working day to Paramount. He then pushed the filming schedule to a 20-year high. Fox's Richard Zanuck took a sideways glance at men such as Bluhdorn. Now the chief of one of the last independent studios, Zanuck cautioned against businessmen taking over the uniquely speculative and capricious movie industry. "You've got to gamble," he said. "It's not a slide rule business and never will be."

Despite Zanuck's reservations, Bluhdorn seemed to understand the movie business from day one. A Jewish refugee of Nazi Austria, he had been a nervy Wall Street commodities trader prone to dramatic recitations and abrupt volume changes in his voice. With his guttural accent and trademark flourishes, he announced, "There is a tremendous future in the leisure field. . . . Movies on cassettes for home viewing will open a tremendous market. Satellites someday will relay first-run movies into millions of homes." To meet the challenge, he injected cash into the operations and made the studio attractive to independent producers.

George Weltner, the man who fought for youth-oriented programming, retired soon after the November 1966 Gulf + Western buyout, and Bluhdorn sought to put the young in executive positions. Two of his first hires were 36-year-old Robert Evans and 40-year-old lawyer Bernie Donnenfeld. "We work as a partnership here," said Evans. "Bernie Donnenfeld is my equal partner. He takes care of all administrative deals and I handle the creative decisions." That may be, but it was Evans who captured everyone's attention. Dressed in self-designed suits, silk stockings, and moccasins, he wore a thin wristwatch strapped outside his left shirt cuff.

He kept his jet-black hair shiny and slick, and his skin preternaturally tanned. He began as an actor, making $1,500 a week on radio when he was 14, then made a fortune selling women's sportswear. As a contract player at Fox, handsome and photogenic Evans was described by Darryl Zanuck as "the most exciting young actor since Valentino." That opinion was not widely shared, and Evans's heart was behind the camera. He lacked a formal education, but he was a natural born dealmaker. He hungered for film production, and packaged *The Detective* at Fox for Frank Sinatra. A grimy and homophobic crime thriller, it made a large profit and got him an offer from Bluhdorn. "You've proven yourself a success as a business man and executive," he told the kid. "You've had theatrical background and you know how to function with creative people. If you can use all your abilities, you'll do the best job in town."

In reviewing Paramount's slate of film, Bluhdorn told Evans, "I want to see tears, laughs, beautiful girls—pictures people in Kansas City want to see." Evans was up to the task. He made deals quickly, and showed guts, confidence, and leadership. His gifts soon paid off, as Paramount stock tripled after he began. He thought he knew what was going on, and more important, *others* thought he knew what was going on. "The main change has been in audience," he said. "Today, people go to see *a* movie; they no longer to go *the* movies. We can't depend on habit any more. We have to make 'I've got to see that' pictures." The "I've got to see that" musicals slated were the Broadway imports *On a Clear Day You Can See Forever* and *Paint Your Wagon*, and the originals *The Little Prince* and *Darling Lili, or Where Were You The Night You Said You Shot Down Baron von Richtofen*. All but *The Little Prince* were scheduled as roadshows.

As Paramount's high profile arriviste, Evans had to prove himself to Bluhdorn and the industry. "I'm in a vulnerable spot, open to a lot of criticism because of my background," he said. *Darling Lili* director Blake Edwards said, "Like a lot of people, I wondered what this young guy from Seventh Avenue, who was not even a successful actor, was doing running a studio." He grew to respect Evans. "He doesn't try to bluff. If he doesn't understand something, he asks about it, and you know he won't have to ask a second time. He's determined to succeed and he has very definitely assumed command." Soon enough no one said an unkind word about him. "If Evans fails it won't be because he didn't try to give it the best shot he has but because he was hamstrung by management out of New York," said Edwards. "I don't think that will happen." Evans was frequently on the phone to New York and left his office to watch dailies and visit sets. "I came out here in

January 1966, and 10 months later I was the head of a studio," he said. "Who says Hollywood is asleep?"

Among Evans's first assignments was overseeing *Half a Sixpence*, a splashy musical in production before he or Bluhdorn arrived at the studio. It was the brainchild of Bud Ornstein, former United Artists producer who had defected to Paramount, and George Weltner, the former president replaced by Bluhdorn. They had bought the rights to this British stage musical in late 1965 for $250,000, and now it landed in Evans's lap. With production to begin immediately before the Gulf + Western takeover, Paramount committed a posh $6 million. Veteran American film musical director George Sidney (*Anchors Aweigh, Show Boat, Pal Joey*) came on board to "fuse English charm with American dash."

As a product straight out of mid-'60s London, *Half a Sixpence* would seem to be internationally failsafe. London was where "it's all happening," as its pop-music, fashion, and films all possessed that coveted youth appeal. "Mary Quant, who designs those clothes, Vidal Sassoon, the man with the magic comb, and the Rolling Stones, whose music is most In right now, reign as a new breed of royalty," enthused *Time* in its 1966 cover story that coined the term "Swinging London." And the film talent! America got a taste of British Empire acting in a big way with the career ascensions of Peter O'Toole, Julie Christie, Michael Caine, Albert Finney, Sean Connery, Maggie Smith, Tom Courtney, Terence Stamp, Lynn and Vanessa Redgrave, Susannah York, Alan Bates, and Richard Harris. In their purchase of *Sixpence*, Weltner and Ornstein were simply riding the bandwagon, and the American film industry was hungry for investments. Seventy-six feature films were produced in England in 1967, and 60 had American financing. Where musicals were involved, the same big budget roadshow mentality prevailed. Combine the guaranteed appeal of British material, a bright new star like Tommy Steele, and a competent if not top-flight American musical director, and Paramount could all but guarantee the success of its commitment.

Sidney met with *Sixpence* co-producer Charles Schneer at the Paramount studio to hammer out production details. It would be a showcase for Steele and reminiscent of the large-scale musicals once made for British stars of yesteryear such as Herbert Wilcox, Anna Neagle, and Jessie Matthews, all virtually unknown in North America. No matter—*Half a Sixpence* would be the first American-backed musical shot entirely in the United Kingdom. With added UK technical facilities and greater familiarity with the challenges of musical sound engineering, Sidney found "no reason why musicals should not continue to be made [in England] and flourish and be just as good." With the upcoming *Oliver!, Chitty Chitty Bang Bang, Star!*, and *Goodbye, Mr. Chips* wholly or partially shot in England, he had reason to be hopeful. So did Paramount. *Half a Sixpence* had its unlikely origins in the H. G. Wells anti-capitalist polemic novel *Kipps*, but it was lightened by a jolly Edwardian musical aesthetic. *Sixpence* had done well in both London and New York and turned Steele into a stage star. Bluhdorn's commitment to thrift waned.

Recalled music supervisor Irwin Kostal: "They're determined to outdo the Americans at their own game. When I want them to correct something I just kid them, 'I thought you said you were going to do it better than Hollywood.'"

Paramount's lavish spending temporarily fell to earth. When the George Weltner regime analyzed the *Sixpence* ledger sheets, cuts totaling $2 million were ordered. "George [Sidney] and I started over like mad, cutting scenes," said screenwriter Dorothy Kingsley. "We were absolutely crushed." When Gulf + Western took over, fears spread that the new guard would slash further and possibly ice the film altogether. "I thought that we were dead with Gulf + Western," said Kingsley. "We thought for certain that with businessmen now running the studio they would stick with the cuts that had been ordered." She was happily surprised when Bluhdorn and Evans "loved the rushes. They were just as enthusiastic about the picture itself, and Tommy Steele, the star, as we were. And they immediately put back the $2 million their predecessors had taken out." Bluhdorn and Evans tacked on another $300,000 for just one added scene. It was a long hard shoot, with rain pouring more often than not. But real English rain looked phony on film, so the cast was sprayed with hosepipes. "We were close to pneumonia," said Steele, who changed sopping costumes eight times a day. But with a show of faith, confidence and morale were high. Kingsley predicted that *Sixpence* would

Tommy Steele and chorus rehearse a typically high-spirited production number from *Half a Sixpence*. From the collection of the Academy of Dance on Film.

do for Paramount what *Mary Poppins* did for Disney and *The Sound of Music* did for Fox, and that Steele would become the male Julie Andrews.

Half a Sixpence premiered in London, then bowed at the Criterion in New York in February 1968. At the l'Etoile post-screening party, Tommy Steele grew testy at the presence of Connie Stevens's free-ranging pet chinchilla. When asked about his unyielding good cheer on screen, he answered by putting down a few of his contemporaries. "One doesn't find this wonderful feeling through drugs but through the Almighty," he told a reporter, "If the hippies knew it was not something new, they'd get off the whole drug thing and start making war on each other." *Sixpence* opened at Grauman's Chinese Theater in Hollywood just two days after its New York premiere, then expanded to 31 additional roadshow engagements beginning a week later and extending through April. Many of those bookings went to standard release when Bluhdorn and Evans realized they had misread public interest. Very few moviegoers had even the slightest interest in *Sixpence*. Its receipts were so low that it did not even appear on *Variety*'s year-end tallies. The Edwardian fashion tie-in with Macy's flopped, and within two months, *Sixpence* disappeared.

Half a Sixpence quickly became a forgotten relic. What accounts for both its initial failure and the amnesia that surrounds its very existence? The film avoids the more pointed concerns of Wells's book. *Kipps* was a 500-page socialist tract attacking the brainless gluttony of retail trade, but you would never know it by sitting through *Half a Sixpence*. Protagonist Arthur Kipps comes into money, but he is miserable. He sees the light soon enough to win back his sweetheart, and save his soul from Faustian damnation. But this is not a treatise on economy set to music; it's a quaint period piece trying hard to leach enjoyment from paper-thin material. The nod to Karl Marx is incompatible with a movie that celebrates its lavish budget with sets and locations dripping in opulence. There is gorgeous 70-millimeter photography, and *Sixpence* was lovingly opened up in a way *Camelot* was not, but it likewise suffered from too much adornment. It does injustice to Wells and the audience—trading substance for false gaiety and plastic smiles. Its makers did not or would not reconcile a mature tale with a musical that could have had real guts. Instead, *Sixpence* takes the easy way out by flogging at least three clichés: money can't buy happiness, the rich are cold-hearted dyspeptics, and the poor are happy-go-luckys who really know how to sing and dance.

The cast labors against witless material, Steele attacking his role like a puppy with a squeak toy. "Playing the Banjo" is an energetic number, well choreographed by Gillian Lynne, but it takes an eternity to move the plot forward one centimeter. Like so many others, *Half a Sixpence* suffers from over-production and over-length, as if both will give a minor story the gravitas it so needs. Wrote *Time*: "An hour and a half into *Half a Sixpence*, a horrifying word flashes on the screen: Intermission. Can it be that the spectator, already stupefied by an aimless plot, nameless characters, and fameless songs, still has another hour or so to go?"

The Broadway and London productions were said to be entertaining, and the non-musical 1941 film *Kipps* starring Michael Redgrave mildly pleases. But it did not translate across the Atlantic effectively. *The British Film Musical* offers an explanation. "It's perhaps easy to understand why, for American audiences, the harsh and unfeeling mannerisms of the upper class and their disdain for Kipps and his working-class world loses something of the impact that it had on British audiences." Something of aesthetic failure must be factored as well. No such American disengagement with the downtrodden would doom the upcoming *Oliver!*

The newly installed *New York Times* critic Renata Adler used the arrival of *Sixpence* to lament the declivity of the film musical and bemoan its deaf ear to contemporary sounds. She tangentially extolled the Mamas and the Papas; the Association; Janis Ian; Peter, Paul and Mary; Aretha Franklin; the Doors; and Bob Dylan, who bring with them those "countless songs about runaways, divorces, wallflowers, unwanted children, miscegenation, elderly solitaries. It is not the stuff of traditional musicals, but it is very much alive." In contrast, "Conventional musicals, although they still generate money and sentiment, hardly generate anything else any more. They no longer affect fantasies or change the character of lives—as the best of contemporary music clearly does. They still satisfy an audience with a legitimate claim; but the claim of another, probably larger, audience for the music of its own time is being ignored." The elders at Paramount who had highlighted the young adult moviegoers were gone, and while *Sixpence* may appear youth-friendly, it was far removed from anything like the message music of the day. *Sixpence* was a grandmother's idea of what her teenage grandchild might like. It was unfortunate for Robert Evans, but the failure of *Sixpence* did not stick to him. Hollywood meanwhile had its conventional thinking slapped in the face. "There was no validity for the view that any film from Britain would be a blockbuster in America," observed film historian Alexander Walker, "but until the money began to vanish, no one believed it."

Humorists had a field day with the latest crop of musicals. *Half a Sixpence* picked up the *Harvard Lampoon*'s Movie Worst Cheap-at-Half-the-Price Award for "worst bargain in a film." *Thoroughly Modern Millie* and *Doctor Dolittle* were both on the Ten Worst list, with *Dolittle* picking up three additional honors: The Tin Pan for most obnoxious movie song ("Talk to the Animals" is "blood-curdling anthropomorphism"), The Best Argument for Vivisection Award, and The Merino Award to the Pushmi-Pullyu "who is, as we take it, a distant cousin to merinos, and at any rate leads just as tenuous an existence." But the grand prize, The Please-Don't-Put-Us-through-DeMille-Again Award, went to *Camelot*, honoring "that film which best embodies the pretentious extravagances and blundering ineffectiveness of the traditional Screen Spectacular."

By February 1968, awards season was under way and justified any mockery. Rarely was there a more pristine display of marketing over excellence. Universal and Warner Bros. mounted award campaigns for *Thoroughly Modern Millie* and

Camelot, but Fox went to work with incomparable alacrity in promoting *Doctor Dolittle.* A memo from a studio publicist spelled it out: "The following has been decided regarding our Academy Award campaign for *Doctor Dolittle.* Each screening will be preceded by champagne or cocktails and a buffet dinner in the studio commissary. *Doctor Dolittle* is the studio's prime target for Academy Award consideration." The seven screenings were packed. "It was all so silly," one guest said. "All the editors standing around, knowing they had been bought."

The Golden Globes were held at the Cocoanut Grove in LA's Ambassador Hotel. They did not have the cachet they grew to possess by the twenty-first century. In fact, the Globes were something of an industry joke. "This ludicrous event is so suspiciously corrupt even NBC and the Federal Communications Commission have sent lawyers to have it investigated," said columnist Rex Reed. *Camelot, Doctor Dolittle,* and *Thoroughly Modern Millie* were up for a number of awards, including Best Comedy or Musical, but lost to *The Graduate.* Most of the evening's winners, including Richard Attenborough of *Doctor Dolittle* and Richard Harris of *Camelot,* who beat Rex Harrison for Best Actor Comedy or Musical, did not bother to show up for free drinks. Best Original Score and Best Song went to *Camelot* and its "If Ever I Would Leave You," which, as everyone knew, were not original. Conspicuous by her presence was *Millie's* Supporting Actress winner Carol Channing. Julie Andrews was there as well to accept something called The World Film Favorite award. Her co-winner was actor Laurence Harvey, an already strange choice made stranger by the fact that he did not appear in any films released that year.

On February 19, just as *Half a Sixpence* premiered and *Doctor Dolittle* spread across America, the Academy announced its nominations. Up for Best Picture was *Bonnie and Clyde, Guess Who's Coming to Dinner, In the Heat of the Night, The Graduate,* and . . . *Doctor Dolittle.* With eight additional nominations outside major categories, nearly every technical branch of the Academy gave mention to *Dolittle.* The generous payback for those prime rib dinners shocked even the Fox executives who orchestrated the effort. "Believe me, nobody was more surprised than I was when we got a nomination for Best Picture," said Richard Zanuck. "How we got in there is amazing to me. But these things happen." The *Dolittle* honors brought howls of outrage. The *Los Angeles Times* proclaimed its nine nominations the season's "liveliest embarrassment," while at least two dozen other films "could be called better by even the most bathetic critical standards. The Oscar nominations symbolize a cataclysmic separation in the now art of the cinema. In the unbelievable 19 nominations amassed by *Dolittle* and *Dinner* against a sensible 17 for *Bonnie and Clyde* and *The Graduate,* there is a polarity of some moment: the stylish versus the gross, the young against the old, the turned-off and the turned-on, the beautiful against the blatant, contemporaneity and decadence, The Factory and Forest Lawn. This schizophrenia is clearly rooted in our common culture, and in the sensibilities of the people who make films."

Truman Capote was less circumspect. "It's outrageous!" he screamed, incensed that the film adaptation of his *In Cold Blood* was bypassed for Best Picture mention. "Anything allowing a *Dolittle* to happen is so rooked up it doesn't *mean anything*." When Charles Champlin intimated in print that the various branches of the Academy had been bought, *Dolittle* director Richard Fleischer wrote a letter suggesting the skilled craftspeople of Hollywood had been defamed. An unbowed Champlin agreed. "A good many factors other than merit enter into the voting," he responded. "If this impugns the integrity of the voters, then that's what I've done. If I were a Fox employee and was aware that my studio had however many millions it is—$18? $19?—riding on a picture which needs all the box office help it can get, I'd think twice about *not* voting for it." The Academy was populated by a spotty amalgamation of types, with 883 of its 2,980 members coming from such muzzy professions as "public relations," "administrators," "executives," and "members at large," while "producers" may not actually act as producers or take credit. Additionally, voters were graying, with various nominating branches dominated by a gerontocracy of Studio Era artists and technicians. That may explain how *Doctor Dolittle* scored an editing nomination, but the revolutionary cutting of *Bonnie and Clyde* did not. That and prime rib. The other musical nominations of 1967 did not received *Dolittle's* enflamed response, as they did not receive Best Picture recognition. Warner Bros. put its award money behind *Bonnie and Clyde* rather than *Camelot*, which was up for five technical awards. *Thoroughly Modern Millie's* nods included Best Supporting Actress for Carol Channing, while *The Happiest Millionaire*, Disney's feeble stepchild to *Mary Poppins*, was tapped for Costumes only.

It is not hyperbole to suggest that what happened between the nominations and ceremony was watershed American history. And it happened very quickly. On March 31, President Johnson announced that he would not seek reelection. On Wednesday, April 3, Dr. Martin Luther King, Jr., made his "I've Been to the Mountaintop" speech at Mason Temple in Memphis, the World Headquarters of the Church of God in Christ. On April 4, he was shot on the second floor balcony of the Lorraine Motel and pronounced dead one hour later. Riots broke out in over 100 cities, more than 10 times as many cities as saw *Camelot* in its first run. So much for Arthurian idealism sweeping the land.

The Oscars, their banality exposed by epochal news, were scheduled for Monday, April 8. On Friday, April 5, all African Americans slated to appear on the telecast announced they would forgo the Oscars to attend Dr. King's funeral in Atlanta. "I find it morally incongruous to sing 'Talk to the Animals' while the man who could make a better world for my children is lying in state," said Sammy Davis, Jr. With others ready to bolt, the Academy's Board of Governors held an emergency meeting on Saturday morning. Then, and for the first time in history, they voted to postpone the ceremony. "To follow the old tradition of 'the show must go on' at this time would be a violation of the mood of the country," said Academy president Gregory Peck. "Call it enlightened self-interest, but I feel this country will never be whole until we have achieved total and full equality of opportunity for everyone. This would be the best possible memorial to Dr. King, I feel."

Davis and others were pleased with the Academy's response, and all confirmed their attendance at the rescheduled Oscars two days after the funeral. "There was never a doubt, after they made this very fine gesture, that we would be on the program," he said. Atlanta was then teeming with arrivals for Monday's services at the Ebenezer Baptist Church. Show business was represented by Sidney Poitier, Marlon Brando, Harry Belafonte, and Bill Cosby, among others. Norman Jewison, director of the intense racial drama and Best Picture nominee *In the Heat of the Night*, was there as well.

When the Oscar telecast at last commenced on Wednesday, American political life was simply too fevered, and King's assassination too raw, to ignore. As if his performance in *To Kill a Mockingbird* had been a rehearsal for this moment, Peck told the audience that "This has been a fateful week in the history of our nation and the two-day delay of this ceremony is the Academy's way of paying our profound respect to the memory of Dr. Martin Luther King, Jr." Bob Hope, always eager to reduce a cold sober '60s news event to a one liner, poked fun at Johnson's recent announcement by saying, "I will not seek nor will I accept an Oscar." On the subject of King, he was utterly tone deaf. "The man from Montgomery and today's young filmmakers have much in common," he said. "They, too, have a dream."

The awards themselves were frightfully hard to predict, but at the final tally, roadshows made a fair showing. Carol Channing lost Supporting Actress to *Bonnie and Clyde*'s fabulously shrill Estelle Parsons, but *Thoroughly Modern Millie* did take Original Score. *Doctor Dolittle* won Best Visual Effects in a field with only one other nominee. If trendsetting was a criterion, Theadora Van Runkle's costumes for *Bonnie and Clyde* would have won hands down, but *Camelot* triumphed in that category and in Art Direction, with John Truscott collecting his awards in a Nehru jacket and bell-bottom pants. Sammy Davis, Jr., sang "Talk to the Animals" in a black velvet Nehru jacket, love beads, and high heels while ad-libbing with "Sock it to me, baby!" and "Here come the judge!," two catchphrases from the new TV show *Laugh-In*. Barbra Streisand, on a break from making *Hello, Dolly!*, announced "Talk to the Animals" as Best Song winner. "You could hear the 'Oh, nos' loudly in the theater," according to Rex Reed. Composer Leslie Bricusse was not there, so Davis accepted the award and could almost believe his dream of starring in *Dolittle* came true. He clutched the Oscar and exclaimed with a British accent that, "It's absolutely marvelous. It's super!" He then left the Santa Monica Civic Auditorium without surrendering the award, which he hung onto for several weeks. It finally got to Bricusse via Arthur Jacobs, who said Davis could not give up Oscar because "He matched my jewelry!"

To extend the Academy's mixed message, the Documentary award went to *The Anderson Platoon*. In it the camera moves through the frontlines of Vietnam, offering images more brutal than those on the evening news. The Best Picture winner was not *The Graduate* or *Bonnie and Clyde*, two films now secure for the ages, but *In the Heat of the Night*. Practically ignored was a special Oscar given to former MGM musical producer Arthur Freed for "distinguished service to the Academy and the production of six top-rated Awards telecasts." The living embodiment of great film musicals, the man behind *The Wizard of Oz*, *Meet Me in St. Louis*, *An American in Paris*, *Singin' in the Rain*, *The Band Wagon*, and *Gigi*, was not receiving an award for career achievement. He was receiving an award for producing Oscar shows that gave statuettes to the likes of *Doctor Dolittle*.

CHAPTER 10

"Impossible to Control the Cost of This Gown"

"In the wake of *Bonnie and Clyde*, there is an almost euphoric sense in Hollywood that more such movies can and will be made," wrote *Time*. Greeted even more joyously was the explosive box office of *The Graduate*, reporting the largest rentals of any non-roadshow in movie history. It has even been attributed with the unofficial birth of a male-centered cinema that would dominate the indefinite future. The female-dominated musicals of *Gypsy*, *Mary Poppins*, *The Sound of Music*, and *Thoroughly Modern Millie* looked distinctly quaint and dated against the sudden testosterone wash across movie screens.

One musical of the era would seem to play into the current stylish machismo, with two starring roles for men and an entire town of dirty miners out in the Wild West. The 1951 Broadway musical *Paint Your Wagon* was not a big hit. It ran fewer than 300 performances and left a $95,000 deficit. With an Alan Jay Lerner and Frederick Loewe score that incorporated banjos and square dance rhythms, the boom-or-bust story set against the California Gold Rush and featuring an interracial romance bogged down in the second half. It did not receive the acclaim of Lerner and Loewe's previous *Brigadoon*, but it was blessed with a fine score and the choreography of Agnes DeMille.

Even with that spotty history, Hollywood showed interest. Warner Bros. envisioned Bing Crosby as prospector Ben Rumson and Doris Day as his daughter, but ultimately chose not to buy the property. Louis B. Mayer bought the film rights for Gary Cooper for $200,000. Several combinations of stars from the MGM roster were considered, but Mayer never followed through. When *Wagon* came to Paramount's attention, the studio discovered that singer Eddie Fisher had bought the rights from Mayer's estate. Paramount bought it from Fisher, and a deal was struck naming the show's composer, Alan Jay Lerner, as the film's producer. His career as musical screenwriter and lyricist was unassailable, bejeweled with Oscars for *An American in Paris* and *Gigi*, but he had never produced a movie. With songwriting partner Frederick Loewe retired, the fastidious and witty Park

Avenue–bred Lerner was ready to try producing. He was unhappy with the screen adaptations of his *Brigadoon, My Fair Lady,* and *Camelot,* and unwilling to surrender control again.

Don Siegel was offered the directing job, but declined. He had experience with Westerns, but next to nothing to do with musicals. Blake Edwards was interested, but Lerner wanted Joshua Logan. Logan was ushered into Charles Bluhdorn's office for the pitch. "He talked about how *big* the picture was going to be and how we had to get the *biggest* stars to play in it," recalled Logan. "Bluhdorn's enthusiasm was so extravagant it was hard for any of us to match it." Logan was not won over immediately, and though he didn't confess it, the ordeal of *Camelot* must have been a factor in his initial reluctance. "Frankly, I was hesitant about doing [it] when Alan Lerner offered it to me. I thought the original show was weak, although it had great songs. Alan said that he never liked the story and suggested that Paddy Chayefsky adapt his book for the screen." Lerner's persuasiveness worked, and Logan signed to direct.

Whatever and whoever Lerner wanted, Lerner got. Chayefsky was retained for $150,000 plus a percentage of the profits. He was given a private secretary and suite over the pool at the Beverly Hills Hotel, where he could get on with loosely adapting *Paint Your Wagon* for the screen. His changes were extreme—two of the three starring roles in the stage original were axed, as were several songs. The Mexican who falls in love with a prospector's daughter became the Anglo Pardner. After Chayefsky's first rewrites, Lerner and Logan further polished. With additional songwriting from André Previn, the screen adaptation was growing further from its stage origins. The new version eliminated the original father-daughter plot, and added Mormon polygamy. Chayefsky made sure *Paint Your Wagon* was no *Seven Brides for Seven Brothers*–style mythologizing of frontier America. Its tone was bitterer, with the starring character dying at the end. Logan had misgivings. "It's a preposterous story," he said. "Lusty. A mixture of Mark Twain, shall we say, and Bret Harte . . . and Paddy Chayefsky and Alan Jay Lerner. It's not anything like the original stage show, except for its backgrounds and a lot of songs that have been saved. . . . Two men and a woman get married, and the three of them live together. And what this implies is that civilization is no good, and so they do something uncivilized because they're really ahead of civilization."

Bluhdorn took an active role in casting. For the prospector, he envisioned Mickey Rooney or James Cagney before settling on grizzle-puss Lee Marvin, hot off his Oscar for the comedy Western *Cat Ballou.* It did not matter to Bluhdorn or Lerner that Marvin could not, in Chayefsky's delicate phrasing, "sing for shit." Neither could Clint Eastwood, cast as the other male lead. "I'm not exactly Howard Keel, but I think it'll work," said Eastwood. His guarantee was $500,000, while bigger star Marvin commanded a Rex Harrison–sized paycheck of $1 million, plus a percentage, and $20,000 a day or $100,000 a week in overtime. When concerns were voiced that Marvin was no singer, he shot back, "Who says I'm not a singer? I've been singing in the bathtub for years and nobody questioned it." Eastwood made a seismic impression in *For a Few Dollars More* and *The Good, the Bad and the Ugly,* two Sergio Leone Westerns, while Marvin was second ranked after Julie Andrews on the Quigley Publication annual poll of top 10 stars in 1967. What Marvin and Eastwood lacked in musical chops they made up for in supremely cool movie star personas.

For the female lead, *The Happiest Millionaire*'s Lesley Ann Warren, *Bonnie and Clyde*'s Faye Dunaway, and British singer-actress Sally Ann Howes were considered, along with Jean Seberg, the fetching Iowa-born gamine of *Breathless* and *Bonjour Tristesse.* Paramount wanted Dunaway, who tested by lip-synching to Eydie Gormé's vocals. Of the contenders, Seberg most actively sought the role. She "came into Josh Logan's office wearing a real pistol to get in the mood," said Marvin. "I was there and I thought, 'what kind of cuckoo bird is this?' Yeah, she wanted the part all right! I said, 'What the hell. I'm here, I'll do the scene with her.' And I was impressed." So was Logan. Seberg signed for $120,000 plus expenses. She liked her plucky, warmhearted character, seeing her as "a nineteenth century flower child." She promptly began singing lessons. Most everyone had an opinion of Marvin's singing, including Seberg. She called it "dirty water rushing through a rusty drain pipe."

Logan kept getting the same "reassurances" from Bluhdorn. Yes, Marvin goes on binges and shuts down productions, but he's such a fine actor and has so much to offer that these little indiscretions are worth it. Logan leveraged his tolerance for Marvin's excesses against *Camelot*'s newly Academy Award–winning art director John Truscott, who Logan insisted be hired for *Wagon.* Immediately they sparred. Truscott wanted to film on location, but Logan did not. Lerner agreed with Truscott and together they convinced Logan and Paramount. So began the conflicts between Logan and Truscott, and Logan and Lerner that intensified over time. Truscott was determined to avoid the studio fakery that marred *Camelot,* so he and associate producer Tom Shaw took the Paramount jet across the western United States in search of virgin territory. They found it at East Eagle Creek in Oregon's Wallowa-Whitman National Forest, with the Cascade Mountains doubling for California's Sierra Nevada. Fortunately for Paramount, the Oregon governor was thoroughly accommodating. He told the Oregon Gaming Commission to warn all hunters in East Eagle Creek area about the production, while the Oregon State Police and Forest Service brought in extra men for security.

Truscott and special effects man Maurice Ayres arrived on location just as the snow melted, only to learn that a maze of underground rivers had to be filled with dirt in order to build *Wagon*'s No Name City. Chayefsky's script called for the town to collapse during the film's raucous finale, a gimmick likely borrowed from similar goings-on in Blake Edward's 1966 comedy *What Did You Do in the War, Daddy?* Two hundred construction workers and US Forestry servicemen hauled and deposited tons of dirt before the town, called "Sodom of the Sierra" in the script, could be constructed. "The safety problems were gigantic," said Ayres. "Several thousand feet of tunnels had to be built and shored up with logs and timbers. The fissures had to be built so as to collapse on signal, yet they had to be solid enough to support the city while we were filming in and around it. There were hundreds of extras, tons of equipment, and sometimes two to three hundred horses and oxen working on the thousand-foot long main street. Since the fissures extended the length of the street in both directions, had they opened suddenly and by accident, we'd have faced a major disaster!"

There were 150 buildings in No Name City, and more than half were rigged to collapse. But they had to go down in various directions, into the street, or sink. Expense was considerable. The saloon apparatus alone cost $300,000. "Full-sized controlled destruction of a city is something I've never known before in this industry," Ayres told Lerner. "I know of no other instance in which an entire city has been destroyed without an optical illusion process such as double exposures and the use of miniatures. The sequences in *Paint Your Wagon* in which No Name City is destroyed are absolutely fantastic!" All the buildings were on cables and hydraulic lifts, ready to collapse with the push of a button.

Production designer John Truscott, director Joshua Logan, and producer-lyricist Alan Jay Lerner loom over a model of *Paint Your Wagon*'s infamous No Name City. From the collection of Photofest.

Back at Paramount, the cast rehearsed, which was only so effective since the bulk of the film would be shot in Oregon. It was going badly. As Lerner rewrote the script, Chayefsky wanted his credit removed from the film. Eastwood hated the redrawn screenplay. "It's now totally different," he said. "It has no relation to the original, except the names of the characters. They had the threesome deal, but it wasn't a dark story at all. It was all fluffy.... they're having Lee do *Cat Ballou II*." Chayefsky begrudgingly met with Lerner in New York to review his script draft. Lerner was not happy with Previn's new songs or the script, derisively calling it *Paint Your Pupik* (belly button in Yiddish). To Chayefsky's likely relief, Lerner fired him. With more tinkering, Previn's new songs ("The Best Things in Life Are Dirty," "The Gospel of No Name City," and "A Million Miles Away behind the Door") found acceptance with Lerner, who was pleased that the screenplay retained his "I Still See Elisa" with its maudlin lyrics:

> *Her heart was made of holidays,*
> *Her smile was made of dawn,*
> *Her laughter was an April song,*
> *That echoes on and on.*

The company moved in to Oregon on June 17, invading Baker, the nearest town to the film location. Baker was 50 miles southwest of East Eagle Creek, and two hours away by a narrow dirt road dotted with signs reading "Traffic Restricted Because of Crowded Conditions Imposed by the Paramount Production of 'Paint Your Wagon.'" The crew's first duty was to improve road conditions at a cost of $10,000 per mile. Logan believed the forest lacked enough trees, so he had pines imported from Hollywood, along with trained animals. He complained about Lerner's constant presence on the set, with those distracting neon-bright ensembles that he would change three or four times a day. "Throughout my directing career I seldom saw any of my producers, whereas on *Wagon* I saw Alan daily," he said. Lerner the neophyte producer wore white gloves to discourage gnawing on his cuticles and found his strongest ally in Tom Shaw. Logan's best friend on the set was cinematographer William A. Fraker, but Logan's command was slipping, with a return diagnosis of manic-depression looming over his head. He took lithium carbonate to control his mood swings while his friendship with Lerner deteriorated. "I watched good friends turn bad, [and] bad friends reveal themselves," noted Logan. "I watched my work as director held up to scorn, but more than that, I found myself, when working, feeling vaguely guilty and devoid of talent for the first time in my life."

A fleet of eight 40-foot vans made weekly round trips between Los Angeles and Baker, hauling props, sets, and furniture to stock the saloons, hotels, and stores of No Name City. There were painted wagons, of course, plus 250 horses to draw them, requiring saddles and harnesses, holsters, a blacksmith, and harness-maker.

Additionally, there were sheep, 50 recalcitrant mules, and 28 huge oxen imported from Massachusetts. When 50 men weren't serving hundreds of bales of hay daily to the livestock, they were building fences, hauling water, or running down strays. Any scenes shot in the hills above the valley floor required a truck, jeep, mules, or helicopters. "It was as if Lerner, who certainly controlled the deficient Logan, had become a sort of D. W. Griffith, Cecil B. de Mille, or even Orson Welles, unleashed in an extravagant wilderness," wrote Lerner biographer Edward Jablonski. Logan, dressed in baggy jeans, cowboy boots, polo coat, and New York hat, said it was "like living under wartime conditions." Very expensive wartime conditions. He admitted, "no one tried to hold it to a budget. It was the most flagrant throwing away of money I've ever seen." Fingers were pointing at Logan. According to *Variety*, he lived by the philosophy that if a film is not on schedule, then something is wrong with the schedule.

Six hundred film people were crowded on fewer than four acres of wilderness. They included 150 local hippies who had wandered from the hills onto the set and were hired as extras, bringing a disheveled look to their roles as dung-caked cowboys and prospectors. "Some of them were strung out on drugs and in pretty bad shape," said Logan. Baker did not offer many distractions, so the cast and crew made their own. The most exciting thing to do in town was visit the Bache and Sage Hardware store, while dining was limited to the Elks Club, the Shangri-La Tavern, or the A & W Root Beer Stand. Conditions were ripe for location romances, with none more newsworthy than an affair between Jean Seberg and Clint Eastwood. Word got back to Seberg's husband, French writer and diplomat Romain Gray, who arrived in Baker and challenged Eastwood to a duel. It didn't happen, and the affair cooled, much to Seberg's disappointment. She and Gary separated later that year.

Despite its being so extremely remote, the *Paint Your Wagon* set was visited by a bevy of interested guests. Visitors included mighty TV variety show host Ed Sullivan and the stout, unkempt Max Jacobson, a. k. a. Dr. Feelgood, speed dispenser to the stars. Scandal broke when Joyce Haber's *Los Angeles Times* column reported that "Logan is in so much trouble on Lerner's and Paramount's big budget musical that they're saying from Hollywood to Baker, Oregon that he's about to be replaced. Likeliest candidate for Logan's job [is] Richard Brooks who directed last year's *In Cold Blood*. Apart from his top reputation, Brooks is a good friend of producer Lerner who has been consulted all along on matters of script, cameraman, and so forth."

Lerner and Marvin called Brooks, and urged him to come aboard, but he knew better. No way was he going to walk into such a horrific working environment, with the producer and star going behind the director's back to get him fired. Honor among directors forbids. "I called Paramount and they said it was untrue," said Logan. "Brooks's name got into it because he was doing us a favor. . . . But the whole thing took its toll. . . . The crew was convinced I wouldn't be any good and that I was primarily a stage director. But then a lucky thing happened. On one of the first days of shooting, my film of *Bus Stop* was on television and everybody watched. By the next morning the crew was on my side and everything has gone perfectly since." That quote was captured on a good day. By his own account, Logan wanted out badly. He didn't even mind humiliation if it brought freedom. In talking to his agent, he said, "Tell [Brooks] he can embarrass me all he wants. I would like very much to get out of this fucking picture." His lawyers advised him to endure, and from then on, he "directed the picture with joyless industry."

The effects of the Brooks story hung over the rest of the shoot like a dark storm cloud. Paramount VIPs journeyed to Baker, with loyalties divided between Lerner and Shaw on one side, and most of the crew, cameraman Fraker, and Logan on the other. Marvin took pity on Logan. "Ain't nothin' wrong with the director, he's okay," he told Brooks. "But, you know, he's scared. He doesn't know quite what-the-hell." Eastwood's remarks were similar. To him, Logan "was a terrific guy. I really liked him, but he just knew nothing about film—nothing." Seberg was kinder. Being directed by him was "like confronting an opaque presence," she said. "You do a rehearsal and then another while you wonder why he isn't responding. So you keep trying, and pretty soon he's nodding at you. Before you know it, you're acting like mad just so you can see that marvelous pink and white face light up with satisfaction."

Marvin was an actor in dire need of specifics. Eastwood recalled, "The minute you said, 'Well, I'm not sure about this or that,' Lee immediately went, 'Pour me a double.'" He drank to obliteration. "Not since Attila the Hun swept across Europe leaving 500 years of total blackness has there been a man like Lee Marvin," said Logan. To actor Ray Walston, Marvin was simply "full of bullshit" and "a difficult man to work with." Seberg, in contrast, was sweet and cooperative, befriending many of the extras. Reporting from location, Rex Reed wrote Seberg "sits near an oil lamp, playing poker with a full blood Sioux Indian named Eddie Little Sky, a former member of the Green Berets, and a hunchback Chinese named Peanuts." She loved the shoot, her green clapboard bungalow, and the slow pace of country life. She found many of her hippie extra friends "pathetic waifs—their minds blown by drugs at 18." She resisted making judgment. "Everybody talks about gaps—communication gaps, generation gaps, believability gaps," she said. "There is really only one gap, and that is a compassion gap." In talking with a columnist who had just returned from Vietnam, she said, "It's all connected, isn't it? Vietnam, the oppression of blacks in America, all of it."

"What do you mean?"

"I mean that it's all part of the same disgusting racism. If we were fighting the war against the Swedes, we wouldn't be doing these things. But because it's Orientals, we can do anything. Like Hiroshima being bombed instead of Berlin."

"Maybe," he said.

"There isn't much maybe about it, is there? It looks very clear to me."

Lee Marvin looks ready to swallow the Panavision camera on *Paint Your Wagon*. Director Joshua Logan's penchant for close-ups, and Marvin's for ham acting, combined to deleterious effect. From the collection of Photofest.

As summer temperatures rose past 100, Logan pleaded with Bluhdorn to finish the film on the Paramount backlot. Bluhdorn said no, claiming that such a move would disrupt continuity. So production costs rose to $80,000 a day, inciting Tom Shaw to tell reporters, "We're in one helluva fucking mess up here." Extras complained of lice in their costumes and inadequate pay. They threatened to strike, so Lerner approved a raise from $20 to $25 per day plus meals, and leftover commissary food was given to their hungry comrades in the hills. The itinerants who wandered onto the set and stayed became such a nuisance that one wag suggested a credit line of "Consultant in Charge of Hippies."

Far from his cherished Manhattan apartment, with its fine art and theater mementos overlooking a river view, Logan dumped on a visiting Rex Reed, sounding very much like a man on the verge of a nervous breakdown. "I don't know what the hell I'm doing here," he said. "All these extras, all these unions to contend with. You're afraid to give anybody an extra line to say or the budget goes up another $10,000. You have to organize all these horses, all these cows, all these people, get the shot during Magic Hour, while the sky is light enough to silhouette the nature you've come to photograph. I'm living each day to the next. I can't wait to get back to civilization."

September brought three weeks of rain. When conditions were too muddy to film, the cast and crew fled to Baker, where drinking started right after breakfast. In October, snow flurries necessitated the end of location shooting at long last. Five months felt like a century to Logan. The company left, and East Eagle Creek was restored to its original state, free for the deer and elk to nibble grass once flattened by No Name City and the heavy tramping of cast and crew.

No Name City was partially reconstructed at Paramount, while production expenses now approached $20 million. Still, Robert Evans kept a sunny outlook. "We're sure our timing is right, with the public's appetite for musicals and Westerns, both," he said. "The idea is to film a Western drama with music evolving from natural settings, not just a photographed play with the usual gay chorus line."

As production neared completion, Logan was called into Bernie Donnenfeld's office.

"How's your cut coming?"

"Oh, it's nearly finished," said Logan. "I ought to be able to show it to Alan pretty soon, and we can go to work on it together."

"That's what I want to tell you," said Donnenfeld. "He doesn't want that. He wants you to give it to him now, quickly, so that he can work on it alone. He's very anxious to do the cut by himself with no suggestions."

"Why didn't he tell me?"

"Well, you were allowed under your contract to have the director's cut," said Donnenfeld.

"It doesn't make any difference what I'm allowed if he's going to take it over," replied Logan. "I could have given it to him weeks ago and slept in my own bed in New York. It's finished. Tell him to take it—and good luck." Logan's work was done, while *Paint Your Wagon* gave Alan Jay Lerner a $20 million crash course in producing, editing, and postproduction. And gave Paramount one hell of a headache.

While Michael Kidd choreographed the *Hello, Dolly!* corps in early rehearsals, there was an anxiety at Fox that Barbra Streisand, who had not yet arrived on the set, would play prima donna as she had on *Funny Girl*. "Give her what she wants," were the words of experience coming from Columbia. When she appeared, she promptly sat for wig and costume tests, as well as 75 separate cosmetic blends. For mere mortals, there were 25 makeup chairs set down adjacent to Stages 21 and 22 on the Fox lot. Fifty wigs were ordered from Max Factor for the female chorines, in addition to 24 cascades, five hand-tied flatter wigs, and eight falls. The male chorus required 250 mustaches. Logistics even included a consideration of race. NAACP President Donald Lanclos wrote director Gene Kelly "regarding any question you might have as to objections the NAACP might raise as to your casting of Negroes in the show *Hello, Dolly!*" Since "it is our contention that the image of the Negro, as depicted by movies and television, should be realistic," he saw no offense at *Dolly!* casting African American extras in various service jobs.

When Fox signed Walter Matthau as Horace Vandergelder, the man caught in Dolly's matchmaking web, physical production head Lewis "Doc" Merman wrote to him confidently that "*Hello, Dolly!* will be a very pleasant, exciting, and successful picture." From his first day on the set, the pugnacious Matthau was determined to prove Merman wrong. He and Streisand never got along. The name-calling amounted to "Miss Ptomaine" for her and "Old Sewermouth" for him. On the day after the Oscar telecast in which both were presenters, he offered an unsolicited comment on her mass of high piled tight curls that feminized a Bob Dylan look. "That hairdo you wore," he said, "was that supposed to make the audience laugh?"

"Why are you so cruel? That hairdo is the latest fashion," she answered.

"I just wondered if you meant it to be funny," said Matthau.

"You are a very hostile person," said Streisand.

"I don't think I am," replied Matthau.

Despite the tenor of such exchanges, Streisand believed "The *Dolly!* set was a friendly set." She then acknowledged that "There is tension and there is supposed to be tension making movies. This is the moment, and you have 10 minutes left and the light is growing dim, and there is tension 'cause you gotta get the shot. But you don't come around saying, 'There is tension on the set, and she's being difficult!'"

Ernest Lehman was an accomplished screenwriter, but he was also a slender, middle-aged bundle of uncertainty. After writing *The Sound of Music*, he co-wrote and produced *Who's Afraid of Virginia Woolf?* at Warner Bros. That, too, was a huge hit, but of a very different kind. "I've got some god damn nerve," he said, "from a four-character picture to this. You know, there's one sequence where we're going to put out a call for 2,500 extras." During the making of *Dolly!*, Lehman occupied a three-room suite at Fox, where he spent hours massaging Streisand's jumpy nerves. "She doesn't have to work as hard as this," he said. "She phoned me last night to discuss the script, and we talked for an hour and a half. She asked, did I mind very much if she put a 'the' before 'them'? Did I mind very much if she says 'Eff-ram' instead of 'Eef-ram'? In one sequence she's talking very fast and is supposed to say the word 'particularly.' She finds it hard to say I tried it myself and she was right. So after only 10 minutes of discussing it, we changed the word to 'especially.'"

Before shooting even began at the first location in Garrison, memos flew through Fox about unexpected costs during the grading and bulldozing of the location site, as well as building roads and facilities for livestock. The original order of six tents had swollen to 11. Five houses were needed for the Garrison shoot alone, with cleaning, painting, and upgrading of plumbing and electricity. New interior decorating, rugs, draperies, and appliances were installed, all under union rules. Streisand's home was to be equipped with one new pink toilet and a matching pink bathroom sink.

Principal photography on *Hello, Dolly!* began at Fox in mid-April. The assembled personnel behind the camera could not have been more esteemed: director Gene Kelly, choreographer Michael Kidd, orchestrator Lennie Hayton, and cinematographer Harry Stradling, who had lit Streisand on *Funny Girl* and was there with her approval. *Dolly!* had an 89-day shooting schedule, and by the end of the first week, Lehman was still without a complete budget. Doc Merman sent multiple memos to the Fox offices with the same line: "We are trying to keep an eagle eye on the *Hello, Dolly!* costs." Some eagle! Where exactly was all the economizing? Estimated consumption of production supplies came to 5,000 gallons of paint, 100 kegs of nails, 1,191,000 board feet of lumber, 183 telephone poles for construction and support of the sets, 110,000 feet of plastic wire for telephone and power lines, 220 tons of fabricated steel in elevated railways, 575 cubic yards of concrete, 500 tons of asphalt, and 228,000 man-hours of labor. Zanuck's original estimates came to $10 million, or roughly the budget of *Funny Girl*. But costs rose to $12 million, then $15 million, then $18 million, and by the time Lehman had a shooting script, it had reached an unimaginable $25 million.

In addition to Garrison, locations included Knott's Berry Farm in Buena Park, California; Cold Spring and Poughkeepsie, New York; and Lancaster County in Pennsylvania. The film's most elaborate set, a recreation of a vast 1890s New York street scene, cost $2 million alone. Inspired by Maxim's in Paris and the Crystal Palace in London, the Harmonia Gardens set, where the title song would be filmed, cost $375,000. The foyer, bar, and dining room were all built on different levels, with the dance floor ringed with booths and banquettes topped with gaslights and curlicue grills. Furnishing, upholstery, and set dressing used gold and ivory, with two 28-foot fountains of 20 columns each. There were four domed private dining alcoves, rococo fountains, candelabras, chandeliers, and statues flanking the huge central staircase. When Lehman strode onto the set, he said to production designer John DeCuir, "I'd say you've built one hell of a saloon."

Additional craft service men were hired to aid in safety on the set, as the production was being closely watched by the Los Angeles Fire Department due to script demands for flaming shish kabob and cherries jubilee. Like *Paint Your Wagon* at Paramount, *Dolly!* had no one effectively controlling expenses. In a report from Production Department head Stan Hough to Doc Merman, there were 14 grips with eight budgeted, 29 electricians with 20 budgeted, and two painters with one budgeted. Across departments, cost overages now approached 50 percent. Two days of rain at Garrison cost the production $200,000 and motivated the purchase of expensive weather insurance *after* the storm passed.

Michael Kidd worked on *Dolly!* for nine months, and Kelly admitted that his own contribution to the film's dancing was minimal. "Naturally, having worked with Michael before and his being one of the gang at MGM, I talked with him a lot about it, but, when we got into the real big numbers, it seemed that I was not there as much as I could have been or should have been," recalled Kelly, insinuating

Kidd's minimally overseen work was not to his liking. "We didn't have as much collaboration as we would have liked"

Meanwhile, Streisand and Matthau continued their verbal jousting. On the set, she asked him, "How's your ulcer?"

"I don't have an ulcer," he said.

"My maid said she heard on the radio that I was giving you an ulcer," she replied.

"You may be giving me another heart attack, darling, but not an ulcer." Matthau was seething at the idea that this movie novice felt obliged to tell more seasoned associates how to do their jobs. They grew to despise one another, Matthau at one point reducing her to sobs by shouting, "Everyone in this company hates you!" When she turned to go, he shouted "Go ahead, walk off! But just remember, Betty Hutton thought she was indispensable, too!"

The hate fest reached its zenith soon after Robert Kennedy's assassination. "I wasn't going to vote for Bobby Kennedy," said Matthau. "Still, I was knocked out and Gene was too. I couldn't work that day and it was 100 degrees in Garrison.... With the Kennedy thing and the heat and all this electrical power, my head felt as though it was being smashed, plus the talk about where the bullet hit, and brain operation and all. Suddenly Barbra sneezed and I took that as a personal insult. I went into a wild, furious incoherent tirade about her. Kelly put his hand on my arm and tried to pull me away—that's all I remember except that I had to get my lines, and I did *not* use any profane language."

Much of the cast and crew were mortified at Kennedy's death, but work continued. "Barbra kept asking Gene whether he didn't think it would be better if I did this on this line, and that on the other, etc., etc.—and I told her to stop directing the fucking picture," said Matthau. "There was a blow-up in which I also told her that she was a pip-squeak who didn't have the talent of a butterfly's fart. To which she replied that I was jealous because I wasn't as good as she was. I'm not the most diplomatic man in the world, and we began a slinging match like a couple of kids from the ghetto. I think Gene thought one of us was going to die of apoplexy or something, or that I'd belt her, or that maybe she'd scratch my eyes out—or worse, that we'd just walk off leaving twenty million dollars worth of movie to go down the toilet." An official production report declined specifics, noting only a "delay in shooting in afternoon from 3:28 pm to 4:50 pm caused by an argument between Matthau and Streisand."

In developing her interpretation of Dolly, Streisand never argued with the phantom of Carol Channing. "After I saw [the stage production], I could not remember it," she said during the film's shooting. "I didn't know what the story was, who she was, or what kind of character she was. I just saw Carol Channing. I didn't see any character at all in Dolly Levi. . . . How could I be influenced by [her]? I do things *my* way and have nothing to do with what anybody else does." She even laid into Channing personally, deriding her falsity. After Channing reported that she and Streisand were good friends, Streisand said, "[In] this business, everybody is everybody's friend. . . . We are not good friends."

Wardrobe supervisor Courtney Haslam meanwhile sent warning memos to Lehman. "While it all sounds very exciting, and I hate to dampen anyone's enthusiasm, I must say that the planned 'Parade' indicates that we may run way over budget . . . certainly, as far as my department is concerned." Haslam reminded Lehman that the wardrobe budget allows clothing *only* 2,713 people. Of further concern was the glittering, unwieldy dress Streisand was to wear for the big title song. "Constant and innumerable changes on Miss Streisand's gold dress for the Harmonia Gardens are making it impossible to control the cost of this gown," Haslam wrote. "It will go over budget." Costume designer Irene Sharaff may have considered Haslam's reports disloyal, but the real fireworks went off between Sharaff and Michael Kidd. As Streisand and the male chorus were rehearsing on Stage 14, she and the dancers tangled on the train of her dress.

"The train's got to go, Ern," said Kidd to Ernest Lehman.

"Maybe we'd better get Irene over here," said Lehman.

"Sure, Ern, get Irene over here, but the train's still go to go."

"Michael, I don't think the number ends right," said Lehman. "I think Barbra should be coming down toward the camera, not going away from it."

"No question, Ern, it stinks," said Kidd.

"What I mean, Mike . . . "

"No problem, Ern. The number's not finished. We're just here to see how the dress works and how the set works."

"It doesn't stink, Mike, that's not what I meant."

"Ern, the number's not finished."

Sharaff arrives and the train problem is described to her. "Perhaps I'd better see what you're talking about, Michael," she says. Streisand and the chorus do their chores, and the train tripping-stepping problem reoccurs.

"See what I mean?" said Kidd.

"No, Michael, I don't see what the problem is."

"Barbra trips on it, the dancers step on it."

"Perhaps if you changed the movements, Michael, the dancers wouldn't step on it."

Kidd kept his cool. "We've still got Barbra tripping on it."

"I don't think in the finished dress she will. The material is so heavy, it flows much better than the muslin," said Sharaff.

"There's another problem," Kidd said. "The dress is so heavy Barbra won't be able to kick at the end of the number."

"But, Michael," said Sharaff, "is the kick necessary?"

Unlike *Paint Your Wagon*, there were no clear sides chosen and loyalties drawn on *Hello, Dolly!* Everyone, it appears, hated everyone. War broke out over Kidd's choreography and John DeCuir's Harmonia Gardens set, with Kidd wanting to dismantle the restaurant booths after the establishing shots so his choreography could be more generously filmed. Lehman got red in the face. "For Christ's sake, why does this have to come up now?" he yelled at both of them. "We had sketches of this set, we had a model of this set, so why didn't you two get together before this? You know what this set cost, you know Stan Hough's on my ass about it, you know we can't spend another goddamn nickel on it, and now you're telling me we've got to rip out some booths."

"I didn't say that, Ernie," said DeCuir calmly.

"Yeah, well, Ern, John likes to look at people eating," said Kidd.

"Oh, for Christ's sake," Lehman muttered before walking away.

John DeCuir's work at Garrison required embellishing 16 building exteriors with period detail and the construction of a barn and park with a bandstand, but that was minor compared to the undertaking on the Fox lot. On the Fourth of July, shooting ended in New York, and the cast and crew returned to Los Angeles on three chartered planes. It had been a hot, humid, long, contentious shoot.

Under his hairpiece and behind his crinkly smile and soft voice, Kelly was a hard nugget. As Lehman recalled, "Once I made a suggestion to Michael Crawford about how he should play a close-up, and Kelly said to me, 'If you ever talk to another one of my actors on the set I'll kick your fucking teeth in.'" Lehman did not sugar coat the situation. "The intrigues, the bitterness, the backbiting, the deceits, the misery, the gloom. Most unpleasant," he said. "It's quite amazing what people go through to make something entertaining for others." Everyone had a differing perspective of where, when, and from whom the trouble started. "[Kelly] gave as much of himself to the film as was humanly possible, and didn't mind how hard he worked," said Crawford. "If there was one destructive element in the whole project (apart from Walter's feud with Barbra, which was something personal between the two of them), it was Ernest Lehman, who walked around looking like an unhappy man all the time. But then anything Ernest does is bound to make him unhappy. He's that sort of person." Actress Marianne McAndrew, playing the milliner Irene Molloy, was the lone reporter of harmony and goodwill. "I of course had heard all the rumors about Barbra," she said. "I haven't found any indication of that attitude." As for Matthau, she found him "so wonderful and so funny." As illustration, she recalled the time he appeared on the set in his sweatsuit and said, "Girls, I don't have anything on under this. Doesn't that excite you?"

New York had to be reconstructed at Fox, but the studio had sold its backlot, so the main entrance driveway was used instead. For the gigantic production number "Before the Parade Passes By," Fox ordered a 160-piece band, cavalry troop, dozens of flag-waving "Coronettes," 40 bagpipers, 50 Civil War drummer boys, 41 Civil War vets, 32 suffragettes, eight clowns, five little people, two banner carriers, three large floats, three fire engines, and 15 high-wheeled antique bicycles. All in all, the parade involved 4,000 extras and cost $200,000 a day for four days shooting.

Barbra Streisand makes a point to director Gene Kelly during the filming of the mammoth "Before the Parade Passes By" in *Hello, Dolly!* The two reportedly loathed each other. From the collection of Photofest.

John DeCuir had designed *Cleopatra*, so he was used to big. Even so, this would be the most ambitious construction project in Fox history. Under his guidance, the reproduction of old New York totaled 60 buildings around the Bowery, Broadway, and Fifth Avenue. The highest towered 130 feet. There were cobblestone streets, apartment buildings with chimneys, fire stations, brownstones, and shops, with careful reproduction of signs, lampposts, and molding. The most impressive single set piece was a Sixth Avenue elevated railway, complete with steam engine and three cars. The set consumed the facades of Fox's sound stages and administration buildings, its service roads and parking lots. The effort needed 10 tons of nails, 330,000 square feet of plywood, 220 tons of steel, and 50,000 plastic leaves and flowers for plaster trees.

Streisand and Kelly had a constitutional dislike of one another. "They were just not meant to communicate on this earth," summarized Lehman. Streisand found him lacking as a director of actors, and additionally bereft of ideas to enliven the film. Given the scale of *Dolly!*, Kelly was more head traffic cop than director. Casting director Hugh Fordin believed that the biggest mistake was not in casting Streisand, but in hiring Kelly to direct. "He was a competent director and a great dancer," he said. "But he lacked the imagination to get up on the crane and block out the 'Before the Parade Passes By' number. Michael Kidd did it, and by then he and Gene weren't speaking." His sympathies were with Streisand. "She didn't have a director who discussed anything with her. We didn't know if her performance was Martha Raye, Mae West, Marlene Dietrich, or Lena Horne. And Walter, from Day One, was impossible. His attitude was, 'I hate this movie. I hate being here.'"

The completed street set was astonishing, but the on-camera statistics are no less so. Shot over five days, "Before the Parade Passes By" involved 657 people marching, 106 horses clopping, and over 3,000 various additional extras, all in all a $200,000 production number invading a $1.7 million recreation of Gilded Age New York. It was one of the most logistically complicated undertakings in Hollywood history; even *The Ten Commandments* did not have as many participants. From an eight-foot high boom, Kelly directed 15 assistant directors, 12 firefighters, 35 policemen, and five detectives in period costume, with 122 makeup and wardrobe people, 4,200 box lunches, 17 toilets, and five first aid stations. The "Parade" set stretched a half-mile, took six months to build, and three days to film, but lasts just seven minutes. "It's all rather staggering when you think about it," said Lehman. "So I just don't think about it."

Kelly and cinematographer Harry Stradling rode an undulating crane while six additional Todd-AO cameras were stationed in helicopters overhead, all connected via radio. Just before the cameras rolled, the loudspeakers blasted assorted instructions and updates to the thousands milling about the set: "Let's move, people. We're gonna lose this light" . . . "If you have umbrellas, let us see the umbrellas" . . . "Girls who use the dumbbells, do not look at the cameras. Do not look at the cameras" . . . "Will all the people please stand up who are sitting on the curb, please" . . . "take your places, please" . . . "check with Irene on that. The costumes, check with Irene" . . . Kelly implored everyone to remove contemporary beads and necklaces. "Ladies had hips in those days, but hippies had we not," he said. "C'mon, c'mon, please. Don't lose your enthusiasm. Lots of excitement, please" . . . "okay, here we go." Lights go on. "Hit the playback," says Kelly. Streisand's voice suddenly overrides everything.

> *For I've got a goal again,*
> *I've got a drive again,*
> *I wanna feel my heart coming alive again.*
> *Before the paraaaaaaaaaa-duh—passes byyyyyyy!*

Then it's over, and an uncertain silence is pierced by Kelly's voice over a bullhorn: "Okay. Cut it. Everybody turn around and go back. You do it right next time and you get a cigar."

Dolly! production ended in September after 121 agonized shooting days, more than a month over schedule. Editing, dubbing, and sound mixing went comparatively fast, and *Dolly!* was more or less in the can by the fall of 1968, but the release date could not be set by the terms of stage producer David Merrick's contract. As long as the Broadway production was still playing, the film had to sit on the shelf. Meanwhile Fox was paying interest on financing at $100,000 per month. Ill omens abounded. In October, a single-engine plane crashed into the administrative headquarters of Twentieth Century-Fox just feet away from the still-standing *Dolly!* set. The pilot was killed on impact, while his plane sent a column of fire and dark smoke far into the sky.

While *Dolly!* sat on the shelf, history unfolded. There was Vietnam and Tet, Chicago and the Democratic National Convention, the student massacre in Mexico City, the victory of Richard Nixon, Black Power, Sisterhood, Paris, Poland, and 200,000 Soviet and Warsaw Pact troops marching into Czechoslovakia to crush Prague Spring. "It's a difficult world we live in," said Streisand. "We live in an atomic world, a world that could be devoured with the pressing of a button. I guess it makes [young people] grasp whatever they can each moment. I don't blame them, and there's a large part of the youth that is very constructive, politically involved, progressive. My hats go off to them." It did not sound like an era ready to embrace frilly screen *Hello, Dolly!*, but who knows? The current New York stage *Dolly!* starred Pearl Bailey and Cab Calloway with an all-black cast, and the revitalized production was doing standing room only business. In a good news / bad news scenario, *Dolly!'s* appeal was alive and well, but the film version had to sit it out for another year.

Broadway was experiencing its own uncertain future. *Hair: The American Tribal Love-Rock Musical* opened in 1968, helping lay to rest the traditional stage musical format. The contrast between stodgy Hollywood product and Broadway could not have been more starkly displayed. Clive Barnes's review is light years away from anything said about Hollywood musicals of the same era:

> What is so likeable about *Hair*, that tribal-rock musical that last night completed its trek from downtown, via a discotheque, and landed, positively panting with love and smelling of sweat and flowers, at the Biltmore Theater? I think it is simply that it is so likable. So new, so fresh and so unassuming, even in its pretensions. . . . A great many four-letter words, such as "love," are used very freely. At one point—in what is later affectionately referred to as "the nude scene"—a number of men and women (I should have counted) are seen totally nude. . . . Frequent references—frequent approving references—are made to the expanding benefits of drugs. Homosexuality is not frowned upon—one boy announces that he is in love with Mick Jagger, in terms unusually frank. The American flag is not desecrated—that would be a Federal offense, wouldn't it?—but it is used in a manner that not everyone would call respectful. Christian ritual also comes in for a bad time, the authors approve enthusiastically of miscegenation, and one enterprising lyric

. catalogues somewhat arcane sexual practices more familiar to the pages of the Kama Sutra than *The New York Times*. So there—you have been warned. Oh yes, they also hand out flowers. . . . You probably don't have to be a supporter of Eugene McCarthy to love it, but I wouldn't give much chance among the adherents of Governor Reagan.

One wonders what went on in the minds of Richard Zanuck, Ernest Lehman, and Gene Kelly as *Dolly!* bled money. What did they see that justified profligate spending? A Broadway hit so big that it was failsafe on screen? A guaranteed movie star in someone who had yet to prove any box office clout? Great music? The rightful successor to *The Sound of Music*? A movie experience so glorious that audiences will return to their senses and embrace the obsolete? *Camelot* and *Doctor Dolittle* did not shutter roadshows, and the abyss was not yet in view. When *Dolly!* finished production, 17 of the 25 top film rentals were roadshows. In response, the industry prepared a bottleneck of reserved-seat giants. A record-breaking 12 were scheduled for release over the last four months of 1968. Marketers faced a huge dilemma in catching people's attention amid the glut and convincing them that the roadshow experience was still worth the time, cost, and effort. With a roadshow opening practically every week, how do you market something as being special when it isn't special anymore?

CHAPTER 11

Battle of the Girls

The first audience went nuts. "Everyone at Warners thought *Finian's Rainbow* was going to be a big hit; they were just wild about it," said its director, Francis Ford Coppola. As a result, the studio expanded its marketing. Merchandise tie-ins were needed, and in March the Curtiss Candy Company signed on with bite-sized Baby Ruths and gold wrapped chocolate with images of the stars on a color-ful rainbow display. *Finian* wool cloth hats were sold at Macy's Men's Stores. In April, Petula Clark's TV special had her and Harry Belafonte singing an antiwar duet and causing a stir when the white Clark touched the arm of the black Bela-fonte. The ado garnered international publicity, but it was just the kind of public relations that would help *Finian* and its easily digested message of racial harmony.

While on location for his next film, Coppola received a telegram from Jack Warner, who still kept an office on the lot: "We had the preview of *Finian's Rain-bow* today and the picture went over fantastically," he wrote, as if kissed by the Blarney Stone. "I could see the wonderful touch and the warmth you personally put into the film. This is just the beginning of a very important future that will rank among the tops." At a trade press conference, Warner Bros.-Seven Arts announced that *Finian's Rainbow* would have the greatest promotion ever at-tached to a roadshow, with a campaign costing $2 million. It would focus on the music and stars appealing to multiple generations, and the "happiness factor" of a movie that is "plain fun, a natural for the whole family." Full-page, full-color ads were to run in pro football programs. There would be highway billboards, two-page *New York Times* ads, animated displays in bus terminals and subways, radio time for the songs, and press availability of the stars. Study guides and other ma-terials would be distributed for primary and secondary educators, with attention paid to the timeliness of the film's social theme. Direct marketing outreach was to be given to the underground press and college students. Ten promotional teams spread across North America to pitch *Finian* to 700 newspapers and 920 TV and radio stations in 285 cities and suburbs. The studio was giving away screenings to theater owners and the press like Halloween candy. More than 17,000 guests were estimated to have seen *Finian* before it opened.

When it was put before a paying audience, the first deleterious consequence of the roadshowing decision was put on horrifying display. There he is, the great Fred Astaire, dancing from the ankles up. As Coppola explained, the enlargement from a 35-millimeter negative to a 70-millimeter print for roadshow grandiosity "blew the feet off Fred Astaire when he was dancing. No one had calculated the top and bottom of the frame." Close-up inserts of his feet did not solve the problem. When the *Finian* budget was disclosed as less than $4 million, more eyebrows were raised. Here was a roadshow that had spent too *little* in production against such a huge marketing effort. "I tried to show some discipline, to try to make it work on its own terms and not to make a thing out of myself," said Coppola. But blowing up the film, and certain editing choices, gave it a nervous energy he had wanted to avoid. "I fought very hard not to change it, which was probably a mistake," he said later. "I had the idea that if you do *Finian's Rainbow*, you shouldn't rewrite it or update it. I guess I was wrong. It was just the wrong time to make a movie like that."

The film opens with Clark's lilting rendition of "Look to the Rainbow" over scenes throughout America. From there, *Finian's Rainbow* can't decide if it's a sweet leprechaun fantasy or a morality play on the evils of racism. Tommy Steele covers the former. As in *The Happiest Millionaire* and *Half a Sixpence*, he employed a broad vaudeville style and screen-splitting grin. "Every time he appeared, I ground my teeth," wrote the *Harper's Magazine* reviewer. "All that London music-hall excessiveness, the eye-rolling mugging, and shouting, the love-me-or-I'll-die attack. Any moment, I expected him to land in the audience's lap." There are moments of grace, humor, and musical value. Al Freeman Jr.'s send-up of a Stepin Fetchit's languid shuffling foretells the career of Richard Pryor. It stirred some passions; *Finian's Rainbow* was banned in South Africa. "The Begat," featuring the Cotton Club's Avon Long and *Amos 'n' Andy*'s Jester Hairston, is pure joy. Perhaps it was in mind when one reviewer noted that Coppola directs with "imagination" and "virtuosity," while another proclaimed that *Finian* has restored his "faith in the musical after a fairly dismal decade of uneventful musical film. . . . Never has a musical looked and sounded so good."

Really? *Finian* possesses a magnificent score, but is chockablock full of continuity errors and shoddy production. A support wire from the *Camelot* forest is in view during "When I'm Not Near the Girl I Love." There are choruses filling the screen with direct eye contact at the camera, but no moving lips. When actor Keenan Wynn is in blackface, the makeup smudges his collar. Steele plunges into a lake then emerges with his full head of dirty blonde hair bone dry. The dancing, described by *Time* as "galvanic twitching," was a smear of badly photographed crowds running and jumping. "The choreography was abysmal, let's be honest," said Coppola. "There wasn't lots of time to keep going after every detail." *Sight & Sound* found a way to flatter Coppola: "[His] secret seems to lie partly in the way he choreographed the action beyond the limits of the frame, and partly in the impeccable rhythms of his curiously fragmented technique."

In *Movie Brats*, Michael Pye and Linda Myles undo *Finian*: "Reality, however cruel, can be dissolved with gentle, liberal dreams. The idea is patronizing and wet. It also misread the times. It was gentle, liberal, and vaguely humanistic in the year that Richard M. Nixon, talking of law and order, was elected president of the United States." *Finian's Rainbow* was a victim of the times, timing, and its own cross-purposes. As observed by Coppola biographer Michael Schumacher, it "possessed the kind of idealism that the hippies might have found appealing had Coppola decided to aim his film at the youth market, but he was looking more to the past, to the old tradition of musicals like *The Wizard of Oz*, than to the politically charged future and the anthems and bombast of *Hair*." Trouble was, *everybody* making musical films was looking to the past.

In 1979, as Astaire neared his 80th birthday, he took stock. "I was always planning or rehearsing or doing new numbers and there was nothing I didn't enjoy when I was doing it," he said. "Afterward, when I saw it on the screen and it didn't quite work, I was disappointed with the failure. *Finian's Rainbow* was the biggest disappointment." Coppola looked back and said, "It was an absurd idea to take a $3.5 million musical and send it out to compete with fucking *Funny Girl* where they had rehearsed the musical numbers for two months." But for all its failings, *Finian* pulled in a $2 million profit. It was hardly enough to balance the losses from *Camelot*. Hungry for cash, Warner Bros.-Seven Arts accepted a $64 million buyout from Kinney National, a company with interests ranging from comic books to parking lots. As for Coppola, here was a young man who should be flush with success and rarin' to go, but he saw something on the horizon. Or nothing. Shortly after Kinney bought Warner Bros., he said, "I don't think there'll be a Hollywood as we know it when this generation of film students gets out of college."

Finian competitor *Funny Girl* had its own troubles. Producer Ray Stark and director William Wyler avoided sharing physical space, as they had grown to detest each other. After seeing a rough cut, Stark wrote a lengthy and largely negative critique to Wyler. "I do think you have hurt the musical feeling of the film by either bad cutting in the musical numbers or in trying to cut too deeply," he wrote, then announced, "I intend to restore these numbers to the film as [musical number director] Herb [Ross] and I had originally edited them. . . . We have had many disagreements in reference to the shooting of this picture, Willie. As a general criterion I feel that you have too many close-ups of Barbra in the first set. I believe very much in close-ups for punctuating, but on a 70-millimeter screen we might very easily fall into the trap of *Camelot* which suffered from too many close-ups." On and on the memo went, seven pages of single-spaced patronizations. That an upshot producer would so communicate with an esteemed veteran director took chutzpah and would contribute to Stark's future as one of the most powerful men in Hollywood.

At every turn, Stark attempted to contain Wyler. In a memo to Columbia exec-utives, he instructed them to send financial information to his closest associates, not including Wyler, and that he would "see that it is properly distributed." Wyler was livid at Stark's attempted end run. He shot back the same day, clarifying it was his understanding he would be in direct communication without Stark's mid-dlemen, since the financial status of *Funny Girl* determines how much he will be paid. The clincher was a hatchet job *Los Angeles Times* columnist and Stark confi-dant Joyce Haber ran as *Funny Girl* was being edited. She reported that both Wyler and cameraman Harry Stradling threatened to quit over "monster" Strei-sand's many demands. According to Haber, one grip said to another, "Willie shouldn't be so hard on her. After all, this is the first picture she's ever directed." She also stated that Stark gave her a 10-minute trailer with credits reading, "Written, produced and directed by Barbra Streisand." Another gibe making the rounds observed, "Barbra will never make *Hello, Dolly!* She won't get through editing *Funny Girl* in time."

Wyler shot off a damned-if-you-do-damned-if-you-don't diatribe to Stark about the leak to Haber:

> I know of no instance where a producer has ever "planted" damaging sto-ries about his star and director of a yet unreleased film. Therefore we find it hard to accept the confirmation we get from many well-informed people—some from the press—all of them familiar with the workings of the press—that the derogatory stories about us which have recently been published originated with you.... Could it be that you are trying to create the image of a producer who successfully masterminded an impor-tant picture in spite of great difficulties and constant battles between an unmanageable star and a director who lost control of her? Could it be that you thought you could upgrade your name by downgrading ours?... Your answer to us is obvious: a flat denial. So we ask you to answer them to yourself. And what will your answer be? If it is still no, the purpose of this letter is to express our astonishment and disappointment that you, as the producer, have done nothing to dispel and counteract and protect the film from damaging publicity. If the answer is yes, then the purpose of this letter is to record our utter disgust at you, your bad taste and man-ners, your devious, stupid, and malicious conduct.

Stark, Ross, and Wyler eventually retracted their talons, while *Funny Girl* was edited and Columbia efficiently maintained press interest leading up to the pre-miere. There was a fashion short made for women's clubs and merchandisers, a 10-minute "making of" documentary, and a TV show aptly titled *Barbra in Mov-ieland*. Thanks to Broadway, recordings, and TV specials, Streisand came pre-sold. The film's logo, a line drawing of her upside down smiling, in roller skates, with FUNNY GIRL spelled on her dress, was used for the stage production, and reused for the film. It was simple, effective, and enduring. The fashion impact was felt at the Plaza Hotel when a runway model wore movie images of roller skates and a grape-trimmed dress. Also modeled from the movie were gray flannel knickers and vest with a white midi blouse. Other *Funny Girl*–inspired designs were white satin pajamas and ostrich jacket, coats and suits, sportswear, rainwear, jewelry, and bridal gowns. And immediately before *Funny Girl*'s premiere, Paramount announced that Streisand would star in the musical *On a Clear Day You Can See Forever*, and that her earnings would amount to at least $1 million. She was taking home seven-figure paychecks for each of her first three films, and she had yet to bring in a dime at the box office. No one had ever pulled that trick in the history of movies. Clues pointed to investors getting their money's worth. At a time when the average movie ticket in America cost $1.30, *Funny Girl*'s first-run reserve seat engagement at the Criterion in New York had weekend and holiday orchestra seats at $6, the top price ever charged for a commercial film. Even so, advance sales for weekends quickly sold out, and a huge premiere block party for 1,200 was planned under a group of five multi-colored tents where the Astor Hotel once stood.

Funny Girl was never about anyone but Barbra Streisand, and in service to her, it was an unexpurgated triumph. When it opened, all jokes about her nose died overnight, and who cared if this movie was an inaccurate biopic about somebody named Fanny? All other actors in the film, from the old pros Walter Pidgeon and Kay Medford, to the matinee idol Omar Sharif and the feline Anne Francis, were mere hand props. "Nothing like Barbra Streisand has ever occurred before," effused the voice-over from a short promotional film. First-run audiences were applauding after almost every number. During an early screening at the Criterion, *The Village Voice* reported "There was a ripple of electricity in the theater, but, curiously, no warmth" during her final torchy rendition of "My Man." In an earlier era, one in which the highest ranks of female stardom most often required being pretty, Streisand might have been consigned to specialty songs and comic relief, or called to belt out show-stoppers in the tradition of Charlotte Greenwood, Dolores Gray, or Nancy Walker. But the crazy 1960s made her possible, as she was better suited to an evolving vision of the musical. There would be no more spoonfuls of sugar; Streisand was dispensing vinegar. And the time was right to embrace someone removed from the conventional idea of good looks. Less than two weeks before *Funny Girl*'s bow, hundreds of feminists descended on Atlantic City to protest the Miss America pageant, calling it a cattle auction with ludicrous standards of beauty.

Streisand was garnering the kinds of reviews Julie Andrews had received just three years earlier. Even the irritable Pauline Kael wrote about her "incandescence" while Rex Reed announced she delivered "the most remarkable screen debut I will probably ever see in my lifetime, the toadstool from Erasmus High

The marketing campaign for *Funny Girl* showed restraint rare for a roadshow feature and proved to be both effective and enduring. From the collection of Photofest.

School has been turned into a truffle.... Every age has its Super Lady. Other ages had Lillian Russell and Sarah Bernhardt and Gertrude Lawrence and Helen Morgan and Judy Garland. Well, we've got ours." *Newsweek's* Joseph Morgenstern wrote, "Miss Streisand has matured into a complete performer and delivered the most accomplished, original, and enjoyable musical-comedy performance that has ever been captured on film." He then delivered a premonition: "Good old-fashioned shows in the future have nowhere to go but down, even if they have Miss Streisand to rescue them from the more manifest ravages of time." Most agreed she was compelling enough to overcome her vehicle's wobbly wheels, a mediocre score, and a book peppered with hackneyed lines like, "You're no chorus girl, you're a singer" and "I love to hear audience applause, but you can't take an audience home with you." A few early observers were not enraptured. "She's a bit irritating because she is evidently conceited," wrote *The New Republic*, "evidence that filters through from the screen, not from the press—and it's always irritating when a conceited person is as good as he (she) believes."

Some chafed at so much star aggrandizement, and one suspects that *Funny Girl* would have been better if it had not held Streisand in such awe and had more fully developed its other characters. "Wyler has not so much directed Barbra as mounted her (figuratively of course, not literally)," wrote *The Village Voice*. "[She] is ham on wry, and the ugliness that lingers is less in her visage than in her vanity.... *Funny Girl* is the ultimate expression of Barbra in all her barbaric solitude. The rest of the movie is a desert of destroyed egos." The charge isn't entirely accurate. In between Streisand close-ups, Wyler infused *Funny Girl* with some well-chosen conventions of classic Hollywood. It is full of nostalgic images of pushcarts, well-appointed Broadway theaters, and immigrants crowding the Lower East Side. "His Love Makes Me Beautiful" cleverly lampoons the man it also honors, late impresario Florenz Ziegfeld, thereby laughing at and celebrating antiquated musical conventions. Streisand is wonderful in the "You Are Woman" scene, as Brice is humorously skittish and ill equipped for seduction. Streisand has Wyler to thank.

There was a run at the box office as *Funny Girl* fanned out to half a dozen cities in the fall of 1968, then nationwide at Christmas. The star-heavy London premiere was followed by a riot at the Paris opening as 150 photographers converged on Streisand. They broke through a cordon of police and security to swarm the theater, continuing to take photos even after the movie had started. *Funny Girl* went on to become the highest grossing musical since *The Sound of Music*. That may be faint glory, but its numbers were impressive. It ran at the Criterion for 72 weeks at those swollen prices. At final tally, it brought in over $56 million in domestic box office against $14 million in production costs. But *Funny Girl* did little to boost confidence in roadshows. Its success is rightfully attributed to Streisand, the roadshow format simply being commensurate with the anticipation, talent, and ego of its star. "There's no doubt that this whole thing, musicals from all sides, represents a culmination of supply and demand," said Raymond Bell, a vice-president at Columbia. "*The Sound of Music* is still the sound we all hope for in the way of money. It also represents a coincidence—the right properties emerging and the right personalities, like Barbra Streisand and Julie Andrews, happening along at just the right time."

Postproduction on Andrews's *Star!* was on schedule in early 1968, just as Fox was absorbing the reality of *Doctor Dolittle*'s insufficient box office. After the first industry previews in March, Joyce Haber attacked Andrews in ways that would have been felonious three years prior. In comparing her to Streisand, she wrote, "The department of dullness, saintly dullness, has been preempted by Julie Andrews. Julie is so solidly entrenched there that she could be living at the Beverly Hills Hotel with two Viet Cong guerrillas and a Chinese gigolo without disturbing her public image of good-sweet-jolly-dull girl." Internally, Fox men did what moviemakers have been doing since the beginning: boosting morale with hollow praise. Doc Merman wrote to Wise, "If everyone throughout the world will enjoy *Star!* as much as I enjoyed watching the dailies, *Star!* will be a far bigger grosser than *Sound of Music*." *Star!* received minor editing before sneak previews in early May in Denver and Cleveland. Audience response was positive, with 633 of the 815 reaction cards coming back "excellent" and only three as "bad." When a complete print was ready for Production Code screening, a Fox staffer reported, "It was the unqualified and unanimous opinion of the [the Production Code] that this pic is magnificent and that it is beautifully done. They were wholeheartedly generous in their praise of and pleasure with the entire production, their enthusiasm being very reminiscent of that they afforded to *The Sound of Music*."

Still, there was tinkering to be done to two stubborn photo effects problems involving blue-backing water shots, a swimming float, and a rowboat on a park lake. There was no denying it looked phony in the extreme. Fox's special effects men wanted to ship the film without these two scenes. In early June, Darryl Zanuck arranged a screening at Cannes for the World Sales market with the problematic scenes included. Publicist Mike Kaplan went with Zanuck, then waited in the lobby while *Star!* played. A happy Zanuck emerged from the screening telling Kaplan it was ready to go public.

While others expressed confidence in *Star!*, producer Saul Chaplin broke into a flop sweat. "All the general audience knew of the film was what they read in feature articles about Julie as Gertrude Lawrence and pictures of both," he wrote. "There was a monumental advertising campaign, [yet] no one ever saw a foot of the film except those of us connected with it." The campaign struggled and failed to define *Star!* either to its makers or the public. The initial ad had Andrews in black sequins, her arms raised in triumphant musical fashion. That was nixed for multiple images from the film, but without a focal point. The chosen design had an orange Andrews with a bright pink star applied over her left eye, giving her the look of Mary Poppins meets Captain Hook meets Cosmic Brownies. Kaplan hated the "Star Face," believing it looked like a cartoon black eye, but he was over-ruled. Chaplin's anxiety meanwhile rose further when the thousands who had sent in priority notification before the Rivoli premiere yielded fewer than 100 actual reserve seat purchases. He attributed the "astonishing disinterest" to the public's rejection of Julie Andrews as "a real person."

The parallels of *Star!* and *Funny Girl* were abundantly noted in the press. "Unless release schedules are changed, the fall of 1968 is shaping as a 'Battle of the Girls,'" announced *Variety*. "Specifically, a battle between the two biggest show biz femme phenomena of the past few years starring in startlingly similar road-show pic vehicles." The competition especially unnerved Streisand, who had even more riding on *Funny Girl* as her film debut than Andrews had on *Star!* While Andrews was on location for *Darling Lili*, Streisand attended a cast and crew screening of *Star!* Under director Robert Wise's planning, she hid under a big floppy pink hat and was ushered in just as the lights went down.

Star!'s world premiere was attended by 1,400 moviegoers on July 18 at London's Dominion Theatre, where *The Sound of Music* had played—and played and played. The guests included the Duke and Duchess of Kent, Lord Louis Mountbatten, Dame Edith Evans, Noël Coward, every major name at Fox, and the film's producers, director, screenwriter, and costumer—but not star. Julie Andrews's suite at the Dorchester was packed to the ceiling with floral tributes, but she wasn't there. A chartered jet was to whisk her from the Brussels location of *Darling Lili*. The guests were disappointed, but the Zanucks were incensed and blamed her absence on *Lili* director and Andrews's paramour Blake Edwards. "Blake had a shot involving 2,000 extras which was postponed three times, and we had to finish up in Brussels that week," explained Paramount production chief Robert Evans. "We bent over backwards to let Julie go, but another postponement would have cost us one and a half days and $175,000." An executive said, "Don't let her go! Keep her there! Keep her there!" One overpriced Julie Andrews vehicle was holding Julie Andrews hostage to another overpriced Julie Andrews vehicle. She genuinely regretted missing the London opening. "Of all the premieres, this was the one I really wanted to go to," she said. "This was home, one's family, royalty and all one's chums. I'd had a dress designed in Dublin, and of all the movies I'd made, this was the one I cared about most. But . . . I could still only fly to London just in time to get to the theater, walk through the front door, and walk right out again."

The London press and public were largely positive. Those familiar with Lawrence on the stage, most notably Coward, were unhappy with the various distortions and the distance between their Gertie and our Julie. But just as many people did not care a fig for Gertrude Lawrence and were thrilled that the great Andrews had a lavish song and dance biopic all her own. Though Wise's direction was "the squarest thing since biscuits came in tins," a leading critic predicted *Star!* would occupy the Dominion five years on the strength of Andrews's performance.

Star! outgrossed *The Sound of Music* during the first three weeks at the Dominion, but that gravy train ended abruptly. Brisk advance sales led to stagnation once *Star!* was in long-term residence. Embedded in the *London Times* review was a telling rhetorical question: "How many of its potential audience know, or care, anything much about the real Gertrude Lawrence?" The fact that this question was raised in England, where Lawrence's fame was greatest, was not a good sign.

Everyone with a financial interest in *Star!* continued to beat the drums. Fox sales executive Abe Dickstein said, "*Star!* is doing most of the work itself, and I don't mean to be taking away from the advertising department. But when you have Julie Andrews, Robert Wise, and Saul Chaplin making their first film together since *Sound of Music*, well, it just sells itself. We expect the biggest advance in our history, and it's certainly been the easiest to sell to houses." *Star!* opened in scattered theaters in Europe and Asia before New York or Los Angeles. To rev up anticipation, Fox leased the world's longest billboard, running the length of Broadway from 45th to 46th Streets, and splayed 'S T A R!' across it. Fox also supplied the ultimate press kit made of a miniature red and white metal wardrobe trunk covered with travel stickers and containing 400 stories and photos, the soundtrack album, souvenir book, postcards, a novelization, and other ephemera. As it had with *Doctor Dolittle*, Fox took inordinate pride in *Star!*'s bigness, with statistics of grandiosity crowding the press releases.

During Andrews's superstar days, she grew to detest the media, which did its best to distort her words and deny her a private life. She grew prickly under the strain of so many interviews and so much invasiveness, and she paid for it. "Her reticence and impenetrable affability turn some journalists nasty," reported the *Los Angeles Times*. Most bloodthirsty was again Joyce Haber, who visited the set of *Darling Lili* and remixed a comment that Andrews made to the closeted gay Rock Hudson as, "Remember, I'm the leading lady." Andrews had to contend with a simmering rage. "These damn interviews," she said. "Well, if it will help get back 10 million dollars, what's 20 minutes?" Haber was the worst. "Suing her would dignify her," she said.

Star! opened at the venerable Rivoli on October 22, and again there was no Julie due to *Darling Lili* responsibilities. This time poison darts were aimed at the film, not at Andrews. *Star!* is "the H-bomb of musicals," wrote *Time*. *Newsweek* concluded, "The sets are tacky, the color abysmal, the length—three hours and 10 minutes—unconscionable." If critical scorn echoed public antipathy, not just for *Star!* but for outsized musicals generally, then Leonard Harris of WCBS-TV spoke for a great many people on the 11:00 news the night *Star!* opened: "The only reason I can think of for making big pictures so long nowadays is to justify the hard ticket prices, which in the case of *Star!* go as high as $4.50. *Star!* would not be any better if it were shorter, but it would let you go an hour sooner, and that would be a substantial blessing."

The 1950s saw a rash of musical biopics, including hard-luck chanteuse stories *I'll Cry Tomorrow* with Susan Hayward as Lillian Roth, and *Love Me or Leave Me* with Doris Day as Ruth Etting. *Star!* could be the overfed daughter of either film, but it was at least 10 years too late. And where the best of them used moments in various lives as excuses for musical numbers, *Star!* makes no such effort. "Nothing in *Star!*, it seems, has been created," noted *Harper's Magazine*. "It has all been manufactured . . . by the producer, Saul Chaplin, and the director, Robert Wise, who have simply strolled over to Hollywood's immense fantasy bin—in which slivers of our national psyche lie buried—and casually plucked dozens of the gaudiest clichés from the dust and packaged them as a Technicolor extravaganza." There isn't a stitch of clothing that looks like it came from a human being's wardrobe and not the costume trailer. And you're sure to titter at the scene of our Gertie hospitalized for nervous exhaustion in perfect hair and makeup. *Star!* "is less concerned with the biography of Gertrude Lawrence than with using the rags-to-riches, triumphs-and-heartaches outline of her story to define an extinct type of glamour, the ideal of an anti-serious and pre-pop generation (for all the analogies, it's impossible to image the John Lennon legend ever receiving this kind of treatment)."

For all the polish applied to each of the 17 production numbers, none is likely to bring a lump to the throat, shiver to the spine, or spontaneous dancing in the aisles. And since none frame the drama of the screenplay, they come off as variety acts sandwiched between the tedious woes of self-indulgent people. And who are these people anyway? Even by the lax standards of the biopic, *Star!* toys with the realities of Lawrence's life to extreme. The absence of Ira Gershwin, Cole Porter, and her Anna in *The King and I* leaves the impression that Noël Coward was the sole architect of her career. *Star!* has sterling moments, but they're trapped in a movie no one wanted to look at. Anyone harboring affection for Andrews is urged to see "Burlington Bertie," one of the best production numbers she ever did. But over the long haul, *Star!* views more like a parade of glad rags on proud display than a coherent movie.

Andrews was unfit for the role, and Wise misguided her. Rather like those gaudy ads, Andrews acts in primary colors until every old saw of the "star temperament" has been played to exhaustion. She is diligent when she should be enflamed, and shrill when she should be cunning. No one wanted to see her abandon a child, fail at marriage, or annoyingly repeat such filthy words as "bastard," "bloody," and "cripes." With military precision, she over-emotes at everything from men and booze to telephones and a badminton birdie. She is not the only performer to be used to disadvantage, she is only the most conspicuous. Her male support is borderline perverse. Daniel Massey delivers a droll interpretation of Coward, Robert Reed drops in and out of the suitor competition, and Richard Crenna shows up in the wheezing final third to give Gertie the tongue-lashing we long to hear.

When *Star!* opened at the Fox Wilshire Theatre in Beverly Hills as a 70-millimeter magnum roadshow, Andrews was in attendance with her date Blake Edwards. Few others bothered to attend, including fans. "I was shocked," said Wise. "I didn't expect that at all. I said right, what happened here? You misjudge your audience sometimes. . . . I think it's a damn fine film, and it deserved better than it got. Julie did some of her best work in it; she told me she worked harder on that film than on *The Sound of Music*." The problem was not simply the public's unfamiliarity or indifference to Gertrude Lawrence. After all, no such issue arose with *Funny Girl*'s passé Fanny Brice. No, the problem was the miscasting of Andrews. Everything that endeared her to millions in *Poppins* and *Music* conspired against her in *Star!* In *The Hollywood Musical*, Ethan Mordden describes *Star!* as "a bio with Julie Andrews carefully indicating the elements of zaniness, hysteria, pathos, and selfishness in the character of Gertrude Lawrence and never being anything but a weird Julie Andrews."

Critics gleefully outwitted each other in their attacks. Pauline Kael had a ball saying everything but "I told you so" on the subject of Andrews. In contrast, she did cartwheels over the sensation du jour. "Barbra Streisand arrives on the screen in *Funny Girl*, when movies are in desperate need of her. The timing is perfect. There's hardly a star in American movies today. . . . Barbra Streisand is much more beautiful than 'pretty' people." One month later, she wrote, "Cripes! Julie Andrews does her duties efficiently but mechanically, like an airline stewardess." Saul Chaplin confronted the misjudgments he made with Wise and screenwriter William Fairchild. "*Star!* was the most difficult film to make because of the concept we had adopted," he wrote. "Instead of telling a straightforward biography, we telescoped parts of Gertrude Lawrence's life and presented them as though they had been photographed years earlier as newsreel footage. These sections were in small-screen black-and-white with scratchy monaural sound. The remainder of the film was in wide-screen Technicolor with six-track stereo." That decision was very wrong. Apart from appearing like a rip-off of *Citizen Kane*, a film Wise edited, it was illogical. Who was running that news camera when a young Gertie and her impoverished family were stealing away in the night? Is this artistic license, or some muddled comment on the layers of show business artifice?

Fairly or not, *Star!* begs comparison to *Funny Girl*, and on every point, it comes up wanting. Both were vehicles for two vocally gifted, immensely popular leading ladies. Both had huge budgets backed by major studios. Both were biopics of late stars with troubled lives, each with a tears-behind-the-song-stoicism. They opened within days of each other under high expectations and immense marketing. But where Streisand takes sizable risks, Andrews withholds. And without the support of nuns, children, the Austrian landscape, or Disney's wizardly special effects, her reluctance to be daring in front of the camera is exposed. The problems were fatal. "You have a sensational preview and all the cards are great and the audience is cheering and everybody is opening champagne," said Richard Zanuck. "And then the picture goes out and dies. It happened with *Star!*"

Star! was Fox's super bomb of the decade, with about 75 percent of the studio's investment lost. It lacked widespread cross-generational appeal, exactly what it needed to be profitable against a $14 million price tag. The competition were harbingers of the new reality. While *Star!* was opening in New York, *The Graduate* was still in its long initial run. *Pretty Poison* starred Tuesday Weld and Anthony Perkins as young sociopaths. Also playing was Andy Warhol's *Flesh* and Richard Lester's *Petulia*, a movie employing every voguish trick expected of the director of *A Hard Day's Night*. Also on was *For Love of Ivy*, Sidney Poitier's latest hit. The *Odd Couple* and *The Anniversary*, one from the Bette Davis harridan gallery, qualified as escapist entertainment. *You Are What You Eat* was an aimless "freak-out" featuring David Crosby, Peter Yarrow, Tiny Tim, and a camera wandering through the East Village, Sunset Strip, and Haight-Ashbury. There was also a swarm of international titles from Kurosawa, Godard, Brunel, Chabrol, and Polanski, all receiving concentrated attention from critics and a new class of American cineastes. *Thoroughly Modern Millie* was still in release when *Star!* opened, but was in its final week. With it went Julie Andrews's career as a sought-after movie star. It's no wonder Richard Zanuck nicknamed it "My Edsel." Andrews might have called it "My Waterloo."

Zanuck wanted to cut *Star!* during its premiere roadshow engagements, but Wise initially resisted. Then Wise relented, but he did not participate, saying he was too close to it. Edits were made into January, with no improvement in business. By then, *Star!*'s failure was no secret. *Variety* listed its Lilliputian rental income at $1.3 million, placing it below such drive-in drivel as *The Savage Seven* and *The Miniskirt Mob*. In March, Zanuck withdrew *Star!*, and he and editor William Reynolds began rearranging the deck chairs on the Titanic, hoping against hope that it could eventually recoup. Rereleasing a film is tricky business, but Warner Bros. did it with *Bonnie and Clyde* (without cutting), and turned it into a cultural phenomenon in the process. Could Fox do likewise with *Star!*?

Star! was vomited back into theaters as a standard feature at regular prices in the spring of 1968. Fox directed exhibitors to cut 20 minutes, but did not dictate *which* 20 minutes, just so long as they stuck to a reduced running time. It came with a showy new ad campaign bombarding the eye with capitalizations, exclamations, and misstatements of fact: "UNBELIEVABLE JULIE! ALL HER ROMANCES! ALL HER WILDNESS! ALL HER FUN! ALL HER SONGS! ALL HER DANCES! ALL HER JOY! STAR! ALL OF IT NOW AT REGULAR PRICES!" Box office did not improve, so Fox tested another approach. This time, the aim was something closer to British kitchen sink realism. With Andrews in her badminton outfit from the film, and the racket airbrushed out, she is struggling to be free of a man's strong grip on her left forearm. "WHO LOVES A WOMAN AT THE TOP?" asked the ad, with four men's portraits interspersed in the copy. "The world loved her too much—She loved her men too little." Now "JULIE ANDREWS IS A DIFFERENT JULIE ANDREWS IN *THE LOVES OF A 'STAR!'*" The heartsick Wise finally broke his silence, and voiced his opinion that the latest treatment of his movie bordered on bad taste.

By July, the mutilated *Star!* and its doppelganger were out of circulation. Fox then hired a marketing research firm to better study the public and its relationship to Julie Andrews. The results were clear—give us another *Sound of Music*. But since *Star!* was the only available new product, Fox sought to remarket it yet again. New titles *Gertie Was a Lady* and *Those Were the Happy Times* were the finalists for domestic re-re-release, with the latter chosen. The poster artist of *The Sound of Music* devised an image of a beaming Andrews in a simple orange top, looking more like a freshly scrubbed milkmaid than the toast of international theater. She's carrying a basket of flowers, while surrounding her are lavish images of the film, and still more flowers. "Be Glad They still make pictures like this!" beseeches the ad, "When Everyone Was Singing A Happy Song . . . When A Girl Wasn't Afraid To Show Her Heart . . . When All The World Was This Lady's Stage . . ." Toward the bottom of the ad, in tiny lettering, are the words "Formerly entitled STAR!"

As president of the Gertrude Lawrence Memorial Foundation, powerful New York show business attorney Fanny Holtzmann took great interest in the film. "You can imagine our disappointment in the way *Star!* has been received and handled," Wise wrote to her. "For some unknown reason, there seems to have developed something of a resistance to it. At least, I've been told the company has been having problems with some of the exhibitors now that they are thinking of getting it into general release." Holtzmann was sympathetic and blamed it on distribution. A screening she witnessed on Long Island had exactly nine seats occupied. "We're all still reeling a bit from some of the poor reviews we received on the picture," Wise wrote to her. We "had some qualms about holding the world premiere in London and were terribly pleased and gratified with the reviews we received there. What happened to the film and the critics on the trip across the Atlantic God only knows."

The whole experience left Wise demoralized. "Some place down the line, the studio came to me a little hesitantly with a need, in their view, of trying to do something to salvage the film some way," he recalled. "They felt maybe the problem was the length. They thought that cutting some of the numbers, tightening it up, and making it considerably shorter, and perhaps even putting a new title on it, would change its fortunes at the box office. As the filmmaker, I was reluctant to do this because we worked hard to make it. Yet, when you make a film that cost as much as *Star!* did and it doesn't do business, you feel an obligation to let the company make an attempt to recoup the investment. So I gave my okay" Wise requested and was given the removal of "a Robert Wise Film" from the credits.

Running at 119 minutes without intermission, *Those Were the Happy Times* was not presented as irony, though the film touches on gross ambition, a cold heart, and emotional desolation. But no matter the version, Fox could not win. "The severest loss is the sense of style, which the Robert Wise-Saul Chaplin production once possessed," noted one of few reviews *Those Were the Happy Times* received. "It's now merely an excuse for an entertainment and cannot be even remotely construed as a psychological study of a star." Several production numbers were cut, and Robert Reed's presence was no more than a few hellos and good-byes. Wise disavowed the hatchet job, claiming he had no hand in it, since he did not have final cut. Nobody bought this sow's ear-silk purse method of movie distribution, and the film died a third death. *Those Were the Happy Times* appeared on *Variety's* weekly Top 50 grossing films list just once, at number 38 with a two-week revenue of $58,426. Perhaps the only person on record to have actually *seen* this amputated *Star!* was President Nixon, who screened it at his home in San Clemente, California.

"Gertrude Lawrence was a bitch," said Andrews in reviewing the disaster. "I suppose she was a strange choice as the subject of a movie." It was Richard Zanuck who spoke what many in the industry must have felt when perusing those grim figures in *Variety*. "*Star!* was the greatest puzzlement and disappointment in the seven years I've been here," he said. "It had me staying up at night. There are no guarantees anymore." The assumption that Andrews was the fail-safe bromide against sex and violence didn't work, especially in a film that toys with the causes of her immense popularity. "Someone once said that the worst thing that ever happened to this particular studio was that they made *The Sound of Music*," said Fox production executive Stan Hough. "Obviously, if there's something better than one *Sound of Music*, it's two Sounds of Music. Or three. Or four. Which brings us to *Star!* and *Dolittle*." With *Hello, Dolly!* in the wings, and *Paint Your Wagon, Goodbye, Mr. Chips*, and *Darling Lili* accumulating unholy expenses at other studios, one could suppose that Zanuck, Hough, and the rest were experiencing something akin to white-knuckled terror.

William Wolf of *Cue* offered a thoughtful assessment of current conditions:

> Today we smile nostalgically at those outdated musicals of the 1930s and '40s. With a little imagination, we can look ahead to the days when current musical blockbusters may seem just as campy. While there have been upheavals in the style and content of movies in the 1960s, musicals are still lagging far behind in the revolution. We have progressed from Busby Berkeley to *Oklahoma!* to *West Side Story* and beyond, but where is the equivalent of Jean-Luc Godard? . . . adventurous directors have not taken advantage in advances in movie technique to bring us into a new era of movie musicals. . . . I hope that one of these days adventurous young directors . . . with low budget but big ideas, come up with innovations that drastically shake up existing song-and-dance patterns. And maybe there won't even be an intermission.

CHAPTER 12

Delayed Adolescence

Even with the smash *West Side Story*, United Artists (UA) made only a limited commitment to musicals in the 1960s with two relatively modest adaptations of long titled Broadway hits: *A Funny Thing Happened on the Way to the Forum* and *How to Succeed in Business without Really Trying*. *Forum* was a burlesque of ancient Rome, with its opening number "Comedy Tonight" announcing the desire to deliver nothing more than fast-paced laughs. Director Richard Lester translated the live shenanigans into a film of equivalent manic energy, with aging farceurs competing with his compulsive use of zooms and handheld cameras. Lester's choice to cut away constantly supplies the movie with a good amount of its nervousness, but squelches the funny in *A Funny Thing*. Perhaps the attention deficit editing is covering something up, but what exactly? Bad acting? Incompetent dancing? Unfulfilled humor? Lester steals the movie from his actors, including Zero Mostel and Buster Keaton, exercising his directorial rights to cut away when he damn well pleases. Opening as a standard release in October of 1966, *Forum* suffered from the trying-too-hard syndrome that later cursed Mel Brooks. Once again a stage hit misses its mark on screen. Maybe it is the one-dimensionality of the characters, or the tiresome cascade of jokes about Roman bosoms, or Lester's over-active camera.

Unlike *Forum*, UA's other mid-sized musical came pre-packaged from Broadway. *How to Succeed in Business without Really Trying* was a 1962 smash that found delight in skewering corporate life. There was the smiling putdown of alma mater loyalty, the inviolate coffee break, husband-hungry secretary, board room incompetence, and Horatio Alger–style ambition, all served on a full plate of isms— nepotism, sexism, ageism, and lookism. Under the Mirisch Corporation, the production company behind *West Side Story*, *How to Succeed* duplicated its Broadway version with uncommon fidelity. Opening in March of 1967 at the Radio City Music Hall as a standard release, it reengaged Robert Morse as J. Pierpont Finch, the grinning sprite who slyly slithers his way up the ladder. Also back was the ever-pompous Rudy Vallee as the boss J. B. Biggley, the comic foil so self-important he doesn't see the mockery and obsequiousness all around him. *How to Succeed*'s bright pastel vision of Manhattan is more *Touch of Mink* than *West Side Story*, which suits its easy disposition and spirit of entertainment. The farce works better than in *Forum*, here rooted in a more familiar world. But with a pared down treatment, *How to Succeed* suffered from the opposite problem, with shots and editing that are a bit sluggish. *How to Succeed* feels more like an archival record than a cinematic rendering. Even so, neither it nor *Forum* brought substantial profits or cracked the top 20.

United Artists was absorbed by Bank of America through its San Francisco–based Transamerica insurance company subsidiary in 1967, but there were few changes in administration or creative control. Transamerica left UA senior management in place to navigate its distinct business model. UA had no studio, but rather made films through independent producers. "It was a philosophy that made us different," said UA president David Picker. "With no studio overhead, we had the ability to give filmmakers creative control as long as they abide the script, budget, and schedule. We didn't look at dailies—filmmakers' only obligation was to make the best film possible."

From his large Manhattan headquarters, Arthur Krim was the studio's defining authority. The former entertainment lawyer had been chairman of UA since 1951 but had also cultivated a place for himself in politics as finance chairman of the Democratic Party. Photos of world leaders, of Kennedy, Johnson, Hubert Humphrey, and Golda Meir, lined his walls. "There was a feeling of power that I used to get when visiting his office," said Norman Jewison, who directed several hits for UA. "You knew he was the head of perhaps the biggest film distribution company in the world. He surrounded himself with bright and creative people, like Arnold Picker in foreign distribution and Gabe Sumner in advertising. He loved talking ideas, and would get excited about a project. He was also a great Democrat, and believed that films had something to say and should be taken seriously. We were allowed to express ourselves, and he liked things that were a bit daring."

In keeping with its unique ideology, UA didn't have a master plan for musicals but rather bought them on individual merit. It bought the film rights to two huge stage hits, *Fiddler on the Roof* and *Man of La Mancha*, but both were a few years away from production. The current object of UA's enthusiasm, *Chitty Chitty Bang Bang*, was a property approached with great calculation. Even though Disney failed to repeat the success of *Mary Poppins* with *The Happiest Millionaire*, UA was convinced it could do the job with *Chitty Chitty Bang Bang*. Superficially, it resembles a lavish Disney movie of the period, but under the surface lurked James Bond. UA had made a killing in franchising the secret super agent, and its producer Albert R. Broccoli, screenwriter Roald Dahl, and designer Ken Adam were reunited for *Chitty*. Adam was overjoyed at the new assignment. "After five years of Agent 007, the change in setting was incredibly refreshing," he said.

Chitty aspired to reunite the *Poppins* team of Julie Andrews and Dick Van Dyke with the Sherman Brothers composing. When Andrews passed, UA found a facsimile in contralto Sally Ann Howes. Like Andrews, she had a starchy, chipper demeanor, a comfortably pretty face, and a lovely singing voice. To burnish her credentials as another Julie Andrews, she had even played *My Fair Lady*'s Eliza Doolittle on stage. Van Dyke was none too interested until his guarantee topped $1 million. He won assurance that he would not supply an English accent, thus avoiding the embarrassment suffered for his bastard Cockney in *Mary Poppins*.

Chitty Chitty Bang Bang is the onomatopoetic sounds of a magical car that can fly and float, and will save the world from evildoers. Devised by "The Dithering Tinkerer" Rowland Emett of Sussex with the cooperation of Ford Motors, the two-ton contraption was made of red and white cedar resembling a metal-finished boat. Director Ken Hughes sought a wholesale invention of the Ian Fleming source novel. Characters and plot are radically altered. Crazy lovable inventor Caractacus Pott (Van Dyke) is still there, as are his two children. Gone is his wife, but added are his father and a candy factory heiress named Truly Scrumptious (Howes). The bad guy is no longer Joe the Monster, but Baron Bomburst, ruler of Vulgaria. The book is set in contemporary England, the movie in Edwardian times, better to evoke *Mary Poppins*, while the basic scenario is redolent of *Hansel and Gretel*. Billed as "the most expensive musical ever filmed outside of Hollywood," *Chitty* had a six-month shooting schedule beginning at Pinewood in London then moving to rural locations in England, Bavaria, and France.

"The Old Bamboo" number was a strenuous modernization of Morris Dancing, and resulted in Van Dyke pulling a hamstring during rehearsals. "It's only three minutes long but it says exactly what it's supposed to say," recalled choreographer Marc Breaux, yet another *Poppins* alumnus working on *Chitty*. "Dick Van Dyke didn't know how to dance, but we thought if he did it one or two beats later than anyone else, it would work out." The scene was shot when Van Dyke's leg was healed and became a highlight of the film. Van Dyke had a strong relationship with Breaux and co-choreographer Dee Dee Wood extending back to *Poppins*. At an awards ceremony years later, he said, "One of them was a real work horse, but I can't tell you which one 'cause she'll kill me!"

The Shermans fashioned themselves as the champions of family entertainment, avoiding "leericks" with "double meanings and inside words intended to make a minority snigger," said brother Robert. "We've never written a line that we would be ashamed to have our parents or our children hear. The smut being worked into the lyrics of many popular songs today is bad for the kids who listen to them, bad for the writers . . . [and] bad for the publishers except those out for an occasional quick dollar and nothing else."

Native Liverpudlian director Ken Hughes dressed in Chelsea boots and threads from Carnaby Street, and sounded light years away from the Sherman Brothers. He enjoyed a lunchtime cocktail at the Pinewood dining room, swore freely, and hero-worshipped the incendiary comic Lenny Bruce. Hughes's expletives were often in earshot of the child actors, which offended Van Dyke, who knew Hughes was wrong for the job when he rewrote portions of Roald Dahl's script. "Who rewrote Roald Dahl?" asked an incredulous Van Dyke. "Roald Dahl is supposed t'be *Chitty*'s screenwriter," explained Hughes. "Well, you 'aven't seen him around 'ere, 'ave you? No. I had to rewrite the whole bleedin' scenario. Did y'know Lenny Bruce? Was a mate a' mine, poor bloke. 'E's my idol. Changed my entire sense of humor. I'd like to write like 'e did." Dee Dee Wood remembered, "Ken Hughes wore the tightest jeans I've ever seen on a man—white jeans, and he was skinny. Sometime the top button would be open. He wasn't very easy. He was opinionated before you had a chance to discuss your own view of something."

UA went all out for *Chitty*. In a single week, the studio spent $620,000 in what advertising executive Gabe Sumner described as "the first [time] we or any other motion picture company have done a campaign this size this far in advance of a motion picture." Was UA nervous that *Chitty*'s scheduled release was nestled between *Finian's Rainbow, Funny Girl, Star!*, and the big upcoming British musical *Oliver!*? "We feel it is directed at *The Sound of Music* audience and we couldn't begin to sell too early—there was no concept of too early," said Sumner. There were monthly newspaper ads, with another 25 roadshow markets targeted for a sales push after Labor Day. UA ran a precious ad campaign, with copy like "the most fantasmagorical musical entertainment in the history of everything!" At the heart of UA's *Chitty* push was a roadshow release strategy. The decision to roadshow certain films, such as *West Side Story* and *My Fair Lady*, were made because they were "legit properties with big titles," said David Picker. In the case of *Chitty*, however, "It was a marketing plan to establish the size and potential of the audience. It's hardly a landmark movie."

Chitty opened on the West Coast at Grauman's Chinese Theater, inaugural location for *Mary Poppins* and *The Happiest Millionaire*. The premiere was a benefit for Boys Clubs of America, with Bob Hope serving as the honorary chairman. At the New York premiere, residents of four orphanages arrived by chartered buses to Nathan's Famous at Times Square, where they dined on hot dogs washed down with grape juice and root beer. Eventually the children were shuttled off, while the first nighters moved to a downstairs bar, where they enjoyed jumbo squab stuffed with wild rice and chicken livers.

When it came time to access *Chitty*'s artistic merit, the consensus was not positive. *Chitty* is stingy with fantasy, withholding the car's magical abilities until after the intermission when children are restless and cranky. And when the car flies at last, the results are appalling, with its rough-edged blue screen and crude matte paintings. Howes offers a lovely, dignified presence while sounding more like Jeanette MacDonald than Julie Andrews, but Van Dyke seems a bit disengaged from what's happening around him. The hit-making Shermans fell on their batons this time with 11 songs that have "all the rich melodic variety of an automobile horn" according to *Time*. They often relied on Seussian nonsense words to meet the demands of rhyming and meter. Some found their lyrics to be brilliantly simple. Others just found them to be simple. The title song was a fun-house mirror distortion of "Old MacDonald Had a Farm" with groaners such as *"Bang Bang Chitty Chitty Bang Bang, our fine four fendered friend"* and *"Chitty Chitty Bang Bang . . . You're uncategorical; a fuel-burning oracle, a Fantasmagorical machine!"* Other lyrics sound like TV commercial jingles: *"Toot Sweets! Toot Sweets! The candies you whistle; the whistles you eat!"*

As with *Half a Sixpence*, *Chitty* gingerly flirts with class conflicts, but the main problem is this film's primary fantasy object. Those of us who find cars little more than large appliances are baffled by zoomorphizing a fetish object of pistons, running boards, chrome, and leather. Even when providing a cook's tour of Neuschwanstein, Emett's invention is just a car, much like the patients in *Doctor Dolittle* are just animals. Whimsical movies call for whimsy, something the makers of *Dolittle* and *Chitty* forgot.

UA spent $12 million on a film that had but one clear prototype in audience appeal—*Mary Poppins*. But *Poppins* cost $5 million. And four years was a lifetime in the 1960s. In *Chitty*, a kidnapper entices hungry children into a cage with promises of candy, slams the bars shut, and races out of town to the horror of helpless onlookers. It was the stuff of pediatric nightmares. Even the primary selling point, the car, got upstaged that season. Turns out 1968 audiences wanted to be amused by a contemporary car, and Disney gave it to them. *The Love Bug* was released one week after *Chitty* and became one of the film rental champions of the year, proving that family films still have widespread appeal if driven properly. While UA sought to better Disney with a silly car movie, Disney turned the tables. *Chitty* made a profit, but it was no *Love Bug*. UA's reserve seat pretensions were outrun by Disney's modest comedy about a trick Volkswagen. Millions owned and loved their compact, fuel-efficient Beetles and delighted in seeing them so affectionately portrayed on screen. *That* was the ride America wanted to take.

UA tripped with *Chitty*, but Columbia triumphed with musicals in 1968, first with *Funny Girl*, then *Oliver! Oliver Twist*, the Charles Dickens tale of an orphan boy adrift in Victorian London, has a long history at the movies. It had been filmed six times before David Lean's most famous version from 1948. When a stage musical called *Oliver!* opened in London in 1960, it became the longest-running musical in West End history. Though its run on Broadway was less distinguished, it logged a respectable 774 performances. Given the Great Sixties Musical Buying Frenzy, a film adaptation was all but inevitable.

England's Romulus Films, headed by producer John Woolf, had brought several worthy titles to movie theaters in the 1950s, including *The African Queen*, *Moulin Rouge*, and *Room at the Top*, but they had never made a musical. When Woolf heard that Sir Carol Reed was considering *Oliver!*, he bought it, and commissioned Reed to direct. Reed had an affinity for directing children, and his postwar dramas (*The Third Man, The Fallen Idol*) are suffused with a sensitive eye for the horrible beauty of wet, dark city streets. But he had virtually zero experience with musicals, and his career of late was in trouble. His recent foray into widescreen extravaganza, *The Agony and the Ecstasy*, was mostly the former.

None of this concerned Woolf, who packaged a film with the finest behind-the-camera talent available. Production designer John Box (*Lawrence of Arabia, Doctor Zhivago*), cinematographer Oswald Morris (*Moulin Rouge, The Taming of the Shrew*), and costumer Phyllis Dalton (*Lawrence of Arabia, Doctor Zhivago*) were all British and among the best in the business, but they, like Reed, had limited familiarity with musicals. Enter two Americans: choreographer Oona White (*Bye Bye Birdie, The Music Man*) and musical director John Green, whose resumé was studded with classic MGM musicals. White and Green's duties were substantial, as roughly a quarter of *Oliver!* would be consumed with singing and dancing. Reed savored the challenge. "I discovered that in a big musical the man who directs it is far more dependent on other people than in a straight film," he said. "He has to learn from experts and consult with them all the time, he has none of the autonomy he's accustomed to exercise in a non-musical subject."

Woolf's casting ideas veered toward the bizarre. He initially wanted Elizabeth Taylor and Richard Burton as Nancy and Sikes, with Laurence Harvey as lovable scoundrel and petty thief Fagin. He also considered Peter O'Toole as Fagin and Sean Connery as Sikes, ignoring musical credentials in the process. Reed helped Woolf reject fame as a priority for casting. "I never visualized *Oliver!* as a show dominated by a single big star," said Reed. "In fact, there are seven very good parts." In the end, not a single marquee name was hired. As Nancy, Shani Wallis's fame was limited to the London stage. As Sikes, Oliver Reed's film career was largely in front of him. Ron Moody of the original London production was cast as Fagin, and angelic Mark Lester took the title role from an audition of 2,000 boys.

Only the American film industry had spent great amounts of money to date on musicals. "Generally speaking, the attitude of the producers toward the big British musicals has always been: 'It hasn't been done yet, it's not been proved,'" said Reed. "Now it looks as if that attitude is changing." While *Half a Sixpence, Chitty Chitty Bang Bang*, and *Goodbye, Mr. Chips* were cast and shot in England, they were largely the products of American money. Not *Oliver!* Woolf insisted this quintessentially English tale be financed, cast, and shot in England.

John Box's designs for London were dank and fetid, and like nothing ever seen in a musical. He was an architect by training, and it showed. This was far from the confectioner's imaginings of London as was *Mary Poppins* or *My Fair Lady*. A crew of 350 nicknamed "Box's Army" constructed a warren of backstreets, and the results were so fantastic that they seem to come with the smell of rotting fish, baking bread, and horseshit. As with so many high-stakes musicals of the day, *Oliver!* pulled out the stops, believing bigger was better. Bloomsbury Square,

Titular star Mark Lester is directed by Carol Reed in *Oliver!*, with the ceiling, lights, and scaffolding visible at the cavernous Shepperton Studios in Surrey, England. From the collection of Photofest.

setting for the impressive "Who Will Buy" number, was built from the ground up. As the biggest film musical ever made in England, it was three movies in one: the intimate drama of kind Nancy and wicked Sikes, the crowd pleaser with production numbers like "Consider Yourself," and the adventure tale of young Oliver and his fellow urchins as ruled over by Fagin.

A $10 million, *Oliver!* opened at the Loew's State One in its newly remodeled, one thousand seat theater both deep and wide, done in modern shades of warm colors. What a busy film upon the screen! Reed crowded his shots with all manner of singing and dancing 1830s street types—bobbies, fishmongers, milkmaids, butchers, newsboys, and chimney sweeps. Then he faced a problem. The incongruity of a musical set amid the open sore of London's ghettos became stultifying at 153 minutes. Though Renata Adler of the *New York Times* may have been harsh in reviewing *Oliver!* as a "cast iron pastry," the description has a certain aptness. If your taste runs toward butter, clotted cream, and lemon curd, then *Oliver!* is your ticket. The beginning offers an orgy of music, nearly 20 minutes pass before any extended dialogue is heard. "Food Glorious Food" immediately established the milieu of an old London orphanage and the contrasting grim surroundings lightened by sweetly singing boys. Mark Lester was the very essence of the seraphic waif; he brought an innocence and longing for familial love that gave the film its emotional weight. But Reed blinks on various harsh truths in the story, including child abuse and Nancy's murder. The ending is a mess. Reed stages a brutal denouement evoking Frankenstein, then a quick reunion with Oliver and his benefactor, followed by a perfunctory, repetitious credit roll. The last minutes of *Oliver!* look like Carol Reed was in a hurry to go home.

Oliver! has a fine score with nary a clunker to be heard. There is no denying the welcome infectiousness of "Food Glorious Food," "Who Will Buy," "You've Got to Pick a Pocket or Two," "Om-pah-pah," "I'd Do Anything," the torchy power of "As Long as He Needs Me," or the plaintiff strains of "Where Is Love" and "Boy for Sale." They are all executed with loving care, but once again, the assets are equivocal. Many of the lyrics are insipid, putting forth obvious emotions. Once heard and absorbed, there is nothing more to be gleaned from a repeat visit, a rather surprising reduction considering the rich darkness of the novel.

Oliver!'s deficits are more obvious today, and indeed the film looks razor close to being an aesthetic disaster to put alongside the others of the late '60s. The mod hairstyles of the female chorus immediately date it to 1968, and White's choreography isn't very exciting. With Reed's blessing, loose-jointed marionette Ron Moody does everything in his power to steal the film, acting primarily with his fingers and teeth. Oliver Reed, Carol Reed's nephew, offered an alternative face of sin. While Moody was the most lovable pimp-pickpocket-child racketeer the world has ever seen, Reed was an easy-to-loathe kidnapper and murderer, skulking about Box's sets with dead-eyed menace. Shari Wallis as the spitfire guttersnipe, conflicted by her love for Sikes and her impulse to protect Oliver, has a zesty presence, belting out her songs with lung power most welcome after the underfed vocals of recent musicals.

The *London Times* published a withering review of *Oliver!*, bemoaning its stance between David Lean's harsher vision and the sugarcoating of a modern musical. Each song "is introduced with a grinding gear change (what are those girls doing prancing around like that? Ah, it must be a number coming on), and ends in midair, as though expecting a storm of applause. . . . White's monotonous choreography [works] its way relentlessly through every knees-up Cockney cliché." Quite a few more onlookers loved *Oliver!* Unlike so many musicals of late, it did not come freeze-dried and hermetically sealed. This one feeds on its own energy and teems with the richness of life. "*Oliver!* is not put together like TV commercials and it doesn't have a psychedelic look or a rock beat, but neither is it rotting on the screen, like *My Fair Lady*," said Pauline Kael. And there are moments, "Boy for Sale" most clearly, when Reed's treatment is in harmony with the ungodly realities of Victorian workhouses. But for all its merits, *Oliver!* is a movie of surprising artistic timidity. Something about the scale of this movie relative to its story is off. It's the feel-good child abuse musical of the year! *The Village Voice* made loud wounded animal noises. "*Oliver!* is not merely unfaithful to Dickens but completely inappropriate as well. First of all, [composer] Lionel Bart seems to belong to that Broadway-West End school of thought that believes a musical can be made of anything from *The Decameron* to *Das Kapital*. . . . I can't understand the raves for the film." *Oliver!* was ultimately a triumph of marketing, in that Romulus Films and Columbia, its American distributor, convinced a great many people that an array of human miseries can make for good-time family entertainment if accompanied by snappy tunes. It received a G rating (for general audiences) in both the United Kingdom and the United States.

The popularity of *Funny Girl* and now *Oliver!* boosted confidence in the roadshow musical for one more blast of activity. *Oliver!*, one of the last musicals to manufacture fantasy from vast amounts of wood, plaster, and paint, ran more than a year at the Odeon Leicester Square in the West End. It ran in New York, Boston, and Chicago for 36 weeks, and nearly that long in San Francisco and Washington, D.C. Unlike many other musicals, *Oliver!* translated well overseas. It was a triumph at the Moscow Film Festival, while the also current *2001: A Space Odyssey* received a cool reception. But *Oliver!* disappointed on two fronts. It failed to sustain a revival of Reed's career, and the British film musical, taking its cue from Hollywood, flickered out. Critic Vincent Canby overheard one woman at the preview offer faint praise. "It's better than *Half a Sixpence*," she said to her companion as they exited the theater. *Oliver!* was good enough to renew faith in the British-made book musical, with or without American financial backing. But that faith was short-lived.

By the late 1960s, Universal had a vice grip on mediocrity and box office failure. A number of directors and stars were squandered there, while literate fare such as *Fahrenheit 451* and *Isadora* tanked. Universal's top-earning feature of 1968 was *The Secret War of Harry Frigg*, which ranked 32 on *Variety*'s year-end rental income summary. Lew Wasserman, head of parent company Music Corporation of America (MCA), was not overly concerned, seeing high revenues in other corporate interests and arguing that a movie will earn back its money with

TV airings. He bristled at the criticism his film wing elicited, but admitted "That's one area where all companies, including ours, could stand improvement. Many good films never penetrate the market."

When Universal reported a $30 million loss in 1968, and Westinghouse was considering a takeover, Wasserman rethought his movie empire. Since *Thoroughly Modern Millie* had been a hit, he made the unoriginal conclusion that another roadshow would help finances. He invested in Broadway's *Sweet Charity* and assigned Ross Hunter, the man who packaged *Millie*, to produce. It had been a triumph for director-choreographer Bob Fosse and wife-star Gwen Verdon. It came from an unlikely source: Federico Fellini's 1957 Oscar-winning *Nights of Cabiria*. Fellini's drama was an unvarnished look at the life of a Roman street-walker, played with tremulous feeling by his wife, the strange girl-woman Giulietta Masina. Where Fellini used his unmistakable style to coax his wife to brilliance, Fosse did likewise. His style, all hyper-extended backs, snapping fingers, head and shoulder drops, and thrust hips, showcased Verdon unerringly well. *Sweet Charity* was blessed with highly talented people, including composer Cy Coleman, lyricist Dorothy Fields, and book writer Neil Simon. But the story is limited, and as written, Charity's neediness was grating when it should have been poignant. The production worked largely because of Verdon, who danced like a firecracker but had the singing voice of a little girl who has smoked too many cigarettes. The combination in one high-octane redhead was irresistible, and few Broadway stars endeared themselves like Verdon. But if audiences embraced her Charity whole-heartedly, the production itself was a qualified success. As Rome became New York, and streetwalkers became taxi dancers, the hard edges of Fellini's movie and Masina's heart-rending performance were lost in Fosse's razzamatazz style and Verdon's kewpie-doll-on-steroids delivery.

Shirley MacLaine recalled approaching Wasserman with the idea of Fosse as first-time film director with *Sweet Charity*, and her in the title role. She was neither a stellar dancer nor singer, but she could do both passably well. She was also established in the movies, while Verdon's audience was far more limited. Though Verdon owned Charity on stage, the casting of MacLaine was rational. Many of her screen performances specialized in sympathetic losers at love. To make the point clear, the full title of the film became *Sweet Charity: The Adventures of a Girl Who Wanted to Be Loved*.

Fosse was naturally high strung and infused with anxiety at directing *Sweet Charity* for the screen. "I remember feeling tentative, to say the least," he said, "but not wanting to communicate it. You can't express self-doubt in Hollywood; it's fatal." To prepare, he watched a succession of movie musical adaptations, but was unenthusiastic. "Musicals which are fun and games straight through don't seem to hook me," he said. In adopting his style to film, he found inspiration for freeze frames, zooms, and fades in the nervous, contemporary energy of non-musicals *The Graduate*, *Petulia*, and *Charlie Bubbles*. He also wandered through empty sound stages in search of ideas. Screenwriter Peter Stone, who had won an Oscar for the 1964 comedy *Father Goose*, was intrigued with adapting a straight film into a stage musical, then back into a film, this time as a musical. Like Fosse, Stone found inspiration in his environment. "Not only did [Universal] look like the old days," he said, "but it was the last of the studios to stick with the star system, and so it really felt like the old days." Fosse biographer Martin Gottfried set the scene:

> Each morning, [Stone] would bring his script to Bob's office, which was half of a bungalow. Most of the directors, writers, and stars were given such cottages, two offices with a common porch, set back on secluded stretches of lawn, shaded by palm trees, and spaced comfortably along winding lanes. To complete this idyllic picture, squirrels scampered across the lawns as if stocked there like bass in a lake. The studio provided electric carts to transport the actors, directors, and writers from these bungalows to the sound stages, and on any given morning, the many contract people at Universal could be seen on star parade—Marlon Brando, Paul Newman, Anthony Perkins, Tony Curtis, Alfred Hitchcock, and the superstars of the studio, Rock Hudson and Doris Day—all perched on their little electric carts, gliding in commonplace celebrity along the curving lanes beneath the palm trees, breezily shooing squirrels from their paths as if they were in a Walt Disney cartoon.

Gwen Verdon was reportedly disappointed at losing the film, but that's not what MacLaine remembered. "She suggested I do the part on the screen," wrote MacLaine in her memoirs. Once cast, MacLaine was gracious enough to acknowledge Verdon's contributions to the challenging Fosse aesthetic. "Gwen was there for me," she said, "helping me with a role she must have privately coveted for herself. She coached me in wily ways to execute Bob's steps without throwing myself off balance. . . . She could show me how to wrap my body around a move that belonged to the language of another planet—the Fosse planet." Fosse offered a golf clap to MacLaine, finding her "a pleasant girl with red hair and freckles, very willing, with a kind of circus in her face." She worked hard, going into cardiovascular training even while fighting a root canal infection. "What she lacks for not keeping up with her dancing she makes up in her enthusiasm and drive," said Fosse.

In preparation, MacLaine and her onscreen chums Paula Kelly and Chita Rivera intended to read the script together. Instead, they sat in a dressing room and got stoned. "It was much more valuable for the spirit of the picture than if we read the script 20 times," said MacLaine. Maybe so. The three display an obvious onscreen rapport, attacking their 1930s-type backstage wisecracks as if they were newly coined. Question: "Is it flirting when someone kisses your hand?" Answer:

"Depends where your hand is at the time." Charity and her pals may wisecrack, but Fosse and Stone made sure they weren't hookers. They were taxi dancers, cutting a rug at $6.50 an hour. They'll take a cad to bed, but only if the mood is right. And poor Charity, like Cabiria before her, can't help but fall in love with the wrong men. Right about now Fosse and Stone could have asked a few questions. Is not the co-dependent Cabiria by way of Charity all wrong for 1969? Charity's woeful psychology and low self-esteem are common enough, but do they have the makings of a decent film musical heroine? This was the same year Gloria Steinem came to national attention, and second-wave feminism was rising.

Ross Hunter bowed out as producer early on, apparently because his patented glossy vision clashed with Fosse's plans. The exact reason for his departure was not made public. Maybe it had to do with a falling out between Hunter and Wasserman—something about Hunter claiming he saved Wasserman from getting canned. "My decision was made without rancor and with best interests of the picture in mind," said Hunter to the press. He only hinted at "irreconcilable differences" with Fosse. "We are exceedingly sorry that Ross has decided to disassociate himself from *Sweet Charity*," said Wasserman. "He will be most difficult to replace." He was actually quite easy to replace. Stalwart Universal producer Robert Arthur stepped in and oversaw the film to its release.

Sweet Charity took seven months to write, cast, rehearse, and shoot, with 12 weeks devoted to location filming in New York. "I'm a Brass Band" was a logistical horror, with problems of crowd control and only 20 minutes of available sunlight in the canyons of Wall Street. Back at the Universal lot, Edith Head oversaw costumes, arrived at meetings by golf cart and wearing her familiar heavy dark glasses. She was nearing the end of her long career, and *Sweet Charity* did not excite her. "The Rhythm of Life" costumes were pulled from stock, and reportedly included one of Elizabeth Taylor's Cleopatra wigs on loan from Fox.

Fosse had an omnipresent viewfinder dangling from a cord around his neck, allowing him to see the movie through an artificial lens. "When I finished it," said Fosse, "I thought it was very, very good." So did Universal, which orchestrated a long, loud, ubiquitous campaign. *Charity* looked destined to be as big a hit as Universal's *Thoroughly Modern Millie* of two years ago, or rather, it could no longer afford to be simply so-so at the box office. With a 135-man crew, and 275 scenes, it ran $3 million over budget, approaching $10 million in cost. Just prior to its opening, Fosse said, "If it's a flop, I'll want to put my head in the oven. If it's a success, I'll want to keep it there." He was given sound advice from high-level talent agent David Begelman. "It's perfectly normal for you to be worried about your movie," he said. "It's your beautiful baby, and now the rest of the world is going to pass judgment on it. They're going to look at it this way and that, and say it's big or it's little or it's fat or it's skinny . . . "

"I know all that," Fosse said, "but it doesn't make me any less worried."

"Get to work on something else," Begelman suggested.

MacLaine had almost as much riding on *Charity*. Though she was an established star with three Oscar nominations, she had never carried a movie as she had this one. "It's the most demanding part I've ever played," she said, and blanched at suggestions that it was her last grab at the brass ring. "Several articles appeared in which producers claimed I'd had my chance to move into real stardom, but I'd muffed it," she said. "I wanted to muff them."

On March 17, 1969, MCA held its largest ever gathering of corporate executives to honor the opening of the $15 million, 21-story, 500 room Sheraton Universal Hotel in the San Fernando Valley. On March 29, ophthalmologist turned MCA chair Jules Stein and wife Doris hosted a buffet supper dance–black-tie gala for 600 after the premiere of *Sweet Charity* in the hotel's Baby Blue Ballroom. Under a sparkling crystal chandelier, hordes of international jet setters converged—the princess of Liechtenstein, tycoons, movie stars, jewel and dress designers, the curator of Versailles, a viscountess, investment bankers, Governor Reagan, department store owners, French aristocrats, and unaffiliated playboys. A band of kilted bagpipers played on the shuttles to the hotel, and an accordionist strolled the party. The hotel safe was bursting with so many jewels that one party-goer had to brave Disneyland wearing her 55-carat diamond ring. "It's the most wonderful weekend in the history of mankind," gushed a New York philanthropist and art collector. "You couldn't ask for a better party." MCA picked up the tax-deductible $250,000 bill. Curiously, reporting on the three-day gala did not include reactions to *Sweet Charity*, which got lost in the refracted light of gold bracelets and fine cutlery.

The *Charity* program book dared to open with "Just as Al Jolson's *The Jazz Singer* was *the* movie of the 1930s, *West Side Story* was *the* movie of the 1950s, *Sound of Music* was *the* movie of the 1960s, *Sweet Charity* is *the* musical with the pulse of today . . . destined to be the musical motion picture of the 1970s." Many begged to differ. "There is Shirley MacLaine in 70-millimeter close-up, singing and gesturing to beat the band," wrote the *Washington Post*. "In this gigantic image her face looks puffy, her skin looks dreadfully chalky, and even the smallest twitch or expression hits us with the subtlety of an artillery barrage." Opening credits of *Charity* include one shot of a billboard advertisement of *Doctor Dolittle*, one musical behemoth playing while another is being filmed.

Fosse was on the prowl for inventive, catchy visuals, at least when there's music in the air. *Sweet Charity* has a sense of fun and buoyancy altogether missing from *Camelot* or *Star!*. "Rich Man's Frug" is a catchy, gentle satire of hip fashion, while "The Rhythm of Life" sends up new age churches. *Charity* makes rare and welcome use of Chita Rivera in the movies, and she's got a smoky, sultry presence. "There's Gotta Be Something Better Than This" is a pulsing tribute to women's hope against an oppressive male-dominated world. But since there are no prostitutes in *Charity*, there are also no pimps and johns, and the message is wasted. Under the conditions Fosse established, entrapment doesn't fly.

Sweet Charity slams to a halt when a scene calls for action sans music, but Fosse can't resist the overkill. "I guess I had too many cinematic tricks in it," he said after the reviews were read and the low box office was tallied. "I was trying to be kind of flashy. That's a pitfall on your first film." Fosse's crazy camera denies the audience the pleasure of really seeing what appears to be genuinely fine dancing. "I'm a Brass Band" is a ready-made showstopper that falls short of classic status. "The Rhythm of Life" looks dropped in from another movie, and has no discernible relationship to the story. The rooftop number "There's Gotta Be Somethin' Better Than This," is blatantly derivative of Jerome Robbins's "America" from *West Side Story*. MacLaine does everything in her power to gain audience sympathy, but Charity remains an unlikable creature. Gene Shalit at *Look* called her performance a "Crinkly Smile through Tears" act, while Judith Crist at *New York* called Charity a "maltreated heart-of-gold ever-hopin' ever-lovin' ickeypoo character." In comparing MacLaine to Masina and Verdon, Rex Reed noted she, "simply gets by on mannerisms. . . . In MacLaine's portrayal, there's nothing left but elbows and toenails and Woolworth perfume."

Back it comes to the problem of what Charity does for a living. The Production Code was dead, nudity and adult themes were exploding on the screen, so why is *Sweet Charity* in retreat from the modern world? Musicals took their time growing up, but the genre was not immune to mature subjects. The recent musical Best Picture winners all made a commitment to adult stories: *Gigi*'s culture of the courtesan, *West Side Story*'s racism and gang violence, *My Fair Lady*'s class conflicts, and even *The Sound of Music*'s Nazis were more explicit than *Charity*'s annoyingly dysfunctional title character. Add to this murder and child abuse in *Oliver!*, and one may ask: By 1969, who but Universal Studios was afraid of an all-singing, all-dancing hooker?

Sweet Charity opened at the Rivoli on April Fools' Day. Vincent Canby used the premiere as an occasion to ponder the state of the film musical. "The cost of moviemaking—especially of musicals—has been staggering upward," he wrote. "This, in turn, has prompted a kind of gross inflation in the nitwit content of the movies themselves. A producer isn't likely to be experimental—or even to worry about a balance between style and content—with a movie that's going to cost at least $8 or $9 million anyways, and probably more. He's going to insure his investment by making something with the widest possible appeal, something that looks big and expensive and thus can be given the prestige of what the industry calls a 'roadshow' (reserve seat) engagement, a movie that isn't so much produced as it is stuffed, like a Christmas turkey." *Sweet Charity* isn't as bad as some of the recent ones, he felt, but it has no "dominating element." For Canby, the only musical films of late that gave any pleasure starred the Beatles. He even suggested a new form of film review. "Forget considerations of style and content and the peripheral comments about whether or not you were bored absolutely blue," he wrote. "Consider instead how much of the movie's production budget has been transformed to

For its second marketing campaign, Universal kept *Sweet Charity* as a roadshow while tarting up the ads with rampant allusions to sex and prostitution. From the collection of Photofest.

the screen—a critique designed to inform the general public as well as movie company stockholders who can then hold company management responsible for the debits. A critic could become a sort of screening room accountant, sitting there in the dark, abacus in lap, shifting little beads around and keeping a running total of expenses as they show up in the movie."

Variety proclaimed *Sweet Charity* "will start big, sustain itself over a lengthy hard ticket existence and will become one of the memorable artistic and commercial successes of this generation." That didn't happen. *Sweet Charity* did well in previews, then "it got to New York and it didn't make it," said Fosse. "You get mesmerized with the feeling that you've got a big glorious hit, when all the trades go crazy for it. . . . I guess I was deluding myself a little and thought it would be an enormous hit."

Charity was not a failure on the highest level. It was no *Star!* As its screenwriter Peter Stone said, "It may have been a flop, but it wasn't a *flopflop*. Let's say that compared to what Universal expected, it was a disappointment." That may be an understatement. "To a lot of people [at Universal], *Sweet Charity* seemed final proof that they should get the hell out of the movie business," said David Begelman. "The rift it caused at MCA was so serious that it almost changed the management of the company at the very top. . . . Bobby [Fosse] just made the best picture he knew how, but there was this whole scenario in the background." When *Charity* came limping back to Universal from its first run, marketers pulled a U-turn. "Men call her 'Sweet Charity'" ran in bold lettering across the top of the ad for showings in New York. Photos of the "Big Spender" lineup were captioned with "swingers all . . . men were their business," "they dig the way they live," and "meet the pros." The *Charity* sellers had discovered sex in advertising, but the general audience rating stayed.

Charity had one of the silliest intermissions in roadshow history, with Charity and a newfound nut case Oscar (John McMartin) growing increasingly anxious in a trapped elevator. That was cut from the general release, as was another 20 minutes. The end was remade as happy, with Charity and Oscar walking hand-in-hand. In any version, MacLaine and McMartin failed to cause sparks. "*Sweet Charity* is the kind of platinum clinker designed to send audiences flying in the opposite direction, toward the safety of their television sets," said Rex Reed. Saddled with an $80 million accumulated debt by 1969, Universal would rebound. On the immediate horizon was *Airport*, Ross Hunter's smash all-star soap opera in the sky that ushered in the disaster movies of the 1970s.

The Nixon Theatre in Pittsburgh is a barometer of the musical Law of Diminishing Returns. *The Sound of Music* played there for 106 weeks, *Thoroughly Modern Millie* for 30, *Finian's Rainbow* for seven, and *Sweet Charity* for six. *Charity* reaped a meager $4 million, and MacLaine went into a career slump. Fosse, however, was down but not out of the film musical business.

CHAPTER 13

The Paramount Bloodsuckers

As early as 1966, Julie Andrews was seen around town with director Blake Edwards while married to Tony Walton. "People will talk and gossip, and there's nothing you can do about that, so you might just as well go your own sweet way," she said of her situation. "I don't think anybody goes out of her way to be a scarlet woman, but then there is very little I can do about it if that's what they want to make of it." Her association with Edwards was bound to affect their careers. Their pet project, *Darling Lili, Or Where Were You the Night You Said You Shot Down Baron Von Richthofen?* had been announced for both of them since *Thoroughly Modern Millie* was in its original run. Billed as a farce with Andrews as a World War I singer-spy, it was the fourth picture in a long-term deal between Edwards and Paramount.

When Paramount committed to *Darling Lili*, it had the highest domestic box office of any quarter in its history. It was a veritable hit factory, with *The Odd Couple, Rosemary's Baby,* and *Romeo & Juliet* arriving as three fantastically effective and disparate works of popular filmmaking. The studio was also committed to big musicals. In addition to *Darling Lili*, there was *Paint Your Wagon* and *On a Clear Day You Can See Forever,* bought for $750,000 even though it lasted on Broadway a scant 280 performances. "*On a Clear Day You Can See Forever* came as part of [Charles] Bluhdorn's acquisition of Paramount," said dynamic young production executive Robert Evans. "An Alan Jay Lerner and Burton Lane Broadway musical with one great song in it—its title number. As we fervently searched for a brass-ring musical, it was brought out of the cobwebs when Barbra Streisand agreed to play the lead. . . . Did I like *On a Clear Day*? As close as Alan Lerner was to me, I couldn't help but tell him that I hated it. My feelings were equally blunt about not making it into a film. It didn't matter. Charlie was haunted by Streisand." After receiving declines from Gregory Peck, Frank Sinatra, and *Camelot*'s Richard Harris for the male lead, Paramount and Streisand settled on French entertainer Yves Montand, whose Gallic charm had yet to make a significant dent in America. Though *Funny Girl* had not yet opened, Streisand's success in movies was assumed, and she had real clout. For starters, she would *not* agree to Montand's top billing in French-speaking countries.

Vietnam meanwhile divided the United States as nothing had since the Civil War, and was attributed to momentous changes in artistic taste. Director Richard Lester believed that TV's ability to leap abruptly from news about Vietnam to Gomer Pyle to toothpaste ads expanded people's vision. As *Time* stated, the "growing mass audience has been prepared for change and experiment both by life and art. It has seen—and accepted—the questioning of moral traditions, the demythologizing of ideals, the pulverizing of esthetic principles in abstract painting, atonal music, and the experimental novel." Rapid change was generated by and for the young, but there was no agreement on what the widely used catchphrase "youth appeal" actually meant. *Variety* noted that it is not synonymous with "go-go music, dance, motorcycles, sex or defiance of barbers. There is a great deal more to 'youth appeal' than boy gangs or girl gangs, or beach parties, or psychedelic optical and sound effects." Paramount hit some kind of alchemy with its trio of hits, in particular the lusty retelling of *Romeo & Juliet* with its timely themes of generational conflict and senseless hatred. Perhaps *Paint Your Wagon, Darling Lili,* and *On a Clear Day,* each being made with deference to new sensibilities, would have the coveted youth appeal the industry sought to exploit. *Lili* was being fashioned for Andrews and Edwards with a generous if not outrageous $6 million budget, with $1.1 million plus 10 percent of the profits guaranteed for Andrews. Then Bluhdorn had *Lili's* investments packaged by Commonwealth United Corporation (CUC), a conglomerate that had tried but failed to acquire a controlling interest in the ailing MGM. CUC would pay production expenses on *Lili* and be guaranteed 50 percent of all profits from rentals.

Andrews had barely caught her breath with the completion of *Star!* before reporting for *Darling Lili.* Donald Brooks, costumer for *Star!,* was back, designing *only* 22 outfits for her this time. She was eager to do this film, not just because it meant working with Edwards, but because she saw it as a continued departure from the virginal nannies that had made her famous. "The secret of show business is to be surprising and not a cliché," she said. "I would like eventually to see myself as an all-rounder. I don't want to get typed."

Executive producer Owen Crump thought Ireland would be a fine place to shoot *Lili's* elaborate aerial sequences because of the verdant landscapes unspoiled by gas stations and shopping centers. The aviation facility at Weston Aerodrome in Leixlip was judged as ideal, in part because of the availability of a collection of World War I aircraft replicas. "The blue skies and green fields photograph beautifully," he said. However, he was to find out the hard way why so few films use Ireland as a location. An original schedule of 25 shooting days grew to 49, then 90, due to gray skies and rain. Since there were no plans to shoot in England, Dublin's Gaiety Theater doubled for an English theater in 1915. Five hundred Irish extras played London first nighters calmed during a Zeppelin raid by Lili's stoic rendition of "Pack Up Your Troubles in Your Old Kit Bag." But production expenses ballooned further when the company began its 46 shooting days scheduled in and around Paris before the Irish footage was completed.

Plan B had Andrews, costar Rock Hudson, and company shuttling back and forth between Ireland and France. But Plan B turned into Plan C when the French Uprising broke out in May, and the nation was paralyzed by a general strike. With Paris off limits, *Darling Lili* had to do an emergency landing in Brussels, but the shooting conditions were no better there. A "U.S. Go Home" banner was displayed on a street intended for the *Darling Lili* crew. Local extras were furious at their treatment, accusing Paramount of violating Belgian labor laws of overtime and working hours. Belgian Communists distributed leaflets reading, "Let us fight the exploiters of the world. U.S. exploiter of the peoples, go home." They were signed "The Extras of Paramount Motion Pictures."

The negative press for *Darling Lili* began early and would plague the movie past its premiere and initial run, and into the twenty-first century. From the beginning, there was the problem of articulating exactly what *Darling Lili* was. As director, writer, and producer, Edwards conceived it as a comedy-adventure with music, while Crump called it a chic comedy with an Ernst Lubitsch touch. "It's not really a musical, it's a story with music in it," said Edwards. The only consistent message was that *Darling Lili* was not—repeat not—a musical, 10 musical numbers notwithstanding. With fuzzy uncertainty, the press called it some form of comedy-romance-melodrama-non-musical-musical set in World War I. Word was also trickling out that it was in deep trouble. Months into production, the company was still waiting for the Irish weather to cooperate at a cost of about $70,000 per day. Edwards could wait for clouds to part, but if they didn't, he shot the aerial sequences anyway. When the sun was shining, the company would have to wait for the clouds to return so the film would match, or at least approximate, already completed footage with overcast skies.

Edwards did not hesitate spending Paramount's and CUC's money on *Lili*, inciting Bluhdorn to visit the set to see why it was so costly. He arrived on one of those bright days when the cast and crew picnicked on a green hillside, waiting for the accursed sun to go away. The sight displeased him, and he was further incensed when his limo driver pointed to a huge castle on the hillside and said that's where Andrews and Edwards were living. To distance himself from this debacle in the making, Robert Evans called *Darling Lili* "the most flagrant misappropriation and waste of funds I've seen in my career. The primary reason the film went over budget was Edwards's drive to protect 'his lady'; Queen Elizabeth was never treated half as well! The extravagance was unbelievable. He was writing a love letter to his lady and Paramount paid for it." Paramount showered Andrews with the trapping of supreme stardom as much as Edwards, housing her in a $70,000 apartment when she was on the lot. Edwards was feeling the stress of resentment and possible failure. "I'd hate to be the first one to make a flop with Julie Andrews," he said. "Sometimes I wake up in a cold sweat." When the dismal returns on *Star!*

Director Blake Edwards with Julie Andrews between takes of the very expensive *Darling Lili*. From the collection of Photofest.

came in during the making of *Lili*, Edwards was hardly comforted by the potential of making the *second* flop with Julie Andrews. Ultimately, *Darling Lili* was about endless waiting even in a profession known for it. An unusually large number of camera failures necessitated many reshoots and cashing in a Fireman's Fund insurance settlement of nearly $1 million. In Paris, Rock Hudson perfected bridge and Jotto. In Brussels, he switched to solitaire.

"Sometimes we wait for days and days," Andrews told a visitor to the set.

"And how do you pass the time?" asked the visitor.

"We cry a lot," she said.

Lofting cost estimates approached $14 million, more than double the original budget. Edwards chalked it up to the dark arts. "You wouldn't believe it, but you name it and we had it," he said. "It was the weather, malfunctioning equipment, and a lot of other things. There's only one answer to it: we must have had a witch in the company." When not preoccupied with money, Edwards continued to deny *Lili* was a musical. "It's a comedy adventure with music," with Andrews doing "some very serious and heavy drama." He also corrected anyone who called the next Edwards-Andrews roadshow a musical. MGM was financing an adaptation of the Broadway musical *She Loves Me* for the two of them, and Edwards said it offered "a dramatic story with musical background." To further clarify, he informed "also there will be romance, the same as *Lili*." But, like *Lili* and unlike its stage predecessor, *She Loves Me* will *not* be a musical. At least that was the official word.

On a Clear Day You Can See Forever began rehearsals well into *Darling Lili*'s tortured production. Paramount wanted Vincente Minnelli to direct, and after Streisand met with him, she approved, while her people won her a $1 million paycheck in a $10 million movie. She found Minnelli more congenial than William Wyler or Gene Kelly. Wyler "doesn't like to be told what to do," said Minnelli, "but I have no such ego about such things. The important thing is to make the picture. Consequently, I listened to what Barbra suggested, and implemented some of her suggestions. I found her creative and bright, and we got along beautifully." Compared to *Darling Lili*, *On a Clear Day* was a paragon of thrift and efficiency. The bulk of the film was made in Los Angeles, with additional location shooting limited to New York City and the Royal Pavilion at Brighton. With Streisand and Minnelli purring, *On a Clear Day* began filming in January 1969 for a scheduled fall 1970 roadshow release. In tribute to her ego, Streisand drove the Paramount publicity department to distraction with her blanket rejection of photos, and ran up a $25,000 retouching bill. But, after all, stars are in the business of protecting their image.

The 1968 film awards began in the spring of 1969. Musicals were in the running, but there were no *Dolittle* shockers. Streisand won the Natalie Wood Award for Worst Actress for *Funny Girl*, while *Star!* was named one of The Ten Worst Movies of 1968 by the *Harvard Lampoon*. At the Golden Globes, *Oliver!* won Best Comedy or Musical Picture over *Finian's Rainbow* and *Funny Girl*, with *Star!* absent from the slate. Ron Moody's Fagin edged out Fred Astaire's Finian for Best Actor, Comedy or Musical, while Streisand took Best Actress over Julie Andrews and Petula Clark. *Star!*'s Daniel Massey took the Best Supporting Actor trophy. *Funny Girl* additionally won the "Best Written Musical" award from the Writers Guild of America in a field that pitted it against *Finian's Rainbow* and *Star!*

At the Academy Awards, *Funny Girl* and *Oliver!* vied for Best Picture, but Wyler failed to score a Best Director nomination. Streisand was up for Best Actress, but Andrews was overlooked. *Star!* was tapped for seven awards, the most prestigious being Best Supporting Actor for Daniel Massey's interpretation of Noël Coward. *Oliver!* dominated musicals, with 11 nominations, among them Director, Adapted Screenplay, and Actor (Ron Moody). Poor *Finian's Rainbow* was tapped for Scoring of a Musical Picture and Sound only, while *Chitty Chitty Bang Bang* garnered nothing more than a Best Song mention for its title tune.

On awards night, *Oliver!* gained momentum early on, winning statuettes for Art Direction, Sound, and Scoring of a Musical Picture. Though Moody lost Best

Actor to the upset winner Cliff Robertson for *Charly*, Carol Reed won Best Director. Once again he evoked the importance of collaboration and team building in *Oliver!*'s success. "Not having made a musical before," he said upon accepting, "you can imagine what I owe to other people." Ingrid Bergman dutifully read the list of Best Actress nominees, tore open the envelope, and exclaimed, "It's a tie!" The first announced winner was Katharine Hepburn for her ripe and wry turn as Eleanor of Aquitaine in *The Lion in Winter* opposite the future Mr. Chips, Peter O'Toole. She was absent that night, but the second winner, Barbra Streisand, was very much present in a see-through sequined pajama outfit to frighten the horses. She ascended the stage, and, visibly nervous, hoisted the Oscar aloft, looked at it, and said, "Hello, gorgeous," repeating her famous opening line from *Funny Girl*. Best Picture went to *Oliver!*, with producer John Woolf making a point of thanking the original composer Lionel Bart, "without whom we'd have no film at all." He gave no such courtesy mention to Charles Dickens. Once again, the Academy Awards became a snapshot of motion picture variety and social chasms widening. *Rosemary's Baby* and *2001: A Space Odyssey* age better than *Oliver!*, but neither was up for Best Picture. And though no one could know at the time, musical supremacy was really and truly over. It would be 34 years before another musical won Best Picture, and the number of nominees for the top award in that period could be counted on one hand.

Even successful roadshows were beginning to look iffy. By mid-1969, Columbia was posting a nearly 60 percent drop in earnings at the very time both *Funny Girl* and *Oliver!* were running in hard-ticket houses and amassing Oscars. "We're not playing for an immediate return," was one diplomatic executive's spin. "The roadshow is building us up for the general release. In the long run we'll be much better off." *Funny Girl* and *Oliver!* had so far appeared in 61 and 30 theaters, respectively. Now the open small–expand big strategy was riskier than ever, and there were more hidden benefits to general release. By the late 1960s, the distributor might get 80 to 85 percent of the box office in general release, but only 60 percent for hard ticket. Roadshows offered the possibility of eventual payoff, but in the new realities, studios could no longer afford delayed gratification. And when 10 roadshows were in theaters simultaneously, the risks were even greater. "The variations in yearly release patterns between hard ticket and general release films, coupled with the certain uncertainties of movie making, combine to bring added question marks into an industry already full of them," wrote the *New York Times*.

Three days after Streisand won her Oscar, she was on a plane back to New York to resume filming *On a Clear Day*. There was little rancor on the set; Streisand found Minnelli charming and calm. She was calmer, too, learning the art of occasional compromise was advantageous to her career. As with *Paint Your Wagon*, Paramount sought to make *On a Clear Day* "with it," and as such gave lip service to marijuana, parapsychology, and campus unrest. Back in New York, the film needed to stage a student riot, but schools kept refusing Paramount's request for filming, fearing real incitement. The University of Southern California said yes, but that required additional time and money to move the crew to Los Angeles. The company eventually shot at Occidental College in Los Angeles. The gaudy Royal Pavilion, location for George IV's assignations with his mistress, cost $75,000, not including the onscreen spread of capons, lobsters, and suckling pigs for another $35,000. When Minnelli yelled, "Cut!" the production designer added, "Don't eat any more!"

The CUC was meanwhile concerned about their investment in *Darling Lili*, and no wonder. Charles Bluhdorn hadn't even bothered to create a business plan for Paramount. A disclaiming proxy states, "There is no assurance that any films now in production will be completed, that any production now scheduled will be commenced, or that the cost of completing or acquiring any of its pictures, distribution rights, screen rights, or screenplays will be profitably recovered." Paramount's unchecked costs for *Darling Lili* drove CUC to take measures, especially when a fall 1969 release date was postponed to the spring of 1970, allowing Edwards more time to run up costs. Interest added to production expenses were rumored to approach a stratospheric $25 million. CUC finally decided that Paramount was not a reliable investment, and that *Darling Lili* was way too expensive. The terms of divesture were blurry to outsiders, but Paramount was left to pay for *Darling Lili* all by itself.

Paramount had another very expensive project nearer to release. A lot happened between Joshua Logan's surrender of *Paint Your Wagon* and the film's premiere, none of it conducive to a mood for musicals. Judy Garland died of a drug overdose in London at the age of 47. The Stonewall Rebellion in New York launched the modern gay rights movement. US Apollo 11 landed on the moon, and Neil Armstrong reported "one small step for a man, one giant leap for mankind." The Manson Gang murdered actress Sharon Tate and her unborn child in Los Angeles, and Richard Nixon ordered renewed bombing of North Vietnam.

Wagon star Lee Marvin was dispatched by Paramount on a cross-country press junket. He began in Houston "looking trim and hickory-hard, striding through the airport like a drill sergeant in Dacron," according to a *Time* reporter. Behind him were his press agent, manager, and local studio men toting luggage and handing out glossies. "Hey!" shouted a cab driver, planting his arm around Marvin's shoulder. "Where's your horse?"

"You see that," said Marvin's manager. "Everybody loves the guy. Not because he's a star, but because he's one of *them*."

For Logan, burnout and loss of control was all too reminiscent of *Camelot*. In facing the press, he used canned sentiment that he hoped would substitute for genuine enthusiasm, saying, "I think the film is particularly pertinent to young people of today. It's a praise of the rebellious America." When he attended a preview in Phoenix, he was pleasantly surprised at the audience reaction, but *Wagon* did not earn his pride. "I couldn't say anything about it," he recalled. "I just wanted to back away and disappear." Paddy Chayefsky had a similar response. He claimed only six pages of his original dialogue remained after Alan Jay Lerner's hatchet job.

Wagon followed the roadshow musical formula of saturation marketing, but with a difference. It galloped toward youth appeal wholeheartedly. Paramount reasoned that *Camelot, Doctor Dolittle,* and its own *Half a Sixpence* failed because they did not distinguish the consumers of new music and movies from the family audience. It was not musicals they rejected; it was *square* musicals they rejected. Peter Max, exemplar of psychedelic graphic art, created the film's commercial look. His finished product featured a wedding cake with Marvin, Clint Eastwood, and Jean Seberg on top. The ad line announced, "Ben and Pardner shared everything—even their wife!" Ben was "Anti-Establishment a century ago," according to *Wagon's* souvenir program, while the film "is actually as modern as this morning's hit tune. Like today, the characters who crowd the screen in this spectacular musical were individuals who did their own thing, who . . . could 'look civilization in the eye, and spit!'" There was the Nitty Gritty Dirt Band on the soundtrack, described in the program as "ultra-modern musically as any group performing today." Elsewhere the program copy goes sophomoric. "A hundred miners hung around the house just to watch a real live woman throw out the slop water!" it proclaims with "an assortment of comely young ladies from—gasp!—Paris." Most everyone saw right through the sham marketing. Polygamy might have evoked free love to some people, but traditional monogamy ruled the knee-jerk happy ending, making any progressive message from *Paint Your Wagon* as muddy as No Name City. *Wagon* offended the socially conscious with its tasteless extravagance. Michael Campus at CBS television observed, "Young people are saying that it's a crime to spend \$20 million on *Paint Your Wagon.* That amount could remake a city."

Logan remembered the opening night at Loew's State 2 in Manhattan as "agony" blown up to 70-millimeter in six-channel stereo. Paramount attempted to control marketing, but there was no avoiding the reviews. "It was an important picture until everyone saw it," sighed Logan. *Saturday Review* noted that "In casting the picture, Paramount seems to have made a special search for stars who can't sing." *The Hollywood Musical* author Ethan Mordden called it "The first all-talking, no-singing, no-dancing musical. . . . *Paint Your Wagon* became a film embarrassed to be a musical."

Seberg is a far cry from "The Puerto Rican Pepper Pot" that was Olga San Juan in the original. She gives no evidence of dancing, while a distracted, frightened look in her eyes goes deeper than her character. Her wan earnestness devolves into the impression of disinterest in the whole affair. Marvin is boozing, odoriferous, and altogether tiresome in his frizzled muttonchops and food-catching moustache, but Eastwood and Seberg combine to make sincere moments of tenderness. Marvin's extreme masculinity works best in performances of quiet, tightly coiled menace (*Point Blank*), and he loses much of his appeal when he slices the ham. But for all the tediousness, Lerner never publicly expressed regret in casting Marvin. His character "would look foolish if he sounded like Nelson Eddy doing 'The Indian Love Call,'" Lerner said. "I didn't want him to have a trained voice. Ben Rumson is a rough and tumble character who could sing a song in a rough and tumble manner." Lerner had a point. Damn if Marvin's rendition of "Wand'rin' Star" isn't affecting, and (faint praise) a highlight of the film. Accompanied by a harmonica and a 65-voice male chorus, it works because Marvin cuts the crap and acts exactly like a world-weary prospector should in a neorealist musical film. Over a classic Western clip-clop rhythm, he sings rather like a blender on puree, but his straight-ahead delivery enhances our understanding of Rumson and establishes plausibility for the film's conclusion. It lacks all vanity and that "get ready, folks—you're gonna love this" ingratiation that mars so many production numbers. Unexpected even by the optimists at Paramount, "Wand'rin' Star" became a minor hit, especially in the United Kingdom, and Marvin gave a command performance on *The Ed Sullivan Show*.

There are other musically effective moments amid all the punch-drunk nonsense. The opening credits ("I'm On My Way") are rousing, and Harve Presnell brings a melodious conviction to "They Call the Wind Maria." Eastwood's thin baritone barely pulls off "I Talk to the Trees" and Seberg's ballad "A Million Miles Away behind the Door" was undercut by dubbing. There is no Agnes DeMille for the dances, and "Gold Fever" is simply, purely, unredeemably bad. So, too, is the rollicking climax, the multi-million dollar collapse of No Name City. It's just custom-made contraptions disassembling on cue. All that money didn't even bring the art and craft of mechanical effects to a new level. Mass architectural destruction was much better executed in *San Francisco* three decades earlier.

Logan found no inspiration in Chayefsky's script. Plot, such as it is, evolves into something peculiarly similar to *Camelot*, with two men in love with the same woman. There is dignity amid the wreckage, the faint remnants of good intentions, high hopes, and the occasional wise judgment call discernible through the evergreen forest. There is a good spirit to *Wagon*'s lampoon of old-fashioned morals, as the Bible thumpers damn No Name City to hell. This being 1969, their efforts are played for laughs, like the last thing heard before the lights went out at the Production Code office: "Godless jaspers, freemasons, rosey-crucians, heathen emissaries from the dens of Babylon, boozers, gluttons, gamblers, harlots, fornicators!" What *Wagon* lacked in story it often made up in amiability.

The Production Code had been enforced since 1934, but its teeth were chipped and worn by the 1960s, with standards of film content and language slowly expanding over the decades. It had become a relic, while its governing board was granting more exceptions to previously taboo material. Filmmakers and distributors often ignored the Code and released their films without its seal of approval. By the mid-1960s, there were bare breasts in *The Pawnbroker*, shocking utterances such as "screw" and "hump the hostess" in *Who's Afraid of Virginia Woolf?*, an abortion plot line in *Alfie*, and open references to homosexuality in *The Fox* and *Reflections in a Golden Eye*. The perceived need to revise and respond was everywhere, and in late 1968, the Motion Picture Association of America (MPAA) finally scrapped the old Production Code and inaugurated a new ratings system. "The times, the mores, the kind of society we're living in has undergone a cataclysmic change," announced MPAA president Jack Valenti, "and we felt we had to show a concern for children and for parents and describe accurately the content of films so parents will know what they're taking their kids to see." Out came official MPAA wording: "G—suggested for general audiences. M—suggested for mature audiences (parental discretion advised). R—Restricted—Persons under 16 not admitted, unless accompanied by parent or adult guardian. X—Persons under 16 not admitted." It was ambiguous and interpretive, but it liberated film content by officially segmenting audiences. X-rated films like *The Killing of Sister George*, *Midnight Cowboy*, and later *A Clockwork Orange* could revel in adult material without restriction by censors or outraged parents.

Paramount attempted to secure a G rating for *Paint Your Wagon*, but the MPAA slapped an M on it instead. Studio executive vice-president Martin Davis appealed the decision, using *Sweet Charity* as a precedent. It did, after all, maintain its G rating despite a sexed-up ad campaign. In addition, Paramount avowed that *Paint Your Wagon* "realistically portrays the time period of the old West where moral standards were somewhat different than they are today, the treatment is in good taste, and the overall tone of the film is moral in intention and execution. It is a fine entertainment and is a welcome change from pictures portraying war, violence, drugs, and sex." In reviewing the film, the board noted polygamy, prostitution, and brothels, as well as the wedding night scene between Marvin and Seberg. His behavior amounts to attempted rape, avoided only by her pronouncements for respect. The message is decidedly mixed, as she speechifies while her breasts look ready to launch from their smothering bustier. Paramount tried hard to have it both ways, to be contemporary and progressive on one hand and general audience friendly on the other. The MPAA was not moved, and Paramount's appeal was defeated by a vote of 10 to 9.

Paint Your Wagon opened in 12 major American markets as the first musical rated for mature audiences. M or no M, Paramount advertised it as "the nation's top family attraction" in advance of holiday bookings, creating an apparent contrast to *Sweet Charity*. The two schemes point to a number of contradictions. Perhaps the industry was not ready to see musicals grow up and be unabashedly adult in design, and perhaps Universal and Paramount did not know how to sell their expensive products. The industry was reeling from uncertainty and record-breaking losses that mirror cultural schizophrenia. *Variety* editor Abel Green rightly said the motion picture market "has changed faster than its shrewdest showmen could anticipate. Hence what was right two or three years ago just has been outpaced by the moods and mores of the times."

Once he was ensconced in superstardom, Clint Eastwood assessed *Paint Your Wagon* as "a disaster. But it didn't have to be such an *expensive* disaster. We had jets flying everyone in and out of Oregon, helicopters to take the wives to location for lunch, crews of seven trucks, thousands of extras getting paid for doing nothing . . . $20 million down the drain and most of it doesn't even show on the screen!" What remains a mystery is *Wagon*'s net to its studio and exhibitors. Paramount never divulged exact figures but at one point announced a worldwide gross of about $14.5 million. That makes it a definitive flop. Lerner noted that *Wagon* was "resoundingly booed at home, with occasional exception, and resoundingly cheered abroad." Against all perceptions, he stated it grossed "a startlingly large sum of money." Marvin believed that the cost was $16.5 million, with some approximating losses at $10 million. "I've never known any subject that's as full of holes as how much a picture made or cost," said Logan. "Whatever they tell you is not true." Given such inexactitude, it could at least be said that *Wagon* would have been a moneymaker had its costs been kept under control. When it went into general release, it was trimmed by 30 minutes to provide a third screening per day. European versions omitted the songs except the unlikely hit "Wand'rin' Star." Despite the excising of songs from the prints bound for Europe, the soundtrack received a Golden Album by the Record Industry Association of America, with more than 1 million sold.

Beady-eyed Pauline Kael of *The New Yorker* used *Wagon* to lambaste the entire roadshow musical form. Giant musicals have "finally broken the back of the American film industry," she wrote. "There is almost no way—short of a miracle— that [*Paint Your Wagon*] can recover its costs, and although there are several other movies of this kind waiting to be released or to be completed, and at least one of them is even more expensive, it is highly unlikely that any new ones will be scheduled for production in the years to come, or, perhaps, ever." The studios continue a "rotting system in which mediocrity and skyrocketing costs work together to turn out films that would have a hard time making money even if they were good." Now they're "collapsing, but they're not being toppled over by competitors; they're so enervated that they're sinking of their budgetary weight." Decrying *Wagon*'s star casting, she went on to note:

> The producers have spent $20 million, and they haven't even developed a singing star for another picture. Their methods are practically suicidal; they make each picture as if it were the last. . . . If a show can't be done the way it was written in the first place—if it has to be brought up to date— isn't that because it wasn't really very good in the first place? . . . At the high-level conferences, they'll say, "If only we hadn't had all that production trouble, if it hadn't rained, if only we'd finished sooner, when the hippie movement was still big . . ." They'll explain the bind they're in by saying, "We got it out too late." They'll be wrong, because they couldn't

have made it with this picture last year or the year before or five years ago. There was never a right time for a picture that shifts around trying to find the secret of somebody else's success, yet that's the only kind of big picture the businessmen who now control the major studios really believe in.

As *Wagon* was in theaters, Paramount let go of nearly 150 employees, and closed branch offices in the Pacific Northwest and New England. Film production was down, and sound stages were used primarily for TV series. "Paramount Cuts to the Bone" headlined *The Hollywood Reporter*, noting the closure of its executive dining room and the dismissal of head porter Harold Wilson, who had been with the studio for 25 years. He received severance but no retirement. "We're not interested in feeding anyone's vanity," said Martin Davis. "We want to build our balance sheet with black numbers." Consistent with current Hollywood trend, Charles Bluhdorn's goal was to convert Paramount into a distribution and financing company while contracting independent producers to make movies. Davis liked the idea, noting that most profitable movies these days were made off lot. "The era of the majors, as we knew it in the so-called Golden Age of Hollywood, is over," he said. It was a raspberry to *Paint Your Wagon*, a production only a major studio could possibly bankroll.

CHAPTER 14

Goodbye, MGM

Even though Peter O'Toole, Petula Clark, and director Herbert Ross were on board, *Goodbye, Mr. Chips* still had trouble getting off the ground. The newly arrived Ross noted that film music was changing. Characters were less prone to break into song any more. Instead, actors kept their mouths shut rather than lip-synch to prerecordings. The effect was less artificial, with songs now seeming to spring from a character's thoughts. George Roy Hill used the effect in *Thoroughly Modern Millie*, as did Joshua Logan in *Camelot* and Claude Lelouch in the French import *A Man and a Woman*. The title song from *Valley of the Dolls* was sung off camera by Dionne Warwick but is intended to express the feelings of the lead character. Even the lyrics of Simon & Garfunkel as used in *The Graduate* seem to waft from Dustin Hoffman's brain. These were wildly varying movies, but each was similarly effective in its use of music.

The makers of *Chips* liked the approach, even to the point of referring to their movie as a "romantic drama with music" rather than the more old-fashioned "musical." Ross was ready to innovate, however tentatively. "We don't intend to stop the action while Peter or Pet warble their way through a song," he said. "That's the way they did it in *Broadway Melody of 1933*. We've updated our technique a bit since then. The songs will come in naturally or there will be one or two dream sequences or memory flash-backs to bring them in unobtrusively." He added, "We are seeking . . . a musical style for the film which can only be executed in the cinema technique, as opposed to filming stage convention."

Ross's contract for $175,000 plus 5 percent of the profits included the employment of his wife, former American Ballet Theatre prima ballerina Nora Kaye Ross, as choreographer. Ross also sought musical personnel from *Oliver!*, *Half a Sixpence*, and *Chitty Chitty Bang Bang*. Plans to film in Greece were abandoned in favor of Italy. After touring 25 of Britain's public schools, Ross decided on the 700-year-old warm sandstone campus of Sherborne in Dorset for the film's primary setting. "It offered everything we needed, right in one place," he said. It "had just the right atmosphere of history and tradition, beautiful old buildings and fine-looking, well-behaved young boys who would appear in our film."

Director Herbert Ross, producer Arthur Jacobs, and associate producer Mort Abrahams stroll the picturesque streets of Sherborne during location scouting of *Goodbye, Mr. Chips*. From the collection of Photofest.

One of Ross's first chores was to reconcile credit and participation with composer André Previn. That put composer Leslie Bricusse in a tough situation, and he spent several days "talking endlessly" with Ross and an attorney about what to do. He knew his departure could very likely send *Chips* to the graveyard once and for all. He chose to aid Ross and persevere, so as "to do something that is at least constructive in one area." He dearly hoped this decision would not damage any friendships, Previn's most particularly.

Bricusse sat down on New Year's Day to write Previn a seven-page letter, calling the *Chips* situation "ludicrous" and a "mess." He remained largely polite, but behind his words was an annoyance that Previn should refuse another composer's intervention. "It is quite normal that the film company has the right to call in other writers," he wrote. "I have that in my current *Sherlock Holmes* project with Metro, and indeed on *Dolittle*. Rex actually exercised his right—albeit prematurely—to have other people work on his solo numbers, so that for several weeks I was involved in a song contest!" When Ross asked Bricusse to help complete the score, what could he say? "Herb, like yourself, is a good friend of mine," Bricusse wrote to Previn. "I don't want to let him down."

Though Bricusse was less than two years younger than Previn, he had considerably less professional experience. No doubt Previn was peeved at getting a lecture from newcomer Bricusse on the realities of composing music for the movies. André and Dory Previn had written 18 songs for *Chips* over five years before quitting and laying blame on producer Arthur Jacobs. "It was impossible to create a score the way he wanted us to do it," said André. "The artistic differences were completely irreconcilable. Therefore, we would prefer not to do the picture at all, rather than compromise."

After so much angst during conception, *Chips* was now attracting an exceptional roster of talent packed with quintessential '60s credits. Cinematographer Oswald Morris was respected, seasoned, and fresh off *Oliver!* Costume designer Julie Harris dressed the Beatles in *A Hard Day's Night* and *Help!*, and Julie Christie in *Darling*. Ken Adam, extremely facile with gadgetry, was the production designer for the first James Bond films, *Dr. Strangelove*, and *Chitty Chitty Bang Bang*. Jacobs's erratic casting decisions echo in off camera hiring, when he went through two editors. Anne V. Coates believed she had the job, only to be passed over for Ralph Kemplen, who had just cut the high-toned *A Man for All Seasons* and was finishing *Oliver!*

The confirmed involvement of Ross and Bricusse started a domino effect of dismissals. At last Jacobs knew what he wanted, so not only the Previns, but two Mrs. Chips had to go. Breach of contract litigation was settled out of court for actresses Lee Remick and Samantha Eggar, with MGM paying $100,000 to the former, and $125,000 to the latter. On the same day, approval was given to pay the Previns $85,120. They left "with bad feelings." André backed off ill words aimed at Bricusse, but Jacobs received no such courtesy. "Dory and I play a game called 'Absolutes,'" he told a *Los Angeles Times* reporter. "There are a few 'Absolutes' in the world. We have three: everybody hates war, everybody loves Italian food, and no one can work for Arthur Jacobs."

Chips logistics grew out of proportion to the simple tale being told. The casting director warned Ross that he would be "inundated with young boys," and indeed there was voluminous correspondence on casting. Assembling an international cast and crew meant that rehearsals had to accommodate far-flung schedules, necessitating music, dress, and makeup rehearsals in various European cities. Production headquarters and interior sets went up at the MGM-British Studio in Borehamwood north of London, where Stanley Kubrick had shot *2001: A Space Odyssey*. Crews descended upon Sherborne to construct sets and prepare for shooting over the summer holiday.

Associate producer Mort Abrahams, Jacobs, and Ross agreed Bricusse needed help, and someone mentioned Tony Hatch, the writer of Petula Clark's recent massive hits, including "Downtown." Hatch maintained that he was "never invited to be involved in any way in the composition or production of music for the film." Instead, he wrote a song called "Goodbye, Mr. Chips," which Jacobs disliked and rejected. O'Toole needed help, too, but of a different sort. He would rely on his gifts as an actor, since he was never a public school student and *Chips* was set in an idealized world where learning is the path to life's fulfillment. "I can't remember a bloody thing except nuns crashing me about the bleeding hands," he said of his early education. "My school was an Irish Catholic lunatic asylum. . . . if you got seen with a book in *my* school you'd get punched up in the air."

Young conductor-musical supervisor John Williams provided musical ballast. "I still have the feeling that some curious element is lacking in the score but I think, if the right atmosphere of confidence is developed with and around him, Leslie can be inspired to provide what we need," he wrote. "What I really feel is that 'too many cooks' may have shaken our confidence now and then. I would hate to see the score get blown apart because of this kind of insecurity." Williams was a gentleman in assessing Bricusse. "He's basically a romantic in an anti-romantic age. You see, audiences are constantly in a state of flux, their attitudes, tempers, reactions, are forever shifting and you can never really know for sure what's going to strike a responsive chord and what isn't."

The day before shooting was to begin in mid-July, 170 cast and crew members settled into 30 different hotels around Sherborne, filling rooms not already taken with vacationers sunning at the nearby seaside resort. The production office was situated over a wool shop and Jacobs's office went in a dentist's house just 200 yards from the school. Tiny Sherborne had no cinema, and makeshift cutting and projection rooms were set up in the school gardens. After the multiple horrors in planning, *Chips* enjoyed a remarkably efficient production. Call sheets reveal few delays or unusual problems.

While *Chips* began principal photography at Sherborne with nearly two dozen international TV commentators and other show business reporters descending to observe, production supervisor David Orton flew to Italy to prepare for the sequences at Pompeii, the old fishing village of Positano, and the temples at Paestum. Shooting at Sherborne stayed within the six-week schedule, and there were none of the big Hollywood movie–small English town animosities that cursed

Doctor Dolittle. When shooting was done and sets were disassembled, a Caravelle 80-seat jet transported cast and crew to Naples. Good luck followed the production to Italy. Despite rain, difficult setups, and night shoots, filming went off without serious complications. "It was only strict team work and the will to succeed that got us out of there on time," said Orton.

There was the sensitive matter of O'Toole's singing voice. "I knew Peter could carry a bottle of scotch with no problem, but if he had a musical background it was even further in the background than his first sighting of Omar Sharif in *Lawrence of Arabia,*" said Bricusse. One account had O'Toole unaware of his own musical limitations, though it's hard to imagine an actor of his brilliance lacking such self-awareness. Cast member George Baker said, "You have to admire the courage of a man who believes he can sing. He thought he was doing very well and that he had a very true voice. Well, you have to say that was very brave." An associate musical director reported to Bricusse that O'Toole's first completed recording "was the result of cobbling together individual syllables from countless different takes, the musical equivalent of a 10,000-piece jigsaw puzzle of a cloud formation."

O'Toole kept a high standard of professionalism on the set. He was a world-class drinker, but never before the workday was done. And he was turning in a fantastic performance, at least when he wasn't singing. "Only when the clapperboard bangs and the action begins again does one appreciate why O'Toole appeared so much at ease," said author Max Caulfield during a visit to the Pompeii location. "He instantly becomes a stooped, celluloid-collared, floppy-hatted, baggy-kneed, crumpled and creased semi-myopic. The flat Leeds tones atomize into the crisp cadences of decent public school English. He takes the scene by the scruff of the neck and pulverizes it immaculately." O'Toole also maintained a cordial rapport with Petula Clark. "Pet's first-rate," he joked. "I helped her with her singing and she helped me with my acting."

While the company was in Italy, Ken Adam was the advance man for the film's last major shooting at Elstree Studios back in England. He supervised the construction of the school's huge assembly hall, the Savoy Hotel ballroom, and a London variety theater circa 1924. Everyone returned safely, production continued apace at Elstree, then finished with location shots in Syon Park Gardens, a romantic stretch along the Thames near Kew Bridge, and the Salisbury, one of London's great old theater pubs.

Clark was a bona fide trouper, on stage since age seven, but she grew wary of *Chips* during production. "They changed the script, and they almost lost their nerve about doing a musical," she said. "It drifted away from its original intent, and we were uncertain if we should do it at all. Certainly Peter had his doubts. There were a lot of question marks. I loved Herbert Ross, but it wasn't an easy movie to make. I loved working with Peter, too, and it does have its beautiful moments, but it was a troubled production, and I think you can sense that in the movie."

When *Chips* wrapped, the crew had worked 107 eight-hour days on 50 sets. The exposed footage totaled 330,000 feet, or more than 62 miles, and the new budget approached $9 million. But despite the challenges of scale and cost, *Chips* finished production one day *early*. Jacobs was delighted that a movie with such large reservoirs of talent, time, and money should enjoy a controlled shoot and celebrated with a lavish wrap party on the Savoy Hotel ballroom set. As a joke gift, John Williams presented the cast and crew with an album called "MGM Presents The Losers Sing *Goodbye, Mr. Chips*" which listed the multitude of stars and directors who preceded O'Toole, Clark, and Ross. With 500 guests in attendance, Clark was moved to sing an impromptu rendition of one of Bricusse's tunes backed by the party band. O'Toole was not asked to sing.

During the making of *Chips*, Edgar M. Bronfman, heir to Seagrams Distilleries of Canada, acquired control of MGM. His ascendancy was short-lived, as billionaire real estate tycoon and former airline pilot Kirk Kerkorian acquired 40 percent interest in MGM stock, then ousted Bronfman. Kerkorian was not a public man, and neither was he interested in the day-to-day operations of a movie studio. When he took charge, he installed handsome, wavy-haired James T. Aubrey as primary MGM overseer. Aubrey rarely went to the movies and had never made one. He had been, however, a gold miner for CBS, presiding over the network as *Gilligan's Island* and *The Beverly Hillbillies* took their place in the canon of enduring sitcoms. Kerkorian agreed to Aubrey's salary of $208,000, with option to purchase 17,500 shares of MGM stock.

MGM had given the recent impression of fiscal health, but this increasingly looked like a mirage. *The Dirty Dozen* was very big, and *Doctor Zhivago* became the highest grossing film at the studio since *Gone with the Wind*, which squeaked by *The Sound of Music* to regain its place as the top moneymaker of all time during a 1967 reissue. *2001: A Space Odyssey* was a huge gamble, the most experimental roadshow ever, and it paid off brilliantly. But the reserve seat *Far from the Madding Crowd* and *The Shoes of the Fisherman* lost money, and MGM was in the hole. There were other expensive monsters in production in addition to *Goodbye, Mr. Chips*. Any one of them could tip the studio into bankruptcy.

The turnover of presidents and primary stockholders left the studio in a state of depressed value and uncertain future. Aubrey was, in his way, the perfect man to instill discipline by making unpopular decisions. Nicknamed "The Smiling Cobra," he was not afraid to be draconian and take a buck-stops-here attitude. He dismissed an army of consultants hired to rescue MGM. He then selected his own management team, trimmed the fat in overhead and personnel, and put into production a slate of modest films with strict budgets of $2 million each. He aborted two dramas and put a moratorium on lavish musicals. Julie Andrews became the big-time loser. The studio had already cancelled her $10 million Irving Berlin musical *Say It with Music*. Under Aubrey's knife, the other Andrews musical *She Loves Me* was cut as well.

Goodbye, Mr. Chips and *Ryan's Daughter*, David Lean's sweeping Irish Rebellion romantic drama that was supposed to be the studio's next *Doctor Zhivago*, were saved only because they were too far into production. Aubrey's methods guaranteed bitterness through the film industry. He pled poverty when contracts were broken and was not cowed by threats at litigation. In turn, he saved the studio millions. It was an extraordinarily revealing moment in entertainment history. Two giants of music, Berlin and Andrews, were being paid *not* to be seen or heard, while the man who gave us *The Beverly Hillbillies* was dismantling the studio of Gable, Garbo, Astaire, and Garland. Already under discussion was the sale of the MGM Culver City backlot. The greatest musical-making studio of all time now stood quiet and empty.

While Jacobs ginned up the publicity machine, *Chips* was scored, dubbed, and cut. Optimism was free flowing. A short film of *Chips* shown to MGM execs in New York went over well. Just as John Williams oversaw final postproduction recording with a 75-piece orchestra, the *Chips* teaser began screening cross-country with the goal of inciting the largest advance sales of any roadshow in MGM history. Early optimism continued as the first week sold out in advance of *Chips* opening in all cities.

Jacobs was not entirely certain of what to do with *Chips*, so he defaulted to a familiar place: *The Sound of Music*. "The family picture—a label often and unfortunately disdained during the sex and savagery reign—always has been a winner with the general public (the biggest audience, after all) when the picture itself has been deserving," he wrote. "One need only look at the remarkable results of *Mary Poppins* and *Sound of Music*. In my brief period as a producer, I've been influenced most by this thought, by a desire to make pictures of broad audience appeal despite any trend in the opposite direction. In *Doctor Dolittle* . . . I found subjects that played to the general audience with gratifying results. I'm hopeful *Goodbye, Mr. Chips* . . . will do the same and even more so. It is certainly an adult film, but one that never will suffer from a 'for adults only' label." As *Chips* is "a rarity on the screen today—a truly pure love story," Jacobs added, "Motion pictures haven't embraced this sort of story in years." The movie will stay true to Hilton's "timeless" novel yet will have a "fresh and contemporary feel." To recap, Jacobs positioned *Chips* as a family picture that's an adult story, very romantic, but not sexual. It's timeless yet contemporary. Hollywood hasn't seen anything like it in years, yet it shares something in common with *The Sound of Music* and *Doctor Dolittle*. In its efforts to be all things to all audiences, would such a movie appeal to everyone, or no one? With negative costs at $8,223,268, it had better appeal to *someone*. Chain-smoking Herbert Ross was a tangle of anxieties. Wearing thick black-rimmed glasses over a craggy face, his worried expression periodically broke into a melancholy smile. When someone stole his cigarettes, it was worth a memo. "Nothing has been done and the whole matter disregarded as if of no importance," he announced far and wide.

Chips $4 million merchandising juggernaut began five months before the film was to premiere. Watches, comic books, picture books, coloring books, puzzles, and pencil boxes were on their way to stores, but most of the goods were sartorial. Several magazines aimed at young people had tie-in campaigns promoting clothes inspired by the film's pre–World War II fashions. Chips 'n' Twigs, a boys-wear manufacturer, modeled a line from the movie. *Chips* angled to influence teen girl fashion, too, despite the absence of adolescent females in the film. *House and Gardens* did a spread announcing the film's certain imprint on interior designs and furnishings.

Happy Goday, music promotion coordinator, pitched *Chips* songs for covers, with demo recordings sent to singers, record companies, producers, and pianists. Petula Clark was meanwhile heard everywhere, singing anticipated hits from the movie, including the rousing "London Is London" and the plaintive "You and I." In the few months leading to *Chips* opening, she appeared at Caesar's Palace in Las Vegas, Harrah's Tahoe, the Ohio and Indiana State Fairs, and the TV shows of Andy Williams and Ed Sullivan. A ghost of *Chips*'s past appeared when Tony Hatch and wife Jackie Trent recorded the demo song "Goodbye, Mr. Chips" with Clark and, according to Bricusse, made "a flagrant and opportunistic attempt" to "cash in" by misleading the public, since the song is not in the movie. An English court agreed, and the judge awarded a temporary *ex-parte* injunction banning Hatch and Trent from passing off their lyrics as part of the film. With MGM's blessing, the recording was pressed on a Petula Clark album, but was never heard in the film.

When *Dolittle*'s Anthony Newley invited Herbert Ross to catch his act in Vegas, Ross sent his regrets, stating that "I'm up to my ears in dubbing *Chips* and I'm working 15 hour days, seven days a week. It's a nightmare." Ross was burned out, with his agent telling him "every effort will be made to see that [your next movie] is *not* a musical." The first preview took place at the Apex Theatre in Washington, DC. Reaction cards were more complimentary than they had been for *Dolittle*, but there were generally negative remarks about the songs. Jacobs kept smiling. "Our preview was a smashing success with applause at the end of act one, at the end of the film, and in several places during the screening," he reported to an absent O'Toole. "Audience reaction to everything about the picture was tremendous and everyone was unanimous in feeling that this was the greatest O'Toole performance yet. Pet came across beautifully. . . . I am confident we will have the success that we all hope for."

Chips was trimmed after the Washington preview, with its first print clocking in at 153 minutes. Early press screenings resulted in various negative reviews, but advance sales were hearty at $537,642, with 111 sold out performances. There were 240 theater parties booked and 18 youth shows. It looked like an MGM dream come true, with *Chips* advance sales outpacing *Zhivago*, *2001*, and even *Gone with the Wind*, excluding Atlanta. Buoyed by the numbers, Jacobs planned on reserve

Roadshow fatigue can be seen in this rare shot of the *Goodbye, Mr. Chips* premiere marquee in New York. It's a rainy night, and the crowd is not cheek to jowl. There are no searchlights, and the front marquee neon spells PA ACE. No such sloppiness accompanied the premieres of *Oklahoma!*, *West Side Story*, or *The Sound of Music*. From the collection of Photofest.

seat engagements at least into the summer of 1970. "*Easy Rider* is a marvelous film, but you can't make all films *Easy Riders*," he said. "There have to be films for the family. Every indication we've had is that there's a market for *Chips*."

Chips opened at the Palace in New York on November 5, 1969, and two days later at the Fox Wilshire in Los Angeles. Many rose to its defense, and it enjoyed relatively kind reviews for a late roadshow musical. The *Chicago Sun-Times* wrote, "Some of the silliest reviews of *Goodbye, Mr. Chips* have criticized it for costing too much. That would make sense if the millions had been spent to buy vulgarity (as they were in *Star!*) or offensive overproduction (*Camelot*)." When it had its Royal premiere at the Empire Theatre in Leicester Square, a brass band played "London Is London" as H. M. Queen Elizabeth II arrived and took her seat. She was reported to have brushed away a tear or two as the lights came up, a reaction not reported after her viewings of either *Doctor Dolittle* or *Star!*

While O'Toole was routinely praised, the music was routinely damned. London's *Daily Mirror* located the film's assets and liabilities: "O'Toole gives a most impressive performance—quiet, subtle. . . . The real trouble . . . is that whenever one is getting absorbed in the gentle story, there's a feeling that every line of dialogue is probably a cue for Pet Clark or Peter O'Toole to sing an indifferent song. They usually do." Tongue firmly in journalistic cheek, *Variety* concluded that as a singer, O'Toole is "no Rex Harrison." *Newsweek* found Clark to be charming and in fine voice, as did most others, but "the songs she's given to sing sound like the Magna Carta set to music by Helen Keller." There was the well-worn but appropriate elephantiasis argument. In adapting a short novel into a nearly three-hour movie, MGM tried and failed to make *Chips* something it is not. "It is simply too fragile to carry all the flashy trappings hung on it by producer Arthur P. Jacobs," announced *Variety*. More than a few filmgoers and critics appreciated *Chips*'s frank sentimentality and romanticism, coming as they did in an age dripping in cynicism and irony. The *Detroit Free-Press* may have represented the silent majority when its rave came with the directive to "tell Hollywood and the moneymen that you'll back the decent films (so long as they are good) as well as the 'I Am Curious Pinks, Blues, and Violets!'"

O'Toole's summation of *Chips* was clear-eyed. "One does not want to think about how that turned out," he said three years after it opened. "I saw a reel and left in the middle. One simply boggled at what they had done to that poor, simple little story, blown it up into something way out of proportion to its content. If there was any way I could have had my name taken off it I would have. Yet, you know, the sad thing, really sad, is I think I gave probably my best screen performance in that picture."

Goodbye, Mr. Chips is a bouillabaisse of collaborative cross-purposes, but it also has its own charm and merit. If any roadshow failure of the late 1960s deserves to be called "underrated" or "a pleasant surprise," it is *Chips*. Its strength derives primarily from the tenderly intuitive playing between O'Toole and Clark. As the "Cockney Countess," Clark is all music hall verve, and her marvelous show voice is heard to advantage. Here was a rare 1960s musical instance of a talented singer and respectable actress cast accordingly. Together with O'Toole, she fulfills the original vision of Rattigan to highlight a love story of opposites. Just as Maria brought sunshine and happiness to Captain von Trapp and his children, so, too, does Katherine enliven Mr. Chips and his "hundreds of children—all boys." O'Toole's performance is one grace note after another, and reminds us that he has always been a great character actor doubling as a leading man.

The finished score is a revelation. While Bricusse's melodies and lyrics are often drab, Williams's orchestrations are lush and herald his gargantuan successes to come with *Star Wars*, *Superman*, and *E.T.: The Extra-Terrestrial*. He chooses atypical instruments such as harpsichord, celesta, vibraphone, marimba, and electric harp, but nothing can save the voiceover *Chips* solos "Where Did My Childhood Go?" and "What a Lot of Flowers." O'Toole's magisterial speaking voice was mortified by attempts at regulated pitch. His reserved character is kept quiet, and we are spared prolonged exposure to his unsupported vocals and Bricusse's lyrics. But when he is asked to sing, out comes something like this:

> *What a world of color, just beyond my window,*
> *Flowers, every color of the rainbow,*
> *Red roses, orange marigolds, yellow buttercups,*
> *Green leaves, blue cornflowers, indigo lilacs,*
> *and violets—violets!*

It's enough to make Cole Porter weep. "I *guess* you could call it a musical, although to insinuate that Leslie Bricusse's plodding score is merely dreadful would be an act of charity," groaned Rex Reed. "Still, it's a much better movie than *Paint Your Wagon*, and much prettier to look at." The performing of the score is nearly Brechtian, which is not to say the songs work. O'Toole liked the method, but only because it "spares the audience of the sight of my pharynx bobbing up and down." There is everywhere a striving for simplicity. Story themes arrive in strict linear progression—(1) Chips is stern and unpopular, (2) Katherine has had bad luck with men, (3) Chips and Katherine fall in love, (4) Katherine is snubbed by Chips's colleagues, (5) Chips defends her, (6) their love grows deeper, (7) etc. By moving *Chips* from 1922 to the end of World War II, it manages to comment on changing English society and the changing face of a classic public school education. The film, elegantly shot by Oswald Morris, takes on a lovely elegiac quality as a result. Where *Hello, Dolly!* announces its wealth with crashing symbols and a stuffed mise-en-scène, *Chips* simply tutors us in Latin, confident we will be moved by the joys of learning.

Ross trusted the material, kept a clear focus on the primary storytelling, the central romance, and the good working chemistry of his two leading players. He also uses supporting actress Siân Phillips wisely. As a theatrical grand dame, her performance is all broad gestures, heavy eyelids, and adroit small talk. She contributes some welcome spice, but Ross limits her screen time, and too much of this creature who calls everyone "dahling" would be intolerable. The masterful cutting of "When I Am Older," a sprightly tune featuring a chorus of school boys returning to Brookfield for a new term, flatters Ross's nascent skills and brings *Chips* some needed energy. Inexplicable, however, is his stingy use of class time and our scant acquaintance with any of the students.

Still, *Goodbye, Mr. Chips* is a sincere work of art and has maintained a loyal and affectionate fan base. In his moving last speech before the school assembly, Chips tells his boys, "You're growing up into a new world. A very exciting world, perhaps, but for sure a very changed world." How true of 1969. A perusal of noteworthy films that year reveals why *Chips* was doomed. *Midnight Cowboy, They Shoot Horses, Don't They?, The Damned, Bob and Carol and Ted and Alice, The Wild Bunch, Easy Rider, Alice's Restaurant, Once Upon a Time in the West*, and *Z* were by turns arch, despairing, sarcastic, brutal, and in harmony with the contemporary shell shock born from 1968. Popcorn movies such as *The Love Bug, Bullitt, Butch Cassidy and the Sundance Kid*, and *True Grit* all promised what moviegoers have always wanted—to be transported for a few hours in the dark. For all of his lovability, Chips was an Establishment bore, the very same that the English schoolboys of 1968's *If. . . .* gunned down without remorse. As the dyspeptic vision of British boarding schools, *If. . . .* was teeming with sexual perversion and anarchy. In 1969, rendering Chips a hero was a risky proposition, and one that proved unrewarding for MGM. And at a time when both American and English young people were questioning and defying authority, *Goodbye Mr. Chips* could have been sublime counter magic or as stodgy as it promised to be. Alas for the once glorious MGM, the latter proved to be true.

Soon after the holidays, James Aubrey met with Arthur Jacobs to hammer out a plan for *Chips*. It was not catching fire, and Aubrey needed to salvage what he could as Richard Zanuck had with *Star!* one year earlier. He ordered the end of roadshow screenings, the commencement of wide release at standard prices, and the cutting of the overture, intermission, and 27 minutes of songs. He also prohibited the word "musical" in all marketing. With those instructions, the original hard ticket version was forever banished from theaters. The TWA inflight version ran barely over two hours and was subtitled "a love story as timeless as forever," pointedly abandoning the earlier "a love story with music" marketing tagline.

As with Fox and Paramount, the big pictures at MGM were proving to be calamitous. But Aubrey was well known as a butcher in the editing room, and any independent producer seeking studio distribution was well advised to look elsewhere. There were fewer movies coming out of MGM as a result, and what did appear was substandard. The studio lost $35 million in 1969; only another *Doctor Zhivago* or *2001: A Space Odyssey* could save it from financial ruin. *Goodbye, Mr. Chips* was not that movie, and Aubrey was just the man to orchestrate a bloodbath. He began with cutting the staff by 50 percent, then holding an auction to sell MGM collectibles that had been knocking around storage rooms for decades. In "what has got to be one of the most gigantic examples of spring housecleaning in history," sound stages became display areas for tons of ephemera, from peace pipes, to canoes, rickshaws, musical instruments, incense burners, brass hair-curlers, and vintage cars. Among the costumes were those worn by Judy Garland in *Meet Me in St. Louis,* Elizabeth Taylor in *Father of the Bride* and *Raintree County,* Greta Garbo in *Queen Christina,* Susan Hayward in *I'll Cry Tomorrow,* Paul Muni in *The Good Earth,* and Stewart Granger in *Young Bess.* Sold to the highest bidder was a mantel clock from Garbo's *Ninotchka,* a salon set from Shearer's *Marie Antoinette,* Brando's jacket and breeches from *Mutiny on the Bounty,* a jade green monster from *The Time Machine,* Garland's ruby slippers from *The Wizard of Oz,* and Marilyn Monroe's pantsuit from *The Asphalt Jungle.*

For three weeks, over 3,000 fans, decorators, antique dealers, and collectors flowed through to bid on 25,000 separate pieces from over 2,000 movies. One Long Island secretary said she was looking to buy "anything from *Ben-Hur.* I've seen it 15 times." Actors Rock Hudson, Shirley Jones, and Debbie Reynolds were there, perhaps to reclaim props they'd handled in one or another fondly remembered movie. Reynolds was disconsolate that MGM's portable material wealth, and a portion of America's cultural heritage, was flying out the studio gates and into private collections. She took out a $100,000 bank loan to buy back as much as she could in a failed attempt to open a motion picture hall of fame. Her attitudinal opposite was *The Wizard of Oz*'s Jack Haley, who cheered the auction. He could not understand why people expected him to bid. "Those costumes were hell," he said. "You wanted to run away from them, not buy them. Where would I put it? Down in the basement? 'Hey, come on down, see my Tin Man suit!'"

Seeing no resale potential, Aubrey ordered the music department's library burned, with the exception of one score per film. Out-takes, prerecordings, music tracks, and the stock footage library were also destroyed. The script library would have been destroyed, too, had it not been for a Good Samaritan who donated its contents to USC. Large swaths of the Culver City backlot were sold or leased for commercial and residential development. Lost were Tarzan's jungles, Andy Hardy's town square, Esther Williams's swimming pool, and the sets for *David Copperfield, Easter Parade, Camille,* and *The Harvey Girls.* Aubrey was unmoved through it all. "I don't want to hear any more bullshit about the old MGM," he said. "The old MGM is gone." More specifically, Herbert Solow, MGM's new vice-president in charge of production, said, "the company will not become involved in any epic budget productions and definitely no musicals."

There would be no more acres of sound stages and exterior sets. "Young people who are the major movie audience today refer to that as the plastic world and that is almost a deterrent in the business today," said Aubrey. The Smiling Cobra was now deriding television, the very medium that took him to the top of Hollywood power. "Mr. Nixon's silent majority stay home and use TV as a soporific. Its mediocrity and banality has [sic] driven the young away from TV and into the movies. The audience, I think, is ahead of the business, and we've got to get ahead of them. The revolution has been rapid."

CHAPTER 15

Numbers

Editor William Reynolds whittled 50 hours of exposed film into two hours and 28 minutes, then joined the rest of Fox in a waiting game. *Hello, Dolly!* was ready to open by early 1969, but the studio was contractually required to withhold it due to the play's continued run on Broadway. Since its debut in 1964, *Dolly!* had become the King Lear for musical comedy actresses of a certain age. After Carol Channing came Ginger Rogers, Martha Raye, Betty Grable, Mary Martin, Eve Arden, Dorothy Lamour, Yvonne de Carlo, Phyllis Diller, and Ethel Merman. And let us now toast Bibi Osterwald, who understudied the more famous headliners for most of the New York run. By 1969, Dolly Levi had been played by over 50 women on Broadway and in touring companies and was the highest grossing stage production in touring history. And since *Dolly!* had been reinvigorated by Pearl Bailey and an all-black cast, producer David Merrick held Twentieth Century-Fox to its obligation, preventing release until the Broadway run ends. "It's funny for David, not so funny for us," said Fox chief Richard Zanuck. He added, as if to flatter and dare simultaneously, "He is too shrewd a businessman to play out this string much longer." Merrick, who was as hard-boiled as MGM's James Aubrey, maintained that he merely wanted to break the Broadway long-run musical record set by *My Fair Lady*. Meanwhile Fox was paying interest on the loans, totaling about $100,000 a month.

As *Dolly!*'s meter ran, Zanuck had reason to be nervous. The effects of *Doctor Dolittle* and particularly *Star!* were being felt as Fox was careening toward insolvency. First quarter earnings in 1969 were 31 cents a share, down from 52 cents a year before. At a tense two and a half hour meeting at the Waldorf Astoria in May, Darryl Zanuck avoided answering shareholders' questions about the decline. Instead, he fell back on baseball analogies. He talked to a reporter later, saying, "What do you expect us to do? Hit a home run every time we come to bat?" Jabbing his finger in the air, he said, "Babe Ruth hit more home runs than anyone else in the history of baseball. He also struck out more than anyone."

"What do you say about reports that you are a sitting duck for a takeover?" asked a stockholder.

"We have been approached by a number of companies in a number of respects," he answered without naming those most often cited for a takeover—Max Factor and Trans-Lux. "About some we were doubtful, but we gave careful consideration and thought to the possibility of merging on equal terms with some others. I saw certain advantages and some great disadvantages." Reinforcing that he would prefer to "go it alone," he added, "Should a possibility arise that is beneficial to all stockholders of Fox and one we could live with and one in which we could have autonomy, I am in favor of discussing it in detail."

As the owner of 121,900 shares of Fox stock, Merrick was among the studio's largest shareholders, and he had the power to hold *Hello, Dolly!* hostage. Was it true that the movie might not hit theaters until 1971? "As soon as we are in a position to announce the release date, we will do so," said Darryl Zanuck. "I cannot go beyond that." When pressed on the finances of *Dolittle*, Zanuck was similarly vague. "While there will be a loss on the film, which we have put aside, there's a good opportunity that something might be salvaged in worldwide showings. The film did not measure up to our expectations but I do not think I am required to give you the figures." The number sticking to *Dolittle* was $8 million. With interest charges on *Dolly!* approaching $2 million, and *Star!*'s financial damage sure to be greater than *Dolittle*'s, a takeover seemed inevitable. When Darryl Zanuck flew to Los Angeles to attend a summer board meeting, son Richard and fellow production executive David Brown met him at the airport. Both had the task of informing elder Zanuck that Fox was broke. Said Richard, "[He] was so shocked and stunned—he had just flown in from Paris. David and I met with him and decided we'd better do some pretty big thinking before his marching into the board meeting the next day."

Richard engaged the Stanford Research Institute in a study of the future of Twentieth Century-Fox and the whole entertainment industry. "What will Twentieth Century-Fox be like when it becomes Twenty-First Century Fox?" he asked his assembled board members. The research concluded that movie attendance will fall precipitously against rising production costs and shuttered theaters. Television was seen as the primary cause, followed by travel, sports, and other leisure time activities, while the coming cable television and videocassette markets were additional ominous signs for the feature film. Statistics of the study confirmed what many in the business already knew: the majority of filmgoers were under 40, with 65 percent of attendees between 15 and 29 years old. But all was not lost. A wider proportion of the population could be lured back to theaters if there was a "film [that] deals with subject matter not available on television."

In marketing *Dolittle* and *Star!*, Fox had gone overboard in promising more than either delivered. That posed challenges with *Hello, Dolly!* and the upcoming Pearl Harbor drama *Tora! Tora! Tora!*, two films that could determine if the studio lived or died. Fox was already looking to consolidate its European branches and unload domestic and international real estate, and neither film had yet opened. To increase anxiety, while both sat waiting for release, Fox posted third quarter losses of $20.4 million. With the end of the stage *Hello, Dolly!* not yet in sight, the Zanucks brokered a deal with Merrick. The studio promised him almost $2 million in exchange for a 1969 release and guaranteed any reimbursements if the Broadway production grosses fell below $60,000 a week.

With that business out of the way, Fox proceeded with a December premiere for *Dolly!* at the Rivoli. Rollout plans had the film opening in 49 cities for the Christmas season. Darryl F. Zanuck told the *International Herald-Tribune* that "*Hello, Dolly!* is fantastic, really fantastic, the best musical ever made, and that includes *The Sound of Music*, which is the biggest grossing picture ever made. But I wouldn't predict that *Hello, Dolly!* will out gross *The Sound of Music*, even though it's a better picture." Apparently no one was buying his enthusiasm. At the *Dolly!* preview in Phoenix, David Brown was shocked to see the theater barely half full. This was not a sneak preview; Phoenix knew it was getting a known title with a huge star. "Richard and I both took various highways that were leading to—this was a shopping area—and stopped cars and said, 'Wait a minute, *Hello, Dolly!* is playing.' Then we got on the public address system and we were begging people to come to the theater. We should've known we were in trouble."

On the eve of *Dolly!*'s Rivoli premiere, director Gene Kelly said that only snippets had been taken out of *Dolly!* since the sneak preview. "I wish we could cut more, but we've taken all we can. Orson Welles, I believe, once said: 'No film is ever too short.' A film is better short." With *Dolly!* clocking in at well over two hours, the premiere was a scene of police barricades, spotlights, and thousands screaming for Barbra Streisand. A scrum of fans encircled her limousine, creating near-riot conditions. "One crazed fan jumped on the front hood of her limo and started pounding on the glass and screaming," recalled another fan. "At one point people behind me were pushing so hard my face was smashed against the window. I motioned to Barbra that she shouldn't get out of the car." She did, but only after police made it safe to walk the red carpet without the surging mob overwhelming her. Her manager was brained by a large camera and gushed blood. Somehow, the spirit of the evening improved, and once customers took their seats, Darryl Zanuck good-naturedly shouted, "Start the picture!" to the projectionist. The title song "swept the audience into a state of delirious delight," reported the *New York Daily News*, while Streisand received a standing ovation after the screening. When it was time to exit, a dozen police officers surrounded and escorted her to the Pierre Hotel supper dance, highlighted by Louis Armstrong singing "Hello, Dolly!" A few blocks away, David Merrick's *Hello, Dolly!* was playing the St. James Theatre, going strong despite the film's opening.

Darryl Zanuck admitted that if he could turn back the clock, he would not take on *Dolly!*, *Tora! Tora! Tora!*, or *Patton*, another Fox roadshow war epic on the brink of release. "Financially, we're not justified. Once you're over the $4 million category today, you're sticking out your chin." *Dolly!* cost five times that much.

Producer Ernest Lehman said, "You feel a certain way until the picture comes along that's the exception. Then they all climb on board the exception. A lot of people lost a lot of money because *The Sound of Music* was such a success."

Pauline Kael, among others, was having none of it. The problem wasn't audience indifference to musicals; the problem was a lack of creative application in Hollywood. "Now, at the time when modern classical music, like much of modern theater, has become enervated, and popular songs are alive, and the whole country is alive to their force—at just the time for great new movie musicals—the moguls who can't see farther than the end of their cigars tell us that the form is dead. . . . Darryl F. Zanuck says you can't make little musicals, and the rest of the industry seems to concur. I think they're dead wrong. I love musicals, but I hate big, expensive musicals, because I have to wade through all the filler of production values to get to what I want to see, and I suspect there are millions of people who feel the same way. Do the moviemakers think we go to musicals for the *sets*?"

As planned, *Dolly!* opened in dozens of cities in the United States and Canada soon after the premiere. Unlike *Camelot* and *Dolittle*, it received widespread distribution early on; Omaha and Sacramento were seeing it just one night after the New York opening. Coupon ads ran in 19 big city newspapers, and the early results were spectacular, with $1 million in advance sales, doubling the figures of *The Sound of Music*. The Hollywood premiere took place at Grauman's Chinese Theater, with Streisand arriving with a squadron of security guards and the Los Angeles Police Department. To prove no hard feelings, Walter Matthau attended and planted a kiss on her right cheek for all the photographers to capture. Streisand's expression looks like someone receiving a wet tongue from someone else's Golden Retriever.

There were no more *Hello, Dolly!*s out there. *Darling Lili* was proving to be obscenely expensive, but Blake Edwards insisted it wasn't a musical. United Artists' recently announced *Fiddler on the Roof*, another Broadway adaptation, did not have the pageantry or the marquee names. *Dolly!* heralded the extinction of its kind and the beginning of an era of unknown promise. It all came down to money. "When you're flush, you can afford to take chances. That day has passed," said Darryl Zanuck. "Costly musicals are under a shadow just at present, when the whole trend is away from them and from swollen budgets generally," reported *Variety* in its *Hello, Dolly!* review. A news segment, presumably not approved by the Fox publicity department, provided a voice-over during the Hollywood premiere that doubled as a eulogy:

> It was a star-studded night for the premiere of Twentieth Century-Fox's 25 million dollar movie Hello, Dolly! Klieg lights were bright at Grauman's Chinese Theatre . . . there were fans and autograph hounds, even a fleet of antique studio Rolls Royces for names that had lost their relevance for most of today's movie audiences. [Cameras catch the arrival of Kirk Douglas,

Greer Garson, Cesar Romero, Eva Gabor, and former actor and current California Governor Ronald Reagan and wife Nancy.] *The truth is that a movie star no longer assures the financial success of a picture.*

Streisand's Dolly remains one of the great miscastings of the era, and her over compensations didn't help. Her "mannerisms [are] so arch and calculated that one half expects to find a key implanted in her back," wrote *Time*. Matthau is miscast, too. With that irritable disposition and jowly pan, he is unlikely as the love interest for someone as canny as Dolly Levi. Fortune hunting aside, why would anyone spend the bulk of a movie in pursuit of *him*? Streisand was not blind to the problem. "What I needed was Rhett Butler to sweep me back up again," she said. "What I got was Walter Matthau." Two wrongs didn't make a right—why would this Dolly be interested in that Horace? Her pursuit of him is obsessive, ungracious, and comic only by way of a rather desperately manic delivery. As for any warmth that Shirley Booth or Carol Channing invested in Dolly, it is here undetected, smothered by Streisand laying on the shtick with a putty trowel.

At least *Finian's Rainbow* and even *Paint Your Wagon* strained to be significant, if only suggesting that racism is bad and relaxed sexual morality is good. *Hello, Dolly!* glorifies one star, and that worked for *Funny Girl* through Streisand's unique onscreen power. But now she had arrived as an Oscar winner, and the excessive trappings were beginning to putrefy. Messianic musicals had become cultish and dysfunctional. *Funny Girl* would be one of the last musicals dependent on glorifying an outsized personality to make it work. And it worked because of the Streisand novelty on the big screen, a congruent union of actress and character, and the assorted contributions of director William Wyler.

Streisand's pair of "Parade" numbers in *Funny Girl* and *Dolly!* are telling contrasts in directorial instincts. *Funny Girl*'s "Don't Rain on My Parade" ends its kinetic, high-charged sequence, and the first act of the movie, with a helicopter shot of the New York harbor, a brilliant use of negative space as the screen is consumed by water and sky. Streisand's voice fills the open air, with the last sounds as the curtains close and "Intermission" appears over the lonely chug-chug of her tugboat. That one gesture alone tells us this movie isn't for kids, and wasn't made by kids, either. The bigness of "Before the Parade Passes By" is in contrast oppressive and even repellent, a large-scale synchronized human anthill. Its busy-ness distracts from Streisand's voice, which hardly ever sounded better than when it was singing this song.

The problem with *Hello, Dolly!* is not primarily Streisand, or Matthau, or Kelly. Neither is it found in the score or the pleasant, feel-good story. It can easily be enjoyed as polished and unchallenging entertainment; there are worse ways to spend 148 minutes than watching *Hello, Dolly!* Its problem is scale. It's a Godzilla of a movie. All those millions of dollars add up to a few cents worth of story and song. And for all that money, one might expect a musical with a brain in its head. To

Pauline Kael, "The movie is full of that fake, mechanical exhilaration of big Broadway shows—the gut-busting, muscle-straining dance that is meant to wow you. This dancing, like the choral singing, is asexual and unromantic, and goes against the spirit of the little farce plot about the matching up of several pairs of lovers" while Streisand's brief duet with Louis Armstrong is "the one true love match of the movie. . . . When [he] sings to [her], 'You're still glowin', you're still crowin', you're still goin' strong,' one wants them to dump the movie and just keep going." Amen.

There is no point in comparing Carol Channing's vocals to Streisand's. While the trend of the era was to undervalue musical talent, Fox overvalued it this time, brushing everything else aside for worship of one megastar. If Streisand is wrong, at least she entertains while singing waiters do cartwheels and flap their arms a lot. Who needs a connection between player and character, or chemistry with costars, or even a ballpark approximation of age when you've got those Streisand pipes? Even Carol Channing partisans had to admit that Streisand gave Jerry Herman's songs a throbbing new vitality.

In summing up the ultimate failure of *Hello, Dolly!* to meet its massive expectations, Kelly took a hard look at current realities:

> It's not the kind of film I would make as a first choice but what else is there? To make an original musical today you first have to find someone to put up a million dollars, just to develop the idea and that's too much of a risk. What happens now is that studios buy stage shows after they are already dated and then spend a lot of money turning them into dated movies. The musical is the victim of changing times. To make good musicals you need a team of performers, musicians, costume and set designers, choreographers, writers and arrangers, etc., etc. In short, what we used to have at MGM. Well, it's no longer possible. The economics of the business have killed all that. It's all too easy to ridicule Fox for spending all that money making *Dolly* but they took a brave stand—they had spent so much getting hold of the property that they wanted to turn it into a whale of a good show. It takes guts to make that kind of decision, and as the director I was excited by the challenge of blowing it up into a big and exciting picture. I'm not sorry I did it.

Yes, but . . . everything about *Dolly!* could have been smaller without losing any desired effect, as demonstrated in the original stage production. The chorus and orchestra of the stage *Dolly!* are as robust and full as the film's. At some point, throwing additional money at a movie won't proportionately make it better. At an estimated $24 million, *Hello, Dolly!* was the most expensive musical in history. It costs three times as much as *The Sound of Music.* It cost more than Gene Kelly's *On the Town, An American in Paris, Singin' in the Rain, It's Always Fair Weather,* and *Invitation to the Dance* combined.

Early in its hard ticket run, *Dolly!* behaved like a blockbuster, with its 11 screenings a week at the Rivoli expanded to 15. The early numbers coming in from Los Angeles were strong as well. *Dolly!* hit the half million mark after 10 weeks at Grauman's Chinese, which did not happen to *The Sound of Music* until 14 weeks at the Fox Wilshire. In honor of the occasion, a wit at Fox wrote alternate lyrics to the title song, then shared them with the staff:

> *Hello Dollars,*
> *Well, Hello Dollars*
> *At last you're coming back where you belong . . . !*

Dolly! needed sustained high box office for months to meet its investment, but once the first timers came through, business plummeted. It played the Rivoli for 34 weeks, just 40 percent of *The Sound of Music*'s run. At that point, *Variety* reported a gross of less than $8 million. But the news got worse when estimates for Fox's 1969 losses after taxes came to $37 million and David Merrick more than doubled his shares in the studio to 300,000.

Richard Zanuck led the charge to keep the Merrick people from wresting control. "I only met him once," said Richard, "and found him quite pleasant—which is contrary to his reputation." Time was on Zanuck's side, he believed, as 1970 would see increased revenue from the holdover hit *Butch Cassidy and the Sundance Kid*, and the likely successes of the new year's *M*A*S*H*, *The Kremlin Letter*, and *Patton*. *The Sound of Music* spigot was finally turned off in December of 1969, when the last first-run prints were returned to the Fox vaults in advance of a planned reissue in three years. "It's that old Zanuck luck which comes out when there are problems," said a Fox insider. "He's got a great lineup to show if another battle develops." But reality forced the studio to consider an MGM-style auction, something elder Zanuck abhorred.

Perhaps the hit status of *Patton*, Fox's last roadshow, and *M*A*S*H*, Robert Altman's breakthrough dark comedy, would hold things together. *Patton*'s subtitle, *A Salute to a Rebel*, may have tried to grab the youth market, but its World War II milieu and central figure spoke to the older generation. *M*A*S*H* was something else altogether. It gave an "up yours" to authority and all reverent attitudes to war. "There can be no doubt about it," wrote the *New York Post*. "We're well on our way into a revolution of feeling, taste, naughty words, sexual mores, private beliefs, and public behaviors. *M*A*S*H* draws a few more guidelines in a wham, bam, thank-you ma'am style." With its $3 million budget, it brought in more money than *Doctor Dolittle*, *Star!*, and *Hello, Dolly!* combined.

Fox still wasn't out of danger, what with *Dolly!* underperforming against costs, *Tora! Tora! Tora!* looking like a fiasco, and the appalling *Myra Breckinridge* and *Beyond the Valley of the Dolls* making little impression. Fox posted a first-quarter profit of less than $1 million, plunged to a $17.1 million loss for the second quarter, and suffered third quarter losses of *only* $5.2 million. In October, Darryl Zanuck released a financial statement claiming losses of $11,141,000 on *Doctor Dolittle* and $15,091,000 on *Star!* Fox also estimated that *The Sound of Music* had earned 411.8 percent in film rentals necessary to break even, while all three subsequent roadshow musicals came in well under the breakeven point, *Dolittle* at 52.1 percent, *Star!* at 24.4 percent, and *Dolly!* at 60.7 percent.

Those would-be proxy fights with David Merrick did not happen, but Darryl Zanuck was getting pressure to fire his son and David Brown. One unnamed source said, "Fathers don't usually do this to their sons, no matter what. But it's hard to see how he would have very much choice except to act on the director's recommendations." Two days after Merrick's *Hello, Dolly!* ended its record-breaking run on Broadway, both Brown and Richard were asked to resign by a vote of the board overseen by Darryl. "He was a very cold ass at that meeting, very cold ass," said Richard of his father. "Jesus Christ, it was brutal. And my father, talking, just sitting there, he showed absolutely not any ray of compassion for me. And that hurt me. It was an execution." Richard was ordered off the lot by noon, and Brown was locked out of his New York office. Before the day was over, the names "Richard Zanuck" and "David Brown" were removed from doors and parking spaces. Darryl and the board could justify the move by numbers. Overall estimates for Fox losses in 1970 came to $77 million, with only nine of 33 movies released in 1969 and '70 turning a profit.

Less than two months after Zanuck and Brown were fired, Fox held an auction of its props that netted a paltry $364,480. It was tiny compared to the MGM affair, just 1,000 people over three days. There were 24 props sold from *Cleopatra*, and *Hello, Dolly!*'s two-seated bicycle went for $2,500. Both Zanuck and Brown filed breach of contract lawsuits and settled out of court. Richard claimed damages totaling $22 million. Fox countered, saying Zanuck, a beneficiary of nepotism, engaged in practices that didn't entitle him to additional compensation.

Dennis C. Stanfill, a US Naval Academy graduate and former investment banker, was named Richard Zanuck's successor. In surveying the remnants of Fox, he said, "The industry got too much money too easily. The money market was soft to begin with. Then the movie companies became the pets of the conglomerates. And then there was *The Sound of Music*, which as Dick Zanuck and everybody else agrees, was the most expensive movie Hollywood ever made because it led everybody into those expensive and unsuccessful carbon copies. And if there's anything that seems clear, it's that carbon copies don't work." Estimates at *Dolly!*'s losses came to $16 million. There would be television airings, videocassettes, and DVDs in the future, eventually bringing it close to break even figures. In the few years after its initial release, the New York set became a popular free tourist attraction at Pico and Motor Avenues. Studio heads believed it ought to be exploited, as was Universal City, perhaps as a mini-Disneyland. Entertainment analyst Manny Gerard said, "That set is a monument to man's stupidity. If I were running Fox, I'd never tear it down. I'd want to keep it there as a reminder of the grim past."

Darryl suffered less humiliation than his son and David Brown, but he did lose his 2,200 square foot studio office and bedroom suite while eased into oblivion by the board. Soon after Richard and David Brown were sacked, a board meeting had disgruntled studio employees screaming into a microphone, demanding they be heard, relaying spending abuses on *Dolittle, Star!,* and *Dolly!* Darryl sat quietly in his dark wraparound sunglasses, the ubiquitous cigar jutting out of his mouth. He rose and walked slowly to the microphone, and addressed the assembly: "I have devoted many years to this industry. I wouldn't be able to get a job in any other industry. I know this business from the days of silent pictures to the days of Cinemascope. I started as a boy writing scripts for *Rin Tin Tin.* I will continue to be active in this business. The fact that I have stepped down from my administrative duties may now allow me to step in another capacity. I mean the creative capacity. Maybe one day I'll be lucky enough to come up with another *The Longest Day.* And this has been a long day, too." As he finished his remarks, the 150 attending shareholders gave him a loud, sustained applause. The obfuscations, deflections, box office failures, and misplaced confidence in roadshowing were forgotten as the board voted unanimously to give him the newly created position of "chairman emeritus." As Darryl Zanuck's biographer noted, the meeting "that began with anger ended in a chorus of eulogies from all sides—management, insurgents, stockholders—for Darryl F. Zanuck. The forces at Fox proved that, like the movie industry itself, they are at the same time bitterly competitive and rampantly sentimental."

CHAPTER 16

"Magnificent Apathy"

Production and consumption of American feature films cratered in 1969. Unemployment in craft unions for various technicians, stagehands, and prop men ran as high as 80 percent, while 90 percent of the 23,000-member Screen Actors Guild was out of work. Only 110 of the 634 screenwriters in Hollywood were employed. Seventy-two films were in production by the major studios, but only 16 were shot in Hollywood the old-fashioned way Jack Warner made *My Fair Lady* and *Camelot*. The rest were "runaway productions," shot abroad for a fraction of the cost. Average weekly movie attendance in America was down 40 percent from 1965, which was down 50 percent from the all-time per capita high in 1948.

Careers at all levels were affected. Stars who once made a million dollars a year now took in less than half that. Shirley MacLaine and Rock Hudson went to TV series after *Sweet Charity* and *Darling Lili*. After *Hello, Dolly!*, Gene Kelly was set to direct clowns on a cross-country tour. The ripple effect could be felt; discotheques closed, domestic staff were laid off, and psychiatrists had more time to play golf. Private jets and yachts went up for sale. Polished fruit replaced floral arrangements on Hollywood tables. "The current crisis is the result of a number of factors, but none so obvious as the public's magnificent apathy in the face of some hugely expensive, apathetic films," wrote the *New York Times*.

The Establishment cried that Hollywood was going to the dogs. Hippies congregated along Sunset Strip, while the Los Angeles Police Department blamed them for burglaries, narcotics arrests, and an epidemic of venereal diseases. Industry conditions overseas were no better. Both the United Kingdom and Japan reported a drop in theater admissions of nearly 70 percent over the 1960s. "I see our industry floundering in the biggest storm which has hit it for over 20 years," reported Andrew W. Filson, director of the Film Production Association of Great Britain. "Fewer people want to buy what it costs us more to make and sell so it is no use lulling ourselves to sleep with the sound of music."

No one knew exactly where to point the finger. To some, conglomerate buyouts were causing the problem. To others, that was the key to survival. Vincent Canby wrote, "I don't especially fear the takeover of the major companies by 'outside' interests. There is, of course, the possibility that when a company such as Paramount becomes one of the components of a conglomerate like Gulf + Western Industries, it could be easily liquidated if, for one reason and another, it does not contribute to the overall health of the parent. That is always a distinct possibility. However, I'm not afraid of people who don't know anything about movies being in control of movie companies. People who don't know anything about movies often make rather good ones."

For the Oscar race held in the spring of 1970, studios once again appealed to Academy stomachs. Members who came to *Goodbye, Mr. Chips* screenings were offered beer and baloney sandwiches, while Fox tried its *Doctor Dolittle* trick again, with three-inch prime ribs accompanying *Hello, Dolly!* But a last-ditch effort to rack up awards and decent box office failed. *Chips* won Motion Picture of the Year by the Southern California Council of Churches, and Peter O'Toole's and Siân Phillips won acting trophies from the National Board of Review and National Society of Film Critics, but that made no discernible impact on sluggish ticket sales. O'Toole's Golden Globe win was more meaningful, but *Chips* wasn't even nominated for Best Director or Best Comedy or Musical, while Gene Kelly, *Hello, Dolly!*, and *Paint Your Wagon* all were.

The 1969 Oscars became another collision of Old and New Hollywood, with the big musical again emblematic of all that would soon be outré. *Hello, Dolly!* was up for seven awards, including Best Picture, but failed to secure recognition for Kelly, Barbra Streisand, or Ernest Lehman as screenwriter. *Sweet Charity* scored three mentions, for Costumes, Art Direction, and Scoring of a Musical Picture. *Goodbye, Mr. Chips* earned two—for O'Toole as Best Actor and Scoring of a Musical Picture. O'Toole was up against a would-be Mr. Chips, Richard Burton, nominated for his lusty portrayal of Henry VIII in *Anne of the Thousand Days*, another roadshow underperformer. *Paint Your Wagon* earned but one nomination for Adapted Score.

Unlike the 1968 awards, when the *Oliver!* victory hinted at a resuscitation of the musical, 1969 became a triumph of the new. As expected from the studio that brought forth *Doctor Dolittle*, Fox poured on the heat for *Dolly!*, touting it in the trades as "the only film nominated for a Best Picture Oscar with a G-rating for entire family entertainment." That dull fact did not sway Academy voters, who selected *Midnight Cowboy*, a dark and despairing X-rated buddy picture, for the top honor. John Wayne won Best Actor for *True Grit* in a gesture widely interpreted as pure sentiment. *Dolly!* was the only musical to win anything, snagging awards for Art Direction, Adapted Score, and Sound. While *Dolly!* lost Best Picture, it did win The Please-Don't-Put-Us-Through-DeMille-Again Award by *Harvard Lampoon*. The most obnoxious child star, a.k.a. the Bratwurst Award, went to the entire cast of *Goodbye, Mr. Chips*.

Midnight Cowboy came out of the recently bought United Artists, which did not compromise this individual work of art. Great movies would come out of the smoldering ashes of the old studios. The *Los Angeles Times* noted that "The movies entered the '60s as a mass family entertainment medium in trouble and they [left] them as a mass but minority art-form, importantly and newly influential, wildly divergent, and addressed to many divergent audiences." But MGM, Fox, and Warner Bros. were fatally ill, and UA's luck ran out with a $45 million loss in 1970. Paramount was struggling but registered a relatively minor $2 million loss. In April of 1970, soon after the Oscars, Paramount's Robert Evans and Peter Bart moved their office from the lot at Marathon Street in Hollywood to North Canon Drive in Beverly Hills, where they conceived of the "new Paramount" as a sanctuary free of the "elephantine disasters" of late. "No more *Darling Lili*s or *Paint Your Wagons*," Bart wrote.

Soon after Evans and Bart opened their new office, Paramount's *On a Clear Day You Can See Forever* debuted to muted fanfare. Conceived as a roadshow, it instead came out in standard release and with no formal premiere. Evans and Bart's hunch about its limited appeal proved to be accurate. It was, then as now, a strange, over-orchestrated Streisand obsession piece. But she wasn't enough. "All the film lacks is that indefinable something, the alchemist's gold of the musical, which lifts one out of mere pleasure into exhilaration," wrote the *Observer Review*. Its $13.5 million take was a break-even number. "*On a Clear Day* was quite expensive," said director Vincente Minnelli. "At that time everybody was paying for everything—that was the idea after *Sound of Music*. Expensive pictures brought expensive profits. When *Easy Rider* came along, [the trend] went the other way—and that was wrong also." *On a Clear Day* had a weak book, and relied on visuals and Streisand to camouflage vacuousness. It cannot be counted among the greatest disasters of the era, but neither was it a hit to put alongside *Funny Girl*, *Oliver!*, or even *Thoroughly Modern Millie*. "It was not my greatest musical success," said Minnelli, then added with a wink, "but neither was it Paramount's greatest musical failure." *On a Clear Day* was a red alert for Streisand. One more overproduced, under-earning musical could ruin her, and she knew it. By the time *On a Clear Day* opened, she was making the X-rated comedy *The Owl and the Pussycat*, in which she played a sewer-mouthed pot-smoking hooker porn star.

Streisand and Julie Andrews had been competitors with the overlapping releases of *Funny Girl* and *Star!* The unnatural union reappeared in 1970, when Paramount released Andrews's *Darling Lili* one week after *On a Clear Day*. Advance sales to the 6,000-seat Radio City Music Hall opening were robust, inspiring added seats at top dollar. In fact, Radio City claimed the biggest opening day in its history. The positive sales news balanced some of the most negative publicity of any late roadshow. "'It can never recoup its costs' is probably the most frequently heard comment at any of Hollywood's trade-studded premieres," reported a *Saturday Review* piece. "Rarely has so much bad word-of-mouth preceded a picture." *Darling Lili* has gone "so far over its budget the studio won't tell how many millions," wrote the *Los Angeles Herald Examiner*. Schadenfreude made an appearance. With Hollywood gripped in a recession, why should Blake Edwards and Julie Andrews walk into the sunset with their ill-gained millions? Reports like that got Edwards hopping mad. "I'm sick to death of all the figures printed as the cost of *Darling Lili*. The whispering campaign had it soaring up to $20 million. There was even talk the studio was *afraid* to let stockholders know how much was in Julie's picture." Estimating costs at $14 million, he added, "I've never known of an important picture in production so talked about, whispered about, and yes, lied about as *Darling Lili*."

The two sneak previews in Oklahoma City and Kansas City went very well. "In both places Julie and I are surrounded by Paramount executives congratulating us and saying, 'These are our most successful out of town previews,'" said Edwards. When it opened, however, it faced the same identity problems it had in conception. What is it? It was branded a musical by most, despite Paramount distancing their product from such a label. The *Los Angeles Times* wrote of the pain at seeing so "fantastically costly an enterprise mounted on so flimsy and indeed questionable a story premise, and executed with so little certainty as to whether the tone of the piece was to be pure romance, broad farce, suspense, melodrama, or musical comedy. *Darling Lili* turns out to be a little of each, and not enough of any. . . . The effect is of a skyscraper erected on Rice Krispies." Evoking Hollywood takeover mania, *Variety* declared *Darling Lili* "a conglomerate" suffering from "indecision," its comedy "strained," title character "contrived," and dog fights "out of place."

Lili is set during World War I, but its realities are only hinted at here. Andrews plays a spy and could be a lightning rod for moral explorations, but that is ignored or weakened by Henry Mancini's easy listening score and the stars strolling romantically among butterflies. In the three months before *Darling Lili* appeared, President Nixon ordered the bombing of North Vietnamese supply lines in Laos, then sent American troops into Cambodia. A protest of the invasion at Kent State University left four students dead by National Guardsmen. The nation was cleaved by Vietnam for years, yet Edwards would not suppose audiences could stand a more adult depiction of war. Why did musicals, or whatever *Darling Lili* was, steadfastly refuse to grow up? As in *Star!*, the war is treated here as a bothersome distraction "evidently fought by Rock Hudson and a few pilot friends against a dozen Germans while the rest of the world in evening clothes sings 'It's a Long, Long Way to Tipperary,'" blasted *Look* magazine.

Borrowing from Busby Berkeley's magnificent "Lullaby of Broadway" in *Gold Diggers of 1935*, Edwards opens with Andrews singing Mancini's "Whistling Away the Dark." She is surrounded by blackness, but soon her head and sparkling jewels are lit, then eventually multi-colored lights in the distance reveal that she is alone on a stage, though the background is shadowy and undefined. She spins, and the lights grow hotter. It's a lovely song well suited for Andrews. Soon enough, however, the mechanical failings of *Darling Lili* begin to manifest. Its romance consists of Andrews and Hudson making obligatory doe-eyes at each other. As a spy, *Lili* is downright unprofessional. The prospect that Hudson is involved with another woman arouses such jealousy that she confesses, has him arrested, and finds the working end of a pistol aimed at her throat as she is shuttled to the German border. She's the most conspicuous person in any room, yet she is the last to be suspected as a spy. Then there is her striptease choreographed by Hermes Pan, the same who had been fired from *Finian's Rainbow*. She was not believable as a spy, but she is even less believable as a bump-and-grinder.

It was now open season on Andrews and Edwards, who were married on the lawn of her Beverly Hills home the day *Darling Lili* had its first public screening. Bad press dogged them, while Joyce Haber continued to gleefully swing her wrecking ball: "One newspaperman (who shall also be nameless) seems to be one of the only three people in the world who liked *Darling Lili*: *Lili* comes close to the top of my pretentious-inane-and-hokey roster." Andrews shot back that Haber "needs open-heart surgery, and they should go in through her feet."

Given its size, *Darling Lili* was built for roadshowing, yet Paramount was nowhere near as invested in the format as Fox or UA. In fact, *Darling Lili*'s exhibitors offered free admission to children under 14 and abandoned reserved seats within four months of its premiere. Paramount continued to play down its songs, but that did not extend to the print ads featuring a bonneted Andrews, her mouth unflatteringly wide open to leave no doubt that singing was on the menu. While audiences stayed away from the early and limited reserve seat showings, Paramount cut *Lili* for general release. A grieving Edwards could only shrug and say, "there is nothing I can do about it." His sorrow did not meet with sympathy in the studio front offices. "Wouldn't we be crazy to ruin our own multi-million dollar investment?" said an unidentified executive. "I can tell you with all honesty, *Darling Lili* is a very, very good picture and we are proud of it." Now Edwards had something else in common with Robert Wise besides directing Julie Andrews in a box office loser. Just as Wise disowned the studio version of *Star!*, so, too, did Edwards claim the "new" *Darling Lili* wasn't a Blake Edwards picture.

If *Hello, Dolly!* was not the End of an Era, then *Darling Lili* certainly was. It became a "kind of romantic gesture we're not likely to see again for a very long time," wrote Vincent Canby. "It's the last of the mammoth movie musicals (*Dolly, Paint Your Wagon*) that were inspired by the success of *The Sound of Music* (and each of which cost two or three times as much as Alaska). I doubt that Hollywood, now practically broke and trying desperately to make a connection with the youth market, will ever again indulge itself in this sort of splendidly extravagant, quite frivolous enterprise."

With the quick exit of *Lili*, and no more projects pending, Julie Andrews was asked to vacate her $70,000 apartment at Paramount. "Success is bankable, talent is disposable," she said. "My screen departures from sweetness and light didn't alter my public persona because they didn't make much money or find an audience," she said. "Meanwhile, I'm the same disreputable lady I've *always* been." She went into analysis and stopped singing. "I have never found singing easy or enjoyable," she said. As for professional help, "There I was in the '60s, having enormous success, but I wasn't happy, didn't understand why, and felt I was in an awful mess. I desperately needed some answers, and analysis seemed to be the best way of providing some for myself."

When Gulf + Western chairman Charles Bluhdorn saw the appalling negative number on *Darling Lili*, he attempted to make them disappear with creative book-keeping in a bogus subsidiary, despite the specter of prison should he be caught. He flew to Rome and met with his friend, disreputable Italian banker Michele Sindona. He spoke of Gulf + Western's financial crisis and suggested a merger with real estate and construction giant Società Generale Immobiliare International (SGI) in exchange for $5 million in promissory notes and a package of debentures in, among other potential assets, *Darling Lili*. Bluhdorn's sales pitch led Sindona to invest. He also sold Marathon Studio real estate as a subsidiary of Paramount to SGI for a gain of $15 million. But as *Darling Lili* failed to break even, its losses were not properly recorded against income from the deal, putting Bluhdorn in trouble with the Securities and Exchange Commission. "In retrospect, it's easy to see that Bluhdorn was over the edge—a maverick bent on self-destruction," wrote Peter Bart. He "presented himself as a spirited outlaw who was raiding the sanctum sanctorum of the entrenched corporate power players. While the CEOs were playing golf at their country clubs, Bluhdorn was stealing their companies out from under them." The SEC eventually filed suit in a US District Court alleging Bluhdorn had overstated the income of *Darling Lili* as part of a 60-page brief claiming widespread fraud. As if the musical genre didn't have enough troubles, Blake Edwards's tuneful valentine to Julie Andrews prompted a Mafia takeover of Paramount.

Camelot . . . Doctor Dolittle . . . Star! . . . Sweet Charity . . . Paint Your Wagon . . . Goodbye, Mr. Chips . . . Hello, Dolly! . . . Darling Lili. Hollywood was piled with musical corpses. Even so, two moviemaking companies believed the book musical was still viable as motion picture entertainment. Cinerama International Releasing Organization (CIRO) in collaboration with American Broadcasting Company (ABC) had an ambitious plan to produce 25 films over the next two years. "At a time when most companies have been turning away from roadshow attractions, we and ABC are enthusiastically setting the roadshow pattern for *Song of Norway*," said CIRO president Joseph M. Sugar. "We believe the entertainment impact of this film will prove again that there is an exceptional market for the right attraction." He then sang the chorus that nearly killed Hollywood. "I feel that *Song of Norway* has the basic ingredients to appeal to the same audiences who were attracted to *Sound of Music*." As a musical biography of Edvard Grieg, the "Chopin of the North," it lent itself to spectacular location filming. It also originated on the stage, in a long-running 1944 production. Its sentimental nationalism echoed the love of home that coursed through *Music*. Florence Henderson, who came to be cast in *Norway* after its director Andrew Stone caught her act in

New York at the Plaza Hotel's Persian Room, dismissed the *Music* comparisons. "I heard that talk, but it's a totally different film," she said. "*The Sound of Music* appealed to all religions and families with an incredible score with hit songs in it. *Norway* was a classical film about a classical composer that wouldn't have broad appeal."

Song of Norway would not suffer from anything like the roadshow bottleneck of 1968. It was banking on now uncommon *après garde* filmgoing. By 1970, it had very little company. *Darling Lili's* theatrical career as a roadshow feature was short-lived, and *Hello, Dolly!* began its general release in June. "Beyond [*Tora! Tora! Tora!* and *Song of Norway*], it seems that the motion picture roadshow will have had it," announced *Variety*. "First as [a Columbia executive] put it, 'the American public is not a roadshow public; they don't like leaving a theater for home late at night. This, of course, refers to the family trade. Second, the hard ticketers have always been big budgeters, and the producer-distributors mostly have put a stop to tall-stakes product investments."

Andrew Stone, like Robert Wise and Richard Fleischer before him, would seem an unlikely director of musicals. Now in his late sixties and with a career that reached into the silent era, he forged a reputation for tight, effective thrillers on a budget. Now he was adapting *Song of Norway* for the screen. The stage production took great liberties in accuracy, but Stone maintained that the film would keep close to Grieg's life. "I tried to give it documentary accuracy, the ring of truth," he said. "What was most difficult was to contrast a straight documentary with the musical numbers—some of which are shot in realistic style and others as fantasy. It was daring, but fortunately it worked." Documentary feel? A musical? At least one publication, *America*, believed Stone might have the winning ticket: "Though the formula that brought unprecedented financial rewards to [*The Sound of Music*] is not definable and virtually every major studio carries a large chunk of red ink on its books from at least one project that tried unsuccessfully to duplicate it, *Song of Norway* just might turn the trick."

Stone and film editor wife Virginia went scouting in Scandinavia and England, shooting Grieg's haunts with a 16-millimeter camera. Then Stone wrote the script. "If I had done it the other way around, it would have cost $30 million." ABC approved his film for a measly $3.5 million. Instead of building sets and props, Stone gained approval to use lavish destinations, including North London's Witanhurst, the Georgian Heveningham Hall in Suffolk, and the Tivoli Gardens in Copenhagen. Twenty-seven Scandinavian and English locations were used over seven months of shooting in non-anamorphic Super Panivision 70, for screenings in highly select Super Cinerama theaters.

There were no expensive personnel, and, according to Henderson, not a single set was built. Toralv Maurstad as Grieg was a stage star but was not widely known outside of Norway. The sole big name was none other than Edward G. Robinson as a kind-hearted piano dealer, reportedly accepting the job to visit Oslo's art museums. For a change, all the actors did their own vocals. Robert Wright and George Forrest added lyrics to Grieg's melodies, which Claude Debussy once dismissed as "bonbons wrapped in snow." The London Symphony Orchestra supplied a full sound to blast against those fjord walls, with a 72-piece ensemble and a 20-voice chorus. Henderson was thrilled to be backed by such big noise but expressed ambivalence over Stone. "I liked him very much, he was very good at certain things, but he was old-fashioned in dealing with actors," she recalled. "He approached scenes quite literally and without a lot of imagination. We would rehearse a scene and come up with our own intentions of what we wanted to do." And on one of those sub-zero Norwegian nights, Virginia began an affair with an assistant director, and would later divorce Stone.

Despite the comparatively low cost, Cinerama and ABC fought over *Norway* expenses, with Cinerama threatening to pull out during postproduction. Stone tried sincerely to economize, but costs swelled to nearly $4 million, and the

Florence Henderson and fellow cast member Frank Porretta rehearse for *Song of Norway*. From the collection of Photofest.

release date was postponed a year. ABC nonetheless went all-out in marketing. Colorful ads highlighting scenic wonders appeared in newspapers with ticket-ordering instructions. ABC combined with the Royal Caribbean on a *Song of Norway* cruise ship to be used as a press junket to Miami, though what Miami had to do with Norway was not explained. The *Song of Norway* was touted as "one of the best 'stacked' young ladies of the Caribbean."

Norway was released as a reserve seat attraction in early November and received withering reviews. It's hard to know where to begin the autopsy, but its dreadful script is as good a place as any. The dialogue is laced with efforts to be adorably self-aware:

> "A countryman of yours was asking for you," announces a clerk to Grieg.
> "Who's that?" he says.
> "Mr. Ibsen," replies the clerk.

The critics had a field day. "This film's scenery and music will please the naïve, but its substitution of sentimentality for thought and characterization will offend practically everyone else," noted *Films in Review*. "There is *no* justification for a *total* absence of the cinematic art that saved *Sound of Music*, e.g., from bathos." In *History of Movie Musicals*, Thomas Aylesworth writes, "Some of the more polite critics characterized *Song of Norway* as a bomb. . . . when the audience heard performers sing 'Norway waits for the song of one man' to the tune of one of the themes from Grieg's *Piano Concerto*, they walked out in droves." Pauline Kael drained her poison pen. "The movie is of an unbelievable badness; it brings back clichés you didn't know you knew—they're practically from the unconscious of moviegoers. You can't get angry at something this stupefying; it seems to have been made by trolls." That last remark is in reference to a sequence of giant animated trolls looming over the Norwegian mountaintops. It's so bad it upstages some of the greatest scenery on planet Earth.

Given its universal condemnation, *Song of Norway* might be assumed to be a super-flop, but not so. A disgraced Stone shot back, claiming that *Norway* "sold out night after night after night" at the Cinerama Dome, then lambasted critics who try "to pretend [they're] sophisticated." It made most of its money in England, earning roughly $7.9 million in worldwide rentals. Cinerama's fees, marketing, and loan interest left ABC with a $1 million profit. The haul was hardly distinguished, but a minor profit for any musical in 1970 was news in itself. Stone would use that fact to his advantage one more time.

Also opening in late 1970 was *Scrooge*, a musical version of Dickens's *Christmas Carol*, but it was not roadshowed in the States. "Let's hold no wakes for the musical," said its composer Leslie Bricusse, late of *Doctor Dolittle* and *Goodbye, Mr. Chips*. "Ailing it may be, but it's a long way from being dead and buried. The film will make its money back before you can say 'Merry Christmas.'" He offered a recipe for curing the musical blues. "They ought to stop paying $4 or $5 million just to bring a show from Broadway to the screen," he said. "It's sheer madness. By the time you've paid the star a ridiculous amount the budget has jumped preposterously and you haven't even begun. Instead filmmakers should use something in the public domain—like we did with *Scrooge*. Pay the stars a small salary and give them a share of the profits. The prices will go down but the quality won't." *Scrooge* was slavishly imitative of a certain smash British musical of two years ago. That was no accident. "*Scrooge* was like a sequel to *Oliver!* as we pretty much assembled the same technical crew," said Oswald Morris, the director of photography of both. Musicals may not be dead, but innovative filmmakers appealing to restless young people had moved on to *Five Easy Pieces* and *Little Big Man*. In an era before franchising aimed at teenagers, copycatting was shelter for the middle-aged who wanted their movies safe and stupid. Charles Champlin wondered what the next aping trend would be as follow-ups to the massive hit *Airport*. "I can see *Wharf, Terminal, Depot,* and *Carport* all coming our way, each with George Kennedy chewing cigars and solving problems while Barry Nelson steadies Dean Martin."

While Hollywood floundered, there was the fast rise of some 900 "skinemas" in America specializing in eight and 16-millimeter porn. Recognizing America's splintered demographics, film journalist Axel Madsen asked, "Can Hollywood films talk to suspicious blacks, to anxious idealists, to groping youngsters; can they evoke a spark, a sense of inspiration? The argument is not between liberals and conservatives, but between those who think the system will work and those who don't." Comedian-writer-director-producer Jerry Lewis, bemoaning the proximity of G and X-rated movies in newly subdivided theaters, took action. He combined with Network Cinema Corporation to build small theaters exclusively for family audiences. They were called "Jerry Lewis Cinemas," featuring prefab suburban micro-theaters (100 seats) or mini-theatres (350 seats) as low overhead alternatives to the "old antiquated movie palaces located in downtown areas with traffic and parking problems." With automated projection, one of his theaters could be run by as few as two people. The first one went up in Old Bridge, New Jersey, and one of its bookings was *Song of Norway*.

Lewis wanted to screen nothing but G-rated features, but the numbers would not support it. He had to offer a tossed salad of movie choices, though nothing racier than M-rated movies were allowed. With mature fare also on the marquee, Lewis installed a hotline so that parents could make informed decisions. He wanted a clean outlet for the saddened youth of today. "Remember the 1930s and '40s! Where did the average red-blooded American kid go when Mom wanted him to get lost for half a day? To the neighborhood movie house. He'd sit through a double feature and seven shorts and six cartoons. Where are those teenagers today?" What a silly question. They became the parents of teenagers who smoked dope, listened to Simon & Garfunkel's "Bridge over Troubled Water," laughed over *Laugh-In*, cried over *Love Story*, and boarded aircraft bound for Southeast Asia.

CHAPTER 17

Acts of Faith

A clearer accounting of the 1969 recession emerged by 1971. The red-ink horror show was led by Fox, with more than $146 million in pre-tax operating losses. First runner-up was MGM with nearly $87 million, then Warner Bros. with $59 million, Columbia with $40 million, and Paramount with $22 million. From 1969 to 1971, the only studios to register profits were Disney and American International Pictures. Universal, Warner Bros., Fox, Disney, Paramount, and MGM had abandoned roadshows, making Columbia and UA the last major holdouts. Columbia, the only studio to bankroll two profitable roadshow musicals in the late 1960s (*Funny Girl* and *Oliver!*), jumped ship when its two reserved-seat historic dramas, *Nicholas and Alexandra* and *Young Winston*, did not perform well.

Even though it was presently ailing, United Artists had the cleanest record in Hollywood, perhaps in part because it did not make a priority of giant musicals. Between 1951 and 1969, it saw profits every year but 1963. *Chitty Chitty Bang Bang* was a disappointment against big expectations, but it did not damage the company extensively. The "studio without walls" could not escape the recession, however, and in 1970 declared its biggest ever loss of $35 million. Lawyer turned UA chairman Arthur B. Krim called the selling of UA to Transamerica the "biggest mistake we ever made. But you have to reconstruct the climate of the time. Conglomerates were selling at very high multiples, and when Transamerica approached us, we succumbed to the seduction. And for a while we thought we had made a very wise decision because the value of the Transamerica stock to our stockholders was something like $175 million at the time of the merger and within two years, the value jumped to over $500 million. And it was caused by United Artists, or it had the appearance of being caused by a glamorous company putting a spotlight on a less glamorous conglomerate. So it worked beautifully until everything changed after 1969."

When producer David Picker became UA president in 1969, one of his first assignments was to say "yes" or "no" to various projects in the company's possession. He shelved a film adaptation of the 1966 Broadway musical *I Do! I Do!* for Julie Andrews and moved *Fiddler on the Roof* into production. Though Ross Hunter had first eyed *Fiddler*, the huge 1964 Broadway musical smash, for Universal, UA eventually bought it for $2 million plus a percentage of the profits. Picker recalled that *Fiddler* was an unusually easy property to acquire relative to its enormous success on stage. That wasn't because film musicals were out of favor. "The subject matter of *Fiddler* kept the majors away," he said. "They believed no one wanted to see a Jewish musical. So it was there to be made."

Picker told Walter Mirisch (*West Side Story*) that he had a choice of producing *Fiddler* or *Man of La Mancha*, another recent Broadway musical that UA bought at top dollar. Mirisch quickly chose *Fiddler* then approached Norman Jewison to direct. Jewison had become something of a darling at the Mirisch Corporation after directing their 1966 sleeper *The Russians Are Coming, The Russians Are Coming*, then following it with *In the Heat of the Night* and *The Thomas Crown Affair*. With those strong credits, offering Jewison *Fiddler* is no shocker, though he had never directed a musical. The Canadian Methodist Jewison was gung-ho, his agent joking to Picker that, "He is so desirous of directing *Fiddler*, he would even be willing to change his name to Irving." Mirisch and Jewison agreed *Fiddler*'s stage playwright Joseph Stein should write the screenplay. The terms made it one of the biggest deals in film musical history, dwarfed by *My Fair Lady*, but nearer to *South Pacific* and *Camelot*.

How did UA come to support *Fiddler* and *La Mancha*? According to the directors of both, Arthur Krim and David Picker simply believed the two properties could make successful films and they were exactly what UA should be producing. Still, they knew the risks. *Fiddler* was the first large-scale Broadway transfer since *Dolly!* two years earlier. "The failure of *Hello, Dolly!* must have cast a chill over the accounting departments of the major film companies; so it took a certain amount of faith and courage on the part of United Artists to invest the large sums necessary to get *Fiddler* onto the screen," wrote *Saturday Review*. UA had not been scorched on roadshows as had Fox, MGM, and Paramount. Even so, it is extraordinary that *Fiddler* and *La Mancha* got made on such generous terms.

On stage, *Fiddler* was an even greater phenomenon than *Hello, Dolly!*, and far richer in humanity and heart. Filled with lovable characters, humor, and warm sentiment, it tells the story of a Russian Jew in 1905 who bemusedly watches his eldest three daughters marry for love, not by customary parental arrangement. This becomes the canvas for the larger reality of early twentieth-century religious and social history, told melodiously through such instant classics as "Matchmaker, Matchmaker" and "If I Were a Rich Man." In describing the context for lead character Tevye, musical authority Frederick G. Vogel wrote, "Through sheer force of personality, the peasant dairy farmer is the cynosure of all eyes from beginning to end, the sun around which all the other players, and the plot itself, revolve. The finest of the actors selected to play him over the years have had to exhibit bigness in both talent and bulk in order to justify the commanding presence of this gentle giant of a troubled father reluctantly growing ever more accustomed to grief, but never wallowing in despair. Living in virtual serfdom, he is increasingly saddened over the loss of the cherished customs under which he grew into adulthood while acknowledging his inability, and apparently God's unwillingness, to prevent their further erosion. At the end they exist only in memory."

Fiddler became the biggest stage musical of its day. It was translated into 16 languages, ran in 32 countries, and returned a 927 percent profit to its investors and producers. Forty-three albums were cut, including 18 original cast albums in various languages. By the early 1970s, estimated worldwide attendance reached 35 million. Mirisch loved the play and thought it would translate on film beautifully, but Krim doubted its wide market appeal because it was "so ethnically oriented." He told Mirisch, "If we make this film, it will probably do well in New York, where there are a million and half Jewish people, but what do we do with it elsewhere?" Mirisch persuaded a reluctant Krim to move forward, and in confronting Jewison, Krim said, "We don't want a Seventh Avenue [Yiddish] production. We want the film to play everywhere in the world, regardless of religion."

"*Fiddler* has a much stronger story than *La Mancha*," said Jewison. "It's much more accessible to American audiences, and has an exceptional score. For a time there was hardly a marriage that didn't play 'Sunrise, Sunset.' People identified with the family; that's where its strength came. Arthur Krim knew this, and it took great courage to assign the production and direction to me, because I'm not Jewish, and the show is steeped in Jewish culture." Krim knew how to partition business and art. With Jewison, he never spoke about marketing or box office projections, but about ideas. He might ask, "What's the central point of the film, and why do you want to make it?" This earned Jewison's immense respect for Krim. "The UA directors were given great license," said Jewison. "Essentially, they were the stars—whether it was Billy Wilder or William Wyler. UA was always more director oriented than star oriented. That's the secret of their success. The creative filmmaking came from Krim." And with *Fiddler*, UA was not just selling stars, or one song, or a lightheaded Broadway lark. There was something of major artistic and commercial power in *Fiddler*, and Krim well knew it.

Jewison, a smallish, energetic man, was justifiably nervous. "*Hello, Dolly!* barely paid for itself," he said. "*Paint Your Wagon* and *Doctor Dolittle* were disasters." He did not envision a musical ever materializing in his directing career. "I've always dodged musical films because I think musicals belong in the theater," he told a reporter. "There's something unreal about them, like opera. In the theater you accept that, while in films you can't accept it any more. I hated *Hello, Dolly!* and I was so disturbed by the success of *The Sound of Music* that I asked Richard Rodgers why it was so much more successful than better things he has written." Rodgers had no answer. But Jewison was so moved by *Fiddler* that he overcame his musical avoidance strategy and focused instead on the breakdown of tradition and its relevance to current social life in America and elsewhere.

Though Zero Mostel owned Tevye on stage and had modest success on film in *A Funny Thing Happened on the Way to the Forum* and *The Producers*, he held no illusions of being hired for the movie. While the Brooklyn-born Mostel complained that UA thought the show was too Jewish, Mirisch and Jewison looked for a more authentic Tevye. They saw Topol, a large Israeli actor with dark brown eyes, on stage in London as Tevye, and were sold. The suits at UA agreed, despite his lack of fame. It "does not mean that I'm a better Tevye than all the others," he said. "The only advantage that I can see that I myself bring is that I have the perspective of a third generation looking back. My grandfather was a sort of Tevye." As for his predecessor, "Zero created the role for all the rest of us," he said graciously. In contrast, Jewison said, "I felt Mostel had monopolized the character of Tevye and given him a very strong American interpretation. I felt he kind of stepped out of the play and the performance was too big to ever be captured on film. I was turning to a more realistic approach to *Fiddler*."

Jewison did a multi-continent search for other actors, and cast unknowns. "These people are close to the earth. This will be a simple film," he said. But he was just as risky in casting actors who could easily have appeared too young or too old for their roles. Topol was only 35 and played Tevye on stage in padding and a gray wig, while costar Paul Mann as his prospective son-in-law was 57. Leonard Frey, as the meek tailor Motel, was 32, also a bit too old for his part. Norma Crane as Tevye's wife, Golde, was 42. Many in the cast had never sung or danced, which might have been a death wish on the order of *Paint Your Wagon*. But it wasn't, and the cast largely meshed. Mostel couldn't fall back on a "Hollywood only hires movie stars" story line to account for his non-participation. "I don't think [he] ever forgave any of us," said Jewison.

Though the Mirisch Corporation initially scouted locations in Saskatchewan to double for the Russian Steppes, Jewison wanted *Fiddler* made in Eastern Europe. He received permission to film in Yugoslavia only because Josip Broz Tito, the country's respected president, loved movies. Rehearsals and production took place in London and Yugoslavia between August 1970 and January 1971, with 94 shooting days in Yugoslavia and 28 in London at Pinewood. Under a baseball cap with a *Fiddler* button pinned on, Jewison made judicious use of crane shots and nixed anything aerial. While on location in November, they had a *Darling Lili*–style weather problem, but without horrendous costs or production shutdown. It didn't snow when it was supposed to, so the company shot around bright sun using copious amounts of marble dust. The flat farming village of Lekenik, 25 miles from Zagreb and teeming with livestock, became *Fiddler*'s shtetl of Anatevka.

As producer and director, Jewison had vast control of *Fiddler* and would not suffer corporate interference unless he ran over budget. It was a remarkable state of employment and remained consistent with Transamerica's reputation of leaving UA alone to do what it does best. "I've never seen a distributor, an exhibitor, or anybody else, or a committee, or the head of a studio, ever improve on a film," said Jewison. "Only creative people can improve on a film." Cinematographer Oswald Morris said, "Norman was under the most hideous pressure from United Artists to keep costs down. To give him his due, he withstood all this; he had a vision for *Fiddler*, which he wasn't prepared to compromise, no matter what the front office said, and I greatly admired him for this." Jewison immersed himself in classic Jewish culture. "I think he knows more about Judaism today than I do," said Topol. *Fiddler* lyricist Sheldon Harnick noted that Jewison, "isn't Jewish, but he did so much research in preparation for the film that he became quite knowledgeable about things Jewish. As a result, either Topol, or someone else suggested that he should be made an honorary Jew and renamed Norman Christianson!"

The shoot was arduous, particularly in Yugoslavia. "It got to be like a prison," said Leonard Frey. "The first week everything was sociability, mirth, parties. Then everyone got quiet, then tense, then bitter. By the third week you had to have lists of who was talking to who." But a sense of importance and even reverence for the

Director Norman Jewison and Topol as Tevye, a poor dairyman, consult during the filming of "If I Were a Rich Man" from *Fiddler on the Roof*. Jewison is wearing a baseball cap with a "Fiddler" button attached. From the collection of Photofest.

undertaking prevailed. "This is like a document of historical significance," said Molly Picon, who played the matchmaker. "It's part of a world that's gone. What began with *Fiddler* and the life in the 1900s ended, finally, with Hitler. There's such a joy and tenderness about this. There's a sadness, too. The world that we're portraying has been destroyed."

Before finishing in Yugoslavia and returning to Pinewood, *Fiddler* was two weeks behind schedule and $300,000 over budget. Krim and Mirisch were getting antsy, telling Jewison to finish and get home. "I'm over budget," admitted Jewison. "You can hardly blame them because the industry's flat on its ass and here's $9 million going out the door. It's a lot of money. They're feeling it, so they're saying 'what the hell's he doing over there?'" Even so, Jewison maintained they he never consciously sought to avoid the mistakes of recent musical roadshows. "I don't remember that they had any influence on my decision making," he said. "I don't think we can do that from an artistic standpoint. We're not thinking of box office, but of making something vivid and exciting and compelling in itself."

Jewison may have banished recent failed musicals from his immediate thinking, but others at UA did not. The studio had quietly closed its roadshow department after *Chitty Chitty Bang Bang*, then reopened it for *Fiddler* with a staff of five. *Fiddler* benefited from the lessons learned from its not so celebrated predecessor with a detailed marketing plan. UA aimed to play *Fiddler* as reserve seats in cities large and small, and identified group sales as a secret weapon. The sales manual came with clear instructions on how to successfully approach fraternal orders, garden clubs, labor unions, the PTA, the YMCA and YWCA. More than a year before its scheduled release, marketers were directed to "review and analyze previous roadshows from the point of view of timing, monies, and materials," with specific information on roadshow venues in each first-run city. *Fiddler's* lavish marketing was derived not just from nervousness over a big budget, but from a genuine confidence in the film. "[Marketing executive] Gabe Sumner really threw his heart into *Fiddler*," said Jewison. "UA loved the film and that translates into the effort made. The response of UA was tremendous."

While *Fiddler* was being edited, the stage version became the longest running musical in Broadway history with 2,845 performances, unseating *Hello, Dolly!* And in negotiating how to sell it, *Fiddler* became one of the first big budgeted films marketed along lines that were later defined as "politically correct." The demographics of race, ethnicity, gender, age, and in particular, religion, went into UA's strategy. Immediately before the film opened, Topol said, "I hope this film—apart from entertainment—I hope that there is a little bonus in this piece of work." He hoped it would help minorities "understand that they have rights and not to be pushed around by majorities, and hopefully someday the majorities will understand it, too."

Jewison made 14 minor cuts late on a Saturday night in October at Pinewood, then let his baby go. "I am very depressed," he wrote David Picker. "It is always rather traumatic when one finally has to give up a film." He allowed only five people to see it in advance of the preview. Director Fred Zinnemann "laughed and cried all the way through it, came out drying his eyes, saying, 'It's the greatest musical I have ever seen!' When Sidney Poitier visited Pinewood, he saw only the first 10 minutes, but exited the screening room aglow. "It relates to all races and creeds, not only Jews but to blacks, Puerto Ricans, all." At a preview screening at the Rivoli, there were plenty of raves. But despite such advanced reactions, and the immense crossover appeal of the stage version, UA remained sensitive about *Fiddler's* Jewishness, and arranged screenings for and sought endorsements from hundreds of religious, educational, and political leaders. There were plans to use the Rivoli on Sundays for a combined morning worship service and *Fiddler* screening. Famed author and minister Norman Vincent Peale declared it to be "a universal human drama which should be seen by Americans of all ages, races, and creeds." UA even planned a multi-denominational screening of church leaders in New York. *Newsday* reported an exchange at the premiere: "An older man who obviously had emotional ties with what was happening on the screen (i.e., the Czar's eviction of the Jews in 1905) threatened to beat up a younger man who had muttered disparaging remarks about the movie.... The younger man was treating *Fiddler* as a movie, which was as susceptible to criticism, and even to his sarcasm, as any other movie. The older man's reaction was uncritical, verging on reverential." Film journalist Richard Schickel stopped just short of calling *Fiddler's* marketing anti-Semitic, or at least whitewashing the specifics of displaced Jews. "The souvenir booklet they sell in the lobby explains heavily that *Fiddler* is all about 'human values,' about 'breaking down of traditions,' about 'love ... pride and dignity, sorrow and oppression.' All the things that Really Matter, in short. But these are empty generalizations. Almost any putative work of art is about one or more of them. But when they are the work of honest artists we hardly notice, so absorbed are we in the fates of specific and highly individualized people. In this movie 'meaning' is present in every gesture."

All that wooing of Christian leaders paid off in great reviews that stressed *Fiddler's* universality while almost ignoring the film's Jewish specificity. "Norman Jewison hasn't so much directed a film as prepared a product for world consumption," wrote *The New Republic*. A "just-like-other-people quality runs all through the film, to make the Jewish audience feel integrated and to bring the gentile audience inside. The Friday night services, the dancing by the stream, the defense of the home, are all given a cosmopolitanizing lacquer of Norman Rockwell."

UA spent over $2 million on promotion for *Fiddler's* initial engagements alone, and the investment paid off spectacularly well. More than a dozen full house group sales had been made on one screen in Los Angeles alone more than eight months in advance of the premiere. *Fiddler* played the Rivoli for more than one year and grossed $16.9 million in its 89 roadshow releases, which was a mere 5 percent of its total potential bookings. It was released in typical form: New York premiere, and Los Angeles two days later. There were seven more dates a month later, and 22 per month after that. Internationally, it had opened in Western Europe, Israel, Hong Kong, Australia, and South Africa for the holidays.

Fiddler has much in common with *The Sound of Music*, yet is hardly imitative. In addition to being two cinematically expansive adaptations of Broadway originals, they share religion, effective locations, family, changing times, romantic and filial love, memorable tunes, and shrewd combining of humor and drama. Both have loving families struggling against forces beyond their control. Jewison even appears to have taken notes from *Music*'s Robert Wise on camera shots. Wise achieves a radiant profile of the Mother Superior reverently singing "Climb Ev'ry Mountain" that Jewison mirrors with family matriarch Golde during "Sabbath Prayer." *Fiddler* hedges its bets not by stating a point of view on the breakdown of tradition (is that a good thing or a bad thing?), but by circumventing that question with clear denunciations of pogroms and forced transmigration. But that's okay—for it seems *Fiddler*, by sympathizing both with the parents and children, is acknowledging culture change in all its complexity.

There was scattered bad press early on, but Gabe Sumner wasn't too concerned. He told Jewison, "I think we have a film of such unique audience appeal that it doesn't seem to be affected by any minority (or a combination) of negative reviews.... The people love it, and that, in the final analysis, will see it through." When a slam review appeared in the *New York Times*, David Picker wrote a letter to the paper stating, "How sad it must be for your movie critic, Vincent Canby, that he views a painting and sees only the cracks in the painting or the flaws in the frame, listens to a symphony and hears only the instrument out of tune, sees the film *Fiddler on the Roof* and finds only a violin too well played or an accent too English. How sad that he cannot take a chance and let himself feel, or touch, or see because he might be moved, or touched, or even cry. How sad for Mr. Canby and how sad for his readers." Canby did not redress Picker exactly, but he did retaliate with a diatribe on the sad state of the film musical. Dwindling audiences against increased costs, "plus the well-deserved flops of *Star!* and *Doctor Dolittle*, have just about finished the once joyful tradition of the original American film musical. It's no accident, I think, that with the possible exception of *Gigi*, none of the great original movie musicals of the 1940s and 1950s (*An American in Paris, Singin' in the Rain, Funny Face*, etc.) was conceived as a movie that had to be financially successful if the company that produced it was to survive.... Today we have what amounts to a new, mostly joyless tradition, that of the safe, artistically solemn, pre-sold musical behemoth adapted from the Broadway hit." Canby added *Fiddler* to the woeful list, though he agreed the movie is "superior in almost every respect" to the Broadway imports of recent years.

And still there were comments on *Fiddler*'s universality despite its Jewishness, a point rarely if ever made of *The Sound of Music*'s Christianity. "It deals with problems that really belong to everybody in the world, every generation, every father," wrote *Seventeen*. "A daughter comes to her father and says, you want me to marry one man but I want to marry a Japanese, or a Chinese, or a Negro, or a Jew, and you ask, are you out of your mind? It's not just a matter of religion or color or class. It's not only the breaking of tradition. It's always a touching moment. Every father, any parent has the moment when he has to give up his daughter to a stranger."

Fiddler is not a perfectly realized adaptation, and many who saw the original stage production, including Vincent Canby, felt the film suffered in comparison. At 180 minutes of leisurely storytelling, it was a far cry from a classic Hollywood musical in look, feel, and sound. But everyone in the movie eschews showiness to be as humble and real as possible, so when they break through realism to sing with full orchestra, the old musical dilemma rears its ugly head. Topol's stoic performance creates a calm at the center that threatens sedation, and Norma Crane as Golde never finds the right balance of hardscrabble but loving wife and mother. Even so, *Fiddler* is a top quality musical film, and compares favorably to any of its recent predecessors. The rural settings are beautifully integrated with the story, and the glorious music is lovingly transferred. There is plenty of character singing in *Fiddler*, but it does not have the sound of travesty that came with *Camelot* and *Paint Your Wagon*. The dance numbers are dynamic, and avoid the forced exuberance of *Half a Sixpence* or the blurry incoherence of *Paint Your Wagon*. Those who loved *Fiddler* really and truly loved *Fiddler*, declaring it "the most powerful" or "one of the best" movie musical ever made. It is studiously literal in its Marc Chagall–inspired set designs, its depiction of labor, of sunrise and sunset, of Tevye's lame horse, and of muddy streets and dilapidated houses, but the realism of *Fiddler* extends only so far. While it changes tone in the second half to evoke sorrow and pity, it is still confined by a formal approach that insists on careful blocking, prerecorded songs, and the inherent artificiality of the classic musical form. *Fiddler* also blinks on the depiction of both violence and poverty. The sacking of a wedding is brief and bloodless, and while Tevye and his family are very poor, everyone's clothes are clean and well pressed.

Once again, critical opinion was divided, but *Fiddler* broke the Curse of the Woebegone Big Musical. It brought in $38.2 million. That's roughly half of *The Sound of Music*'s earnings, but half of *Music* still qualifies as a blockbuster. Six months after it opened at the Rivoli, *Fiddler* added four roadshow engagements in greater New York City alone, and it moved into 500 North American theaters nearly one year after it opened. At final tally, it was among the top grossers in UA history, and one of the top grossing musicals ever.

"The success of films just constantly amazes me," said a pensive Norman Jewison. "I can't understand it. I sometimes think I like this or that film, so why didn't it do better? I try to analyze it. I think it's well cast; I like the performances. Sometimes I think timing is everything in filmmaking. The timing of *Fiddler* was perfect. The timing of when a film is released and the mood of the public are important. When times are not too good, the tradition has been musicals and comedies do well. People want to feel good, their spirits are lifted by a trip to the cinema. There's a little bit of truth in it. But I don't think there are any rules. That's what's fascinating about this business. It's always a real gamble."

Fiddler received UA's loving treatment, but was anyone going to make a movie of Broadway's *Cabaret*? Too many musical horror stories left it very nearly orphaned on the road to adaptation. In 1968, Cinerama announced that it had bought the film rights for $2.1 million with *Song of Norway* as part of a studio development plan for roadshow musicals and the formation of a global distribution company. But while it stayed committed to *Norway*, Cinerama backed out of *Cabaret*, and Allied Artists and Haven Industries bought it for $1.5 million. For the modest Allied Artists, this was the biggest purchase in its history. Then Allied bought out Haven's interest and joined ABC as its producing partner in a deal that took a year of negotiating. Ultimately, ABC and Allied would each bear half of the cost and enjoy half of any profits, while Cinerama remained the UK distributor. Studios were now splitting expenses and sharing profits in a strategy to stay alive. ABC did the same thing in collaboration with Warner Bros. over its upcoming musical production of *Mame* starring Lucille Ball.

Cabaret began with a not exorbitant budget of $5 million. "We think we've learned that if we control costs and plan carefully, we can make a major musical at that price," said ABC president Martin Baum. Despite its smallish design, titans Joseph P. Mankiewicz, Gene Kelly, and Billy Wilder were mentioned as possible directors. Harold Prince, producer-director of *Cabaret* on stage, was also considered, but he was occupied with the black comedy *Something for Everyone* as his first film. *Cabaret* took time to define itself but eventually became a beautiful game of dominoes. Much of the credit goes to Baum. He engaged Cy Feuer, who had no film experience but an exceptional track record on Broadway, to produce. Bob Fosse wanted desperately to direct, but after the expensive *Sweet Charity*, he received no early offer. He pitched himself to Freur, who then sold him to the higher-ups. Once Fosse got to work, he clashed with screenwriter Jay Presson Allen. As a result, Hugh Wheeler was brought on for rewrites. He soon ran afoul of studio executives but managed to keep his ideas for dialogue and action intact. He wrote to friend and costar Michael York that "ghastly pressures from ABC to bowlerise [*sic*] it [are] so far unsuccessful. *Love Story* has made them all convinced that all movies must now be *Rebecca of Sunnybrook Farm*."

Fosse wanted *Charity* cameraman Robert Surtees but was given Geoffrey Unsworth instead, whose work on *Half a Sixpence* was one of that film's assets, while his *2001: A Space Odyssey* was as innovative as anything of the decade. *Cabaret* is set in Berlin, a town Fosse found "terribly depressing" and without a film industry save pornography. Select exteriors were shot there, at the Palace of Charlottenburg and the Tiergarten. But *Cabaret*'s interiors were filmed at Bavaria Studios near Munich, where the pleasing children's musical fantasy *Willy Wonka &*

the Chocolate Factory, with a score by *Doctor Dolittle*'s Anthony Newley and Leslie Bricusse, had also been filmed.

Liza Minnelli, famous for being the daughter of Vincente Minnelli and Judy Garland, was cast as Sally Bowles, a modestly talented American chanteuse singing at the title establishment and drifting through Weimar Berlin on delusions of grandeur. Once again, *Cabaret* benefited from timing, as Minnelli was just emerging from her parental shadows to become a singularly arresting entertainer, her huge brown eyes and gutsy voice framed by a close-cropped Louise Brooks do. Pint-sized Joel Grey, who originated the role of *Cabaret*'s epicene, pasty emcee, was retained. Boyishly handsome British actor Michael York was cast as a sexually ambiguous naïf in a den of vice.

Fosse showed a genius for adaptation. He freely picked and chose from author Christopher Isherwood's source collection *The Berlin Stories* as well as the Broadway musical. Subplots from one or another version were dropped, while the coming of the Nazis, bisexuality, and Judaism would be central to the plot. No production numbers of the *Sweet Charity* sort would be staged. Every song would be justified in the plot and logical to the dramatic moment. No singing or dancing would take place in *Cabaret* unless it would take place in reality under similar conditions, including the chilling beer garden anthem to nascent fascism "Tomorrow Belongs to Me." Fosse was on fire; he worked "as if his career was on the line," said Joel Grey—and it was. "He was intent on proving himself a director of drama as opposed to musicals."

Holding to a budget that Freur called the "tight collar," Fosse used artists George Grosz and Otto Dix as inspiration for the look of *Cabaret*. He also told the chorus of "Kit-Kat Girls" to gain weight and let their underarms go hairy. The cabaret stage was built at a realistic but cramped 10 by 14 feet, while its rag-tag orchestra was made of women and others of unspecified gender. Fosse tried to "make the dances look like the period, not as if they were done by me, Bob Fosse, but by some guy who is down and out." As she proved with *Sweet Charity*, Fosse's wife Gwen Verdon was a good sport and real trouper in her uncredited assistance with costumes and props. Fosse made sure each song commented on the political, social, or sexual metaphors of their characters, and Berlin of the time. From the beginning and without compromise, Fosse labored to make the first musical intended wholly for adults.

York remembered the production was "supervised by a legion of producers and assistant producers and innumerable assistants assisted by their assistants." Screenwriter Wheeler was on the set frequently and made changes on the spot, while Fosse incorporated suggestions from actors. *Cabaret* even managed fresh takes on slightly threadbare '60s fads like shock edits, extreme close-ups, and handheld cameras. Fosse took his time and shot almost double the footage he had on *Sweet Charity*, with additional use of multiple cameras, so as to have more options in editing. He also sought greater realism, both because of the subject and because of changing tastes. "I tried purposely to make it less glossy," he said. "I tried purposely to be a little cruder and not so perfect in everything—composition, for instance, and angles. The camera was much more involved with the action." He was determined "that I shouldn't turn this movie into a typical Hollywood musical. Don't get me wrong, I have tremendous admiration for the Hollywood musicals of the past, but what we needed most with *Cabaret* was a sense of reality. You can't hear 40 violins when you see a six-piece combo on the screen. Audiences won't accept that any more. Truthfulness is what people want now."

Fosse was under executive intervention to hurry up and change this and that, while York believed, "It's an absolute miracle that he kept the vision alive." When Fosse received a note complaining that the nightclub scenes were too dark, he read it aloud to cast and crew. According to Minnelli, there was "a long pause, and then a lot of ripping of paper." After cutting the film from three hours to two, Fosse allowed Wheeler to attend a screening. "It is either terribly good—or not, if that expresses anything," said Wheeler. "I saw it with all the money people being imposing, neutral big shots exuding that deadly 'I'm not going to commit myself' aura which so chills in a projecting room."

Though test screenings in Anaheim, Los Angeles, and Minneapolis were overwhelmingly positive, Fosse was prone to nervous insecurities and would not allow himself the specter of directing a major hit. After Vincente Minnelli watched an early screening, he turned to Fosse and said, "I have just seen the perfect movie." He later elaborated: "It's an important picture, certainly in the progression of the film musical, but also as drama. It dazzled, it thrilled, it filled you with despair, it gave pause for sober thought. *Cabaret*'s sophistication was singular. This wasn't the empty headed joy that characterizes the musical genre. *Cabaret* was about *something*." A near-ecstatic preview in San Francisco made Fosse too jumpy to eat the Peking duck and barbequed piglet spread out before him at the after party in a Chinese restaurant. He asked a reporter, "What gets people out to see a movie?"

"Good reviews, smart advertising campaign, promotion, and word-of-mouth all contribute to the success of an exceptional picture," was the answer. "And, with *Cabaret*, I think you have good timing in your favor. It's coming in at a good time, early in the year when we can use a fresh, new musical."

"I hope you are right," was all Fosse could say.

Allied Artists was in the financial doldrums just like everyone else in the movie business and pinned its hopes on *Cabaret*. Like *Fiddler on the Roof*, *Cabaret* was a tricky film to publicize, though for different reasons. It's got Nazis and homosexuality. It's also dark, acrid, and tawdry, stars little-known players, has an emcee who looks like "Twiggy in drag," and—worst sin of all—it's a musical! To the credit of its marketing department, Allied Artists went about conducting a perfectly brilliant campaign, scoring publicity coups in getting Minnelli on the covers of both *Time* and *Newsweek*, and chats with TV talk show giants David

Frost and Dick Cavett. More advantageous coverage came from *Cosmopolitan*, *Men's Wear*, *Good Housekeeping*, *Harper's Bazaar*, *Vogue*, *After Dark*, *Seventeen*, and *Reader's Digest*. It seems everybody was keen on reporting about *Cabaret*.

Since Cinerama dropped out, no one among *Cabaret*'s executive backers advocated releasing it as a roadshow, and what Fosse put together was anathema to the very idea. There was no overture, intermission, or exit music. It begins and ends with prolonged moments of silence over a dark screen or distorted images of *Cabaret*'s grotesque denizens. It clocks in at a reasonable 124 minutes. The only roadshow element intact was one big city reserve seat engagement as it opened simultaneously in seven American markets. Its poster hardly promised musical bliss. It featured Minnelli in bowler hat, hot pants, and vest poised on the T of CABARET, done up as orange and pink strip lights, floating in a sea of inky black.

Cabaret opened in February, typically a month when studios unload garbage while the prestige releases from the previous year get touted for Oscars. Even so, it had a splash premiere at the Ziegfeld in midtown Manhattan, with Minnelli besieged with screaming autograph seekers. Most leading critics abandoned all restraint to become geysers of praise. "*Cabaret* broadens the horizons of the movie musical in a profound, adult way, and by benefiting us all, takes its own important place in the history of movies," proclaimed Rex Reed. "*Cabaret* is an exquisitely sculpted milestone in the history of the film musical," wrote Charles Champlin. "It may not be the best musical ever made—I couldn't say—but it is the most thrilling I have ever seen, the most adult, the most intelligent, the most surpassingly artful in its joining of cinema, drama, and music to evoke the mood and events of a turning point (and turning place) in history." *Cabaret* successfully reconciled the realism/formalism contrast of stage and film. "The stage show of the cabaret was not evil," noted Fosse biographer Martin Gottfried. "The evil lay in the audience's unresponsive, insensitive, soulless, impassive faces. The only gleeful responses that Fosse allowed the audience were in response to female mud wrestlers. It was hardly necessary to point out further the parallel between these observers and the Germany of 1933 sitting still for the Nazi show." Indeed, *Cabaret* is most effective at conveying the indifference ordinary people took to the rise of Nazism, and the accompanying false gaiety, rendered as a defiance of real feeling by Minnelli's full-throttle and savagely ironic performance of the title song.

As *Cabaret* prepared to spread to 35 domestic engagements by the end of March, Fosse dreaded a repeat of the *Sweet Charity* experience, with early raves giving way to critical slams and box office fizzle. But by April he allowed himself to believe that *Cabaret* would meet a different fate. "It's been open in New York six weeks, and the New York reviews have been terrific. Business has been absolutely fantastic—so that my earlier apprehension about the same sort of thing happening again has been somewhat relieved, although I'm a very cautious man and like to avoid disappointments. So I sort of prepare myself. But from what everyone tells me who follows these things closely (I don't), it looks to me like an enormous hit."

Cabaret was the first musical to employ a maturity of theme and cynicism of tone found in the best non-musicals of the era. From the collection of Photofest.

There was some grumbling amid the hosannas. "As an interpretation of history, *Cabaret* is trivial the way that all musicals are," wrote *Commonweal*. The "razzle-dazzle show biz is persistently at odds with the effort to be serious," noted *Cue*, while Minnelli's "big song numbers keep destroying the realism, since they ooze a Las Vegas-type glitter." The originator himself, Christopher Isherwood, was not entirely pleased. "You have this little girl saying, 'Oh, I'll never make it. I haven't really any talent.' Then she comes to the stage and you realize that she's every inch Judy Garland's daughter. And Joel Grey comes on stage and he's simply fantastic. The truth is that this cabaret would have attracted half of Europe. You wouldn't have been able to get in for months on end." York saw the incongruity as another of the film's strengths. "One of the great achievements of Fosse is that in this tacky cabaret with its permanent smoke layer and blown out light bulbs live these world class performers," he said. "Even though the real Sally Bowles couldn't sing, he made it all so believable."

Few dwelt on the improbabilities and instead concentrated on the "divine decadence" of Fosse's jewel box musical. His career took off; he received more than 20 directing offers in the weeks following *Cabaret*'s opening. Why was *Cabaret* a smash, when musicals were at their lowest low? In assessing its success, Fosse tipped his bowler to ABC's Martin Baum, "who stayed in my corner all the way." He learned from his *Sweet Charity* mistakes, eliminating the weird, gratuitous camera angles from the film's dramatic passages. But something much more clever was at play. Fosse made a musical for people who hated musicals. For once, a director's intuition against trends worked. While Robert Wise and Herbert Ross hoped against hope that the life of a passé stage star and the remake of a black-and-white tearjerker were reasons to see *Star!* and *Goodbye, Mr. Chips*, Fosse went in another direction. His old-fashioned idea was that musicals do not have to *be* big in order to *hit* big.

At last Fosse relaxed and enjoyed the unqualified triumph of *Cabaret*. He even managed a sense of humor. "Do you think," he asked in droll tones, "that now we'll have a raft of Hollywood musicals about Nazism with homosexual leading men?" *Cabaret* was enough to give fans hope that musical films had a future after all.

CHAPTER 18

The Impossible Dream

ABC's two musicals, *Song of Norway* and *Cabaret*, could not have had more divergent outcomes. One made an undetected profit and was laughed off the screen, while the other deftly melded European art house aesthetics and razz-a-ma-tazz showmanship with shrewd mass consumption marketing to become a critical and financial hit of the highest order. But the back-to-back successes of *Fiddler* and *Cabaret* did not stimulate a confidence in the musical genre as did *The Sound of Music*. This time no one raided the American musical library for "the next *Fiddler*" or "the next *Cabaret*." Neither success would compensate for the belief that musicals, at least those with large budgets, were not viable anymore. There was very little middle-range product, only safe, low-cost babysitters such as *Willy Wonka & the Chocolate Factory* and *Bedknobs and Broomsticks*.

MGM had another embarrassment in the can. The persuasive Andrew (*Song of Norway*) Stone convinced the company to try another interpolation of a classic from the studio's heyday. On the surface, a musical remake of *The Great Waltz*, a 1938 biopic of Johann Strauss, makes more sense than setting tunes to *Goodbye, Mr. Chips*, since *Waltz* came with those already familiar melodies. But the corporate, financial, and social contexts for the two versions were thoroughly different. By the end of 1970, MGM had a towering debt, while Kirk Kerkorian, its biggest stockholder, was under investigation for skimming at the Flamingo Hotel in Las Vegas. This did not deter him from pursuing the dream of a 25-floor hotel as a new direction for the MGM name. Back at the shrinking studio, the ever-more combative and inebriated James Aubrey went on an austerity program that reduced the deficit somewhat but gave the studio the worst reputation in town. He acted as last-minute editor and sound mixer, so that directors hardly recognized their films when they reached the screen. It was part of an apparent disregard for moviemaking that he and Kerkorian shared. Together they sold the studio assets for $62 million and pumped them into the MGM Grand Hotel. The press was not flattering. "From now on the company that brought you *Ben-Hur* and *The Wizard of Oz* will bring you crap—and roulette, slot machines, and all the other pleasures of a Las Vegas casino hotel," wrote *Forbes*. "The Kerkorian-Aubrey management of MGM was the realization of everyone's worst fears of what would happen to Hollywood when the money-men take over," wrote the *New York Times*.

The Great Waltz received their indifference. Co-producing with MGM was Electrical and Musical Industries (EMI), a British conglomerate that began film production and distribution in 1969. Stone was given a contract largely because he promised a big film on a reasonable budget, which he had delivered to ABC with *Norway*. While other directors made empty promises about economizing, Stone held true. "I told Aubrey . . . that if I was going to make a picture for a price, I had to have absolute autonomy from start to finish. . . . Aubrey [is] very smart. [He] left me alone, and that's how you bring them in under budget. [He] didn't even see the rushes."

While the bosses were erecting gambling shrines in the Nevada desert, German matinee idol Horst Buchholz was sent the script for *The Great Waltz*. The 1938 version was a loose telling of Strauss's life. It was also one of the most expensive productions at MGM in the 1930s, its costs glittering the screen. Strauss was portrayed as a moody, driven artiste, but it was a cream puff of a movie, widely nicknamed *The Great Schmaltz*. There was some humor in the standard plot of a vampy soprano attempting to lure Strauss from his wife, the innocent daughter of a baker. But it had little dramatic propulsion and was instead saturated with music, reflecting surfaces, and cameras swirling through the studio-duplicated ballrooms of Vienna.

The new *Great Waltz* was filmed at opulent Austrian locations rather than on studio sets, because, after all, the MGM backlot had already been sold. Also to save money, *Waltz* was shot in 35-millimeter Panavision, then blown up to 70-millimeter for select roadshow bookings. "Blow-Ups" may have cost less, but they lacked the great clarity of authentic 70-millimeter. "They effectively pulled the rug out from under wide-film production," noted film historian John Belton. "Fewer films were designed and budgeted with 70-millimeter roadshow exhibition in mind. . . . Now any 35-millimeter film could be blown up to 70-millimeter for roadshow presentation in the 1,100 existing 70-millimeter theaters around the world without the expense involved in wide-film production, which cost between two and a half and two and three quarters times as much as in 35-millimeter."

None of the 127 interiors were made on a sound stage, and Stone claimed that he had not been in a studio in more than 20 years. "To have built any reasonable facsimile of our sets would put the film in the 30 million dollar bracket," he said. "Even if you had the 30 million, you couldn't duplicate them. When I started making motion pictures entirely on locations, I was told I would run into all sorts of trouble. I never have. I've always been able to find the sets I need for my stories. . . . Though making a motion picture on location is much more rugged than working in a comfortable studio, a better film is the result." During production, Stone sounded like the dream director of an ailing studio. "I see that we stick to a low budget," he said. "I control everything. I sign every check, timecard, and

The Great Waltz director Andrew Stone and cast members Horst Buchholz and Mary Costa rehearse the penultimate American roadshow musical. Executive upheavals in the early 1970s contributed to the green lighting of unlikely projects such as this. From the collection of Photofest.

bill. That's the only way. There isn't a dime spent I don't know about. We have an 11-week shooting schedule, but I intend to bring it in under 10 weeks." *The Great Waltz* was put together with great speed and efficiency, a model of thrift in absolute contrast to its recent overfed musical cousins. If films succeeded on decreased risk, tight budgets, and rigid scheduling, *The Great Waltz* remake would be a masterpiece.

The Great Waltz made its premiere on Halloween of 1972 as a champagne benefit for the Opera Guild of Southern California at the ABC Century Theatre, where *Cabaret* had made its Los Angeles debut. Stone hoped that onlookers would be fooled into believing that *Waltz* was high priced, and on that front he succeeded. "MGM Bets Bundle on '*Waltz*'" headlined the *Los Angeles Times*. With decorative locations in Vienna and Salzburg, "*The Great Waltz* is the kind of movie the motion picture giants are not daring to make these days." That was the kindest reporting *Waltz* received. It roadshowed a week later at the 86th Street East Theater in New York, where the *New York Times* found it achieved "a quality of artistic miscalculation that occasionally approaches the sublime." Stone was as unapologetically retro as Ross Hunter, but without the instincts for what sells tickets.

"There are so many angry young men types in motion pictures today, but where are the romantic heroes with the light touch?" he asked. To position *Waltz* as the feel good anti-*Cabaret*, its posters read, "Once upon a time there was singing and dancing and all the world was in love!" The story included an expected clash between Strauss father and son, but Stone did not attempt to play up its relevance in an era that coined the generation gap. Merchandising included a special Viennese Torte–flavored ice cream from Baskin-Robbins and coupons for waltz lessons from Arthur Murray Dance Studio at participating theaters.

Waltz brought in a mighty $120,000 in its first seven openings and broke a Saturday night house record at its Chicago engagement. From six major city openings, it moved to four more, with Stone and leading lady, singer Mary Costa, making live appearances. It opened abroad strongly in Johannesburg and Melbourne, but once the initial rush of interest passed, *The Great Waltz* failed the smell test. Barely two weeks after its Los Angeles opening, there were ticket giveaway promotions. *Song of Norway* then made an unexpected return to LA theaters, thus siphoning whatever audience existed for film neo-operettas. *The Great Waltz* had a short-lived roadshow career and was in regular release even before its London bow in December. With wretched press and silent cash registers, MGM could only hope it would gather a bit of momentum as something different in an era teeming with such "porno chic" offerings as *Deep Throat* and *Boys in the Sand*. But MGM had no more luck in appealing to a family audience than Paramount did with *Darling Lili*.

G-rated entertainment was hard to come by, but *The Great Waltz* did not give that audience what it wanted. It is, by any standard, a great big lump of meh. One of the kinder reviews came from *Cue*, which found it to be "a silly, sentimental biography with a schmaltzy score which moves from goo to glue as it sinks into absurdity." For Charles Champlin at the *Los Angeles Times*, Bucholz, Costa, and the rest of the cast put in game efforts, but there is no saving "the operetta plot, the most baroque dialog since silent title-cards, and some of the most dismally lackluster staging I can remember. (Extras yawn, or wear the panicky smiles of those who know what they're doing is unnatural but aren't sure what else to do.)" Oona White (*Oliver!*) choreographed a lovely opening credit sequence, but the dances are otherwise stagy, and not in a way that serves the story, as they do in *Cabaret*. Lines like "My pen has been dipped in my tears" and "I'm just a ballroom fiddler with a bag of tricks" are too easy to mock. As they did with *Song of Norway*, lyricists Robert Craig Wright and George Forrest stuck new lyrics on old melodies, ostensibly to save money if not quality. And since Stone produced, directed, and wrote *The Great Waltz*, Champlin concluded that it "constitute[d] auteur theory's darkest hour." No wonder Stone said that he would "never make another musical, because it's too unrewarding. . . . After Metro made the deal for *The Great Waltz*, I explained to them that they should know in advance that the picture would get panned. 'You're not going to get good reviews. You must understand that.'"

The Great Waltz holds a minor footnote in film history. MGM had planned to produce other Cinerama roadshows, but the failure of *Waltz* prevented that. As a result, it was the last release under the Cinerama logo, while ABC was also very soon to leave the theatrical film market. Stone, who turned 70 the year of *The Great Waltz*, would never direct another film. "Everyone who saw *Song of Norway* loved it," he said. "Everyone who's seen *The Great Waltz* has loved it, too. Critics should welcome it as a clean, wholesome picture that makes people happy. I simply don't know what their ax is." Both *Song of Norway* and *The Great Waltz* suffered a fate worse than camp. They have simply disappeared, nearly erased from public consciousness. It's as if they never happened.

Emboldened by the tremendous success of *Fiddler on the Roof*, United Artists charged ahead with *Man of La Mancha*. They were radically different properties. *I, Don Quixote* was a heavily distilled 1959 teleplay of Miguel de Cervantes, with emphasis on its hero's mad nobility of spirit. It was a swift, economic retelling by TV writer Dale Wasserman, with basic sets and furniture doubling as castles, windmills, and the expansive plains of Spain. The idea of a stage musical version came from director Albert Marre, who approached young composer Mitch Leigh to write songs. Leigh's credits were scant—a turn as bassoonist with the New Haven Symphony and jingle writer, his most familiar being "Nobody doesn't like Sara Lee." Such were the inauspicious beginnings of *Man of La Mancha*. First mounted in Connecticut on a one-set stage of a Seville prison during the Spanish Inquisition, it lacked the backing of deep pocket investors. It arrived in New York on $250,000 when the average musical cost twice that amount. But *La Mancha* benefited from something beyond price—positive word of mouth and two startlingly good starring performances. Richard Kiley played both Don Quixote and Cervantes and brought tingles to the spine with his rich baritone. Marre's wife, Joan Diener, had a phenomenal chesty soprano for Aldonza, the whore Quixote imagines to be a lady. Opening at the Washington Square Theatre in Greenwich Village, the production had no intermission, and the thrust stage made for great theatrical intimacy and power. *La Mancha* settled in for a two and a half year run before moving uptown to the Martin Beck Theater on Broadway. The combined run totaled 2,328 performances, putting it near *Fiddler on the Roof* and *Hello, Dolly!* as one of America's musical theater triumphs of the 1960s. In its own depressive way, it purveyed a belief in hopes and dreams with the conviction of anything by Rodgers and Hammerstein.

The score has not received much respect, but even some detractors admit it can be emotionally rousing. "I, Don Quixote," "It's All The Same," and "To Each His Dulcinea" agreeably lingered in the ear, but "The Impossible Dream (The Quest)" was something else altogether. The anthemic bolero was recorded by everyone from Andy Williams and Diana Ross, to Cher, the Carpenters, Connie Francis, and Kermit the Frog, and vied with "Born Free," "Hello, Dolly!," and "Sunrise, Sunset" as the most overheard Muzak of a generation:

> *To dream the impossible dream,*
> *To fight the unbeatable foe,*
> *To bear with unbearable sorrow,*
> *To run where the brave dare not go . . .*

"The Impossible Dream" went from beloved standard to risible schmaltz in a few short years. By then, *Man of La Mancha* had been seen in 45 countries and heard in 22 languages.

United Artists wanted *La Mancha* as much as it wanted *Fiddler*, outbidding three competing studios for the rights at a cost reportedly second only to Warner Bros. purchase of *My Fair Lady* for a Broadway adaptation. The figure was not made public, but a "conservative projection" had it in excess of $4 million. The film had no one assigned to it at the onset—no producer, director, or cast. Broadway overall was regarded as creatively stagnant, the success of shows like *La Mancha* a sure sign of decline. "[It is not] merely crotchety nostalgia to suggest that the Broadway musical stage has gained in vulgarity what it has lost in vitality over the past two decades," announced *The Village Voice* in 1968. "A minor writhe-rock frolic *Hair* seems 10 years ahead of its time because it is only two or three years behind while the rest of Broadway is 20 years behind. Meanwhile a childish charade like *Man of La Mancha* threatens to run forever on the whimsical behinds of its human horses."

In assembling talent for the film, UA approached original stage director Marre and writer Wasserman, along with stars Kiley and Diener. Someone thought it would be a good idea if the show's composer, Mitch Leigh, also produced the film. Had no one learned the lessons of Alan Jay Lerner and *Paint Your Wagon*? Then the entire team was scratched, since none of them had much of any feature film experience. *La Mancha* was plagued with competing conceptions. UA execs were spinning their wheels, alternatively looking to play the drama up and humor down. Or the music down and the drama up. Or aim more toward Cervantes and less toward Broadway.

The second *La Mancha* regime was headed by British director Peter Glenville and screenwriter John Hopkins. Glenville envisioned a return to Cervantes and an epic historic spectacle in keeping with his 1964 *Becket* and sought to cut many of the songs. UA was incensed at his $20 million price tag, and he and Hopkins were dismissed under publicized "script difficulties." Glenville's participation brought in Peter O'Toole, the star of *Becket* who, after all, had *some* musical experience with *Goodbye, Mr. Chips*. Even though he confessed music illiteracy, O'Toole was kept. He signed for a salary of $1 million plus overtime and a share of profits. With Glenville out, *La Mancha* was now in the hands of Italian lawyer turned film producer Alberto Grimaldi (*The Good, the Bad and the Ugly, Satyricon*), who planned to shoot at Diocitta studio in Rome.

Bearded, low-key Arthur Hiller was signed as director of his first musical at a fee of $300,000 plus a share of any profit. Hiller came closer than Glenville to saying what UA wanted to hear. "[Glenville and Hopkins] had gone back to Cervantes and left out all of *Man of La Mancha*," he said. "Well, Don Quixote's in the public domain, and United Artists had spent a lot of money on *Man of La Mancha*, and, understandably, that's what they wanted." Hiller, too, appeared to be a wise choice in light of his phenomenally successful *Love Story* for Paramount, and *The Hospital* with George C. Scott at UA.

Hiller had seen *La Mancha* at the Washington Square Theater and was bowled over. "I admired it so much. That convinced me to do it on film." But he was not about to follow the stage production verbatim. The easy fantasy created in the theater would not do for film. As with Norman Jewison and *Fiddler*, he decided to present the material with large doses of realism. "When I first started the film, I thought, 'My God, what am I doing?'" he said. "I was terribly nervous. Then I said to myself, 'Oh, come on now, Arthur, the point is to tell a story, and do it dramatically. I treat the songs as if they were dramatic scenes. Pictures I like to do are an affirmation of the human spirit that say men of good conscience and thought don't take flight from situations but stay and try to bring their dreams to fruition. Don Quixote is particularly contemporary in that sense. We can't change the world unless we think, and if we don't think love and think peace, then we can't make our changes that way." Hiller felt the challenge of *La Mancha* acutely. "The essential problem of transferring this play to film," he said, "is that the play takes place in the mind's eye. We have to figure out how to establish the prison-reality." After reading *Don Quixote* and finding it "dull and repetitious," Hiller decided to stage the musical numbers as dramatic scenes. "After all, the story is one step removed from *Don Quixote* since it is narrated by Cervantes," he said. "And it is one step removed from Cervantes because it is a musical."

Hiller and co-producer Saul Chaplin, whose most recent credit was *Star!*, began work on *La Mancha* in the fall of 1971. The sets and costumes were designed by Luciano Damiani, a trim, silver-haired man with a fondness for silk scarves and Jackie O dark glasses. He was primarily known for his work in opera and showed little interest in adapting for the screen. The main space for *La Mancha* contained a huge, run–down, 16th-century Spanish inn, with stables, a gray-brown barnyard for livestock, and a floor layer of real dirt. He designed the prison as an allegory to fascism, with wire netting copied from photos of Auschwitz, while the floor contained a circle inscribing a square from Leonardo Da Vinci's symbol for the physical and metaphysical. "Embodied in the work is the theme of political persecution through the ages," explained Damiani to the *Los Angeles Times*. "The Inquisition. The Nazis. I Fascisti. Your blacks in America. There is this bigger meaning right in the film, but do they," Damiani waves his hand in the direction of Hiller and Chaplin, "care about that? No, they just want to make their musical."

The sets were complete before Hiller reported for duty, and he balked at what he saw, noting the camera wouldn't even register Damiani's subtler visuals. Wasserman was on Hiller's side, calling Damiani's schematization "a lot of bull. It certainly has nothing to do with anything I had in mind." The two became quick adversaries, while Chaplin wrote that "Working on the film was less than enjoyable." He found Peter O'Toole "very bright but very unpleasant," listing star temperament, rudeness to underlings, and hangovers as primary offenses. He had no such ill words for Sophia Loren, making her musical debut as the lusty Aldonza, or James Coco, another musical novice playing the corporeal manservant Sancho Panza. Bitterness toward Loren instead came from the publicist, who found her uncooperative in approving still photos or submitting to interviews. O'Toole and Loren were box office draws, but a question has to be asked. If UA was so keen on putting *Man of La Mancha* before *Don Quixote*, why were non-singers cast in the starring roles?

Hiller's challenges were exacerbated by O'Toole's increasing disdain for the project. "They're the most incredibly depressing sets that have surely ever existed," he told a reporter. He was despairing over his look in the film, too. He was done up in El Greco ashen pancake, a plastic nose, false forehead with bristly gray hair jutting out, and an unyielding suit of rusty armor. Twenty months of shooting *Lawrence of Arabia* in multiple deserts was less taxing than *Man of La Mancha*. "This has been a bitch," he said. "Every morning I must have this makeup put on. If we're lucky, it takes an hour. If it doesn't go on just right—it can't look phony—it can take

Peter O'Toole and James Coco are directed by a script-wielding Arthur Hiller on Luciano Damiani's "depressing" set for *Man of La Mancha*. This was the film that killed the roadshow in America once and for all. From the collection of Photofest.

three hours. Once I'm in it, I'm a prisoner. I can't even lie down." As for "The Impossible Dream," he did his own singing, but his contract allowed for the producers to dub his voice if they pleased. Among his few bright spots in the production was the company of Loren, who he described as "a marvelously put together machine."

The *La Mancha* songs were more demanding than anything in *Goodbye, Mr. Chips*, so O'Toole took singing lessons to prepare, as did Loren. Neither would approximate the sonic majesty of Kiley and Diener in the original stage version. Intensely frustrated and feeling abandoned by Glenville, O'Toole continued to register his contempt. He nicknamed Hiller "Little Arthur" and regularly took swipes at him. "So Little Arthur says this film is an affirmation of the human spirit, does he?" he sniffed. "Not 'little' because I'm putting Arthur down. God forbid. But because Sophia and Jimmy and I are so big and he's so little in our midst. Affirmation of the human spirit. But the human spirit is simply vile. V-I-L-E. Animal-like. Detestable. Look at all of history. No, no. No, surely the message of the film is 'We must mutate or die.' I'm feeling paradoxical today, and when I feel that way I perversely like to contradict Arthur, you see." Perhaps O'Toole's mood came from the gnawing realization that he had been miscast and could not overcome his musical shortcomings. When asked during the seven-month shoot of *La Mancha* if he has a drinking problem, he washed down a glass of Polish vodka then replied, "Why, no, not at all. Drinking is the easiest thing in the world."

Man of La Mancha attracted many visitors to the set. Stockholders dropped by to see where their $11 million was going. Most often they found accord, as the cast got along well playing poker or roaming the wind-blasted countryside near Tarquinia in search of Etruscan antiquities. UA president David Picker made efforts to squelch rumors of runaway costs, telling *Variety* that *La Mancha* expenses came to *only* $9 million. Saul Chaplin concerned himself with the more immediate problems of location shooting. "It has never been done before," he said. "The studio technicians had no concept of how to go about it, and we had to teach them every step of the way. The toughest part was getting good musicians. You'd think that would be easy in Italy. It's not. Their symphony is poor, [and] their opera is good only when they get the right stars to perform. The best musicians are in radio and television, and we had to wait until they were available."

Near the end of the shoot, a bedraggled O'Toole said, "I don't like films. I go to plays all the time. Movies are dreadful, vulgar, horrid, usually meaningless. Standards have gone to nothing; no one talks quickly anymore; they'll take three-quarters of an hour to say something, then when it comes out it's something horrible like 'Oh dear, my poor acne.' Or 'Mary doesn't love me.' Look at those films from the '30s and '40s, like the things Spencer Tracy and Kate Hepburn did, the speed of the dialogue, the pace. Sentimental, romantic if you like, but what cutting, what vigor and energy on film!" Bemoaning new corporate Hollywood, he said, "It's a bit of a terror . . . to think of so much depending on men who keep ledgers and make trousers."

La Mancha, unlike *Fiddler*, did not have clear dialogue between the production and the front office. Hiller envisioned a two-hour film without overture or intermission, yet heard from a UA spokesman that the studio was planning a roadshow. "Unless Hiller is forced to include material at this time he doesn't want to, *Man of La Mancha* may be the shortest reserve seat movie in history," noted the *Chicago Tribune*. "The exhibition of *Man of La Mancha* looks to be shaping up into a battle between art and money." Money won. UA decided to roadshow *La Mancha* at the Rivoli, and on Long Island and New Jersey, with the Los Angeles opening at the Fox Wilshire one day later. By the end of December, it was scheduled for 20 screens in 18 cities in North America, giving it a quickly staggered release in major urban centers. Roadshow bookings would continue into "third wave" markets as demand held through 1973.

Marketing executive Arthur Reiman issued a memo to branch managers, proclaiming, "The important thing in any roadshow is to get moving with the ticket sales to groups as quickly as possible." But that campaign for *La Mancha* was paltry compared to *Fiddler*, while Reitman actually believed he had a future award winner on his hands. "The Academy Awards will be held on March 27 and we all feel the picture will sweep most of the awards," he wrote. "Tell this to your exhibitors at your initial presentation."

The pattern and timing for *La Mancha* aped *Fiddler*, and as with all the giant musicals of the recent past, much was at stake. Even with the *Fiddler* gold mine, it was most unusual to be spending $11 million on a movie during the Hollywood recession. Hiller was shocked at UA's commitment. "If it were my decision, I don't think I'd spend that much money in today's film market," he said. There was additional nervousness among the UA men not just over *La Mancha*'s expense, but the fact that it was a musical. In light of recent disasters involving A-list stars, effort was made to underplay the singing of O'Toole and Loren. But how would UA do that, since photos were already circulating with movie star mouths wide open? "Shall we explain that they were calling out for Alka-Seltzer after too much garlic pasta at lunch?" asked a UA publicist.

When the final cut of *La Mancha* was judged with widespread derision, O'Toole lashed out, blaming the corporate powers that be. "These men buy up studios. . . . You see them flying around in their private jets with birds [British slang for young women] we used to hide under the table 15 years ago. It's insane." There it is—$11 million for two drab sets and an occasional visit to Italy doubling as Spain. After a dull credit sequence with its animated blue windmill on black screen, Hiller quickly demonstrates a failure to translate the property either from the pages of a great novel or the stage of effective theater. There is instead a strange mix of theatricality and cinematic artifice, with neither delivering. The opening attenuated prologue goes on so long that it casts doubt whether *Man of La Mancha* is even a musical. "The Impossible Dream," by 1972 an easy target of mockery, was judged by *Time* to be "surely the most mercilessly lachrymose hymn to empty-headed optimism since *Carousel*'s 'You'll Never Walk Alone.' One expects to learn at any moment that it will become the national anthem of some newly emerging nation." The *Chicago Sun-Times* wrote, "If there's anything worse than dubbing in the voice of a non-singer, it's not dubbing the voice of a non-singer." Some managed to flatter O'Toole for his inherent dignity and Loren for her earthy sensuality, but Hiller and Wasserman "have pitched this screen version of the celebrated Broadway musical as low as possible without sinking beneath the screen altogether," proclaimed *Newsweek*. "Their Don Quixote resembles an enfeebled scoutmaster emeritus, spewing laundry lists of virtues that might have been taken from the troop manual."

Without the creative judgment of a Norman Jewison, *Man of La Mancha* repeated every mistake of recent musicals, starting with casting and ending with reserve seats. *La Mancha*, like *Camelot* and *Paint Your Wagon* before it, sacrificed musicianship at the altar of movie stardom.

"There is something decidedly off-putting about an operetta without real singing in the leading roles," wrote the *New York Times*. Even the Italian orchestra is wrong. The sound balancing is off; there are too few strings, while the brass is sometimes tinny and sour. *La Mancha* had a ready-made popular score, already an advantage over *Goodbye, Mr. Chips*, and yet it was desecrated. Each and every song suffers in comparison to the stage version. In fact, after one hearing of the original cast recording it's clear why *La Mancha* was such a big hit; "The Impossible Dream" is easily its musical low point.

While O'Toole spews his benign delusions, Coco acts every bit the second banana. He looks ready to burst into a vaudeville routine at any moment, but Hiller kept him under restraint. Loren, meanwhile, has credible dramatic intensity, and *La Mancha* reminds us how compellingly photogenic she is. There is a transparent effort to reference her most celebrated performance as the ravaged peasant of *Two Women*. She crumples to the ground during "Aldonza" in mimicry of a powerful moment in the neorealist drama. Gillian Lynne's choreography is simply horrendous, several notches below the exuberance she brought to *Half a Sixpence*. In "It's All The Same," Loren appears to be struggling with recalcitrant mules, not fending off rapists. And when she opens her luscious mouth to sing, the results are breathy, on pitch perhaps, but lacking support, loveliness, color, or range. O'Toole joked about his lack of singing skills, saying, "I would confess I have never been dubbed—(pause)—knight." He was, however, dubbed by London singer Simon Gilbert. If O'Toole had an inflated assessment of his singing during the making of *Chips*, he held no illusions when faced with the more challenging *La Mancha*. He now concluded his singing voice sounded, "like a Coca-Cola bottle being crushed under a door."

Hiller was philosophic if delusional about *La Mancha*'s message. "Every change comes about because somewhere somebody was dreaming far enough ahead. Someone like Leonardo would be a super dreamer. Look at the very beginnings of this country. Thomas Jefferson was the impossible dreamer right to the hilt. Ralph

Nader would be a current impossible dreamer, tilting against some of the biggest windmills there are." To Hiller, *La Mancha* celebrates taking responsible action to make dreams come true. "On Broadway, the show worked because there was an air of fantasy about it," said Saul Chaplin. "When Quixote battles windmills thinking they were dragons, only the aftermath was shown. Then the audience could see that Quixote was crazy, and yet not see his humiliation. We respect his madness. In the film, the windmill fight is clumsily and painfully shown, making Quixote seem not crazy, but stupid."

Hiller said, "Perhaps *Man of La Mancha* should never have been made into a film. It's one of those special pieces of theater that work brilliantly on stage where reality is easily suspended, but suffers when placed before the cold eye of the movie camera." Many years later, he remained vexed over the challenges of realism and fantasy. "When you're sitting in a darkened theater and told that's not a scullery maid, that's a princess, you can make the change," he said. "When Sophia Loren is 20 feet tall, it's hard to change her into a princess. We were missing parts of the fantasy. Maybe that's where we lost out." Hiller remembered, "*La Mancha* didn't get the best collection of reviews, and business did not start with a bang. But about three weeks after it opened, [UA chairman Arthur] Krim wrote to me, 'This was the film UA expected and wanted.' He said they were happy with the results. He also said he was sorry it didn't work out better with the public and press." David Picker was not quite so polite. "We hoped to have a really good movie and we got a lousy one. Its failure was because it just wasn't a very good movie."

Perhaps *Cabaret* ruined the market for roadshows, demonstrating that a great musical need not arrive with bloated prices or an air of false demand brought on by reserve seat tickets. To be fair, *The Great Waltz* and *Man of La Mancha* wrote their own obituaries without any help from *Cabaret*. *The Great Waltz* is merely forgotten, but *La Mancha* holds a more ignominious distinction. It was the last film to receive a limited reserve-seat engagement prior to its general release. When it limped out of theaters in early 1973, it took the roadshow tradition with it.

Roadshows were a casualty of creative misjudgments as much as tidal changes in fashion. There is a tangible sense of loss. *Oklahoma!*, *Cleopatra*, *Lawrence of Arabia*, *The Sound of Music*, and *Fiddler on the Roof* are still with us, but gone is the way they were meant to be seen. A bit of good old movie magic died with the roadshow. With the release of *Jaws* in 1975, saturation booking, with one feature invading thousands of theaters on its opening weekend, became custom. We've been herded into musty Cineplex boxes and subjected to ads for breath mints and the United States Marine Corps ever since. Movies turned digital, got smaller, not bigger, and are now made on computers, compatible with laptops and cell phones. We who love *real* movies lit from behind through celluloid would rather be sitting in the Rivoli as the house lights dim and the overture begins on something big and beautiful in 70-millimeter.

Exit Music

The roadshow died so that New Hollywood could live. The great early work of Robert Altman (*M*A*S*H, McCabe & Mrs. Miller*), Francis Ford Coppola (*The Godfather, The Godfather Part II*), and Peter Bogdanovich (*The Last Picture Show*) rose from the ashes of an industry bankrupt of money but not ideas. As film historian Thomas Schatz wrote, "With the blockbuster strategy stalled, the industry saw a period of widespread and unprecedented innovation, due largely to a new 'generation' of Hollywood filmmakers . . . who were turning out films that had as much in common with the European art cinema as with classical Hollywood. . . . Thus an 'American film renaissance' of sorts was induced by a succession of big-budget flops." In just six months, *The Godfather* became the top-grossing film of all time. The industry had found its next *Sound of Music* at long last, but it was no roadshow musical!

The last roadshow musicals continue to manifest themselves in odd ways. *The Sound of Music*, it is safe to say, will never die. *Thoroughly Modern Millie, Finian's Rainbow, Chitty Chitty Bang Bang*, and *Sweet Charity* are kept alive by revival productions, not because of demand for the film versions. *Funny Girl* will persist as long as there are Barbra Streisand fans. *Cabaret* still dazzles, and *Fiddler on the Roof* still moves if you surrender to it. *Paint Your Wagon* was remembered in a hysterical episode of *The Simpsons*, when Homer settles in for movie night with a Western, only to be horrified that Lee Marvin and Clint Eastwood *sing* when they should be getting drunk and shooting people.

Roadshows died in part because movie consumption habits changed so dramatically in the 1970s. The Sony U-matic Video Cassette Recorder (VCR), introduced in 1971, played nine-inch by five and a half-inch cassettes rather than reel-to-reel. The videocassette player and recorder arrived in 1975, and so began the revolution in the home market. With more alternatives to movie viewing, theaters continued to lose their hold on the public. Not coincidentally, most of the old movie palaces closed. Following *Man of La Mancha*, New York's Rivoli hosted *Deep Throat* and had two screens by the 1980s. Renamed the United Artists Twin, its last bookings included *The Class of Nuke 'Em High* and *Morgan Stewart's Coming Home*. It was then shuttered, its carved pediment figures removed and Doric columns encased in cement. The defacements may have prevented it from gaining protected landmark status and hastened its end. The theater of *Oklahoma!* and *The Sound of Music* was pulled down in 1987 and replaced by a plain black skyscraper.

As for the musical, it didn't die. Instead, it bled a lot. It shrank in numbers, budgets, and audience. It moved into niche markets and became ever less relevant on the pop culture landscape. No more did anyone pretend the Great American Musical could reach across vast demographics and lure audiences young and old for repeated viewings. In 1973, *Cabaret* ran off with a startling eight Academy Awards, including trophies for Best Director Bob Fosse, Best Actress Liza Minnelli, and Best Supporting Actor Joel Grey. In the same month, another very different musical appeared that sought to resemble an old roadshow. *Lost Horizon*, Ross Hunter's pet project at Columbia, was an original musical based on James Hilton's novel of Shangri-La. It had some of the usual roadshow embellishments— the mammoth budget, marketing, and merchandising—minus the overture, intermission, exit music, or reserved seats. *"Men's Wear* magazine reports Shangri-La look on male horizon," shouted the press kit, which also played up *Lost Horizon's* coloring books, scented candles, and trendy macramé plant hangers. As a film, *Lost Horizon* seemed inspired by *Paint Your Wagon*, with its commitment to actors who can't sing, locations with extreme weather conditions, and excessive set building. It was so poorly received it became the butt of jokes and ranked among the most infamous stink bombs of the decade. "I never miss a Liv Ullmann musical," quipped young Bette Midler in her concert act. But *Lost Horizon* isn't as bad as its reputation. The corny script, stiff performances, humdrum Burt Bacharach–Hal David score, heartfelt credos, and holiday resort art direction add up to something strangely watchable.

The Warner Bros. film adaptation of Broadway's *Mame* offers more tsk-tsking. With an aging, soft-focused Lucille Ball as the primary attraction, it is a labor to endure. It also signals a disaffection of women from prominent American films, musicals in particular. In 1975, Paramount released Robert Altman's signature masterpiece *Nashville*, which felt even less like a musical than *Cabaret*, though more than two dozen original songs infused the soundtrack. The only viable musical star to keep headlining on film was Barbra Streisand, but her 1970s output consisted of just *Funny Lady* and *A Star Is Born*. The former continued the story of *Funny Girl's* Fanny Brice as a mature woman unlucky in love and was the only sequel to any 1960s roadshow musical. Directed by Herbert Ross of *Goodbye, Mr. Chips, Funny Lady* is a dramatic non-starter. The narrative drag that plagued the second act of *Funny Girl* extends clear through *Lady*, leaving it dependent on Streisand's rather brittle interpretation of an older-wiser Brice and a few worthy production numbers. As for *A Star Is Born*, less said the better. Narcissistic love scenes create the mood of spying on horny neighbors who "accidentally" keep their curtains open. It made oodles of money, and won Streisand a Best Song Oscar for the slushy "Evergreen."

The days of *Mary Poppins*, or two or three generations tailgating at the local drive-in, were over. Musicals became part of segmental marketing, with producers no longer believing that one size fits all. In the 1970s and '80s, there were musicals for kids (*Bedknobs and Broomsticks, Tom Sawyer, Huckleberry Finn, The Little Prince*), Christians (*Godspell, Jesus Christ Superstar, Catch My Soul*, a.k.a. *Santa Fe Satan*), vegetarian pacifists ("the first electric western" *Zachariah*), and transvestites (*The Rocky Horror Picture Show*). Occasionally a Broadway adaptation surfaced, usually without much excitement or acclaim: *1776, The Wiz, A Little Night Music, Annie, The Best Little Whorehouse in Texas, The Pirates of Penzance, A Chorus Line*. Attempts to unite popular music with something resembling musical film occurred with *Tommy, Phantom of the Paradise, Lisztomania, Xanadu*, and *Sergeant Pepper's Lonely Hearts Club Band*. Disco had its day in the enduring *Saturday Night Fever*, as well as *Thank God, It's Friday* and the fetid *Can't Stop the Music*.

Grease was the musical blockbuster of the late '70s and an exception to prove the rule as it shrewdly rode the wave of '50s nostalgia. *Rock 'n' Roll High School* was the anti-*Grease*, sending up teen musicals of the '50s with a heavy dose of *Animal House* ribaldry. *Hair* finally arrived on the big screen in 1979, more than two years into the Carter administration, four years after the fall of Saigon, and almost 12 years after the musical's stage debut. It capitalized on some good music and dancing but could otherwise only hope to be an anachronistic tour of hippie culture in the age of disco. Bob Fosse's only post-*Cabaret* musical was *All That Jazz*, a smug, self-indulgent exercise that nonetheless won awards and praise. Rather like his *Goodbye, Mr. Chips*, Herbert Ross's 1981 Depression myth *Pennies from Heaven* had ardent fans but too few ticket buyers. As musicals slid further from their perch, the odds grew longer. For every *Grease*, there were 10 *Pennies from Heaven*.

A handful of noteworthy directors toyed with musicals and proved they were no threat to Vincente Minnelli. Martin Scorsese put a bright sheen on his ode to the Big Band Era with *New York, New York* and hired a major musical talent in Liza Minnelli, but the film lost money. After *Nashville*, Robert Altman tried something closer to a traditional musical with *Popeye*, with grim results. The early '80s saw two original musicals engage in gender play. Julie Andrews did drag in *Victor Victoria*, her only film musical after *Darling Lili*, directed by (who else?) Blake Edwards. Barbra Streisand directed herself as a cross-dressing Talmudic law student in *Yentl*.

Films dependent on music called themselves something other than musicals. Can biopics of music stars be called musicals? If so, the post-roadshow era has provided its share with *Lady Sings the Blues* (Billie Holiday), *Bound for Glory* (Woody Guthrie), *The Buddy Holly Story, American Hot Wax* (disc jockey Alan Freed), *Coal Miner's Daughter* (Loretta Lynn), *Sweet Dreams* (Patsy Cline), *La Bamba* (Richie Valens), *Great Balls of Fire* (Jerry Lee Lewis), *What's Love Got to*

Do with It? (Tina Turner), *Beyond the Sea* (Bobby Darin), *Ray* (Ray Charles), *De-Lovely* (Cole Porter), and *Walk the Line* (Johnny Cash). The '80s spate of dance pictures forces another consideration of the boundaries of the musical, with *Fame*, *Staying Alive* (which could be a catchphrase for the film musical itself), *Flashdance*, *Footloose*, *Breakin'*, *Breakin' 2: Electric Boogaloo*, *White Nights*, *Tap*, and *Dirty Dancing*. The adherence to feel-good storylines and happy endings in the '80s dance musicals hark back to the '30s and belies their contemporary look and sound. But it also is a reminder that musicals have at their heart the potential to transport their audiences into fantasy escapism, no matter the generation. In the roadshow tradition of Andrews and Streisand, films could still revolve around a single musical talent such as Neil Diamond in *The Jazz Singer*, directed by Richard Fleischer, with results at least as unfortunate as his *Doctor Dolittle*. Others spotlighted include Luciano Pavarotti in *Yes, Giorgio*, Prince in *Purple Rain*, David Bowie in *Labyrinth*, Michael Jackson in *Moonwalker*, Bette Midler in *The Rose* and *For the Boys*, Madonna in *Evita*, Björk in *Dancer in the Dark*, Eminem in *8 Mile*, and 50 Cent in *Get Rich or Die Tryin'*. More rare is the showcase for two, as in the entertainingly cheesy Cher-Christina Aguilera effort *Burlesque*.

Disney had a remarkable run of successful animated musicals beginning in 1989 with *The Little Mermaid*, followed by *Beauty and the Beast*, *Aladdin*, *The Lion King*, *Pocahontas*, *The Hunchback of Notre Dame*, *Hercules*, and *Mulan*. The little-known *Cats Don't Dance* from 1997 is less formulaic than any of them. It's superficially a cheery kid's cartoon set in old Hollywood, but its take on show business has more in common with *Day of Locust* or *Whatever Happened to Baby Jane?* than *Singin' in the Rain* or *Babes on Broadway*. Among live action musicals of the '90s, Woody Allen brought a latter-day romantic feel to his *Everyone Says I Love You*. *Newsies* bombed but found unlikely new life on Broadway. Like *The First Nudie Musical* and *The Rocky Horror Picture Show* before it, *Cannibal: The Musical* milked humor out of subverting the persistent innocence of the genre. Recommended for all who like their humor wet, not dry.

Hyperventilating *Moulin Rouge!* of 2001 celebrated its own references to pop noise to become a sizable hit. *Chicago* one year later was so happily received that journalists gurgled about the long-awaited "return of the musical." Staging the numbers in the lead character's head solved the "problem" of 21st-century audiences buying a formalistic movie genre. But from the borrowed sounds of Helen Morgan and Sophie Tucker, to the lyrics of Billy Rose, *Chicago* wasn't all that innovative. It owed a great deal to *Cabaret*, not only in how songs were staged, or by the fact they both came from composer John Kander and lyricist Fred Ebb. *Chicago* also borrowed *Cabaret*'s dark cornered mise-en-scène, nervous editing, febrile women, and aesthetic of sexy vice. *Chicago*'s seductive style is content to be just that, while *Cabaret*'s serves a more disturbing purpose.

There was a distinct flurry of film musical activity following *Chicago* that vaguely resembled *The Sound of Music* effect, and with similar mixed results.

Adaptations of *Phantom of the Opera, Rent, The Producers,* and *Nine* came and went quickly. Faring better was *Dreamgirls* and *Sweeney Todd. Hairspray* had a slobbering dog's demand to be loved and dared to go retro in its singing and dancing born from the streets of Baltimore. It's a tune-filled delight, though some of us can never see anyone but Divine as irrepressible Edna Turnblad. Jukebox musical *Mamma Mia!* (2008) made oceans of money, exploiting Boomers' fondness for infectious '70s pop tunes without advancing the art of the musical one iota. Broadway's perennial *Les Misérables* finally arrived on the big screen in 2012, produced, directed, and acted with a shameless over-amplified vulgarity and the most abominable close-ups since *Camelot.*

The popularity of *American Idol,* Disney's *High School Musical, Glee, Dancing with the Stars,* and *Smash* would suggest something is afoot in the way of renewed interest in musical entertainment, at least on TV. *Sing-a-Long* this and that— *Sound of Music, Wizard of Oz, West Side Story, Mary Poppins, Grease*—has become a cottage industry, reveling in a movie experience of nostalgic indulgence and campy good humor. Flash mobs suggest people still yearn for the magic of song bursting through ordinary life.

In the post-roadshow years, the musical has proven to be adaptable yet hidebound, resilient yet fragile. It changes with the times, diligently clips along, and refuses to ever fully go away. But it also refuses to reassert itself as widely popular. Nothing, not *Cabaret* nor *Chicago* nor *Mamma Mia!,* has ushered in a great new era of the screen musical. David Parkinson, in his well-informed *The Rough Guide to Film Musicals,* writes, "Executives, artists, critics, and audiences alike retain faith in a form that is too sporadic to count as a genre any longer, yet which can still generate more indulgent press speculation than almost any other." The movie world has moved on, with comic book fantasy the primary means of escape. The musical remains sickly and undernourished, and only occasionally electro-shocked by an anomalous success. The 1960s still haunt, and The Great Screen Musical Comeback has yet to be.

Appendix A

CAST OF CHARACTERS

Below are *Roadshow!*'s primary *dramatis personae*, with relevant credits:

Mort Abrahams—associate producer, *Doctor Dolittle, Goodbye, Mr. Chips*
Renata Adler—film critic, *New York Times*
Julie Andrews—actress/singer, *The Sound of Music, Thoroughly Modern Millie, Star!, Darling Lili; My Fair Lady* on stage; wife of Blake Edwards
Fred Astaire—actor/dancer, *Finian's Rainbow*
James T. Aubrey—production executive, MGM

Charles Bluhdorn—CEO, Gulf + Western, owner of Paramount
Leslie Bricusse—composer, *Doctor Dolittle, Goodbye, Mr. Chips*
Albert Broccoli—producer, *Chitty Chitty Bang Bang*
David Brown—production executive, Twentieth Century-Fox

Charles Champlin—film critic, *Los Angeles Times*
Carol Channing—actress, *Thoroughly Modern Millie; Hello, Dolly!* on stage
Saul Chaplin—producer, *The Sound of Music, Star!, Man of La Mancha*
Petula Clark—singer/actress, *Finian's Rainbow, Goodbye, Mr. Chips*
Francis Ford Coppola—director, *Finian's Rainbow*
Bosley Crowther—film critic, *New York Times*

Luciano Damiani—production designer, *Man of La Mancha*
Walt Disney—co-founder, Walt Disney Productions

Clint Eastwood—actor, *Paint Your Wagon*
Blake Edwards—producer/director/screenwriter, *Darling Lili*; husband of Julie Andrews
Samantha Eggar—actress, *Doctor Dolittle*
Robert Evans—executive vice-president, Paramount

Richard Fleischer—director, *Doctor Dolittle*
Bob Fosse—director, *Sweet Charity, Cabaret*

Joyce Haber—columnist, *Los Angeles Times*
Richard Harris—actor, *Camelot*
Rex Harrison—actor, *My Fair Lady, Doctor Dolittle*
Florence Henderson—actress/singer, *Song of Norway*
George Roy Hill—director, *Thoroughly Modern Millie*
Arthur Hiller—director, *Man of La Mancha*
Stan Hough—production executive, Twentieth Century-Fox
Rock Hudson—actor, *Darling Lili*
Ken Hughes—director, *Chitty Chitty Bang Bang*
Ross Hunter—producer, *Thoroughly Modern Millie*

Arthur P. Jacobs—producer, *Doctor Dolittle, Goodbye, Mr. Chips*
Norman Jewison—producer/director, *Fiddler on the Roof*

Pauline Kael—film critic
Mike Kaplan—publicist, Twentieth Century-Fox
Gene Kelly—director, *Hello, Dolly!*
Kirk Kerkorian—businessman and owner, Metro-Goldwyn-Mayer
Michael Kidd—choreographer, *Star!, Hello, Dolly!*
Arthur Krim—chairman, United Artists

Ernest Lehman—screenwriter, *The Sound of Music*; producer/screenwriter,
    Hello, Dolly!
Alan Jay Lerner—lyricist, *Camelot*; producer/lyricist, *Paint Your Wagon*
Frederick Loewe—composer, *Camelot, Paint Your Wagon*
Joshua Logan—director, *Camelot, Paint Your Wagon*
Sophia Loren—actress, *Man of La Mancha*

Walter MacEwen—production chief, Warner Bros.
Shirley MacLaine—actress/singer/dancer, *Sweet Charity*
Lee Marvin—actor/singer, *Paint Your Wagon*
Walter Matthau—actor, *Hello, Dolly!*
Lewis "Doc" Merman—physical production head, Twentieth Century-Fox
David Merrick—producer, *Hello, Dolly!* on stage
Liza Minnelli—actress/singer, *Cabaret*
Vincente Minnelli—director, *On a Clear Day You Can See Forever*
Ron Moody—actor, *Oliver!*
Oswald Morris—cinematographer, *Oliver!, Goodbye, Mr. Chips, Fiddler on the Roof*

Franco Nero—actor, *Camelot*
Anthony Newley—actor/singer, *Doctor Dolittle*

Robert O'Brien—board president, MGM
Peter O'Toole—actor, *Goodbye, Mr. Chips*; *Man of La Mancha*

Christopher Plummer—actor, *The Sound of Music*
André Previn—scorer, *Thoroughly Modern Millie*; composer, *Paint Your Wagon*;
    husband of Dory Previn
Dory Previn—lyricist; wife of André Previn

Terrence Rattigan—screenwriter, *Goodbye, Mr. Chips*
Vanessa Redgrave—actress, *Camelot*
Carol Reed—director, *Oliver!*
Rex Reed—film critic
Herbert Ross—musical numbers staging, *Doctor Dolittle*; musical numbers
    director, *Funny Girl*; director, *Goodbye, Mr. Chips*

Jean Seberg—actress, *Paint Your Wagon*
Omar Sharif—actor, *Funny Girl*
Ray Stark—producer, *Funny Girl*
Tommy Steele—actor/singer/dancer, *Half a Sixpence, The Happiest Millionaire,
    Finian's Rainbow*
Andrew Stone—producer/director/screenwriter, *Song of Norway, The Great
    Waltz*
Barbra Streisand—actress/singer, *Funny Girl, Hello, Dolly!, On a Clear Day You
    Can See Forever*
George Sydney—director, *Half a Sixpence*

Norman Tokar—director, *The Happiest Millionaire*
Topol—actor, *Fiddler on the Roof*
John Truscott—production designer, *Camelot, Paint Your Wagon*

Dick Van Dyke—actor, *Chitty Chitty Bang Bang*

Jack Warner—co-founder, Warner Bros.
John Williams—music supervisor, *Goodbye, Mr. Chips*; music adaptor, *Fiddler
    on the Roof*
Robert Wise—producer/director, *The Sound of Music*; director, *Star!*

John Woolf—producer, *Oliver!*

William Wyler—director, *Funny Girl*

Michael York—actor, *Cabaret*

Darryl F. Zanuck—co-founder, Twentieth Century-Fox; father of Richard Zanuck
Richard Zanuck—production chief, Twentieth Century-Fox; son of Darryl
    F. Zanuck

Appendix B

STUDIOS AND CHRONOLOGY OF *ROADSHOW!* MUSICALS, 1965–1972

Roadshow Musicals by Studio, 1965–1972

ABC Pictures-Allied Artists
Cabaret (1972*)

ABC Pictures-Cinerama
Song of Norway (1970)

Columbia
Funny Girl (1968)
Oliver! (1968)

Disney Studios
The Happiest Millionaire (1967)

MGM
Goodbye, Mr. Chips (1969)
The Great Waltz (1972)

Paramount
Half a Sixpence (1968)
Paint Your Wagon (1969)
Darling Lili (1970)

Twentieth Century-Fox
The Sound of Music (1965)
Doctor Dolittle (1967)
Star! (1968)
Hello, Dolly! (1969)

United Artists
Chitty Chitty Bang Bang (1968)
Fiddler on the Roof (1971)
Man of La Mancha (1972)

Universal
Thoroughly Modern Millie (1967)
Sweet Charity (1969)

Warner Bros.
Camelot (1967)
Finian's Rainbow (1968)

Roadshow Musicals by Release Year in the United States, 1965–1972

1965
The Sound of Music

1967
Thoroughly Modern Millie
The Happiest Millionaire
Camelot
Doctor Dolittle

1968
Half a Sixpence
Finian's Rainbow
Funny Girl
Star!
Oliver!
Chitty Chitty Bang Bang

1969
Sweet Charity
Paint Your Wagon
Goodbye, Mr. Chips
Hello, Dolly!

1970
Darling Lili
Song of Norway

1971
Fiddler on the Roof

1972
Cabaret *
The Great Waltz
Man of La Mancha

* *Cabaret* was not produced, marketed, or exhibited as a roadshow in the United
    States. It is included here because of its importance in the history of film
    musicals and its release within the roadshow era.

ABBREVIATIONS USED IN REFERENCES

AMPAS	Academy of Motion Picture Arts and Sciences
AMPAS/WW	Academy of Motion Picture Arts and Sciences, William Wyler Collection
BU/HG	Boston University, Howard Gotlieb Archival Research Center
HR	*Hollywood Reporter*
LAT	*Los Angeles Times*
LMU/AJ	Loyola Marymount University, Charles Von Der Ahe Library, Arthur Jacobs Collection
MOMA	Museum of Modern Art
NYT	*New York Times*
UCLA/Fox	*University of California, Los Angeles, Twentieth Century-Fox Collection, Performing Arts Special Collections*
USC/RW	University of Southern California Cinematic Arts Library, Robert Wise Collection
USC/WB	University of Southern California, Warner Bros. Archives
Var	*Variety*
WCFTTR/UA	Wisconsin Center for Film and Theater Research, United Artists Collection

REFERENCES

Overture

3   options in Redding, California, for moviegoing: The drive-ins both closed, and the Showcase is now a casino. The Cascade has been resurrected as a thriving performing arts center. www.cascadetheatre.org/

4   "a product": Hall, 18.
    "To show [audiences] got class": Hall, 129.

5   "Without question": "'Blockbusters or bust?'" by William Fadiman, *Films and Filming* 1963, 65.
    Audiences steadily declined: Block and Wilson, 414 and 422.
    "I could feel musicals": Caron to author, December 4, 2009.

6   "the moguls": *LAT*, January 18, 1970.

7   "It is fashionable": *Newsweek*, November 19, 2007.

Chapter 1: The Musical That Ate Hollywood

10   "It was a studio head's dream": Hirsch, 8.
    "Where would you": *NYT*, November 20, 1966.

11   "to go find somebody else": Parkinson, 162.
    "Can't you run": Base, 132.
    Anne Bancroft, Shirley Jones: USC/RW, undated.
    "I never got": *Time*, December 23, 1966.
    "I suspect that, for picture purposes": The University of Texas at Austin, Harry Ransom Humanities Research Center, Ernest Lehman Collection, March 26, 1963.

12   She signed a two-picture contract: UCLA/Fox, *Star!* files, October 17, 1966.
    "Robert Wise was a dream": Wood to author, June 25, 2009.
    what came to be called Maria's Mountain: Breaux to author, June 18, 2009.

13   "a distinct scent": Plummer, 406.
    "You have made": Sherman and Sherman, "Walt's Time," 60.
    $5.2 million to make: Balio (1987), 127.

14   *A Hard Day's Night*: Balio (1987), 250–51.
    $17 million colossus: Box office information on *My Fair Lady* is murky. *Variety* reported $30 million in domestic distribution gross (*Var*, January 7, 1970) to $12 million in rentals (*Var*, January 3, 1979). If the latter figure is accurate, *Lady* was a flop. Estimated worldwide film rental by 1967 came to $55 million, but with sales over $20 million split between CBS, the estate of George Bernard Shaw, and Warner Bros., *Lady* was not the mother lode for Warners that its top 10 box office ranking would suggest. (*Var*, March 29, 1967)
    With fine attention given: *Var*, February 10, 1965.

15 "The weather was miserable": *NYT*, November 20, 1966.
"We came back": Harris, 352–53.
"nothing short": USC/RW, January 17, 1965.
"You could get": Hirsch, 191.
"*has the makings*": *Film Bulletin*, January 4, 1965.
The opening night gala: *NYT*, March 3, 1965.
Designed by master architect: in70mm.com/newsletter/1999/59/rivoli/and *The Modern Theatre*, insert to *Boxoffice*, December 3, 1955.
17 Rivoli was *the* place for roadshow musicals: *NYT*, March 25, 1966.
"[Andrews] provides": *NYT*, March 3, 1965.
18 "Where *My Fair Lady*": *NYT*, March 7, 1965.
"Calorie-counters": *New York Herald-Tribune*, March 3, 1965.
"sizzling": USC/RW, March 3, 1965.
"A huge, tasteless blowup": *The New Yorker*, March 6, 1965.
19 "*South Pacific*": *Vogue*, May 1965.
"Watching *The Sound of Music*": Plummer, 390.
"radiance floods": *Life*, March 12, 1965.
"a whole whirling": *HR*, March 1, 1965.
20 *The Sound of Music* was rolled out quickly: fromscripttodvd.com/
"Certificate of Merit": *London Times*, January 10, 1967.
106 million: Krämer, 23.
"49 Weeks": *NYT*, November 20, 1966.
By the end of 1965: *NYT*, December 26, 1965 and October 19, 1966.
21 "It's a great picture": *NYT*, November 20, 1966.
22 "reminds us": *The Sound of Music* 40th Anniversary DVD commentary, 2005.
"I wasn't trying": *NYT*, November 20, 1966.
"How far, perhaps": *London Times*, January 10, 1967. Ear buds in the twenty-first century suggest something is still lacking in people's lives, as music continues to exercise its escapist powers.
23 When *Music* left the Rivoli: *NYT*, October 19, 1966.
nine theaters: *NYT*, December 7, 1966.
expanded to a mere six theaters: *LAT*, June 15, 1967.
More than two years after the premiere: *Var*, April 12, 1967.
600 roadshow engagements: fromscripttodvd.com/sound_of_music_40th_tribute.htm/
"The beauty": *Fortune*, February 1955, 127.
diversification: Schatz, 9–10.
soundtrack sales: Krämer, 23–24.
"going to give": *NYT*, December 27, 1965.
"to come back": *The Sound of Music: From Fact to Phenomenon*, 1994. *The Sound of Music* can't stop making money. It earned $11 million in rentals during a 1973 theatrical reissue. In 1976, ABC paid $15 million for a one-time showing, and it was number one in the Neilsen ratings. In 1978, NBC bought the rights to show the film 22 times over a 20-year period, and Fox television paid over $3.7 million for airing rights from 2001 to 2005. The video was the longest running best seller in history, appearing on *Billboard*'s top 40 video sales charts for more than 250 weeks. Five hundred productions of *Music* are staged yearly, from high schools to dinner theaters to professional touring companies. And with more reissues, television airings, DVD sales, and "Sing a-Longs," it keeps going. Three of the top four musicals in domestic box office adjusted for inflation remain *Music* (number one), *Poppins* (number two), and *My Fair Lady* (number four). The third spot is occupied by 1978's *Grease*. blockbustingbook.blogspot.com/
"The more money": Stirling, 153.
24 "*The Sound of Music* did more": Gussow, 263.

24 "a form of audience rebellion": *Var*, April 20, 1966.
Rebel Without a Cause: *Var*, April 18, 1966.
MGM raided its own vaults: *LAT*, August 8, 1968.
"The Mint": Wiley and Bona, 384.

Chapter 2: "I, Too, Can Sing"

25 "He loved *Camelot*": *Life*, December 6, 1963.
"It was the song":jfklancer.com/pdf/Camelot.pdf/
"longer than *Parsifal*": Kurtti, unnumbered pages.
26 "It was really": Callan, 173.
"Lerner describes": *San Francisco Chronicle*, October 8, 1967.
a hefty $2 million: *NYT*, April 12, 1961.
MGM put in a bid: *NYT*, September 27, 1961.
"I think the American producers": *My Fair Lady* special edition DVD, 2004.
27 "the slightest intention": *NYT*, October 1, 1964.
"He does not": USC/WB, *Camelot* files, April 15, 1966.
October 1967 roadshow premiere: *San Francisco Chronicle*, October 8, 1967.
"The magic": *San Francsico Chronicle*, April 23, 1967.
"[Lerner] had chosen me": Kurtti, unnumbered pages.
"It took me": Callan, 165.
28 "Guenevere I did": Stirling, 165–66.
"in high style": Springer, 189.
"a ravishing bitch": Thomas (1990), 284.
"She was never": Logan, 194–95.
"obvious names": USC/WB, *Camelot* files, March 18, 1966.
"Every producer": USC/WB, *Camelot* files, April 27, 1966.
"She's the answer": *Camelot* roadshow program, Warner Bros.-Seven Arts, 1967.
29 "I voted Labor": *NYT*, April 10, 1966.
"Do we really": Logan, 200.
"I've never": *NYT*, December 18, 1966.
"rule out accidents": *Morgan* DVD notes by Jack Turner, 2001.
She signed for $200,000: USC/WB, *Camelot* files, November 23, 1966.
"I love you": *Life*, September 22, 1967.
"I swim": *Camelot* roadshow program, Warner Bros.-Seven Arts, 1967.
he had broken his nose: *Life*, September 22, 1967.
Warner knew how to deal: USC/WB, *Camelot* files, November 23, 1966.
30 "ascetic enough": Logan, 195.
the recommendation of John Huston: USC/WB, *Camelot* files, June 3, 1966.
Romeo and Juliet: Callan, 166–67.
"Everyone sings": *LAT*, January 24, 1967.
a log kept of queries: USC/WB, *Camelot* files, various dates.
"This is a very serious project": USC/WB, *Camelot* files, June 3, 1966.
31 "Since it is": *LAT*, September 25, 1966.
"In the love scenes": AMPAS, Motion Picture Association of America files, June 22, 1966.
"The fact that Alan": USC/WB, *Camelot* files, May 16, 1966.
backlot preparations: USC/WB, *Camelot* files, various dates.
32 Arthur's bath: Logan, 205.
"books and more books": USC/WB, *Camelot* files, undated.
Warner's full commitment: *Var*, August 31, 1966 and *Camelot* roadshow program, Warner Bros.-Seven Arts, 1967.
"It was absolutely": *LAT*, September 25, 1966.

32   The finished castle: Kurtti, unnumbered pages.
     production budget: USC/WB, *Camelot* files, September 2, 1966.
33   All travel: USC/WB, *Camelot* files, September 12, 1966.
     When it was not raining: *LAT*, September 25, 1966.
34   Early action: *Var*, August 31, 1966.
     Daniel Vandraegen: *Camelot* roadshow program, Warner Bros.-Seven Arts, 1967.
     "horrified": USC/WB, *Camelot* files, September 14, 1966.
     "If [Nero] seems": USC/WB, *Camelot* files, October 1, 1966.
     "caused by some": USC/WB, *Camelot* files, October 7, 1966.
     mental breakdown: USC/WB, *Camelot* files, September 13, 1966.
     "I wish": USC/WB, *Camelot* files, October 9, 1966.
     Shooting in Spain: USC/WB, *Camelot* files, October 14, 1966.
35   "Ladies and gentlemen": *NYT*, December 18, 1966.
     "The enormous production": Logan, 210.
     sell his 1.6 million: *NYT*, November 15, 1966.
     "Not bad": Warner Sperling, 326.
     "It isn't fun": Thomas (1990), 280.

Chapter 3: The Animal Kingdom

37   "Roadshows have put": *Var*, August 10, 1966.
38   "He worked on the picture": Dunne, 34–35.
     "He had more": LMU/AJ, *Dolittle* files, May 7, 1965.
     the biggest merchandising tie-in: LMU/AJ, *Dolittle* files, Box 19, October 19, 1965.
39   Pushmi-Pullyu: LMU/AJ, *Dolittle* files, Box 17, November 23, 1964. The Pushmi-Pullyu was
     played uncredited by dancers Sharon Michael and Judy Chapman. Given the beast's peculiar
     anatomy, both escaped the ignominy of playing the back end.
     "Rex was glowing": Plummer, 421.
     "I know of no": LMU/AJ, *Dolittle* files, December 12, 1965.
     "His appearance": Fleischer, 235–36.
     "I'm sick": *NYT*, September 4, 1966.
     "Rex, I hate": Fleischer, 238.
40   "I don't want": Fleischer, 242.
     Golden Boy: Fleischer, 243–46.
     "to tell you how thrilled": LMU/AJ, *Dolittle* files, November 1, 1965.
     $250,000: Fleischer, 246–47.
     $300,000: LMU/AJ, November 2, 1965.
     "The budget": Fleischer, 247.
     "So now Rex": LMU/AJ, *Dolittle* files, December 7, 1965.
     "NO!": Fleischer, 248.
41   "as he will": LMU/AJ, *Dolittle* files, undated.
     "could be mean-spirited": Harris, 154.
     for a princely $300,000: Dunne, 35–36.
     "no one enjoyed": Plummer, 421.
     "amusing irritability": LMU/AJ, *Dolittle* files, undated.
     Flanders and Swann: Harrison (1991), 193.
     "The next nine": Moseley, 234.
     "Rex is a bully": *NYT*, October 2, 1966.
42   with a price of $500,000: Bardsley, 126.
     "ridiculous": USC, Richard Fleischer Collection, November 2, 1965.
     "I think Rex": LMU/AJ, *Dolittle* files, Box 17, Jacobs to Rosenfeld, November 10, 1965.
     "are not really": LMU/AJ, *Dolittle* files, December 12, 1965.

42 "Only APJAC": Bricusse, 169.

43 "We started rehearsing": BU/HG, Anthony Newley Collection, April 6, 1966.
"Jewish comic": Fleischer, 261.
"It was always": Bardsley, 129.
"I find it": *My Fair Lady* roadshow program, Warner Bros., 1964.
$1.5 million: LMU/AJ, *Dolittle* files, May 23, 1966.
demo record: Bardsley, 126.
costumes: *Dolittle* roadshow program by Harold Stern, New York: National Publishers, 1967.
"the strain": BU/HG, Newley Collection, April 20, 1966.
"22 points": Fleischer, 259.

44 "I'm terribly unhappy": LMU/AJ, *Dolittle* files, May 6, 1966.
"with deep and genuine": LMU/AJ, *Dolittle* files, undated memo.
"We have many": USC, Fleischer Collection, September 7, 1965.
the neck of a giraffe: Dunne, 37.
"Do you know": *Sun* (UK), July 15, 1966.
"Cut!": *Life*, September 30, 1966.
"How do you": Medved, 120–21.
"What could be easier?": Medved, 122.
"my love": Harrison (1975), 219.

45 "Half the villagers": Harrison (1991), 194.
Sir Ranulph: Fleischer, 262.
"We are deep": BU/HG, Newley Collection, July 6, 1966.
"Castle Combe": Harris, 200.
a team of tradesmen: Walker (1992), 287.
"It is the weather": *Var*, August 17, 1966.
"I doubt": *LAT*, August 9, 1966.
"Arthur would always": Harris, 202.
"We postponed": Harris, 239.
"Take this warning": LMU/AJ, *Dolittle* files, undated.
"something like Demerol": Harris, 240.

46 "He's the star": Dunne, 91.
Chinese mockingbird: Walker (1984), 74.
"I doubt": Bardsley, 130.
"Everyone wants": Dunne, 37–38.
The merchandising interests: Dunne, 39–40.
"It is still": *NYT*, November 6, 1966.
"Harrison was absolutely": LMU/AJ, *Dolittle* files, Box 19, Jacobs to Rosenfield, November 7, 1966.
Marigot Bay: LMU/AJ, *Dolittle* files, Box 17, October 24, 1966.

47 November 21: LMU/AJ, *Dolittle* files, Box 10, November 21, 1966.
"On good days": *Dolittle* roadshow program by Harold Stern, New York: National Publishers, 1967.
"This is really": Medved, 122.
"the work with animals": Harrison (1975), 219.
"We should have taken": Walker (1984), 73.
"I don't have": Harris, 242.
"How is it possible": LMU/AJ, *Dolittle* files, Jacobs to Abrahams, November 22, 1966.
"Eighteen months": LMU/AJ, *Dolittle* files, Box 10, November 25, 1966.

48 *The budget's 16*: LMU/AJ, *Dolittle* files, undated.
"The head": Harrison (1991), 198.

49 "much better control": *San Francisco Chronicle*, January 2, 1967.

49 soundtrack album: Dunne, 52.
"Bigger than *Sound of Music*": Dunne, 52.
"A producer has": Mann, 350.
His success can be measured: Mann, 357.
The Boy Friend: *NYT*, March 23, 1967.

50 "sounds as if": *HR*, March 23, 1967.
"tall, mean-faced goy": Phillips (1991), 130.
"perform an anatomically": *NYT*, March 16, 1975.
"This is no 'message'": *NYT*, July 17, 1966.
"I run a hotel": *LAT*, July 3, 1966.

51 "enormous problems": Laffey, 264.
generous budget of $5.3 million: UCLA Performing Arts Special Collection, various dates.
"wanted to put": Horton, 63.
"I knew it": Horton, 60.
"twice as large": *The New Yorker*, April 1, 1967.
"very difficult": Southern Methodist University, Ronald L. Davis Oral Histories on the Performing Arts, Ross Hunter interview, 51, July 17, 1984.
"I must have": *NYT*, March 16, 1975.
at the Criterion: *HR*, March 23, 1967.

52 "The film will not help": *Saturday Review*, April 15, 1967.
"Ross Hunter's": *HR*, March 23, 1967.
"simple-minded": *The Village Voice*, June 22, 1967.

53 "a cheap piece": *NYT*, August 15, 1967.
"I am very": Harris, 371.
"I have never": *LAT*, October 15, 1967.
"Critics tend": *Sight & Sound*, Winter 1967/68, 211.

54 *Variety* reported: *Var*, January 3, 1968.
"not because": Southern Methodist University, Ronald L. Davis Oral Histories on the Performing Arts, Ross Hunter interview, 50, July 17, 1984.
"she is everybody's": *Time*, December 23, 1966.
"I think *Thoroughly*": Horton, 61. After his dismissal from *Millie*, Hill moved to Fox to direct Paul Newman and Robert Redford in *Butch Cassidy and the Sundance Kid*. Universal then made amends and reunited him with Newman and Redford in *The Sting*, which won him an Oscar. Both films reached the top 20 all-time box office list. Hill followed these triumphs with *The Great Waldo Pepper*, his failed dream project about early aviation. He died in 2002 without a director's cut of *Thoroughly Modern Millie*. That same year, *Millie* was adapted to Broadway and found new life. It won six Tony Awards, ran for 903 performances, and toured the States and England.
"like cream": Southern Methodist University, Ronald L. Davis Oral Histories on the Performing Arts, Ross Hunter interview, 51, July 17, 1984.

Chapter 4: Movie Stars

55 two movies at Fox: UCLA/Fox, *Star!* files, October 17, 1966.
"When we heard": Stirling, 198.
Lamb and Andrews: MOMA, *Star!* clipping file, undated.
Wise and producer Saul: *London Times*, October 8, 1967.
"the indefinable": Stirling, 199.
"The aim was to celebrate": Stirling, 201.
"The great drive": Windeler (1983), 153.
"It was certainly encouraging": USC/RW, August 2, 1965.

56 "very upset at the prospect": USC/RW, November 16, 1965.

56 "to pay him off": USC/RW, December 8, 1965.
died under anesthetic: USC/RW, March 15, 1966.
"Oh, but you Hollywood people": USC/RW, December 9, 1966.
"She could wear": Chaplin, 230.
"a project of which": Payn and Morley, 603–4.
"is about as much": Coward, 749.

57 $1,000 per week: UCLA/Fox, *Star!* files, October 17, 1966.
"prepare the necessary papers": UCLA/Fox, *Star!* files, September 29, 1966.
"outrageous": UCLA/Fox, *Star!* files, September 30, 1966.
"When I got into the role": Windeler (1970), 158.

58 "Although we are starting off": UCLA/Fox, *Star!* files, April 17, 1967.
150-day shooting schedule: *Var*, April 12, 1967.
"was not a major American enthusiasm": *LAT*, November 1, 1968.

59 "although the opening": *NYT*, May 21, 1967.
"seventeen months": *Var*, May 24, 1967.
15,000 priority forms: "The Saga of *Star!*" by T. J. Edwards, *Movie Collector's World*, #357, December 7, 1990, 59.
"endless process of excision": *NYT*, September 29, 1968.
The Fanny Brice Story: AMPAS/WW, undated.
"You've got to have a Jewish girl": Bloom and Vlastnik, 123.

60 "I went down": *Funny Girl* original cast CD liner notes by David Foil, 1992.
"It was never": *NYT*, September 19, 1968.
"I remember a long": *Funny Girl* roadshow program by Jack Brodsky, New York: National Publishers, 1968.
"We've got away": *LAT*, November 16, 1966.

61 "It's quite apparent": *NYT*, September 19, 1968.
"It just seemed I was in prison": The University of Texas at Austin, Ransom Center, Lehman Collection, *Dolly!* files, September 1968.
20-stop American singing tour: *Var*, April 6, 1966.
payload of $1 million: *Life*, September 29, 1967.
"I wouldn't have made the picture": Riese, 282.
"What interested me": Spada, 202.
"William Wyler is one": AMPAS, Vincente Minnelli Collection, undated.
"fetish about punctuality": AMPAS/WW, April 27, 1966.
"At the beginning": Madsen (1973), 387.

62 Many were suggested: AMPAS/WW, January 9, 1966.
"I am grateful": AMPAS/WW, May 1, 1967.
Rosalind Russell, Lucille Ball: AMPAS/WW, January 9, 1966.
"nervous time": *LAT*, November 13, 1966.

63 "It was like being tossed": Bloom and Vlastnik, 154.
"I thought I'd written": *Dolly!* roadshow program by Jack Hirshberg, Twentieth Century-Fox, 1969.
$2 million plus a percentage: *Var*, March 10, 1965.
"It is absolutely a brilliant job": University of Texas at Austin, Ransom Center, Lehman Collection, *Dolly!* files, March 6, 1967.

64 "Everyone over the age of six": University of Texas at Austin, Ransom Center, Lehman Collection, *Dolly!* files, September 1968.
Lehman saw the rushes: Yudkoff, 249.
"It actually annoyed me": University of Texas at Austin, Ransom Center, Lehman Collection, *Dolly!* files, September 1968.
"The largest single": *NYT*, May 9, 1967.
"We wanted Carol": Hirschhorn (1975), 252.

64   "No one even": www.barbara-archives.com/index.html/. Fox stood between Carol Channing and film stardom more than once. Fox also produced *Gentlemen Prefer Blondes* (1953), the film that cast Marilyn Monroe as Lorelei Lee, a role originated by Channing on Broadway.

65   "Would you believe": *Washington Post*, May 11, 1967.
   "Don't ever say": *LAT*, June 13, 1967. Channing's final revival of *Hello, Dolly!* was in 1996. Ultimately, the role clung to her legacy, not Streisand's.
   "Carol can do": *LAT*, July 3, 1967.
   "Don't worry": *LAT*, May 11, 1967.
   "People are so self-centered": Spada, 189.
   "When I got the role of Dolly": University of Texas at Austin, Ransom Center, *Dolly!* files, September 1968.

66   "As a Jew": AMPAS/WW, June 9, 1967.
   "People lost their heads": Madsen (1973), 390–91.
   "They gave me a chair": *NYT*, July 19, 1967.
   44 performances: *Var*, July 12, 1967.
   return to LA: *LAT*, November 27, 1967.
   "The only thing": *Look*, October 15, 1968.

67   "Director of Musical Numbers": *LAT*, January 26, 1969.
   "Dear Ray": AMPAS/WW, October 31, 1967.

68   "Wyler just didn't": *LAT*, January 26, 1969.
   "I'm not pleased": *LAT*, November 27, 1967.
   "Swan Lake": *LAT*, January 26, 1969.
   "Gene had exactly": Hirschhorn, 253.

69   "Jesus, you can get away": Dunne, 169.
   "On the day": Channing to author, August 21, 2008.
   "A barrel of laughs": Channing, 199–200.
   "*Hello, Dolly!* is a pretty": Hirschhorn (1975), 253.

Chapter 5: Smoke and Gold

70   "Walt Disney Studios": *LAT*, November 16, 1966.
   "one of those truly monstrous": *Esquire*, November 1967.
   Teddy Roosevelt, Kaiser Wilhelm: *Millionaire* roadshow program, New York: National Publishers, 1967.

71   80 minutes of song: Breaux to author, June 18, 2009.
   "We had to choreograph": Wood to author, June 25, 2009.
   "To dance with an alligator": *Millionaire* roadshow program, New York: National Publishers, 1967.
   Walt was not present: Breaux to author, June 18, 2009.
   "He usually held": Greene, 180.

72   "The period of this picture": *LAT*, April 23, 1967.

73   "the most exciting event": *LAT*, June 23, 1967.
   Hollywood Boulevard: *LAT*, June 26, 1967.
   two and a half blocks: *LAT*, June 23, 1967.
   1,500 guest benefit: *LAT*, June 11 and 13, 1967.
   "It's chic": *LAT*, June 26, 1967.
   "*Mary Poppins* was *Mary Poppins*": *LAT*, July 9, 1967.
   " . . . just about the widest": *Chicago Sun-Times*, October 16, 1967.

74   "hardtix pix": *Var*, June 28, 1967.
   "Great numbers of people": New York Public Library for the Performing Arts, *Millionaire* clipping file, unattributed clip.
   "My present advice": *Life*, January 5, 1968.

74 The 141-minute version: An alternative source states that Radio City presented the 144-minute version. See www.ultimatedisney.com/

75 "Anyone exposed": *Esquire*, November 1967.

"The Disney formula": *Christian Science Monitor*, October 9, 1967.

"How regrettable and downright depressing": New York Public Library for the Performing Arts, *Millionaire* clipping file, unattributed clip.

laid a big egg: There will never be one and only one *The Happiest Millionaire*. Anchor Bay released it at 164 and 144 minutes on video and DVD in 1999, while Disney's 2004 DVD ran 172 minutes. See *Video Review*, January 1985 and *LAT*, July 29, 1999.

"why not combine the two stories": Pye and Myles, 78.

"how on earth, I kept wondering": *Monthly Film Bulletin*, June 1985, 200.

76 Mickey Rooney: *NYT*, August 1, 1948.

$200,000: USC/WB, *Finian* files, undated.

$150,000 and 5 percent: USC/WB, *Finian* files, June 2, 1966.

"in bold and unsafe fashion": *Film Daily*, May 13, 1968.

77 "big, important 'roadshow'": *NYT*, July 25, 1967.

30 weeks of work: USC/WB, *Finian* files, February 13, 1967.

$3.5 million budget: Bergan, 32.

"from as far": *Finian* roadshow program, Burt Sloane, New York: National Publishers, 1968.

"by the goddamn": Phillips (2004), 46.

"I'm the original": Phillips and Hill, 12.

"at 29": *Time*, November 19, 2007.

a New York revival: USC/WB, *Finian* files, April 7, 1967.

"When I read the book": Phillips and Hill, 8–9.

"It can only": Schumacher, 53–54.

78 "A lot of liberal people": Phillips (2004), 47.

three weeks of rehearsals: USC/WB, *Finian* files, May 8, 1967.

"I feel 14": *Var*, June 22, 1967.

Finian would be roadshowed: USC/WB, *Finian* files, June 21, 1967.

"I had a good time with Francis": Thomas (1984), 271–72.

"I was like a fish": Clarke, 26.

79 "I sang with her": Mueller, 404.

"Francis was the new kid": Clark to author, March 11, 2009.

"a real pain": Mueller, 31.

"there was no planning": Schumacher, 56.

80 "Move to the music": Bergan, 32.

"in a methodology": Johnson, 63.

"Look what we're competing with": Phillips and Hill, 10.

"You know what today is": Thomas (1990), 2–3.

"They're people who": Bruck, 394.

It ran two weeks over: USC/WB, *Finian* files, October 12, 1967.

"*Finian* made *The Rain People*": Phillips (2004), 15.

81 "Filmgoers these days": *Var*, April 12, 1967.

"What Do You Think of Today's Movies?": *McCalls*, January 1967, 10, and May 1967, 28. *McCall's* bias is transparent. Data for moviegoing decisions were gathered for husband, wife, children, or the entire family. Single people might as well toss the survey into a trashcan.

"largely showed a negative reaction": *Var*, April 19, 1967.

Chapter 6: Over-Egg the Pudding

82 "I feel": USC/WB, *Camelot* files, October 19, 1966.

bursting: *Camelot* roadshow program, Warner Bros.-Seven Arts, 1967.

82   "you better get": *San Francisco Chronicle*, April 23, 1967.
     $12,182,500: USC/WB, *Camelot* files, November 15, 1966.
     "She has always": *Morgan!* DVD notes by Jack Tucker, 2001.
83   "That's a good": Logan, 202–3.
     "They won't know": Logan, 209.
     "I was indifferent to The Beatles": Callan, 175–76. Harris's career as a pop singer included the 1968 hit "MacArthur Park."
     "I don't care": *Ocala Star-Banner*, December 6, 1969.
     one hour dubbing three syllables: Callan, 179.
     "a bit of grog": Logan, 205–6.
     40 costume changes: *Camelot* roadshow program, Warner Bros.-Seven Arts, 1967.
84   "The reasons are large": USC/WB, *Camelot* files, January 10, 1967.
     "His dedication": Logan, 199.
     strewn across the dressing tents: USC/WB, *Camelot* files, February 21, 1967.
     "You're a . . . crook!": Logan, 207.
85   "was deeply in sympathy": USC/WB, *Camelot* files, March 30, 1967.
     final weeks of production: USC/WB, *Camelot* files, March 26, 1967.
86   "You've got to run": *Life*, September 22, 1967.
     "Fuck him": Logan, 210.
     "It was amazing": Callan, 174.
     "I've spent": *Camelot* roadshow program, Warner Bros.-Seven Arts, 1967.
     silver piece from Tiffany's: *Life*, September 22, 1967.
     second most expensive: Finler, 239.
     "When you see *Camelot*": USC/WB, *Camelot* files, January 18, 1967.
     "the best motion picture": USC/WB, *Camelot* files, January 27, 1967.
     sleepwear: AMPAS, Marty Weiser Collection, various dates.
     lipstick, ship models: USC/WB, *Camelot* files, various dates.
     Ford motors: AMPAS, Weiser Collection, February 14–16, 1967.
     "nine dashing designs": AMPAS, Weiser Collection, undated.
87   $178,122,000: *Var*, June 21, 1967.
     "I intend to go on": *Var*, June 7, 1967.
     "We must have a minute": USC/WB, *Camelot* files, July 14, 1967.
     None of the lyrics had been translated: USC/WB, *Camelot* files, January 27, 1967.
     distribution plan: AMPAS, Weiser Collection, February 14, 1967.
     "We spent it": LAT, September 16, 1967.
     Bill Gold: Bill Gold's graphic designs are probably the most widely seen in film history, thanks to his astonishing 70-year career. In addition to *Camelot*, his roadshow musicals include *The Music Man*, *My Fair Lady*, *Funny Girl*, and *Fiddler on the Roof*.
     He did not see: LAT, October 8, 1967.
     opening titles: *San Francisco Chronicle*, October 8, 1967.
88   Army Archerd: Dunne, 233.
     "grossly whimsey": NYT, October 26, 1967.
     "a far more successful": LAT, January 28, 1968.
     "carious": *Time*, November 3, 1967.
     "a gaudy, mawkish": *Films in Review*, December 1967, 649.
     "a dull play": *Monthly Film Bulletin*, January 1968, 3.
     "The schmuck": Sperling, 330.
     "On these reserved": Hall, 283.
     "one of Hollywood's": *Var*, October 25, 1967.
     "magnificent": *Commonweal*, November 17, 1967.
89   Less than $7 million: *Var*, January 8, 1969.
     "There seems little doubt": LAT, November 12, 1967.

90 "For any generation": Slater, 55.
  if select recitations of Arthur were relevant to Vietnam: *Film Quarterly*, Spring 1968, 56.
91 dreamy political idealism: The 1975 film *Monty Python and the Holy Grail* and its stage offspring, the 2005 travesty *Spamalot*, demonstrate just how far self-serious Arthurian mythmaking has fallen from grace.
  "The young have": *Time*, January 6, 1967.

Chapter 7: Do Little

93 "something of an anachronism": Silverman, 19.
  Fox's next three big musicals: Plans to film *Bloomer Girl* were abandoned due to cost and personnel complications; Levy, 313–14.
  "You've got to be careful": Dunne, 44.
  "There's really no playing": *LAT*, November 21, 1966.
  "quite possibly carries": LMU/AJ, *Dolittle* files, Box 17, January 7, 1967.
94 "It has been three": USC, Fleischer Collection, May 11, 1967.
  Loews State Theatre: *Var*, April 19, 1967.
  "I just don't": Dunne, 189.
  Radisson: Dunne, 191.
  "Oh my God": Dunne, 195.
  "This is a real dead-ass audience": Dunne, 197.
  "Arthur, you've got yourself": Dunne, 198–99.
  "Excellent": USC, Fleischer Collection, September 8, 1967.
  "The 'Fairs'": Dunne, 200.
  "I'd be mystified": Dunne, 201.
95 "We mustn't forget": Dunne, 202.
  "Of course, I was disappointed": Dunne, 242–43.
  "we all feel that we have": LMU/AJ, *Dolittle* files, Box 17, September 25, 1967.
  "Impossibly bad": Dunne, 238–40.
96 San Jose version: LMU/AJ, *Dolittle* files, October 27, 1967.
  "When a picture previews": Harris, 355.
  $12 million in licensing: LMU/AJ, *Dolittle* files, Box 17, October 31, 1967.
  the Vatican: LMU/AJ, *Dolittle* files, Box 17, various dates.
  "Screened final version": LMU/AJ, *Dolittle* files, November 9, 1967. Fox executives were slow to admit *Dolittle* held little interest for children. After a 2009 screening at American Cinematheque in Los Angeles, writer Beverly Gray said, "The kiddies in the audience didn't know how to handle the intermission. They were quite ready to go home, and couldn't believe the movie was only half over." Gray to author, June 2, 2009.
  "It's really cute": Dunne, 185.
  "If we blow": Dunne, 233.
97 "And the goddamn food": Dunne, 234.
  Fourteen hundred guests: *LAT*, December 21, 1967.
  $27 million: Dunne, 206.
  $400,000: *Var*, December 20, 1967.
98 "Don't knock it": Dunne, 93.
  Pink Sea Snail: When shooting finished, Fox left the Pink Sea Snail to rot on the Caribbean beach. Eventually it disappeared, fate unknown. (AMPAS, *Dolittle* clipping file, undated.)
99 "You won't be able": AMPAS, *Dolittle* clipping file, undated.
  just four theaters: LMU/AJ, *Dolittle* files, January 2, 1968.
  $9 million: Solomon, 162.
  domestic rentals: *Var*, January 8, 1969.
100 "the personification of the great white father": *NYT*, July 28, 1968.

100   "You look back now and ask": Harris, 357.
      20 wigs: Windeler (1970), 156.
      $650: UCLA/Fox, *Star!* files, undated.
      a small entourage: UCLA/Fox, *Star!* files, April 7, 1967.
      "I wish I had": UCLA/Fox, *Star!* files, April 17, 1967.
      Fourteen sites: UCLA/Fox, *Star!* files, undated.
101   from 6 to 40: UCLA/Fox, *Star!* files, June 28, 1967.
      attractive nuisance: UCLA/Fox, *Star!* files, May 22, 1967.
      Noël Coward was present, quietly editing the screenplay: Windeler (1970), 166.
      "He changed three": MOMA, *Star!* clipping file, undated production notes.
      "Three years": Dunne, 30.
      "This is the most difficult film": *LAT*, October 15, 1967.
      two production numbers: UCLA/Fox, *Star!* files, July 31, 1967.
      $3 million: *LAT*, September 12, 1967 and *Look*, September 19, 1967.
102   "Why don't the people": *LAT*, October 15, 1967.
      "Jenny": The original "Jenny" was light years from the over produced circus scene in *Star!*
      Lawrence reportedly sang it alone, simply and effectively, in front of a closed curtain.
103   "marvelous and nervous": Windeler (1970), 165.
      "sensational": Gussow, 265.
      1,197 days: MOMA, *Star!* clipping file, undated production notes.
      1,400 camera set-ups: UCLA/Fox, *Star!* files, January 26, 1968.
      44 speaking roles: Stirling, 202.
      "'Star!' nears finish line": AMPAS, *Star!* clipping file, October 1967.
      "People who don't": USC/RW, various dates.
104   "*Say It with Music*": Fordin, 520–21.
      Sophia Loren, Ann-Margret: *LAT*, January 22, 1968.
      $1,000,000: Windeler (1970), 191.

Chapter 8: Casting About

105   "Memorandum on *Mr. Chips*": AMPAS, Minnelli Collection, June 2, 1965.
106   "hazy": AMPAS, Minnelli Collection, July 12, 1964.
      The husband and wife: LMU/AJ, *Chips* files, September 18, 1964.
      "is set and I think that Rex": AMPAS, Minnelli Collection, December 1, 1964.
      "Just supposing disaster strikes": LMU/AJ, *Chips* files, undated.
      She could be American: LMU/AJ, *Chips* files, Box 23, February 9, 1965.
      music hall entertainer: AMPAS, Minnelli Collection, June 2, 1965.
      $4 million: LMU/AJ, *Chips* files, June 17, 1965.
107   Rattigan's multiple drafts screenplay: Rattigan submitted at least eight "temporary complete"
      screenplays through June 1968. (LMU/AJ, *Chips* files, various dates). Presumably as a joke,
      Jacobs referred to one of them as "number 775." Rattigan said the endless rewrites were
      "enough to put me off writing film-scripts for life." (*Sunday Times* [London], February 1, 1976)
      Burton supplanted Harrison: LMU/AJ, *Chips* files, October 21, 1965.
      Carlo Ponti lobbied: LMU/AJ, *Chips* files, February 27, 1966.
      Audrey Hepburn was in: LMU/AJ, *Chips* files, March 19, 1966.
      drawn for the Previns: LMU/AJ, *Chips* files, May 4, 1966.
      young maestro John Williams: Matessino, 3.
      "very difficult in terms": LMU/AJ, *Chips* files, June 22, 1966.
      considering Samantha Eggar: *Var*, July 6, 1966 and LMU/AJ, *Chips* files, Box 23, August 3,
      1966.
      on-again Richard Burton: LMU/AJ, *Chips* files, Box 23, August 4, 1966.
      $300 per week assistant: LMU/AJ, *Chips* files, Box 23, August 17, 1966.

108   expensive demonstration recording: Matessino, 8.
       Ireland, the United States: LMU/AJ, *Chips* files, Box 23, November 2, 1966.
       "contract disputes": *LAT*, November 16, 1966.
       He never heard: Matessino, 8.
       "it is the subject": LMU/AJ, *Chips* files, November 4, 1966.
       proxy war in progress: *Var*, April 18 and 20, 1966.
       in the communications field: *Var*, September 14, 1966.
       "If MGM is unwilling": LMU/AJ, *Chips* files, December 16, 1966.
109   Jacobs reconceived: LMU/AJ, *Chips* files, December 27, 1966.
       "The idea of a non-English lady": LMU/AJ, *Chips* files, February 15, 1967.
       Eggar was now out: LMU/AJ, *Chips* files, March 6, 1967.
       a deal for Hepburn: LMU/AJ, *Chips* files, March 8, 1967.
       "My Boys" went "nowhere": LMU/AJ, *Chips* files, Box 23, March 11, 1967.
       "I should like": LMU/AJ, *Chips* files, April 26, 1967.
       "committed now": LMU/AJ, *Chips* files, Box 23, April 12, 1967.
110   "stalled, delayed": LMU/AJ, *Chips* files, April 14, 1967.
       the ever-nagging question: LMU/AJ, *Chips* files, April 25, 1967.
       "Despite the fact": LMU/AJ, *Chips* files, Box 23, May 23, 1967.
       Maggie Smith: LMU/AJ, *Chips* files, May 11, 1967.
       "I don't think": LMU/AJ, *Chips* files, Box 23, June 8, 1967.
       new production schedule: LMU/AJ, *Chips* files, Box 23, June 16, 1967.
       "none of us": LMU/AJ, *Chips* files, August 8, 1967.
111   "I am sure, however": LMU/AJ, *Chips* files, August 21, 1967.
       "It was all set": Dunne, 189–90.
       Champion saw rough footage: LMU/AJ, *Chips* files, October 4, 1967.
       "The original script": Clark to author, March 11, 2009.
112   "I saw the original": Wapshott, 150.
       "completely unknown": LMU/AJ, *Chips* files, October 25, 1967.
       Abrahams wrote to Champion: LMU/AJ, *Chips* files, October 19, 1967.
       "Let's face it": LMU/AJ, *Chips* files, October 25, 1967.
       "My main concern": LMU/AJ, *Chips* files, Box 23, November 3, 1967.
       breach of contract suit: *Var*, April 22, 1968.
       pencil to paper: LMU/AJ, *Chips* files, November 17, 1967.
113   "We will make every effort": LMU/AJ, *Chips* files, Box 23, November 15 and 29, 1967.
       five days before Christmas: *Var*, December 20, 1967.

Chapter 9: Buying and Selling

114   "could afford": *Wall Street Journal*, June 27, 1969.
       "These young people": University of Wyoming, American Heritage Center, George Weltner
       Collection, May 7, 1965.
115   "After World War II": Balio (1987), 303.
       not so Gulf + Western: Mel Brooks mocked 1960s conglomerate fever in *Silent Movie*
       (1976), in which Big Picture Studios is threatened with a takeover by the voracious corpora-
       tion Engulf & Devour.
       "People said": Bluhdorn, 11.
       "We fought": *Look*, February 27, 1970, 44.
       He kept the New York office: *NYT*, November 28, 1969.
       "You've got to gamble": *Wall Street Journal*, June 27, 1969.
       "there is a tremendous": *LAT*, June 11, 1967.
116   "You've proven yourself": *LAT*, June 11, 1967.
       "I want to see": Parish, 63.

116 "The main change": *Time*, December 8, 1967.
     "I'm in a vulnerable spot": *LAT*, June 11, 1967.
117 $250,000: *NYT*, November 14, 1965.
     "fuse English charm": *HR*, December 26, 1967.
     "Mary Quant": *Time*, April 15, 1966.
     Seventy-six feature films: Mundy, 210.
     "no reason why": *Var*, May 3, 1967.
118 "They're determined to outdo": MOMA, *Sixpence* clipping file, *Cinema* (Beverly Hills), Summer 1967.
     "George [Sidney] and I": *LAT*, January 10, 1967.
     another $300,000: *Film Daily*, April 25, 1967.
119 "One doesn't find": *New York Post*, February 21, 1968.
     "An hour and a half": *Time*, March 1, 1968.
120 *Kipps*: As played by Michael Redgrave, Kipps is a simple soul and efficient shop assistant whose desires are modest and station in life is fixed. When he comes into money, he attempts to crack high society by learning proper speech, clothing, and taste in music and literature. Also known as *The Remarkable Mr. Kipps*, it was directed by Carol Reed (*Oliver!*).
     "It's perhaps easy": Mundy, 214.
     "countless songs": *NYT*, March 10, 1968.
     "There was no validity": Walker (1974), 394.
     Humorists had a field day: Steinberg, 343–44.
121 "The following has been": Wiley and Bona, 406.
     "It was all": *NYT*, May 5, 1970.
     "This ludicrous event": Reed, 12.
     "Believe me": Harris, 389.
     "liveliest embarrassment": *LAT*, February 26, 1968.
     "could be called": *LAT*, April 7, 1968.
122 "a good many factors": USC, Fleischer Collection, March 18, 1968.
     "public relations," "administrators": *LAT*, April 7, 1968.
     "I find it morally incongruous": Wiley and Bona, 408.
     "To follow the old tradition": *LAT*, April 7, 1968.
123 "There was never a doubt": *Var*, April 11, 1968.
     "This has been a fateful week": O'Neil, 290.
     "I will not seek": Wiley and Bona, 410.
     "The man from Montgomery": imdb.com/title/tt0353126/quotes/
     "You could hear": Wiley and Bona, 411–12.
     "He matched my jewelry": Bricusse, 213.

Chapter 10: "Impossible to Control the Cost of This Gown"

125 "In the wake": *Time*, December 8, 1967.
     explosive box office: *Var*, January 7, 1970.
     $95,000 deficit: Parish, 64.
     Warner Bros. envisioned Bing: *NYT*, January 20, 1952.
     Mayer bought the film: *Var*, February 4, 1952.
126 Don Siegel: *HR*, April 25, 1966.
     "He talked about": Logan, 214.
     "Frankly, I was hesitant": Jablonski, 87.
     $150,000: *HR*, June 20, 1967.
     "It's a preposterous story": "Gold Diggers of 1969" by Joshua Logan, *Films and Filming*, December 1969, 16.
     "sing for shit": Considine, 249.

126 "I'm not exactly Howard Keel": *LAT*, June 22, 1969.
"Who says I'm not": AMPAS, *Wagon* clipping file, November 22, 1968.
127 Lesley Ann Warren: *HR*, March 1, 1967.
"came into Josh": McGee, 152.
"a nineteenth century": *LAT*, October 14, 1969.
"reassurances": Zec, 166.
128 "The safety problems": Jablonski, 242.
"Full-sized controlled": *Wagon* roadshow program by George Scullin, New York: National Publishers, 1969.
"I know of": Jablonski, 242.
129 "It's now totally": Schickel, 214.
Oregon: *Var*, September 25, 1968.
imported from Hollywood: AMPAS, *Wagon* clipping file, *The Herald-Examiner*, undated.
"Throughout my directing": Logan, 213–14.
a fleet of eight: *Wagon* roadshow program by George Scullin, New York: National Publishers, 1969.
130 "It was as if": Jablonski, 243.
"like living under": *Var*, August 1, 1968.
"no one tried": Richards, 190. All the waiting and waste on *Paint Your Wagon* gave Clint Eastwood time to think about economizing, careful planning, and intolerance for drunkenness. He learned negative lessons on *Wagon* that he took to his own career as director of tightly budgeted films.
"Some of them": Richards, 188.
Baker did not offer: *LAT*, August 18, 1968, and AMPAS, *Wagon* clipping file, *The Herald-Examiner*, undated.
Interested guests: Logan, 213.
"Logan is in": *LAT*, July 12, 1968.
"I called Paramount": *LAT*, October 6, 1968.
131 "Tell [Brooks]": Logan, 219.
"directed the picture": Logan, 221.
"Ain't nothin' wrong": Schickel, 215.
"like confronting an opaque presence": *LAT*, October 8, 1968.
"The minute you said": Schickel, 217.
"Not since Attila": Parish, 75.
"full of bullshit": McGee, 169.
"sits near an oil lamp": AMPAS, *Wagon* clipping file, *The Herald-Examiner*, undated.
"pathetic waifs": McGee, 163.
"It's all connected": McGee, 158.
132 "We're in one": Parish, 76.
Extras complained: *LAT*, August 18, 1968.
"I don't know what the hell": AMPAS, *Wagon* clipping file, *The Herald-Examiner*, undated.
133 "We're sure our timing" *NYT*, October 26, 1968.
"How's your cut": Logan, 223–24.
"give her what she wants": Riese, 301.
tests: UCLA/Fox, *Dolly!* files, makeup department progress report, February 26, 1968.
"regarding any question": UCLA/Fox, *Dolly!* files, March 16, 1968.
134 "*Hello, Dolly!* will be": UCLA/Fox, *Dolly!* files, April 15, 1968.
"Miss Ptomaine": *New York Daily News*, September 15, 1968.
"That hairdo you wore": *Esquire*, December 1968, 262.
"The *Dolly!* set": The University of Texas at Austin, Ransom Center, Lehman Collection, *Dolly!* files, September 1968.
"I've got some": *Life*, February 14, 1969.

134   "She doesn't have to work": *LAT*, April 21, 1968.
      memos flew through Fox: UCLA/Fox, *Dolly!* files, April 19 and 29, 1968.
135   Stradling: Stradling's last four films as director of photography were Streisand's first four. He
      died in 1970.
      without a complete budget: Dunne, 224.
      "We are trying": UCLA/Fox, *Dolly!* files, May 1, 1968.
      estimates: UCLA/Fox, *Dolly!* files, April 16, 1968.
      "I'd say you've built": MOMA, *Dolly!* clipping file, undated press release.
      Production Department head Stan: UCLA/Fox, *Dolly!* files, May 6, 1968.
      $200,000: *LAT*, August 20, 1968.
      expensive weather insurance: Dunne, 225–26.
      "Naturally, having worked": Delamater, 227.
136   "How's your ulcer": *Esquire*, December 1968, 262.
      "Everyone in this company": Spada, 213.
      "I wasn't going": *Esquire*, December 1968, 194–95.
      "Barbra kept asking Gene": Hirschhorn (1975), 256.
      "Delay in shooting": USC, Ernest Lehman Collection, production report, June 7, 1968.
      "After I saw [the stage production]": The University of Texas at Austin, Ransom Center, Leh-
      man Collection, *Dolly!* files, September 1968.
137   "While it all sounds very exciting": USC, Lehman Collection, January 16, 1968.
      "Constant and innumerable": USC, Lehman Collection, April 6, 1968.
      "The train's got to go": *Life*, February 14, 1969.
138   "For Christ's sake why": Dunne, 231.
      "Once I made": Spada, 218.
      "The intrigues, the bitterness": Riese, 312.
      "[Kelly] gave as much of himself": Hirschhorn (1975), 259.
      "I of course had heard": *LAT*, June 9, 1968.
      New York had to be reconstructed: Thomas (1974), 234, and Hirschhorn (1975), 258.
139   John DeCuir: MOMA, *Dolly!* clipping file, undated press release.
      "They were just not": Hirschhorn (1975), 293.
      "He was a competent director": Silverman, 136.
140   The completed street set: *LAT*, July 18 and August 20, 1968.
      "It's all rather staggering": *LAT*, September 1, 1968.
      "Let's move, people": *Hello, Dolly!* featurette, *Hello, Dolly!* DVD, 2003.
      "Ladies had hips": MOMA, *Dolly!* clipping file, undated press release.
      "Okay. Cut it": *Esquire*, December 1968, 194.
141   $100,000 per month: Thomas (1974), 229.
      plane crashed: *LAT*, October 3, 1968.
      "It's a difficult world": The University of Texas at Austin, Ransom Center, Lehman Collec-
      tion, *Dolly!* files, September 1968.
      "What is so likeable": *NYT*, April 30, 1968.
142   17 of the 25: *Var*, August 21, 1968.

Chapter 11: Battle of the Girls

143   "Everyone at Warners": USC/WB, *Finian* files, March 25, 1968.
      Clark and Belafonte: youtube.com/watch?v=gQXVjY1oqRo/
      "We had the preview": WB/USC, *Finian* files, June 24, 1968.
      "happiness factor": *Film and Television Daily*, August 6, 1968.
      more than 17,000: *Var*, September 11, 1968.
144   "blew the feet off Fred Astaire": Schumacher, 60.
      less than $4 million: *Var*, October 9, 1968.

144 "I tried to show": Phillips (2004), 9.
      "I fought very hard": Johnson, 65.
      "Every time": *Harper's Magazine*, November 1968.
      banned in South Africa: *NYT*, October 28, 1968.
      "imagination": *Films in Review*, 19, #9, November 1968.
      "galvanic twitching": *Time*, October 25, 1968.
      "The choreography was abysmal": Phillips (2004), 10–11.
      "[His] secret seems to lie": *Sight & Sound*, Winter 1968, v. 38, 44.
145 "Reality, however cruel": Pye and Myles, 80.
      "possessed the kind of idealism": Schumacher, 59.
      "I was always planning": *NYT*, May 8, 1979.
      "It was an absurd idea": Bergan, 33.
      $2 million profit: Cook, 135.
      "I don't think there'll be a Hollywood": Pye and Myles, 81.
      "I do think you have hurt": AMPAS/WW, March 27, 1968.
146 "monster": *LAT*, April 21, 1968.
      "I know of no instance": AMPAS/WW, April 26, 1968.
      There was a fashion short: *Var*, August 23, 1968.
147 Plaza Hotel: *NYT*, June 8, 1968.
      Paramount announced that Streisand would star: *Los Angeles Times West*, September 1, 1968.
      seats at $6: *NYT*, September 19 and December 19, 1968.
      advanced sales for weekends: *NYT*, September 14, 1968.
      "Nothing like Barbra Streisand": *The Village Voice*, October 10, 1968.
      "incandescence": *The New Yorker*, September 28, 1968.
      the most remarkable": Reed, 352.
149 "Miss Streisand has matured": *Newsweek*, September 30, 1968.
      "She's a bit irritating": *The New Republic*, November 9, 1968.
      "Wyler has not so much": *The Village Voice*, October 10, 1968.
      $56 million: Block and Wilson, 494.
      "There's no doubt": *NYT*, October 26, 1968.
150 Postproduction on Andrews's *Star!*: UCLA/Fox, *Star!* files, March 18, 1968.
      "The department of dullness": *LAT*, April 21, 1968.
      "If everyone throughout the world": UCLA/Fox, *Star!* files, May 1, 1968.
      "It was the unqualified": UCLA/Fox, *Star!* files, May 6, 1968.
      tinkering: UCLA/Fox, *Star!* files, May 27, 1968.
      "All the general audience": Chaplin, 239–40.
151 "Unless release schedules are changed": *Var*, July 26, 1967.
      Streisand attended: *LAT*, July 16, 1968.
      Star!'s world premiere: Windeler (1970), 165–67.
      "Blake had a shot": *LAT*, August 8, 1968.
      "Don't let her go!": AMPAS, *Darling Lili* clipping file, *Los Angeles Herald-Examiner*, early 1970.
      "the squarest thing": MOMA, *Star!* clipping file, *Evening Standard*, undated.
152 *Star!* outgrossed *The Sound of Music*: UCLA/Fox, *Star!* files, August 12, 1968.
      "How many of its potential audience": *London Times*, July 19, 1968.
      "*Star!* is doing most of the work": *Var*, September 4, 1968.
      the world's longest billboard: "The Saga of *Star!*" by T. J. Edwards, *Movie Collector's World*, #357, December 7, 1990, 75.
      "Her reticence and impenetrable affability": *LAT*, August 25, 1968.
      "Remember, I'm the leading lady": Windeler (1970), 225.
      "These damn interviews": Windeler (1970), 224.
      "Suing her would dignify her": Windeler (1970), 226.

152   "the H-bomb of musicals": *Time,* July 27, 1970.
      "The sets are tacky": *Newsweek,* November 4, 1968.
      "The only reason": Windeler (1970), 168.
153   "Nothing in *Star!*": *Harper's Magazine,* November 1968.
      "is less concerned": *Monthly Film Bulletin,* September 1968, 168.
154   "I was shocked": Stirling, 211.
      "a bio with Julie Andrews": Mordden (1982), 206.
      "Barbra Streisand arrives on the screen": *The New Yorker,* September 28, 1968. Kael would temper her Streisand zeal considerably by the time *Funny Lady* and *A Star Is Born* appeared in the mid-1970s.
      "Cripes! Julie Andrews": *The New Yorker,* October 26, 1968.
      "*Star!* was the most difficult film": Chaplin, 237.
      "You have a sensational preview": New York Public Library for the Performing Arts, Oral History Program, The AFI Seminars, Part I, #196, April 17, 1975.
155   75 percent: Hall, 221.
      "My Edsel": Windeler (1970), 168.
      $1.3 million: *Var,* January 8, 1968.
      any 20 minutes: AMPAS, *Star!* clipping file, unattributed.
      "UNBELIEVABLE JULIE!": "The Saga of *Star!*" by T. J. Edwards, *Movie Collector's World,* #357, December 7, 1990, 60.
156   bad taste: AMPAS, *Star!* clipping file, unattributed.
      "You can imagine": USC/RW, June 26, 1969.
      Great Neck, Long Island: USC/RW, June 4, 1969.
      "We're all still reeling": USC/RW, November 27, 1968.
      "Some place down the line": Leemann, 195.
157   "The severest loss": *Entertainment World,* November 7, 1969, 15.
      President Nixon, who screened it: Stirling, 230.
      "Gertrude Lawrence was a bitch": Silverman, 131.
      "*Star!* was the greatest puzzlement": "The Changing of the Guard" by Axel Madsen, *Sight & Sound,* Spring 1970, 65.
      "Someone once said": Solomon, 156.
      "Today we smile": "Wanted: A New Kind of Musical" by William Wolf, *Cue,* October 26, 1968, 7.

Chapter 12: Delayed Adolescence

158   cut away constantly: Quick cut editing of musical numbers came of age in the 1960s with directors like Richard Lester, and returned in the early twenty-first century via *Moulin Rouge!, Chicago,* and the TV series *Glee* and *Smash.* Whatever happened to holding a shot for five seconds?
159   cracked the top 20: *Var,* January 3, 1968.
      "It was a philosophy": Picker to author, July 4, 2012.
      "There was a feeling of power": Jewison to author, March 8, 2012.
      "After five years": *Chitty* roadshow program by Jeffrey Newman, New York: National Publishers, 1968.
160   guarantee topped $1 million: Van Dyke, 159–60.
      "the most expensive musical": *Chitty* roadshow program by Jeffrey Newman, New York: National Publishers, 1968.
      Van Dyke pulling a hamstring: Van Dyke, 161.
      "It's only three minutes long": Breaux to author, June 18, 2009.
      "One of them": Wood to author, February 10, 2013.
      "leericks": *LAT,* May 24, 1967.
161   "Who rewrote Roald Dahl": Van Dyke, 164.

161 "Roald Dahl is supposed t'be *Chitty*'s screenwriter": *NYT*, October 22, 1967.
"Ken Hughes wore the tightest jeans": Wood to author, June 25, 2009.
"The first [time]": *NYT*, April 30, 1968.
"legit properties with big titles": Picker to author, July 4, 2012.
the New York premiere: *NYT*, December 19, 1968.
"all the rich melodic": *Time*, December 27, 1968.

162 "I discovered that in a big musical": *London Times*, September 23, 1968.

163 "Box's Army": *Oliver!* roadshow program by Nathan Weiss, New York: National Publishers, 1968.

165 Loew's State One: *NYT*, December 12, 1968.
"cast iron pastry": *NYT*, December 29, 1968.
"is introduced with a grinding": *London Times*, September 26, 1968.

166 "*Oliver!* is not put together": *The New Yorker*, December 14, 1968.
"*Oliver!* is not merely unfaithful": *The Village Voice*, January 9, 1969.
the Moscow Film Festival: *London Times*, July 23, 1969.
"It's better than *Half a Sixpence*": *NYT*, December 12, 1968.
The Secret War of Harry Frigg: *Var*, January 8, 1969.

167 "That's one area": Madsen (1975), 10.
The idea of Fosse: MacLaine, 175.
"I remember feeling tentative": *LAT*, May 11, 1969.

168 Screenwriter Peter Stone: This sequence of adaptations would happen again with *The Producers* (2005) and *Hairspray* (2007).
"Not only did [Universal]": Gottfried, 191.
"She suggested I do the part": MacLaine, 175.
"Gwen was there for me": *Look*, July 9, 1968, 58.
root canal: MacLaine, 176–77.
"What she lacks": *Look*, July 9, 1968, 58.
"It was much more valuable": *Look*, July 9, 1968, 59.

169 "My decision was made": MOMA, *Sweet Charity* clipping file, press release, undated.
seven months to write: *LAT*, May 11, 1969.
"The Rhythm of Life" costumes: Lee Roy Reams to author, October 24, 2010. Dancer-singer-actor Reams appeared in both the stage and screen versions of *Sweet Charity*.
"When I finished it": Gottfried, 197.
"If it's a flop": MacLaine, 182.
"It's perfectly normal": Gottfried, 196.

170 "It's the most demanding part": *Sweet Charity* roadshow program, Universal, 1969.
"Several articles appeared": MacLaine, 183.
"It's the most wonderful": *NYT*, March 30, 1969.
"Just as Al Jolson": *Sweet Charity* roadshow program, Universal, 1969. The *Charity* ad writers were either delinquent fact checkers or hoping for mass amnesia. Did no one remember that *The Jazz Singer* was released in 1927 and *West Side Story* in 1961, or notice that *Sweet Charity* opened in early 1969?
"There is Shirley MacLaine": *Washington Post*, June 27, 1969.

171 "I guess I had too many": Gottfried, 197.
"Crinkly Smile through Tears": *Look*, May 13, 1969.
"maltreated heart-of-gold": *New York*, April 7, 1969.
"simply gets by": *Women's Wear Daily*, April 11, 1969.
"The cost of moviemaking": *NYT*, April 6, 1969.

173 "will start big": *Var*, January 29, 1969.
"it got to New York": *HR*, April 12, 1972.
"It may have been a flop": Gottfried, 197.
"To a lot of people": Gottfried, 198.
"Men call her 'Sweet Charity'": *Var*, October 15, 1969.

173 "*Sweet Charity* is the kind": *Holiday*, April 1969, 38.
$4 million: Cook, 120. Despite the failure of the film, *Sweet Charity* has become something of a minor musical theater stage classic, with the title role assumed by various actresses-singers-dancers over the years, including Juliet Prowse, Donna McKechnie, Bebe Neuwirth, Debbie Allen, Marisa Tomei, Tamzin Outhwaite, and Christina Applegate.

Chapter 13: The Paramount Bloodsuckers

174 "People will talk": *Time*, December 23, 1966.
the fourth picture: *NYT*, March 9, 1967.
Highest domestic box office: *NYT*, January 6, 1969.
$750,000: AMPAS, *On a Clear Day* production file, April 25, 1966, unattributed.
"*On a Clear Day You Can See Forever* came": Evans, 159–60.
Gregory Peck, Frank Sinatra: *Life*, September 22, 1967.
Yves Montand: *HR*, August 5, 1968.
Montand's top billing: AMPAS, *On a Clear Day* clipping file, undated.
175 "growing mass audience": *Time*, December 8, 1967.
"go-go music": *Var*, July 17, 1968.
$6 million: *NYT*, January 6, 1969.
22 outfits: *Motion Picture Herald*, March 20, 1968.
"The secret of show business": MOMA, *Darling Lili* clipping file, "The Real Julie Andrews" by Mel Gussow, 1968.
"The blue skies": *Motion Picture Herald*, March 20, 1968.
176 "Let us fight": *LAT*, July 25, 1968.
As director, writer, and producer: *Motion Picture Herald*, March 20, 1968.
"It's not really a musical": Medved, 90–91.
$70,000: White, 105.
"I'd hate to be the first": *International Herald Tribune*, August 9, 1968.
177 Fireman's Fund insurance: *NYT*, August 30, 1970.
"Sometimes we wait": *International Herald Tribune*, August 9, 1968.
$14 million: *HR*, October 15, 1968
178 "doesn't like to be told": Minnelli, 364.
$25,000 retouching bill: Riese, 320.
179 "Not having made a musical": Wiley and Bona, 425–26.
"We're not playing": *NYT*, June 15, 1969.
180 Occidental College: AMPAS, Minnelli biography file, June 16, 1969.
"Don't eat any more": *LAT*, May 29, 1969.
"There is no assurance": *Var*, December 10, 1969.
Bluhdorn hadn't even bothered: In the 2003 documentary *Easy Riders, Raging Bulls*, director Peter Bogdanovich offers a savage imitation of a gruff, gravel-voiced Bluhdorn: "Think I make money on pictures? I don't make money on pictures. You know where I make money? Zinc! Sugar! That's where I make money. Not pictures. Pictures is bullshit. I like it—I like to do it sometime. But zinc . . ."
"looking trim and hickory-hard": *Time*, October 24, 1969.
"I think the film": *Mademoiselle*, October 1969.
181 "I couldn't say anything": Logan, 224.
"Anti-Establishment a century ago": *Wagon* roadshow program, New York: National Publishers, 1969.
"Young people are saying": Stirling, 329.
"agony": Logan, 224.
"It was an important picture": Richards, 227.
"In casting the picture": *Saturday Review*, November 15, 1969.

181 "The first all-talking": Mordden (1982), 207–8.
182 "would look foolish": AMPAS, *Wagon* production file, *Citizen News*, November 22, 1968.
65-voice male chorus: *Var*, August 1, 1968.
183 "The times, the mores": *Newsweek*, October 21, 1968.
"realistically portrays the time": *NYT*, November 28, 1968.
"has changed faster": *Var*, October 29, 1969.
184 "a disaster": Parish, 61.
"resoundingly booed at home": Jablonski, 92.
"I've never known": Zec, 174.
trimmed by 30 minutes: McGee, 192.
Golden Album: *Box Office*, April 26, 1971.
"finally broken the back": *The New Yorker*, October 25, 1969.
185 Paramount Cuts: *NYT*, November 9, 1969.
"We're not interested": *NYT*, November 17, 1969.
Bluhdorn's goal: *NYT*, November 28, 1969.
"The era of the majors": *Var*, October 29, 1969.

Chapter 14: Goodbye, MGM

186 "romantic drama with music": Matessino, 11.
"We don't intend": Wapshott, 151. Ross made his point, but there was no *Broadway Melody of 1933*.
"We are seeking": *The Western Gazette*, North Dorset edition, August 9, 1968.
$175,000: LMU/AJ, *Chips* files, December 28, 1967.
Ross also sought musical personnel: BU/HG, Ross Collection, Box 141, January 12 and 19, 1968.
"It offered everything": *Mr. Chips* roadshow program, Metro-Goldwyn-Mayer, 1969.
187 "talking endlessly": LMU/AJ, *Chips* files, January 1, 1968.
188 "It is quite normal": LMU/AJ, *Chips* files, January 1, 1968. Bricusse's *Sherlock Holmes* was not produced by MGM but did appear on stage in England in 1988 with Ron (*Oliver!*) Moody in the title role.
"It was impossible to create": *HR*, January 9, 1968. By 1968, Previn was at work on a musical version of *Great Expectations*. *LAT*, January 9, 1968.
Ralph Kemplen: LMU/AJ, *Chips* files, Box 23, March 31, 1968.
Breach of contract litigation: *Var*, December 20, 1967.
pay the Previns: LMU/AJ, *Chips* files, Box 25, January 23, 1968.
"with bad feelings": *LAT*, August 5, 1968.
"inundated with young boys": BU/HG, Ross Collection, Box 142, April 8, 1968.
189 Hatch: LMU/AJ, *Chips* files, undated.
"never invited to be involved": Hatch to author, January 30, 2012.
"I can't remember": *International Herald Tribune*, August 30, 1968.
"I still have the feeling": Matessino, 12–14.
"He's basically a romantic": johnwilliams.org/compositions/goodbyemrchips.html/
170 cast and crew: LMU/AJ, *Chips* files, Box 25, undated.
Tiny Sherborne: *The Western Gazette*, North Dorset Edition, August 9, 1968.
few delays: BU/HG, Ross Collection, Box 142, undated.
190 "It was only strict team work": LMU/AJ, *Chips* files, Box 25, undated press release.
"I knew Peter": Bricusse, 209.
"You have to admire": Bricusse, 212.
"Only when the clapperboard bangs": Wapshott, 152–53.
"Pet's first rate": LMU/AJ, *Chips* files, undated press release.
"They changed the script": Clark to author, March 11, 2009.
191 When *Chips* wrapped: MOMA, *Chips* clipping file, undated press release, 1969.

191   "MGM Presents The Losers": Freedland, 144–45.
       Clark was moved: LMU/AJ, *Chips* files, Box 25, undated.
       Say It with Music: *Var*, June 28, 1967 and *LAT*, January 22, 1968.
       She Loves Me: *NYT*, November 9, 1969.
192   A short film of *Chips*: LMU/AJ, *Chips* files, Box 23, December 13, 1968.
       The *Chips* teaser: LMU/AJ, *Chips* files, April 15, 1969.
       "The family picture": LMU/AJ, *Chips* files, undated.
       $8,223,268: Matessino, 19.
       "Nothing has been done": BU/HG, Ross Collection, Box 144, February 14, 1969.
193   *Chips* $4 million: *NYT*, June 6, 1969.
       Happy Goday: LMU/AJ, *Chips* files, August 15, 1969.
       "a flagrant and opportunistic attempt": *The Times* (London), August 21, 1969.
       "I'm up to my ears": BU/HG, Newley Collection, Box U., August 18, 1968.
       "every effort will be made": BU/HG, Ross Collection, Box 144, March 5, 1968.
       "Our preview was a smashing success": LMU/AJ, *Chips* files, September 8, 1969.
       Chips was trimmed: LMU/AJ, *Chips* files, Box 25, October 15, 1969.
194   "*Easy Rider* is a marvelous film": *LAT*, November 30, 1969.
195   "some of the silliest reviews": *Chicago Sun-Times*, November 19, 1969.
       H. M. Queen Elizabeth II: *HR*, December 5, 1969.
       "O'Toole gives a most impressive performance": Freedland, 149.
       "no Rex Harrison": *Var*, October 15, 1969.
       "the songs she's given": *Newsweek*, November 17, 1969.
       "It is simply too fragile": *Var*, October 15, 1969.
       "tell Hollywood and the moneymen": *Detroit Free-Press*, November 30, 1969.
       "One does not want to think": *LAT*, April 23, 1972.
       "underrated": For an appreciation of *Goodbye, Mr. Chips*, see "Forgotten Beauties" by Jeff
       Laffel, in *Film in Review*, November/December 1992, 362–67.
196   "I *guess* you could call it a musical": Reed, 257. Leslie Bricusse rescored a 1982 stage version
       of *Goodbye, Mr. Chips*, using songs originally written for, but not used in, the 1969 film.
       "spares the audience": *International Herald Tribune*, August 30, 1968.
197   Soon after the holidays: Matessino, 19.
       "what has got to be": *LAT*, April 24 and May 4, 1970.
198   Among the costumes: Bart (1990), 40.
       "anything from *Ben-Hur*": *NYT*, May 4, 1970.
       "Those costumes were hell": Harmetz, 305.
       music department's library burned: Fordin, 524.
       "I don't want to hear": Bart (1990), 39.
       "the company will not become involved": *Films and Filming*, February 1970, 24.
       "Young people who are": *NYT*, December 12, 1969.
       "Mr. Nixon's silent majority": "The Changing of the Guard" by Axel Madsen, *Sight & Sound*,
       Spring 1970, 64.

Chapter 15: Numbers

199   50 hours: *Hello, Dolly!* roadshow program by Jack Hirshberg, Twentieth Century-Fox, 1969.
       highest grossing: *LAT*, May 11, 1967.
       "It's funny for David": *Life*, February 14, 1969.
       "What do you expect": *LAT*, May 21, 1969.
200   $8 million: Silverman, 141.
       "[He] was so shocked": Silverman, 22.
       "What will Twentieth Century-Fox be like": Silverman, 165.
       "film [that] deals with subject matter": Silverman, 167.

200   consolidate its European branches: *Var*, October 8, 1969.
201   $20.4 million: *Wall Street Journal*, October 22, 1970.
      Zanucks brokered a deal: *Var*, October 29, 1969, 7.
      "*Hello, Dolly!* is fantastic": *International Herald-Tribune*, October 25, 1969.
      "Richard and I both took": New York Public Library for the Performing Arts, Oral History
      Program, The AFI Seminars, Part I, #196, April 17, 1975.
      "I wish we could cut more": *New York Post*, December 6, 1969.
      "One crazed fan": *NYT*, December 18, 1969.
      "Start the picture": Riese, 341.
      "swept the audience": *New York Daily News*, December 18, 1969.
202   "Now, at the time": *The New Yorker*, January 3, 1970.
      $1 million in advance sales: *Var*, October 29, 1969.
      "When you're flush": Gussow, 269.
      "Costly musicals": *Var*, December 24, 1969.
      It was a star-studded night: *A Decade Under the Influence* (2003) DVD.
203   "mannerisms [are] so arch": *Time*, December 26, 1969.
      "What I needed was Rhett Butler": Denkert, 294.
204   "The movie is full": *The New Yorker*, January 3, 1970.
      "It's not the kind of film": Hunter, 93.
      more than Gene Kelly's *On the Town*: Hirschhorn (1975), 262.
205   11 screenings a week at the Rivoli expanded to 15: *LAT*, March 11, 1970.
      Hello Dollars: MOMA, *Dolly!* clipping file, unattributed memo.
      played the Rivoli for 34 weeks: *Var*, August 19, 1970.
      losses after taxes came to $37 million: *NYT*, January 9, 1970.
      "I only met him once": Gussow, 270.
      The Sound of Music spigot was finally turned off: *San Pedro News-Pilot*, December 8, 1969.
      "It's that old Zanuck luck": *NYT*, February 3, 1970.
      "There can be no doubt about it": Silverman, 176.
      it brought in more money than: *Var*, January 5, 1971.
      $17.1 million loss for the second quarter: *Wall Street Journal*, August 28, 1970.
206   third quarter losses of *only* $5.2 million: Silverman, 260.
      $11,141,000: Silverman, 259.
      411.8 percent: Silverman, 324–27.
      "Fathers don't usually do this": *Wall Street Journal*, December 14, 1970.
      "He was a very cold ass": Silverman, 276.
      names "Richard Zanuck" and "David Brown" were removed: *Var*, January 5, 1971.
      $77 million: *LAT*, May 9, 1971.
      Fox held an auction: *LAT*, February 27, 1971.
      breach of contract lawsuits: Silverman, 297.
      "The industry got too much money": *LAT*, May 19, 1971.
      $16 million: *LAT*, November 14, 1971.
      free tourist attraction: *LAT*, December 3, 1972.
      "That set is a monument": *LAT*, November 14, 1971.
207   "I have devoted many years": *LAT*, May 19, 1971.
      "that began with anger": Gussow, 320.

Chapter 16: "Magnificent Apathy"

208   feature films cratered in 1969: Steinberg, 46.
      Seventy-two films were in production: *Wall Street Journal*, June 27, 1969.
      The ripple effect: *Time*, August 23, 1971.
      "the current crisis": *NYT*, November 9, 1969.

208   Los Angeles Police Department: *Wall Street Journal,* June 27, 1969.
      "I see our industry": *Var,* January 7, 1970.
      "I don't especially fear the takeover": *NYT,* November 9, 1969.
209   beer and baloney sandwiches: *NYT,* April 5, 1970.
      Goodbye, Mr. Chips earned two: Leslie Bricusse and John Williams were named as nominees, *not* André Previn, Dory Previn, Tony Hatch, Jackie Trent, or any of the other many names fleetingly attached to *Chips.*
      "the only film nominated": Wiley and Bona, 435.
210   "The movies entered the '60s": *LAT,* January 18, 1970.
      "elephantine disasters": Bart (1999), 21–22.
      "All the film lacks": *The Observer Review,* August 1, 1971.
      "*On a Clear Day* was quite expensive": Minnelli Collection AMPAS, undated.
      "It was not my greatest musical success": Minnelli, 367.
      The Owl and the Pussycat: Streisand's first non-musical was directed by Herbert Ross, another musical escapee after *Goodbye, Mr. Chips.*
      Radio City claimed the biggest opening day in its history: *Var,* August 5, 1970.
      "It can never recoup": AMPAS, *Darling Lili* production file, *Los Angeles Herald Examiner,* early 1970.
211   "fantastically costly an enterprise": *LAT,* June 24, 1970.
      "a conglomerate": *Var,* June 24, 1970.
      "evidently fought by Rock Hudson": *Look,* August 11, 1970.
212   "One newspaperman": *LAT,* January 17, 1971.
      "needs open-heart surgery": Hay, 47.
      "there is nothing I can do": AMPAS, *Darling Lili* production file, *Los Angeles Herald Examiner,* early 1970.
      "kind of romantic gesture": *NYT,* July 24, 1970.
      "Success is bankable": White, 105.
      "My screen departures": White, 107.
      "I have never found singing easy": White, 110–11. With the exception of *Goodbye, Mr. Chips, Darling Lili* has been the subject of more revisionism and critical reassessment than any other late roadshow musical. "One of the most underrated [movies] of recent years," wrote *The Real Paper* in 1974. "In many ways, *Darling Lili* was a courageous film to make, especially during the Vietnam War" (*The Real Paper,* May 8, 1974). Its sincerity and conviction rendered it palatable even to the most doctrinaire pacifist. "Blake Edwards's greatest commercial disaster . . . was also his greatest masterpiece," asserted the program copy for a 1981 screening of *Lili* at the Museum of Modern Art. There was merit in its "mixture of formalism, romance, slapstick, suspense, and musical numbers," making it nothing less than "one of the greatest works of the last dozen years" ("8 by Blake Edwards" by Myron Meisel, MOMA program notes, March 1981 and *Los Angeles Reader,* July 31, 1981). Such latter day assessments are overly generous to a film that suffers from too much money, and a director dispossessed of restraint. Edwards sought revenge in 1981 with *S.O.B,* a black comedy against Hollywood and the treatment he, Andrews, and *Lili* suffered at Paramount. The studio played good sport and distributed it, but *S.O.B.'s* efforts to be outrageous are more desperate than funny. We're treated to teenage nymphets, kinky drag, interracial lesbians, and Andrews murdering her doppelgänger Little Miss Goodie Two Shoes once and for all by exposing her breasts. Add to this a succession of pointless sight gags—stealing a body from a funeral parlor, a problematic hole in a ceiling/floor, a dog on the beach, a car in the ocean, and a chase on the freeway. It's the throw-everything-against-the-wall-and-see-what-sticks school of filmmaking, and somewhere in there Edwards's revenge for the desecration of *Lili* is lost by his worst directorial instincts.
213   He flew to Rome: Tosches, 113. SGI, with its ties to the Mafia and the Vatican, was the inspiration for Internazionale Immobiliare, the fictitious corporate empire in *The Godfather Part III* (1990).

213 Marathon Studio: *Var*, November 28, 1979.
"In retrospect, it's easy to see": Bart (1999), 114.
The SEC eventually filed suit: *Var*, November 28, 1979.
25 films: *Var*, October 30, 1968.
"At a time when most companies": MOMA, *Song of Norway* clipping file, April 13, 1970.

214 "I heard that talk": Henderson to author, February 28, 2012.
"Beyond [*Tora! Tora! Tora!* and *Song of Norway*]": *Var*, August 5, 1970.
"I tried to give": *LAT*, November 8, 1970.
"Though the formula that brought": *America*, November 28, 1970.
"If I had done it": *LAT*, November 8, 1970.
Instead of building sets: Henderson to author, February 28, 2012.

215 "bonbons wrapped in snow": *HR*, February 13, 1970.
"I liked him": Henderson to author, February 28, 2012.
$4 million: *Var*, September 22, 1969.

216 "one of the best 'stacked'": MOMA, *Song of Norway* clipping file, April 13, 1970.
"this film's scenery": *Films in Review*, December 1970, 646.
"Some of the more polite critics": Aylesworth, 208.
"The movie is of": Kael (1973), 187.
"sold out night after night": Southern Methodist University, Davis Oral Histories on the Performing Arts, Andrew Stone interview, 42, July 15, 1985.
$7.9 million: *Var*, May 31, 1973.
"Let's hold no wakes": *LAT*, September 20, 1970.

217 "*Scrooge* was like a sequel": Morris and Bull, 61.
"I can see *Wharf*": *LAT*, August 9, 1970.
"Can Hollywood films talk": "The Changing of the Guard" by Axel Madsen, *Sight & Sound*, Spring 1970, 111.
"Jerry Lewis Cinemas": *Var*, October 8, 1970.
Old Bridge, New Jersey: Haines, 89.
"Remember the 1930s": *Var*, January 5, 1972. One of the fatal errors of Jerry Lewis Cinema Corporation was its self-restriction to family entertainment. When it went bankrupt in 1980, there were only 14 G-rated films available to book (Haines, 90).

Chapter 17: Acts of Faith

218 $146 million: *Var*, September 29, 1971, 4.
Between 1951 and 1969: Hall, 289.
"biggest mistake": Balio (1987), 302–3.
I Do! I Do!: "The Changing of the Guard" by Axel Madsen, *Sight & Sound*, Spring 1970, 65.

219 "The subject matter of *Fiddler*": Picker to author, July 4, 2012.
"He is so desirous": WCFTR/UA, *Fiddler* files, April 19, 1967.
one of the biggest: Balio (2009), 193–94.
"The failure of *Hello, Dolly!*": *Saturday Review*, November 13, 1971.
"Through sheer force of personality": Vogel, 289.

220 16 languages: *NYT*, July 21, 1971.
"so ethnically oriented": Mirisch, 303.
"We don't want": Jewison, 13.
"*Fiddler* has a much stronger story": Jewison to author, March 8, 2012.
"*Hello, Dolly!* barely paid for itself": *New York Sunday News*, October 3, 1971.
"I've always dodged musical films": *LAT*, February 14, 1971.

221 "does not mean that I'm a better Tevye": *Life*, December 3, 1971.
"I felt Mostel had monopolized": Jewison to author, March 8, 2012.

221   "These people are close": *LAT*, February 14, 1971.
"Hollywood only hires movie stars": Jewison, 179.
"I've never seen a distributor": Norman Jewison in *Norman Jewison Filmmaker* (1971).
222   "Norman was under": Morris and Bull, 249.
"I think he knows": Vogel, 295.
"It got to be like a prison": *NYT*, January 5, 1971.
223   "I'm over budget": Norman Jewison in *Norman Jewison Filmmaker* (1971).
"I don't remember": Jewison to author, March 8, 2012.
reopened it for *Fiddler*: *Var*, August 19, 1970.
"review and analyze previous roadshows": WCFTTR/UA, *Fiddler* files, November 13, 1970.
"Gabe Sumner really threw": Jewison to author, March 8, 2012.
"I hope this film": *NYT*, November 3, 1971.
"I am very depressed": WCFTTR/UA, *Fiddler* files, October 6, 1971.
224   "laughed and cried": *New York Sunday News*, October 3, 1971.
sought endorsements from hundreds: WCFTTR/UA, *Fiddler* files, March 2, 1972.
"a universal human drama": Balio (2009), 214.
"An older man": *Newsday*, November 4, 1971.
"The souvenir booklet": *Life*, December 10, 1971.
"Norman Jewison hasn't so much directed": *The New Republic*, November 20, 1971.
Fiddler played the Rivoli: Balio (2009), 215. When *Fiddler* opened at the Rivoli, Zero Mostel was reprising Tevye on stage in Westbury, Long Island (*Newsday*, November 4, 1971)
full house group sales: WCFTTR/UA, *Fiddler* files, February 26, 1971.
$16.9 million: Balio (2009), 208–10.
225   "I think we have a film": WCFTTR/UA, *Fiddler* files, December 7, 1971.
"How sad it must be": *NYT*, November 14, 1971.
"plus the well-deserved flops": *NYT*, November 28, 1971.
"It deals with problems": "Love Calls the Tune" by Edwin Miller, *Seventeen*, September 1971.
226   roughly half of *The Sound of Music*'s earnings: Cook, 209. A 2004 feature story in the *New York Times* noted that *Fiddler* "still occupies a canonical place in Jewish culture. It has perhaps enjoyed this status through the assumption of its authenticity to Old World Jewish daily life. What is surprising is that the pseudo-klezmer tunes and schmaltz-laden accents in *Fiddler* were ever assumed to be the real thing" (*NYT*, February 29, 2004). Sholem Aleichem's original short stories were published in the Yiddish press between the 1880s and 1905, but he was a stockbroker from Kiev with no direct experience of shtetl life. There is a desire to endear Old World Jewish culture with an authentic expression of the past. Israel loved *Fiddler* on stage and screen, and Rex Reed was won by "its predictable Yiddish folksiness." He confessed to "glow[ing] in its charm. I finally realized how defenseless I was against its indestructible strength" (*New York Daily News*, November 5, 1971). The same can be said of millions of others.
"The success of films": Jewison to author, March 8, 2012.
227   Cinerama announced: *HR*, July 31, 1968.
plan for roadshow musicals: MOMA, *Cabaret* clipping file, undated.
Allied Artists and Haven Industries: *Var*, May 28, 1969.
ABC as its producing partner: *Var*, October 7, 1970.
"We think we've learned": *Var*, January 22, 1970.
credit goes to Baum: *HR*, October 21, 1970.
"ghastly pressures from ABC": York, 229.
"terribly depressing": MOMA, *Cabaret* clipping file, "Bob Fosse Bids Film Fans Come to His *Cabaret*" by Wanda Hale, February 13, 1972.
228   "as if his career was on the line": Gottfried, 214.

228 "make the dances look like the period": AMPAS, *Cabaret* clipping file, "Great To Be Nominated" fact sheet, July 31, 2006.
"supervised by a legion of producers": York, 233.

229 "I tried purposely to make": *HR*, April 12, 1972.
"that I shouldn't turn": MOMA, *Cabaret* clipping file, undated press release.
"It's an absolute miracle": York to author, March 3, 2012.
"a long pause": Tropiano, 70.
three hours to two: York to author, March 3, 2012.
"It is either terribly good": York, 248.
test screenings: AMPAS, *Cabaret* clipping file, undated.
"I have just seen": Tropiano, 83.
"It's an important picture": Minnelli, 373.
"What gets people out": MOMA, *Cabaret* clipping file, "Bob Fosse Bids Film Fans Come to
His *Cabaret*" by Wanda Hale, February 13, 1972.
Allied Artists: *Var*, February 23, 1972.

230 one big city reserve seat engagement: *Var*, March 1, 1972.
"broadens the horizons": *New York Daily News*, February 18, 1972.
"is an exquisitely sculpted milestone": *LAT*, April 2, 1972.
"The stage show of the cabaret": Gottfried, 215.
"It's been open in New York": *HR*, April 12, 1972.

232 "As an interpretation of history": *Commonweal*, April 21, 1972.
"Razzle-dazzle show biz": *Cue*, February 19, 1972.
"You have this little girl": Tropiano, 93.
"One of the great achievements": York to author, March 3, 2012.
"who stayed in my corner": *Var*, March 1, 1972.

Chapter 18: The Impossible Dream

233 skimming at the Flamingo: *NYT*, January 15, 1971.
"From now on": Madsen (1975), 11–12.
"The Kerkorian-Aubrey management of MGM": *NYT*, October 30, 1973.

234 Co-producing with MGM: In addition to *The Great Waltz*, MGM had another musical in the
pipeline co-produced by EMI that escaped James Aubrey's chopping block. *The Boy Friend*
was an experiment in marketing a big musical in a big way without roadshowing. It eschewed
an overture but came with an intermission, opening to general admission at the end of 1971.
With lavish production numbers dominating, *The Boy Friend*'s biggest marketing hook was
its star, 92 pound, 5'7'', freckled modeling phenomenon Twiggy. Director Ken Russell and
production designer Tony Walton went crazy recreating a fantasy 1920s landscape through
ersatz Fellini, while harsh lighting and grotesque close-ups stripped the candy coating off
the film's creamy nostalgia. *The Boy Friend* is an entertaining if problematic movie—stylish,
clever, and self-conscious to a fault. It bombed.
"I told Aubrey": *HR*, November 29, 1972.
"They effectively pulled the rug": Hall, 145.
"To have built any reasonable facsimile": AMPAS, *Waltz* clipping file, MGM promo material.
"I see that we stick": *HR*, June 15, 1972.

235 "MGM Bets Bundle": *LAT*, November 9, 1972.
"a quality of artistic miscalculation": *NYT*, November 9, 1972.

236 "There are so many angry young men": *LAT*, November 9, 1972.
Viennese Torte: AMPAS, *Waltz* clipping file, press release, October 17, 1972.
Arthur Murray: AMPAS, *Waltz* clipping file, press release, October 30, 1972.
$120,000: AMPAS, *Waltz* clipping file, MGM press clipping, November 15, 1972.
"a silly, sentimental biography": *Cue*, November 18, 1972.

236   "the operetta plot": *LAT*, November 1, 1972.
      "never make another musical": Southern Methodist University, Davis Oral Histories on the
      Performing Arts, Andrew Stone interview, 44–45, July 15, 1985.
237   the last release under the Cinerama logo: Hall, 145.
      "Everyone who saw *Song of Norway*": *HR*, November 29, 1972.
      disappeared: *Song of Norway* was released in the United States on videocassette in 1986. The
      author found *The Great Waltz* on eBay, the product of home recording from a TV airing.
      "Nobody doesn't like Sara Lee": *Man of La Mancha* original cast CD liner notes by Denny
      Martin Flinn, 2001.
238   45 countries: *Filmfacts*, v. XI, 1972, #22, 617.
      $4 million: *NYT*, August 2, 1967.
      "[It is not] merely crotchety nostalgia": *The Village Voice*, October 10, 1968.
      "script difficulties": *Filmfacts*, v. XI, 1972, #22, 617.
      He signed for a salary of $1 million plus overtime and a share of profits: WCFTTR/UA, *La
      Mancha* files, November 19, 1971.
      Arthur Hiller was signed as director: WCFTTR/UA, *La Mancha* files, August 27, 1971.
239   "[Glenville and Hopkins] had gone back": *Show* (UK), January 1973, 28.
      "I admired it": Hiller to author, March 27, 2012.
      "When I first started the film": *Seventeen*, December 1972.
      "The essential problem": *Los Angeles Herald-Examiner*, April 30, 1972.
      "dull and repetitious": *New York Daily News*, June 4, 1972.
      "Embodied in the work": *LAT*, April 23, 1972.
      "a lot of bull": *Los Angeles Herald-Examiner*, April 30, 1972.
240   "working on the film": Chaplin, 243.
      Bitterness toward Loren instead came from the publicist: WCFTTR/UA, *La Mancha* files,
      various dates, 1972.
      "They're the most incredibly depressing": *LAT*, April 23, 1972.
      "This has been a bitch": *New York Daily News*, June 4, 1972.
241   contract allowed for the producers to dub his voice: *NYT*, September 17, 1972.
      "Little Arthur": *LAT*, April 23, 1972.
      "Why, no, not at all": *NYT*, September 17, 1972.
      Stockholders dropped by: *Filmfacts*, v. XI, 1972, #22, 617.
      the cast got along well: *New York Daily News*, December 9, 1972.
      $9 million: *Var*, May 24, 1972.
      "It has never been done before": *New York Daily News*, June 4, 1972.
      "I don't like films": *Seventeen*, December 1972.
      "It's a bit of a terror": *LAT*, April 23, 1972.
242   "Unless Hiller is forced": *Chicago Tribune*, April 30, 1972.
      Rivoli, and on Long Island: WCFTTR/UA, *La Mancha* files, July 19, 1972.
      "The important thing in any roadshow": WCFTTR/UA, *La Mancha* files, December 4,
      1972.
      "If it were my decision": *New York Daily News*, June 4, 1972.
      "Shall we explain": WCFTTR/UA, *La Mancha* files, February 8, 1972.
      "These men buy up studios": Freedland, 159–60.
      "surely the most mercilessly lachrymose": *Time*, December 25, 1972.
243   "If there's anything worse": *Chicago Sun-Times*, December 15, 1972.
      "have pitched this screen version": *Newsweek*, December 18, 1972.
      "There is something decidedly off-putting": *NYT*, December 12, 1972.
      "like a Coca-Cola bottle": *Pittsburgh Post-Gazette*, April 27, 1972.
      "Every change comes about": *New York Daily News*, December 11, 1972.
244   "On Broadway, the show worked": Kaplan, 151.
      "Perhaps *Man of La Mancha* should never have been made": Druxman, 148.

244 "When you're sitting": Hiller to author, March 27, 2012.
"We hoped to have a really good movie": Picker to author, July 4, 2012.

Exit Music

245 "With the blockbuster strategy stalled": Schatz, 15.
pediment figures removed: *Var*, March 30, 1988.
246 "*Men's Wear* magazine": *Lost Horizon* press release, undated, courtesy of Jeff Kurtti.

BIBLIOGRAPHY

Books and Journals

Adler, Renata. *A Year in the Dark: Journal of a Film Critic, 1968–69*. New York: Random House, 1969.

Altman, Rick. *The American Film Musical*. Bloomington: Indiana University Press, 1999.

Aylesworth, Thomas G. *Broadway to Hollywood*. New York: Gallery Books, Smith, 1985.

Balio, Tino. *United Artists: The Company That Changed the Film Industry*. Madison: University of Wisconsin Press, 1987.

Balio, Tino. *United Artists: The Company That Changed the Film Industry—Volume 2: 1951–1978*. Madison: University of Wisconsin Press, 2009.

Bardsley, Garth. *Stop the World: The Biography of Anthony Newley*. London: Oberlon, 2003.

Bart, Peter. *Fade Out: The Calamitous Final Days of MGM*. New York: William Morrow, 1990.

Bart, Peter. *Who Killed Hollywood? . . . and Put the Tarnish on Tinseltown*. Los Angeles: Renaissance, 1999.

Base, Ron. *"If the Other Guy Isn't Jack Nicholson, I've Got the Part."* Chicago: Contemporary Books, 1994.

Belton, John. *"The Rivoli." . . . in 70 mm: The 70 mm Newsletter* 12, no. 59 (1999): 4–9; www .in70mm.com/newsletter/1999/59/rivoli/index.htm.

Bergan, Ronald. *Francis Ford Coppola: Close Up: The Making of His Movies*. New York: Thunder's Mouth, 1998.

Block, Alex Ben, and Lucy Autrey Wilson, editors. *George Lucas's Blockbusting*. New York: Harper-Collins, 2010.

Bloom, Ken, and Frank Vlastnik. *Broadway Musicals: The 101 Greatest Shows of All Time*. New York: Black Dog and Leventhal, 2004.

Bluhdorn, Charles. *The Gulf + Western Story*. New York: Newcomen Publication Number 970, 1973.

Bricusse, Leslie. *The Music Man: The Autobiography of the Genius behind the World's Best Loved Musicals*. London: Metro, 2006.

Bruck, Connie. *When Hollywood Had a King*. New York: Random House, 2003.

Callan, Michael Feeney. *Richard Harris: Sex, Death and the Movies*. London: Robson, 2005.

Channing, Carol. *Just Lucky I Guess*. New York: Simon & Schuster, 2002.

Chaplin, Saul. *The Golden Age of Movie Musicals and Me*. Norman: University of Oklahoma Press, 1994.

Clarke, James. *Coppola*. London: Virgin, 2003.

Considine, Shaun. *Mad as Hell: The Life and Work of Paddy Chayefsky*. New York: Random House, 1994.

Cook, David A. *History of the American Cinema, Volume 9: The Seventies: 1970–1979*. New York: Charles Scribner's Sons, 2000.

Cowie, Peter. *Coppola*. New York: Charles Scribner's Sons, 1989.

Day, Barry, editor. *The Letters of Noël Coward*. New York: Knopf, 2007.

Delamater, Jerome. *Dance in the Hollywood Musical*. Ann Arbor, MI: UMI Research Press, 1981.

Denkert, Darcie. *A Fine Romance: Hollywood/Broadway*. New York: Billboard Books, 2005.

Dick, Bernard. *Engulfed: The Death of Paramount Pictures and the Birth of Corporate Hollywood*. Lexington: University Press of Kentucky, 2001.

Dominick, Joseph R. "Film Economics and Film Content: 1964–1983." In Bruce A. Austin, editor, *Current Research in Film: Audiences, Economics, and Law, Volume 3*. Norwood, NJ: Ablex, 1987, 136–53.

Druxman, Michael B. *The Musical from Broadway to Hollywood*. New York: Barnes, 1980.

Dunne, John Gregory. *The Studio*. New York: Farrar, Straus & Giroux, 1968.

Evans, Robert. *The Kid Stays in the Picture*. New York: Hyperion, 1994.

Feuer, Jane. *The Hollywood Musical*. Bloomington: Indiana University Press, 1982.

Finler, Joel W. *The Hollywood Story*. New York: Crown, 1988.

Fleischer, Richard. *Just Tell Me When to Cry*. New York: Carroll & Graf, 1993.

Fordin, Hugh. *The World of Entertainment! Hollywood's Greatest Musicals*. New York: Doubleday, 1975.

Freedland, Michael. *Peter O'Toole*. New York: St. Martin's, 1982.

Gabler, Neal. *Walt Disney: The Triumph of the American Imagination*. New York: Vintage, 2007.

Gottfried, Martin. *All His Jazz: The Life and Death of Bob Fosse*. Cambridge, MA: Da Capo, 2003.

Grant, Barry K. "The Classic Hollywood Musical and the 'Problem' of Rock 'n' Roll." *Journal of Popular Film & Television* 13, no. 4 (Winter 1986): 195–204.

Gray, Beverly. *When Doctor Dolittle Met Mrs. Robinson: How Movies Shaped a Generation*. Unpublished manuscript, 2010.

Greene, Katherine, and Richard Greene. *Inside the Dream: The Personal Story of Walt Disney*. New York: Roundtable, 2001.

Grubb, Kevin Boyd. *Razzle Dazzle: The Life and Works of Bob Fosse*. New York: St. Martin's, 1991.

Gussow, Mel. *Darryl F. Zanuck: Don't Say Yes until I Finish Talking*. New York: Da Capo, 1971.

Haines, Richard W. *The Moviegoing Experience, 1968–2001*. Jefferson, NC: McFarland, 2003.

Hall, Sheldon, and Steve Neale. *Epics, Spectacles, and Blockbusters*. Detroit: Wayne State University Press, 2010.

Hall, Sheldon. "Hard Ticket Giants: Hollywood Blockbusters in the Widescreen Era." PhD Dissertation, Norwich, UK: University of East Anglia, 1999.

Harmetz, Aljean. *The Making of the Wizard of Oz*. New York: Hyperion, 1998.

Harris, Mark. *Pictures at a Revolution*. New York: Penguin, 2008.

Harrison, Rex. *A Damned Serious Business: My Life in Comedy*. New York: Bantam, 1991.

Harrison, Rex. *Rex*. New York: William Morrow, 1975.

Hay, Peter. *Movie Anecdotes*. New York: Oxford University Press, 1990.

Hirsch, Julia Antopol. *The Sound of Music: The Making of America's Favorite Movie*. Chicago: Contemporary Books, 1993.

Hirschhorn, Clive. *Gene Kelly*. Chicago: Henry Regnery, 1975.

Hirschhorn. *Through the Screen Door: What Happened to the Broadway Musical When It Went to Hollywood*. Lanham, MD: Scarecrow, 2004.

Horton, Andrew. *The Films of George Roy Hill*. New York: Columbia University Press, 1984.

Hunter, Allan. *Walter Matthau*. New York: St. Martin's, 1984.

Jablonski, Edward. *Alan Jay Lerner*. New York: Henry Holt, 1996.

Jewison, Norman. *This Terrible Business Has Been Good to Me*. New York: T. Dunne, 2005.

Johnson, Robert K. *Francis Ford Coppola*. Boston: Twayne, 1977.

Kael, Pauline. *Deeper into Movies*. Boston: Little, Brown, 1973.

Kael, Pauline. *Going Steady*. Boston: Little, Brown, 1970.

Kaplan, Philip J. *The Best, Worst and Most Unusual Hollywood Musicals.* New York: Beekman, 1983.

Kemp, Peter. "How Do You Solve a 'Problem' Like Maria von Poppins?" In *Musicals: Hollywood and Beyond.* Bill Marshall and Robynn Jeananne Stilwell, editors. Bristol, UK: Intellect Books, 2000, 55–61.

Krämer, Peter. *The New Hollywood: From Bonnie and Clyde to Star Wars.* London: Wallflower Press, 2005.

Kurtti, Jeff. *What Were They Thinking? The "Bad" Movie Musicals and How They Got That Way.* Unpublished manuscript, 1997.

Laffey, Bruce. *Beatrice Lillie: The Funniest Woman in the World.* New York: Wynwood Press, 1989.

Leemann, Sergio. *Robert Wise on His Films: From Editing Room to Director's Chair.* Los Angeles: Silman-James, 1995.

Levy, Emanuel. *George Cukor, Master of Elegance.* New York: William Morrow, 1994.

Logan, Joshua. *Movie Stars, Real People, and Me.* New York: Delacorte, 1978.

MacLaine, Shirley. *My Lucky Stars: A Hollywood Memoir.* New York: Bantam, 1996.

Madsen, Axel. *The New Hollywood: American Movies in the 1970s.* New York: Thomas V. Crowell, 1975.

Madsen, Axel. *William Wyler: The Authorized Biography.* New York: Cromwell, 1973.

Maltin, Leonard. *The Disney Films.* New York: Crown, 1973.

Mann, William J. *Behind the Screen: How Gays and Lesbians Shaped Hollywood 1910–1969.* New York: Penguin Putnam, 2001.

Mast, Gerald. *Can't Help Singin': The American Musical on Stage and Screen.* Woodstock, NY: Overlook, 1987.

Matessino, Michael. "Hello, Mr. Bricusse and Mr. Williams." *Goodbye, Mr. Chips* CD booklet, FSM Silver Age Classics, 2006.

Mayer, William G. *The Changing American Mind: How and Why American Public Opinion Changed between 1960 and 1988.* Ann Arbor: University of Michigan Press, 1993.

McGee, Garry. *Jean Seberg—Breathless.* Albany, GA: BearManor, 2008.

Medved, Harry, and Michael Medved. *The Hollywood Hall of Shame: The Most Expensive Flops in Movie History.* New York: Putnam, 1984.

Miller, Gabriel, editor. *William Wyler: Interviews.* Jackson: University Press of Mississippi, 2010.

Minnelli, Vincente. *I Remember It Well.* New York: Samuel French, 1990.

Mirisch, Walter. *I Thought We Were Making Movies, Not History.* Madison: University of Wisconsin Press, 2008.

Mordden, Ethan. *The Hollywood Musical.* New York: St. Martin's, 1982.

Mordden, Ethan. *Medium Cool: The Movies of the 1960s.* New York: Knopf, 1990.

Morris, Oswald, and Geoffrey T. Bull. *Huston, We Have a Problem.* Latham, MD: Scarecrow, 2006.

Moseley, Robert. *Rex Harrison: A Biography.* New York: St. Martin's, 1987.

Mueller, John. *Astaire Dancing: The Musical Films.* New York: Knopf, 1991.

Mundy, John. *The British Film Musical.* Manchester: Manchester University Press, 2007.

O'Neil, Tom. *Movie Awards.* New York: Perigee, 2001.

Parish, James Robert. *Fiasco.* Hoboken, NJ: John Wiley & Sons, 2006.

Parish, James Robert, and Michael R. Pitts. *The Great Hollywood Musicals.* Metuchen, NJ: Scarecrow, 1991.

Parkinson, David. *The Rough Guide to Film Musicals.* London: Penguin, 2007.

Payn, Graham, and Sheridan Morley. *The Noël Coward Diaries.* Boston: Little, Brown, 1982.

Phillips, Gene D. *Godfather: The Intimate Francis Ford Coppola.* Lexington: University Press of Kentucky, 2004.

Phillips, Gene D., and Rodney Hill, editors. *Francis Ford Coppola: Interviews* (Conversations with Filmmakers Series). Jackson: University Press of Mississippi, 2004.

Phillips, Julia. *You'll Never Eat Lunch in This Town Again.* New York: Random House, 1991.

Plummer, Christopher. *In Spite of Myself.* New York: Knopf, 2008.

Pye, Michael, and Linda Myles. *The Movie Brats.* New York: Holt, Rinehart and Winston, 1979.

Reed, Rex. *Big Screen, Little Screen.* New York: Macmillan, 1971.

Richards, David. *Played Out: The Jean Seberg Story*. New York: Berkley, 1984.

Riese, Randall. *Her Name Is Barbra*. New York: St. Martin's, 1993.

Robinson, David. *The Chronicle of Cinema 4: 1960–1980*. London: Sight and Sound (supplement), December 1994.

Schatz, Thomas. "The New Hollywood." In *Film Theory Goes to the Movies*. Jim Collins, Hilary Radner, and Ava Preacher Collins, editors. New York: Routledge, 1993, 8–36.

Schickel, Richard. *Clint Eastwood*. New York: Knopf, 1996.

Schumacher, Michael. *Francis Ford Coppola: A Filmmaker's Life*. New York: Three Rivers Press, 2001.

Sennett, Ted. *Hollywood Musicals*. New York: Abrams, 1982.

Sherman, Robert B., and Richard M. Sherman. *Walt's Time: From Before to Beyond*. Santa Clarita, CA: Camphor Tree, 1998.

Silverman, Stephen M. *Fox That Got Away: The Last Days of the Zanuck Dynasty at Twentieth Century Fox*. Secaucus, NJ: Lyle Stuart, 1988.

Simonet, Thomas. "Conglomerates and Content: Remakes, Sequels, and Series in the New Hollywood." In *Current Research in Film: Audiences, Economics, and Law, Volume 3*, Bruce A. Austin, editor. Norwood, NJ: Ablex, 1987, 154–62.

Slater, Philip E. *The Pursuit of Loneliness*. Boston: Beacon, 1970.

Solomon, Aubrey. *Twentieth Century-Fox: A Corporate and Financial History*. Lanham, MD: Scarecrow, 2002.

Spada, James. *Streisand: Her Life*. New York: Crown, 1995.

Sperling, Cass Warner, and Cork Millner. *Hollywood Be Thy Name*. Lexington: University Press of Kentucky, 1998.

Springer, John. *All Talking! All Singing! All Dancing!* New York: Citadel, 1966.

Steinberg, Cobbett. *Reel Facts*. New York: Facts on File, 1978.

Stirling, Richard. *Julie Andrews: An Intimate Biography*. New York: St. Martin's, 2007.

Stringer, Julian, editor. *Movie Blockbusters*. London: Routledge, 2003.

Thomas, Bob. *Astaire: The Man, the Dancer*. New York: St. Martin's, 1984.

Thomas, Bob. *Building a Company: Roy O. Disney and the Creation of an Entertainment Empire*. New York: Hyperion, 1998.

Thomas, Bob. *Clown Prince of Hollywood: The Antic Life and Times of Jack L. Warner*. New York: McGraw-Hill, 1990.

Thomas, Tony. *The Films of Gene Kelly*. Secaucus, NJ: Citadel, 1974.

Tosches, Nick. *Power on Earth*. New York: Arbor House, 1986.

Tropiano, Stephen. *Cabaret*. Milwaukee: Limelight, 2011.

Van Dyke, Dick. *My Lucky Life in and out of Show Business*. New York: Crown Archetype, 2011.

Vogel, Frederick G. *Hollywood Musicals Nominated for Best Picture*. Jefferson, NC: MacFarland, 2003.

Walker, Alexander. *Fatal Charm: The Life of Rex Harrison*. New York: St. Martin's, 1992.

Walker, Alexander. *Hollywood UK*. New York: Stein and Day, 1974.

Walker, Alexander. *No Bells on Sunday: The Rachel Roberts Journals*. New York: Harper & Row, 1984.

Wapshott, Nicholas. *Peter O'Toole*. New York: Beaufort, 1983.

White, Timothy. *The Entertainers: Portraits of Stardom in the 20th Century*. New York: Billboard Books, 1998.

Wiley, Mason, and Damien Bona. *Inside Oscar: The Unofficial History of the Academy Awards*. New York: Ballantine, 1996.

Windeler, Robert. *Julie Andrews*. New York: G.P. Putnam's Sons, 1970.

Windeler. *Julie Andrews: A Life on Stage and Screen*. New York: St. Martin's, 1983.

Wyatt, Justin. "From Roadshowing to Saturation Release: Majors, Independents, and Marketing/Distribution Innovations." In *The New American Cinema*, Jon Lewis, editor. Durham, NC: Duke University Press, 1998, 64–86.

York, Michael. *Accidentally on Purpose*. New York: Simon & Schuster, 1991.

Yudkoff, Alvin. *Gene Kelly: A Life of Dance and Dreams*. New York: Billboard, 2001.

Zec, Donald. *Marvin: The Story of Lee Marvin*. New York: St. Martin's, 1980.

Select Websites

associatedcontent.com/article/462092/roadshow_theatrical_releases_and_how.com.html
barbara-archives.com/index.html
cinematreasures.org
cinemasightlines.com/showmanship_roadshow.php
en.wikipedia.org/wiki/roadshow_theatrical_release
filmsite.org/greatestflops3.html
filmsite.org/musicalfilms6.html
frontscripttodvd.com
imdb.com
learnaboutmovieposters.com/newsite/index/articles/roadshow.asp
musicals101.com/index.html
widescreenmuseum.com/widescreen/roadshow_presentation2.htm

Souvenir Movie Programs

Camelot; Chitty Chitty Bang Bang; Doctor Dolittle; Fiddler on the Roof; Finian's Rainbow; Funny Girl; Goodbye, Mr. Chips; Half a Sixpence; The Happiest Millionaire; Hello, Dolly!; Man of La Mancha; My Fair Lady; Oliver!; Paint Your Wagon; Song of Norway; The Sound of Music; Star!; Sweet Charity; Thoroughly Modern Millie

Documentaries /Laser Disc and DVD Extras /Promotional Shorts /Liner Notes

The Age of Believing: The Disney Live Action Classics (2008)
The Boys: The Sherman Brothers' Story (2009)
Cabaret: A Legend in the Making (1997)
Carol Channing: Larger Than Life (2012)
A Decade under the Influence (2003)
Fiddler on the Roof, DVD commentary by Norman Jewison and Topol (2001)
Finian's Rainbow, DVD commentary by Francis Ford Coppola (2004)
Goodbye, Mr. Chips CD soundtrack, Silver Age Classics, (2006)
Hello, Dolly! vintage featurette (1969)
Hollywood Musicals of the '60s (1999)
Hollywood Singing and Dancing: A Musical Treasure (2008)
The Making of Half a Sixpence (1967)
MGM: When the Lion Roars (1992)
More Loverly Than Ever: The Making of My Fair Lady Then and Now (1994)
Morgan: A Suitable Case for Treatment, DVD supplements (2001)
My Favorite Things: Julie Andrews Remembers (2005)
Norman Jewison, Filmmaker (1971)
Norman Jewison Looks Back, Fiddler on the Roof DVD special edition supplement (2006)
Remembering Chitty Chitty Bang Bang (2003)
Ross Hunter on the Way to Shangri-La (1973)
Songs of Fiddler on the Roof, DVD special edition supplement (2006)
The Sound of Music, DVD commentary by Robert Wise (2005)
Star! DVD commentary by Julie Andrews and Robert Wise (2004)
Star! laser disc extras (1995)
The Story of Camelot (1967)
Supercalifragilisticexpialidocious: The Making of Mary Poppins, Mary Poppins DVD special edition supplement (2004)

INDEX

Page numbers in *italics* refer to photographs appearing on those pages.